REMBRANDT: *King David*

The
CHRISTIAN
BOOK
OF
KNOWLEDGE

The

CHRISTIAN BOOK

Editor
DON CLEVELAND NORMAN, A.B., Th.B., D.D.

Assistant Editor
JOSEPH HOWARD NORMAN

Art Editor
WILLARD G. SMYTHE, F.I.A.L.

Picture Editor
MATHILDA SCHIRMER, Ph.B.

Layout
CHARLES BOZETT

Maps
ELLEN MIKALS

OF KNOWLEDGE

Volume Two

CONSOLIDATED BOOK PUBLISHERS Chicago, Illinois

LIBRARY OF CONGRESS CATALOG CARD NUMBER: 68-54682

STANDARD BOOK NUMBER: 8326 - 2000-9

Printed in the United States of America

Foreword

IN THE FIRST VOLUME of THE CHRISTIAN BOOK OF KNOWLEDGE you have had many vistas of God's Word opened to you in exciting new ways.

You have walked with Bible heroes and heroines amid the lush beauty and in the desert places of their own lands. The entire setting of many an old and wonderful Bible story has come alive for you in the vivid photographs of Bible Lands today that are sprinkled throughout the text.

Moreover, you have found the pictures depicting incidents in the lives of Bible heroes and heroines to be as varied as the lives of the Old Masters or later artists who painted them. But you have also found that each reproduction, whether in full color or in black and white, has carried an impact all its own. Each one reflects a particular artist's interpretation according to his understanding of the Bible hero or event recorded. Taken all together, you have received definite visual impressions of Bible men, women, and events that cannot be erased.

Now, as you read Volume II, you will find the same quality and quantity of pictorial material that you have found so helpful in Volume I.

Lessons for Today's Living

Among the special features in Volume I of THE CHRISTIAN BOOK OF KNOWLEDGE, one that has provided you with most inspiration for living your life at its highest peak of service is probably the section found at the end of each Bible story, *Lessons for Today's Living.*

Volume II continues the high standard of quality material used in this section that was set by the first volume. Again Guideposts Associates, Inc., Carmel, N.Y., has given permission to reprint selections from *Guideposts Magazine.* Specific credits and copyright dates appear in the introduction to each selection. Some of the stories included are by or about

Bobby Richardson, All-Star baseball player; J. Edgar Hoover, director of the Federal Bureau of Investigation; Captain William R. Anderson, commander of the nuclear submarine *Nautilus;* and Justin Fisher, son of a merchant who achieved success in the face of a series of misfortunes. Despite the diversity of these stories, they all have a unifying common denominator: reliance on a firm faith in God during time of crisis. You will find the titles and the authors listed in the Table of Contents.

Fleming H. Revell Company publications have constituted another helpful source of material for this section. Chapters from three Revell books have been used, by permission, in Volume II. They are: "It Takes Courage To Be Yourself" and "Be a Good Winner" from *That Girl in Your Mirror,* by Vonda Kay Van Dyke (© 1966 by Fleming H. Revell Company, Westwood, N.J.); "Does Faith in God Insure Success in Business?" from *The Christian in Business,* by John A. Mitchell, Jr. (© 1966 by Fleming H. Revell Company); and "The Heart of a Champion" and "Response to the Challenge" from *The Heart of a Champion,* by Bob Richards (© 1959 by Fleming H. Revell Company).

"Where Courage Begins," by Richard Tregaskis, award-winning foreign correspondent of World War II and popular author, is reprinted from the *Family Weekly Magazine,* (© 1964), by permission of Paul R Reynolds, Inc., 599 Fifth Avenue, New York, N.Y., 10017.

From Zondervan Publishing mission has been received from *Archaeology and O Contemporaries,* by Jam Zondervan Publishing Michigan). Dr. Kel of excavations i drawn from hi edge to pr Bible per *mous C'*

(© 1964 by Zondervan Publishing House), is the work of an able and well-known author who is represented in Volume II of THE CHRISTIAN BOOK OF KNOWLEDGE by "John Fletcher's Miracle-Filled Life."

You will find the page numbers for the above by consulting the Table of Contents, which lists the title and author of stories used in *Lessons for Today's Living*. All credits and copyright dates are contained within the introduction to each excerpt.

Other Features

The special features that accompanied each Bible story in Volume I have been continued in Volume II. Through the beauty and simplicity of its language, the *Introduction* to each story will again prepare your mind and heart for the story that follows. And when you have finished reading the chapters, you will again find that the *Places, Questions, Answers, Further Facts,* and *Outline(s)* will aid in your understanding of each story in its relation to the others.

A unique chapter in Volume II of THE CHRISTIAN BOOK OF KNOWLEDGE is "A History Bridge Between the Testaments." The material therein provides a link between the closing events of the Old Testament and the opening days of the New Testament. This time-span of four hundred years is often neglected, yet the history of this period is important to a full understanding of the world at the time of Christ's birth. This chapter at the end of Volume II is a fascinating account of the men and nations that rose to power, of the changes that took place in the ancient world, of the conquered and the conquerors; but, most of all, it is the dramatic story of the events and the people whom God used to prepare the world for the coming of His Son, Whose life is told in Volume III.

In providing for you the wonderful array of choice items, briefly previewed above, members of the staff of THE CHRISTIAN BOOK OF KNOWLEDGE have sought to give the same dedicated service that characterized their work in Volume I.

THE PUBLISHERS

Table of Contents

TABLE OF CONTENTS

TABLE OF CONTENTS

TABLE OF CONTENTS

List of Illustrations

PLATES IN FULL COLOR

MAPS AND DIAGRAMS

ILLUSTRATIONS

ILLUMINATED SECTION IN COLOR

Saul

OTHING IN THE LIFE OF THE ISRAELITES required that they have a king to rule over them, except their desire to be like the nations around them. Saul stands upon the pages of Israel's history as an object lesson in the real meaning of their choice. He was a revelation to the people of what the possession of a king like those of the nations around them really meant. Saul was a man of enormous physical strength, yet fitful and failing from first to last; a man of undoubted mental acumen, yet a man of moods who finally became a madman; a man whose spiritual life was characterized from the beginning by slowness and, at last, a man so devoid of spiritual illumination and power that he turned his back upon the Lord and consulted a witch.

Look at the kingdom under Saul. After he was chosen, the people were for a time practically without a king. He manifested his weakness by "hiding among the stuff," when he ought immediately to have taken hold of the scepter. Others interpret that story differently. They affirm that Saul was a man of such extreme modesty that, after he was appointed, he went back to work in quietness without taking the kingdom. Such modesty is sin. It is as great a sin to urge modesty and keep in the background, when God calls to the foreground, as it is to go to the front when God's appointment is to the rear. Then came the period of the wars—conflicts that ultimately ended in terrible disaster. Under Saul's reign the kingdom became thoroughly disorganized.

The closing chapter in the First Book of Samuel is draped in sackcloth and covered with ashes. It tells the tragic story of the last act in the life of a man who was a ghastly failure. Defeat at the hands of the Philistines drove Saul to utmost desperation. Saul died by his own hand physically, as he had already perished spiritually to the noble purposes and possibilities of his life through his own sin and folly.

Despite all this, Saul and his son Jonathan were subjects of a beautiful and plaintive lament by his successor, David, who felt so strongly about the Lord's anointed—the king—that he required his singularly beautiful song to be taught to the people, lest they think of their first king in his final defeat and fail to remember his early victories. In view of this, David could sing with fervor, "Thy glory, O Israel, is slain upon thy high places" (2 Samuel 1:19).—G. Campbell Morgan, *Living Messages of the Books of the Bible* and *Searchlights from the Word*

CASTAGNO: *The Youthful David*

PRECEDING PAGE

The Youthful David

by ANDREA DEL CASTAGNO (1423-1457) *Italian School*

National Gallery, Washington, D. C. (Widener Collection)

And David put his hand in his bag, and took thence a stone, and slang it, and smote the Philistine in his forehead, that the stone sunk into his forehead . . . and took his sword, and drew it out of the sheath thereof, and slew him. I SAMUEL 17:49,51

ONE OF THE LEADING PAINTERS of the Florentine Renaissance, Castagno worked for anatomical accuracy and variety of bodily movement in his figures. The victorious David—one of the favorite symbols of the young Florentine republic, which liked to think of itself as a "giant killer," too—shows such verve and skillful observations of detail that it comes as something of a surprise to find that the pose was borrowed from an ancient Roman statue. The unusual shape of the picture is due to the fact that it was painted as a processional shield. Parades of every sort are still a popular public spectacle in Italy and, in the 15th century, they were decked out with costumes and floats designed, often, by the most famous artists of the day.

1

THE PEOPLE CHOOSE SAUL

THE AIR WAS TINGLING with excitement throughout the land of Israel. All roads led to Mizpeh that day as every family from every tribe headed there. In obedience to Samuel's orders, they were to assemble in Mizpeh to choose a king! And, despite Samuel's warning, they were certain that all their troubles would be over if only they had a king to lead them.

In those days, when important decisions were to be made, great dependence was placed on drawing lots because the people believed that God directed the hand of the person drawing them. So it came as no surprise to the people when Samuel announced that this would be the method used to select their king. After all the tribes except Benjamin had been eliminated, Saul slipped quietly away and hid. He *knew* who would be chosen. Saul, the prospective king, had suddenly become Saul, the shrinking violet!

From his hiding place nearby, Saul listened momentarily to the drawing as family after family from his tribe were eliminated. Soon, however, he was deep in thought. He remembered well that day when Samuel had anointed him as the man the Lord had chosen to become Israel's first king. He also recalled that the signs Samuel had given him as proof that he really was the Lord's choice had happened exactly as predicted. He had met the two men near Rachel's tomb who told him the donkeys had been found. At the oak of Tabor he had met the three men going to Bethel to worship God. One of them had been carrying three goats, another had been carrying three loaves of bread, and the other had been carrying a skin of wine. And one of them had given him two loaves of bread. He had also met the band of prophets near Gibeah and had prophesied among them.

Saul's hiding place was not as good as he had imagined, because his reverie was suddenly interrupted by someone shaking his shoulder. Looking up, he saw Samuel and some of the people standing around him. Samuel spoke.

"The last lot has been drawn," he said, "and God has chosen you to be Israel's first king. Come now, and let me present you to all the people."

What an impressive sight Saul made as he stood there on the platform, head and shoulders above any of his subjects! There was a great ovation as Samuel moved forward to speak to the people.

"Hear me, all of you!" he cried, "I have listened to your request and, by the guidance of the Lord, I was able to find a king for you and anoint him as the man God has chosen to rule over you. I present him now, King Saul, son of Kish, from the city of Gibeah!"

These words had hardly ended when a mighty roar arose from the crowd, as everyone shouted in unison:

"God save the king! Long live the king!"

Samuel finally managed to restore some semblance of order among the teeming multitudes, who were wildly enthusiastic in their joy. He then continued his speech.

"You have known me since I was a lad, serving in the Lord's Tabernacle," he

"Saul Prophesies with the Prophets" by J. James Tissot. The Old Testament, Illustrated. The multitudes were surprised at the wisdom of young Saul's prophecies when he joined a group of prophets after Samuel anointed him.   M. de Buffan & Co.

said. "During none of this time have I ever oppressed you, or cheated you, or taken a bribe from any of you. Now that you have a king, remember my last solemn warning: Things will go well with you and your kingdom as long as you obey the Lord and keep His commandments. If, on the other hand, you ever rebel against God and refuse to serve and honor Him, both you and your king shall be destroyed. As for me, I shall continue to pray for you and to help you in every way possible. God bless the king!"

At the close of Samuel's speech the people disbanded and returned to their homes. Most of them were happy to have Saul as their king, but he was confronted immediately by a group of dissidents. They rudely asked, in the hearing of the new king: "How can this man save us from our enemies?"

King Saul was soon to show them.

After his coronation, Saul established the temporary capital of the kingdom in his home town of Gibeah. While there the new king received some terrible news. East of the Jordan some of his people were in dire straits. Messengers from Jabesh-gilead reported that Nahash, cruel and inhuman king of the Ammonites, had camped near their city. One of the conditions for a peace treaty was that all the men in the city should have their right eyes put out. When Saul heard of this demand, he became white-hot with anger! However, he calmed down somewhat upon hearing that the elders had been able to negotiate a truce for seven days with King Nahash. He had been willing to

grant this respite because he was certain that no one would come to the rescue. How wrong his guess was to prove!

There was a flurry of activity at Saul's headquarters. He had sent his own messengers throughout the kingdom on a massive and urgent recruitment program. The recruiters, armed with dire threats of reprisal by Saul against anyone who refused to rally behind him, quickly enlisted all the able-bodied men in Israel.

When word of the success of the drive reached Saul, he turned to the messengers who had come to him and said:

"Return to your city and tell your elders that by noon tomorrow I, Saul, king of Israel, with my armies will have liberated their city and will have defeated the Ammonites."

Saul divided his men into three companies and, on a forced march throughout the night, arrived at the camp of the Ammonites during the morning watch. Then began the massacre of King Nahash and his men. The battle raged until noon, as Saul and his men inflicted heavy casualties on the Ammonites. Those who survived the attack were so scattered that no two of them remained together.

In triumph, King Saul led his armies back to Gibeah. He now had the support of all the people, as he firmly resolved to maintain a large standing army. Never again would Israel be caught so defenseless and unprepared.

Based on the story in the Bible:
1 Samuel 8:1—12:25

2
SAUL'S SON, JONATHAN

AT THE BEGINNING OF HIS REIGN King Saul had everything going for him. He was a handsome man, a great leader, and a powerful warrior. He drew deep loyalty and affection from those around him. Abner, his cousin and most important captain, was devoted to him. So was his son Jonathan and, even when Saul did wrong, Samuel's heart went out to him in sorrow.

How different things were now! Poor Saul was almost submerged in troubles. His once proud and triumphant army had been reduced, either by defection to the enemy or by desertion, to a small band of 600 men. And, to make matters worse, the Philistines were on the rampage again and had gained control of virtually all Israel. They even had garrisons up on the highlands and were keeping the Israelites in a state of constant terror. The people often had to hide in caves and holes in the rocks, as they had done during the days of Gideon. Visitors to Palestine today can explore many of these caves and underground dwellings.

Underneath a pomegranate tree on the outskirts of Gibeah, Saul had pitched his royal tent. A few miles north of him, in a valley named Michmash, the main body of the Philistine army was camped. A major battle was certain to occur in a few days. Saul, by scraping the bottom of his military manpower barrel, had called up some reserves and he hoped that the war would not begin until they arrived in camp. Then he would have about three thousand men. The king's hopes, however, were doomed to disappointment. His very own son would touch off the spark early the next morning.

The sun had barely risen when Prince Jonathan lifted up his eyes to the top of a nearby hill. Just as he expected! The Philistine garrison was still camped there between two crags. This meant that he must follow through on the decision he had made last night. The time for action had come! So, without saying anything to his father, he turned to his armor-bearer and spoke:

"Come! Let's go up to the garrison and dislodge our enemies from their lofty heights. Perhaps God will be on our side. If He is, it matters little whether there are many with us or only the two of us."

His armor-bearer answered immediately: "Do whatever you wish. You can count on me to be with you all the way."

Little did Jonathan dream that this capricious caper would almost cost him his life, on the orders of his own father! As they moved stealthily up the hill, Jonathan told his aide:

"This is how we shall know if the Lord is with us. We shall no longer hide from the men at the garrison. When they see us, if they tell us to linger awhile until they can come down to us, we shall know that this is not our day and make a hasty retreat to the foot of the hill. On the other hand, if they tell us to come on up, we shall know that God will give us a victory."

They moved forward boldly now and soon were within sight of the Philistines, who promptly greeted them with taunts and jeers, shouting in raucous voices:

"Well, well, well! Look at the two brave Hebrews! They have come out of the holes where they have been hiding to visit us. Come on up here, and we will show you something!"

These were the very words Jonathan wanted to hear, so he promptly accepted their invitation. When they reached the summit, Jonathan became almost like a whirling dervish as he struck down man after man after man with his heavy cane. His aide followed closely behind him and gave the finishing stroke to each man who had fallen. Soon twenty bodies had been

"Jonathan at the Assault of the Philistines" by J. James Tissot. *The Old Testament*, Illustrated. Jonathan and his armor-bearer bravely enter the garrison.   M. de Buffan & Co.

piled up, and the remainder of the garrison had fled in terror to the main army camp. Their terror became infectious, and confusion piled on top of confusion among the Philistines when a sharp earthquake rocked the valley. The earth opened up and literally swallowed thousands of the men!

Jonathan and his aide were astounded when they reached the site of the Philistines camp. What had started out to be a simple mission of overthrowing the garrison at the top of the hill had turned into an overwhelming victory over all Philistines.

Saul, who had been watching all the proceedings, wondered who could have started the battle prematurely. He gave an order to Captain Abner: "Call the roll and find out who is gone!"

The roll call was completed. Jonathan and his aide were missing! Although Saul did not know it yet, the two Israelites had found a ready-made fifth column among the Philistines. Most of the defectors had rallied behind Jonathan and had turned upon the people who had granted them asylum. As Saul continued to watch the fleeing, panic-stricken Philistines, his excitement grew. He called his army together and said:

"As soon as the Philistines pass by, we shall join in on the chase. So that we may eliminate as many of the enemy as possible, I command that no one eat anything until nightfall. If anyone does, he shall be summarily executed."

The people continued their chase-and-kill operation throughout the long, hot day. During the day, Jonathan led a group of the men through a forest where honey was dripping around them. Since he had been away from camp when his father had issued his thoughtless command, Jonathan had not heard of it. The soldiers gazed in horror as he paused momentarily, ate

7

"Jonathan Eats, in Violation of Saul's Command." Saul had ordered his people to fast until nightfall, threatening death to anyone disobeying him. Unwittingly, Jonathan ate honey; but, by interceding, the people saved him from execution.

some of the honey, and refreshed himself. One of the men told Jonathan that his father had ordered no one to eat until nightfall.

Jonathan answered swiftly: "My father overlooked one thing when he issued his careless command. An army travels on its stomach. Far more Philistines would have been killed today if you had stopped to eat some of the food that we captured from them."

Despite this good advice, none of the men dared disobey the king. When darkness finally came, the famished Israelites

8

began to slaughter the cattle and eat them, without even allowing time for the blood to run away. When Saul heard what was going on, he ordered two altars to be built. One was for a thanks offering to God, and the other was so that the people could bring the animals to it and kill them according to Mosaic regulations. The manner in which they had been eating the meat was strictly forbidden by the law of Moses.

With the sacrifices made and his men's hunger abated, King Saul now wished to know if God wanted him to resume his chase of the Philistines. He asked Ahiah, the priest, to get instructions from the Lord. When Ahiah failed to receive an answer from God, Saul became perturbed. He was convinced that someone in the crowd had committed a sin, and it seemed that the drawing of the lot would be the only way he could find out who it was.

As the drawing of the lots began, Saul and Jonathan sat on one side of the flickering camp fires and the army sat on the other side. One by one, the men were proven innocent. Now the choice was down to two people: the prince and the king! The air was filled with a deathly silence when Saul solemnly drew lots between himself and his son. Jonathan was chosen. Saul then asked Jonathan sternly: "Tell me, my son, what you have done!"

Jonathan answered sadly: "Alas! I only ate a little honey, and now I must die!"

Poor Jonathan! He had expected to return to camp a hero. Instead, he was soon to hear his father sentence him to death.

The king turned to his son and said: "I have made a solemn vow. You shall surely die!"

When the army heard these words, they rebelled against the king's decision and shouted angrily: "God forbid that Jonathan, the man who brought about this victory, should die! Not even a hair on his head shall fall to the ground. The Lord has surely been with him this day."

Thus it was that the army rescued Jonathan that night and he did not die. That night also marked the start of Saul's long slide downward.

Based on the story in the Bible:
1 Samuel 13:1 — 14:46

SAUL REJECTED, DAVID CHOSEN

GOD WAS BECOMING EXASPERATED with Samuel. Long ago He had told the prophet that Saul no longer pleased Him. Despite this firm decision, Samuel had taken no action either to notify Saul or to go about the business of selecting a new ruler. Instead, he had spent the days and nights weeping and mourning for Saul because of his great love for the king. The day finally came when God had to speak firmly to Samuel.

"How much longer are you going to sit around in sackcloth and ashes mourning for Saul?" He asked. "You know that I have irrevocably rejected him from reigning over My people. Arise now, fill your horn with oil, and go to the home of Jesse in Bethlehem. I have chosen a king from among his sons."

It will be recalled that Ruth the Moabitess had married Boaz and that her baby was named Obed. He had a son named Jesse, who was a sheep-farmer on the very land that once belonged to Boaz. Jesse had eight sons, the youngest of whom was named David. Since he was the youngest, it was his job to watch over the sheep. David thus followed in the footsteps of Moses, Jacob, and other early Hebrew leaders whose hard lot was that of being a shepherd.

When Samuel arrived in Bethlehem, he went immediately to the home of Jesse and told him that he had come to make a sacrificial offering to God. Jesse knew that this meant a feast afterward, so preparations for it were begun immediately. After the sacrifice had been offered and the feast was over, Samuel called Jesse and his sons to him and blessed them.

"What a handsome group of men!"

Samuel thought as he stood there waiting for God to reveal His choice to him. Suddenly God spoke to Samuel.

"David Presented to Samuel" by J. James Tissot. *The Old Testament,* Illustrated. At Samuel's request, Jesse brought his youngest son, David, to meet him.   M. de Buffan & Co.

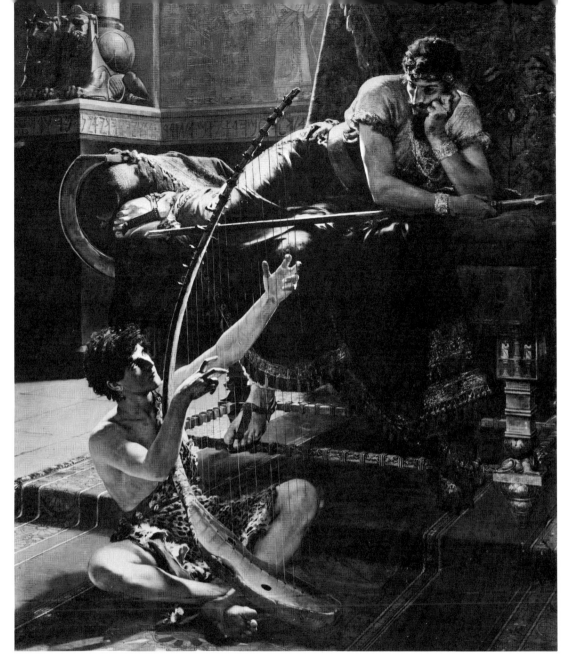

"*David and Saul*" by Julius Kronberg. National Museum, Stockholm. When Saul became depressed, he called on David to play the harp for him. The beautiful music would calm and relax the troubled king.
National Museum

"Physical appearance will not have such a high priority this time," He said. "Today I shall look into the heart of each man. Now you may ask the brothers to pass before you."

One by one, the sons passed before Samuel and, to his amazement, God disqualified each of them for one reason or another.

"Do you have any other sons here?" Samuel asked Jesse.

"Yes, my youngest son, David, is out in

11

the field keeping watch over the sheep," Jesse replied.

"Send for him at once!" Samuel ordered. "We shall remain standing until he gets here."

Jesse sent for David and presented him to the prophet. Samuel sat down with a sigh of relief. Standing before him was a handsome, clear-eyed, tanned, and healthy young man. Then God spoke to Samuel.

"Arise and anoint him," He said. "This is the man I have chosen."

Samuel took the horn of oil and anointed David in the presence of his father and his brothers. The Spirit of God descended upon the shepherd lad and, in his heart, he knew that this was a red-letter day for him. God had chosen him for some great purpose.

Upon Samuel's return from Bethlehem, he proceeded immediately to Saul's palace to fulfill the second and sad part of the mission God had given him. Saul listened in shocked disbelief as Samuel spoke these dire words:

"God has told me to tell you that He is no longer pleased with you as king of His people. He has firmly declared that, in due time, you will be replaced by a man after His own heart."

Saul was depressed. From the day Samuel proclaimed that awesome message, the king remained in his royal chambers most of the time. On those rare occasions when he did venture out, he acted so strangely that his servants feared that he was losing his mind. One day they went to Saul with a suggestion.

"We are worried about you," they said. "We believe that you need a man who is skillful at playing the harp to come here and remain as your constant companion. Then, when you feel these fits of depression coming on, he could play beautiful music for you and drive away your blues."

Saul was pleased with the idea, so he asked if anyone knew of such a man. One of the servants answered promptly:

"I know just the man for you. His name is David, son of Jesse, and he lives in Bethlehem. He is an excellent player, good looking, and God is with him."

Saul sent for David immediately. Poor Saul. Little did he know then that he was bringing the successor to his throne to the palace! When David entered the royal chambers and bowed before Saul, a feeling of mutual admiration sprang up instantly between the young shepherd and his king.

All the servants waited anxiously to see what effect the music would have on their king. The moment of truth was near, because Saul had sent for David to play for the first time. The servants' anxiety was set at ease as the first strains of David's melodious music filled the air. His music was composed of such exquisite sounds as the song of the birds and the whispering of the wind. Saul seemed to receive instant relief, as the dark clouds of gloom drifted away.

In no time at all, David became a court favorite. He and Jonathan formed an inseparable friendship, and Saul was feeling better and happier than he had felt in many a day.

Based on the story in the Bible:
1 Samuel 15:1 — 16:23

4
GOLIATH VERSUS DAVID

SAUL WAS STILL HAVING TROUBLE with the Philistines. He was now engaged in what seemed to be a losing campaign against them. The battle lines were drawn, with the Valley of Elah separating the two armies which were camped on mountains on opposite sides of the valley. In order to save lives, it was sometimes customary in those days for each army to choose a champion and let these men fight it out alone to decide the outcome of the battle. The Philistines had already made their choice, and he was a giant of a man. His name was Goliath and he was over ten feet tall.

Early each morning and late each afternoon, Goliath walked down the mountain and boldly marched back and forth across no man's land as he roared out his challenge:

"Choose a man and let him come down here and fight with me. If perchance he should win and kill me, my army will surrender. On the other hand, if I prevail

The Valley of Elah lies in the hill country about 15 miles southwest of Jerusalem between Socoh and Azekah. David's first experience in battle occurred here during a campaign against the Philistines.
© Matson Photo

and kill your man, your army will surrender. Don't tell me you are afraid of me!"

When Saul and the Israelites saw the size of the man and heard his words, they were indeed afraid. Even Saul, who stood head and shoulders higher than any of his people, dared not accept the Philistine's challenge.

One day Saul was astounded when David told him quietly: "Let no man have heart failure because of Goliath. I will go and fight him!"

After Saul had caught his breath, he answered sternly: "You can't go out and fight that giant. You are still a youth, with no war training, and he is an experienced warrior."

David realized he was taking on a tremendous responsibility. If he failed, not only would he lose his life but his people would fall still deeper under the dominion of the Philistines. However, he was so strongly convinced that God wanted him to fight Goliath that he tried to think of some persuasive argument to cause Saul to change his mind.

"When I was a shepherd watching over my father's flocks, bears and lions sometimes came and took one of the lambs," he began. "I chased these animals, saved the lamb and, with God's help, killed these wild beasts when they attacked me. Yes, I have killed both lions and bears, and it will be the same with this Philistine, especially since he has openly defied the army of the living God. I know that the Lord will save me from this giant."

David spoke so sincerely and with such quiet conviction and power that Saul finally changed his mind. Excitement ran riot throughout the camp when the king announced that David had volunteered to fight Goliath. Preparation for the contest was soon completed. At first, Saul dressed David in his own armor, helmet, and

sword. David had already mapped his battle strategy, however, so he resorted to a bit of subterfuge when he told Saul that he could not go along with the idea of using the armor and sword because he had never tried them out.

During David's years as a shepherd he had practiced hours upon endless hours with his sling. He had become such an expert with it that he could hit a nail on the head with a pebble from a distance of fifty paces, the equivalent of fifty yards as distance is measured today. David's secret weapon was his sling.

A Modern David. A shepherd boy of today demonstrates the technique of using the sling-shot in the manner in which David of old slew the Philistine giant.   © Matson Photo

"David Slings the Stone" by J. James Tissot. *The Old Testament,* Illustrated. David offered to face the Philistine warrior, Goliath. He used the sling and stone to overcome the giant and gain victory for the Israelites.   M. de Buffan & Co.

The first championship fight was soon to start. Goliath had fully expected the Israelites to send out their biggest warrior, armed and dressed in armor like himself, if they answered his challenge at all. He gasped with amazement when he saw the choice they had made. It was a young lad dressed in simple shepherd's clothing, and the only visible weapon was a staff or cane. Goliath thought to himself that it would be easy for him to kill the lad. Little did he know that Death in the shape of the young shepherd was drawing closer and closer to him!

Both armies watched the proceedings intently as David reached the valley, paused momentarily at a small stream, picked up some smooth pebbles, and put them in his pouch. As David drew nearer to the giant, what looked like the most unequal contest ever staged began. At first, it was a war of words. Threats and counterthreats rang through the valley. Each fighter declared that he would kill the other and chop up his body so fine that it could be fed to the birds.

David was now about fifty yards away from the giant. It was time for action. The shepherd lad took his sling and a pebble from his pouch. He aimed for a small opening in Goliath's helmet. The stone sped straight and true, and it sank into the giant's head. The knockout punch was delivered! The huge giant toppled slowly to the ground and lay prone on his face in the dust of Elah Valley. David rushed to the spot, removed Goliath's sword from its sheath, cut off the giant's head and held it up by the hair for all to see. The Israelites' hearts beat high with joy as they let out a mighty cheer for their champion. As for the Philistines, their hearts shrank with terror as they looked on their dead and headless champion.

Saul and his army were on the way to the Philistine camp to accept their surrender. On reaching the camp, however, Saul found that the Philistines had not kept their part of the bargain. They were already on a wild, frenzied flight to one of their fortified cities. Saul and his men chased them to the gates of Ekron but were unable to catch up with them. On their return, Saul's army collected the spoils of victory from the Philistine camp and returned victoriously to their own camp. David had proven once more that little things can mean a lot.

Based on the story in the Bible:
1 Samuel 17:1-53

5
SAUL'S JEALOUSY OF DAVID

WHETHER SAUL KNEW that God had selected David as his successor, or whether he just guessed it, is not recorded. However, it is known that his jealousy of David grew stronger day by day. Saul was truly a man of many moods and passions. There were days when he loved David as much as he loved his own son. On those days the king would do anything for his brave young warrior. Then there were days when Saul bitterly hated him and openly expressed the hope that David would be killed in one or another of his battles with the Philistines.

David was so successful in all the assignments which Saul gave to him that he rose rapidly through the ranks and soon earned the right to be leader of all the armies of Israel. Following his promotion, David scored victory after victory over his enemies. Upon each victorious return from battle, the women came out of their homes and danced, played their timbrels, and sang this song:

"Saul has slain his thousands,
And David has slain his ten
thousands."

Every time he heard this song Saul became infuriated, because it showed clearly that his popularity was waning and that David's was steadily rising.

Early in their acquaintanceship, David and Jonathan formed a friendship pact in which both of them pledged to remain friends as long as they lived. This pact was to be tested sooner than they expected. Saul had heard *that* song again and, in a fit of rage, ordered his servants to find David and kill him on sight. Jonathan rushed to his friend immediately, told him of his father's orders and suggested that he remain in hiding during the night.

The next morning Jonathan and his father came out of the palace for their daily stroll. Jonathan made a powerful appeal to his father, as he attempted to effect a reconciliation between him and David.

"Why are you determined to kill David?" he asked. "He has done you no harm. Instead, his every action has been for your interest. Surely you haven't forgotten that morning when he stood alone in the valley, faced Goliath, and killed him. Don't you remember that the death of the giant resulted in the freedom of all your people from the cruel oppression of the Philistines? Has it been so easy for you to forget the rejoicing of the Israelites and the celebrations they held throughout the land because God had once again saved them from their enemy?"

Saul was so impressed by his son's eloquent plea that he promised him that David would not be killed.

During this period of reconciliation Saul permitted his youngest daughter Michal, who loved David, to marry him. Saul gave the young couple an elegant house not far from the palace so that David could be summoned quickly to the royal court in the event that the king needed to listen to some music.

Late one afternoon Saul called David to the palace to play for him. David selected a lyre and was playing beautiful

"David before Saul" by Rembrandt. Frankfurt. Saul became suspicious of David because of his popularity. The king, in a sudden flare of jealous anger, once hurled his javelin at the young musician. National Archives, Brussels

soft music when, suddenly and without warning, Saul threw his javelin at him! David was so startled at this turn of events that he dropped his lyre, rushed out of the palace, and raced to his own home. Thus it came about that Saul's jealousy of David turned into murderous hatred for him.

Saul fully intended to kill David the next morning, so he sent some guards to surround his house in order to prevent him from leaving during the night. After David told his wife what had happened at the palace, they walked over to the window and were looking out into the semi-darkness when the guards arrived.

Michal's mind was swirling with ideas. She was certain that her father, who must surely be losing his mind, would leave no stone unturned until he killed her husband. She knew that something must be done immediately to thwart this obsession. Finally, she thought of a plan which she believed would work.

First, she got a rope and, after David had kissed her goodbye, Michal lowered him from a window to the ground. After assuring herself that David had made good his escape, she made certain that he would have a good headstart. She placed a dummy on his bed and covered it so that, if the guards came up to make an on-the-spot inspection, they would think the decoy on the bed was David.

The next morning, when Saul learned of David's escape and Michal's deception, he became furious. He strode angrily over to his daughter's house and stormed at her: "Why did you help my enemy escape? Why did you deceive my guards?"

In order to appease her angry father, Michal pretended that David had threatened to kill her if she did not help him escape. Upon hearing this explanation, Saul returned to the palace and began making plans for the capture and execution of David. Poor Saul! Little did he realize that his house would soon topple and that, even now, two of his children were in league with David and against *him!*

Shortly after forming their friendship pact, David and Jonathan selected a cave some distance from the palace as a secret meeting place. It would be used to enable them to keep in touch with one another in the event that Saul followed through on his threat either to attempt to kill David or to drive him away from the palace. After fleeing from the palace that night, David went to Ramah and visited Samuel

RUBENS: *The Judgment of Solomon*

PRECEDING PAGE

The Judgment of Solomon

by PETER PAUL RUBENS (1577-1640) *Flemish School*

Royal Museum of Fine Arts, Copenhagen

*And the king said, Divide the living child in two, and give
half to the other.* I KINGS 3:25

THE DRAMATIC PORTRAYAL depicting the climax in the story of
Solomon and the two women who claimed the living child is
typical of the dynamic style of Ruben's painting. His mastery of
figure drawing, his solid composition, and his knowledge and use
of color and lighting enabled him to convey the emotional impact
of the moment. Rubens was recognized as the leading Flemish
painter in the Baroque style and one of the greatest painters of
all time. An extraordinarily vital and versatile man, Rubens com-
bined his successful artistic career with an equally successful
one as a diplomat. His work was in such demand that he employed assistants to execute his designs and thus fill the commis-
sions he received. He carefully controlled the work of these
assistants and added the finishing touches where necessary. In
this way he was able to produce an outstanding number of paint-
ings, while still maintaining a high standard.

"David Makes His Escape" by J. James Tissot. *The Old Testament,* Illustrated. David received so much praise from the people that Saul became insanely jealous and plotted to kill him. But David's wife Michal helped him to escape the king's guards who had surrounded their house.   M. de Buffan & Cc.

for a few days, giving him a report on happenings at the palace. David then decided to return to the secret meeting place, in the hope that Jonathan would come there, too.

It happened just as David had hoped. Not long after he reached the cave, Jonathan arrived. After renewing their vow of friendship, David asked if Saul was still angry with him.

Jonathan replied: "I do not know, for he hasn't spoken about you lately. However, there is a three-day feast at the palace starting tomorrow, and I'm sure he is expecting you. If you stay away, as I think you should, I'll cover for you. Then I'll return here and let you know what's on my father's mind."

It was agreed that the next visit should not be a personal one because Saul might become suspicious and have Jonathan followed, thereby learning where David was hiding. Therefore, it became necessary for the friends to develop a plan whereby Jonathan could let David know Saul's attitude toward him. Their solution of the problem was simple but good. David would remain in hiding in the cave. Jonathan would return to the field near the cave with a young arrow-chaser and his bow and arrows. Then he would shoot the arrows and send the young boy after them. If Jonathan shouted to the lad that the arrows were behind him, David would know that all was well. On the other hand, if he shouted to his young arrow-chaser that they were in front of him, David would know that he was in great danger.

The three-day feast had begun. When Jonathan entered the banquet room, his father and Captain Abner were already seated and he noted that, surely enough, his father had prepared a place for David. However, Jonathan knew that this was a feeble attempt to lure David out of hiding so that he could be captured and killed.

19

"Saul Casts a Javelin at Jonathan" by J. James Tissot. *The Old Testament*, Illustrated. Jonathan loved David as a brother and tried to defend him. He succeeded only in enraging his father who tried to kill him, too.　　M. de Buffan & Co.

No mention was made of David's empty chair during the first day of banquet, but the second day was to be far different.

Events on the second day of the feast began innocently enough. The guests had arrived, had been served, and had started eating. Little did Jonathan dream that, within the next few minutes, he himself would bear the brunt of his father's wild outburst of anger! Jonathan noticed the scowl on his father's face when he looked at David's empty chair for the second straight day. Saul turned to his son and asked, "Why hasn't the son of Jesse come to dine with me? He wasn't here yesterday, and today he is still missing."

Jonathan replied, "I granted him permission to go to Bethlehem to be with his own family during the three-day feast."

Saul was almost hysterical as he shouted to his son: "You son of shame and perdition! I know that you have chosen the son of Jesse instead of me. Don't you realize that you can never be king as long as the son of Jesse lives? Go now and bring him to the palace, for he shall surely die."

Instead of leaving, Jonathan again pleaded for David's life. In the midst of this plea, Saul arose abruptly and went to his weapons-rack. There he picked up his javelin and then, to the amazement of all the guests, he hurled it at his son! Saul's aim was still bad, so Jonathan was unhurt. More in sorrow than in anger, he looked upon his poor, pitiful father. Surely, Saul's madness had reached its climax. Jonathan gave his father another glance, walked firmly out of the room, and no longer participated in the feast.

The next morning, with his bow and arrows and the young lad beside him, Jonathan stood in a field near the cave. He sent the youngster some distance away and quietly shot the three arrows over his head. Then Jonathan called out: "My boy, the arrows are in front of you!"

As soon as the lad disappeared from sight, David threw caution to the wind and rushed out of the cave to greet Jonathan. The friends spoke their sad farewells. Jonathan returned to the palace; but David was an outlaw, and he fled for his life.

Based on the story in the Bible:
1 Samuel 18:1 — 20:42

6
SAUL OUTLAWS DAVID

THE TRAGIC LAST DAYS of Saul's life were spent in the bitter though vain attempt to capture David and kill him. When he fled from Saul's palace, David became an outlaw and faced instant death if the king's men ever found him. The same fate would befall anyone known to have aided or befriended him. David made his first stop at Nob, one of the priestly cities of the Levites. Leaving outside the city the few companions who had aligned themselves with him, he went to the shrine of Ahimelech, priest of the city.

David knew that he and his companions could not survive, even for a few days, unless he could secure some food and a weapon. Ahimelech was surprised when he recognized his visitor and listened to his unusual request, so he asked: "Why are you, the leader of the king's armies, away from the palace, alone, weaponless, and without food?"

David did not dare tell the priest the real reason for his presence in Nob, so he resorted to subtlety.

"I am on an important top-secret mission for the king," he replied, "and the matter is so urgent that there was no time to procure either food or a weapon. Now, what do you have for me that is available immediately?"

Since he knew David's status at the court, as well as the fact that he was the king's son-in-law, Ahimelech accepted the story as true. The kindly priest told David that the only bread in the Temple was the holy bread and the only weapon was the sword of Goliath. Ahimelech offered both of them to David, who gratefully accepted them.

David hurried out of the city to rejoin his companions, congratulating himself on the ease with which he had deceived the priest. Little did he know that this deception and the kindness of the priest would cost the lives of Ahimelech, his priests, and his entire household! The entire transaction had been watched by Doeg, one of Saul's spies. The informer would soon make his report to Saul, who would take drastic vengeance on the house of Ahimelech.

After leaving Nob, David and his men headed in a southwesterly direction into the wilderness of Judah. When they

"David and Ahimelech" by J. James Tissot. *The Old Testament*, Illustrated. David received holy bread and the sword of Goliath from the priest of Nob.   M. de Buffan & Co.

reached the cave of Adullam, they pitched camp and prepared to fortify the place. Soon David's small band increased to four hundred men. Debtors, malcontents, and other men flocked to the cave of Adullam. Even David's father, mother, and brothers fled to David's camp. He was concerned about the safety of his parents, so David decided that the first order of business was to find a sanctuary for them. He remembered that his great-grandmother Ruth had come from Moab, so he took his parents to the city of Mizpeh in that land and asked the king to care for them as long as necessary. The king readily agreed, and David returned to his men at the cave.

Shortly after David's return to camp, he received the shocking news of the massacre of the priests of Nob. Abiathar, a son and the only priest who had escaped Saul's fury, told David that the king was so enraged on learning of the aid given the outlaw that he ordered Doeg the Edomite to kill Ahimelech, his priests, and all his people. Altogether, eighty-five people were slain. David was disconsolate when he heard of the slaughter, especially so since his deception had led the priest into aiding him. He expressed his regrets to Abiathar.

"It is my fault," he said. "I have been the cause of the death of all your people. You must stay here with me, because we are both in the same boat now. Saul is seeking to kill the two of us. You will be safe with me as long as I live."

David was preparing to engage in his first battle for Israel after becoming an outlaw. He had just learned that the Philistines were fighting against the frontier town of Keilah and were robbing the people of their grain. God gave David His approval of the battle so he went out confidently, confronted the enemy, decisively defeated the Philistines, and took many of their cattle. Then he returned to Keilah. In the meantime, Saul learned that David and his men had come out into the open and were camped in Keilah. He decided to besiege the city and capture David.

Back in Keilah, David heard that Saul and his vast army were marching toward the city to lay siege to it until David and his men were delivered to them. Since he and his band had just liberated the city from the Philistines, David was confident that the people would show their gratitude by protecting him. He was stunned when God revealed to him that the people would turn him over to Saul. After receiving this startling information, David lost no time in leading his men out of the city into the mountainous country where they could hide in caves and strongholds. Saul called off his plans to besiege Keilah when he learned that, once again, David had eluded his clutches.

Saul continued his relentless search for David, combing the mountains for him every day. However, God was with the outlawed warrior and he craftily evaded every trap.

One day, while still in hiding in the mountains, David had the unexpected happiness of seeing his friend Jonathan once more. Again, they renewed their vow of friendship. Then, in an attempt to cheer David up, Jonathan said: "Have no fear that my father will find you. He knows that you will be the next king of Israel, and that I shall be your right-hand man."

David watched Jonathan until he disappeared from sight, and then he went back to his hiding place. David could not know that this was the last time he would see his friend alive.

Based on the story in the Bible:
1 Samuel 21:1 — 23:18

7
DAVID'S LIFE IN THE WILDERNESS

DAVID'S FLIGHT FROM SAUL brought him into contact with many communities in southern Palestine. Another result of his flight was that many mighty men gathered around him. In addition to being brave and loyal to David, these men were trained to be ambidextrous in hurling stones and shooting arrows. The outlaw chieftan drew men to him and trained them thoroughly.

Late one afternoon, David sat near the entrance to his cave deep in thought. He remembered a few of the many things that had happened to him since he had fled from Saul's wrath. Three of his men had risked their lives by going through the Philistine lines to the gate of Bethlehem in order to bring him a drink of water from the well there.

He recalled that night when Saul, weary and exhausted, had stumbled accidentally into the very cave where he and one of his men had been hiding. Saul had gone to sleep, and David had been given a golden

"David Refuses To Kill Saul." One night Saul entered a cave to rest. It was the very cave in which David was hiding. David cut off a piece of Saul's robe to prove that, although he could have slain Saul as he slept, he would not harm God's anointed king.

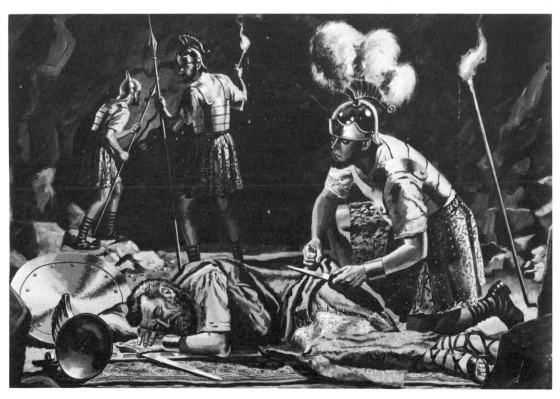

opportunity to end the struggle then and there. However, he had only cut off a piece of Saul's robe to prove to the king that he, too, had been in the cave.

Finally, he remembered that time when the Ziphites had betrayed him and his men and Saul had almost captured him. Saul's army had been closing in for the kill when a messenger had come to the king and had told him that the Philistines had launched a massive attack on the land of Israel. Saul had given up pursuit of David and had gone to fight the invaders. Grateful for his deliverance, David had named the place Sela-hammahlekoth, which means, "Rock of Escape."

David's meditations were interrupted when one of his men came to him with the report that the camp was running out of food. David knew that the servants of Nabal, a very rich man who owned three thousand sheep and one thousand goats, were shearing his flocks nearby. In fact, David and his men had appointed themselves as unofficial guardians of the shepherds, the servants, and the sheep. Many a night they had driven off marauders, armed robbers, and wild beasts. Feeling reasonably certain that Nabal would gladly give him some supplies in exchange for these services, David selected ten young men to deliver a message to the wealthy man.

The spokesman for the messengers advanced toward Nabal and bowed politely.

"We have come to you on behalf of our captain and leader, David, the son of Jesse," he said. "He sends his greetings and best wishes to you and all your household. Your shearers are camped near our camp and, ever since they have been there, David and his men have protected them from attacks by raiders and wild animals. Now, he needs some help from you. There is a food shortage at our camp,

and our captain respectfully requests that you give us all the surplus food and supplies that you have at your camp."

Nabal, whose name literally means "churlish fool," lived up to his name.

"Who is this David, and who is this son of Jesse?" he answered with scorn. "As far as I know, you could be a band of slaves who have run away from your masters. Anyway, pray tell me, why should I take the bread, water, and meat that I have prepared for my workers and give it to you who have come from I know not where?"

At first, David listened in shocked amazement as his messengers made their report to him. Then he became furiously angry. Still boiling with rage, he called all his men together.

"Nabal shall pay with his life for what he has done this day!" he declared. "Not only so, but all his household shall perish. What he could have given to us cheerfully and peacefully, he shall now give to us at the point of a sword. All of you get your swords and put them on. Two hundred of you must remain here to guard our camp; the other four hundred will follow me."

In the meantime, back at Maon, one of Nabal's shepherds had just reported to Abigail about the rudeness and discourtesy that her husband had shown to David's messengers. He confirmed that, time after time, David and his men had saved Nabal's flocks from robbers and wild beasts. He also told Abigail that David would be merciless in his revenge for her husband's affront and ingratitude.

Abigail knew she must act, and act fast, if she wished to save her household from David's vengeance. Quickly, she gathered two hundred loaves of bread, two skins of wine, five sheep already dressed, five measures of parched corn, one hundred clusters of raisins, and two hundred cakes of figs. Then she called her servants.

"*Abigail Brings Food to David.*" School of Rubens. Pinacothek, Munich. Nabal refused to give David's men anything to eat, but Abigail secretly brought food and drink to David and asked him to forgive her husband.

Pinacothek

"Load this food on donkeys and go out to meet David," she said. "After you have given it to him, tell him that your mistress, the wife of Nabal, will soon arrive to speak with him."

Abigail's strategy of appeasement before actual encounter is reminiscent of Jacob's action, centuries before, when he feared the vengeance of his brother. Unfortunately, her plan misfired because she failed to calculate the speed of one rider versus the speed of the caravan. Consequently, she and the food met with David at the same time.

David was still furious as he led his men out of the wilderness. Each time he thought of how Nabal had returned evil for good, anger was rekindled in his heart. When he rounded a curve on the road to Maon, he found his way blocked by a caravan of donkeys, loaded with food and led by the most beautiful woman he had ever seen.

Abigail dismounted quickly, approached David, curtsied politely, and began the most moving and most impressive plea recorded in the Bible:

"Let me, my lord, take the blame for my husband's sin. Pay no attention to the foolish actions of this wicked ingrate, Nabal. When you become king, you will be glad that you do not have blood-stained hands. Please take the food that I have brought for you and return to your camp."

David listened attentively as the lovely lady pleaded with him. His anger died down, his heart softened, and he spoke to her gently.

"I sincerely thank the Lord that He sent you to meet me this day," he said. "If you had not come, Nabal and all his men would have been killed before tomorrow morning. I gratefully accept the gifts that you offer. Now, return in peace to your own home."

Nabal was having a feast when she returned home, so Abigail waited until the next morning to tell him what she had done. Nabal was paralyzed with horror at the thought of what might have happened. Ten days later he had a massive and fatal "stroke."

When David learned that Nabal was dead, he sent some of his men to Abigail's home to tell her that he had fallen in love with her at the moment he first saw her, and that he would consider it a great honor if she would marry him. Like all good love stories, David's romance with Abigail ended happily. She agreed to go to David's camp with the messengers, and the two lovers were married.

While still in the wilderness, David was married again, this time to a woman from Jezreel. Her name was Ahinoam. However, he lost his first wife, Michal, because Saul had given his daughter to another man—a fact David was to learn later.

Based on the story in the Bible:
1 Samuel 23:19 — 25:44

SAUL'S LAST CONTACT WITH DAVID

S AMUEL DIED AND WAS BURIED in Ramah, his home town. All the people of Israel mourned for him." What a brief obituary for so great a man! His passing was to have yet another result. After Samuel's death, Saul's determination to destroy David became an obsession. No other thought entered his deranged mind. He openly declared, "If David is in Israel, I will not leave a stone unturned until I have found him and killed him."

Again the Ziphites betrayed David. They went to Saul and told him where David was hiding. Saul quickly selected three thousand of his ablest men and, with Abner in command, began a forced march which brought them near the place where David and his men were camped, late in the afternoon. By the time they had pitched camp, it was almost dark.

David's lookouts reported the arrival of Saul and his army in the valley below. Then they reported in quick succession that the men had pitched camp, eaten supper, and gone to their tents for a night's rest.

David was alone at one of the lookout posts. He watched the campfires slowly flicker out. Soon the encampment was dark and silent, and he returned to his men. To the surprise of all, David called for a volunteer to go with him to Saul's camp. Abishai, son of his sister Zeruiah, answered the call.

David and his nephew moved silently among the tents of the enemy. At last they came to the king's tent and looked inside. Saul and Abner were fast asleep. Abishai whispered to his uncle: "God has put Saul at our mercy. Let me go in and kill him with his own spear."

David saw that he must restrain his impulsive nephew, so he replied: "You must not kill Saul! Despite his hatred for me

"David Stops on a Hill" by J. James Tissot. *The Old Testament,* Illustrated. David took Saul's spear and flask while he slept, but did not harm him. M. de Buffan & Co.

and his many weaknesses, he is still our king, anointed by the Lord. God will not hold guiltless the person who takes his life. In the course of time, his day to die will come; or, perhaps, he will be killed on the battlefield. Get his spear and bottle of water, and we will return to our camp."

The next morning David stood on top of a hill overlooking the king's camp and shouted to Saul and Abner to attract their attention.

"Who are you that calls the king?" Abner shouted in reply.

"What a brave and valiant man you are, Abner!" David retorted, his voice tinged with sarcasm. "Your chief responsibility is to guard and protect the king. Yet, last night one of my men and I were in Saul's tent and you were fast asleep. You deserve to die, Abner, for sleeping on guard duty. But now, look! Here is the king's spear, and here the bottle of water that was by his side."

Saul thought that he recognized David's voice, so he called out: "Is this the voice of David?"

"It is my voice, O king!" David replied. "Why do you continue to pursue me? What wrong have I done you? If God has stirred you up against me, let us make a sacrifice to Him; but if it is your advisers, cursed be they before the Lord. Now, therefore, let not the king of Israel come out to seek my life, like a hunter looks for a partridge in the mountains."

After hearing these words Saul, perhaps for the first and last time, looked deeply into his heart and saw himself as he really was.

"I have sinned greatly, my son!" he cried to David. "Please come back to the palace with me. I promise that I shall never again try to harm you, because you spared my life last night. I have played the fool, and have erred exceedingly."

As the echo of their voices faded away, the two men went their separate ways— David back into the wilderness, because he could not believe that Saul had really changed so greatly, and Saul, back to his palace.

Just as David had surmised, the truce lasted only a few days. Saul was on his trail again, and David was tired of running. Moreover, he was becoming increasingly concerned about the welfare of his family and the families of his men. David carefully considered these problems and decided that the only solution was to leave Israel and go to the land of the Philistines.

David stood before Achish, Philistine king of Gath. He had just offered the service of himself and his men to Achish, if the king would give him a city in which all their families could settle.

Achish was delighted to welcome this brave warrior and his band of defectors. He promptly granted asylum to David and his men and gave them the city of Ziklag. As soon as they had established themselves there, David and his men made one cruel raid after another on communities in the surrounding territory. After each sortie, Achish would ask David where the scene of attack was, and David would pretend to the king that he raided some of the border towns of Israel. Achish believed David and began to trust him more and more. This deception was soon to bring David a real problem.

In response to a call from Achish, David and his men hurried to the palace. The king came out and spoke to them: "I have just completed plans for a major campaign against the Israelites. David, you and your men shall go with me and my army, for I have appointed you to be my personal bodyguard as long as you live."

David found himself in an awkward position. Was it possible that he would fight with the Philistines against his own

people? The lords and commanders of the armies were not as naive as Achish; they were distrustful of David and his men. They themselves solved David's dilemma when they went to Achish and told him sternly: "David and his men shall not go with us to the battle!"

After Achish had dismissed them, David and his band returned to Ziklag. They were grief-stricken to find that the city had been looted and burned by the Amalekites and that all their women and children had been carried off into captivity. They wept until there were no more tears; then they started out in hot pursuit of the Amalekites, caught up with them, and killed all of the enemy except four hundred young men who escaped on camels.

All the women and children were rescued unharmed, and everything that had been taken was recovered. In addition, all the flocks and herds of the Amalekites were seized and driven in front of the people as they started their return journey to Ziklag.

Based on the story in the Bible:
1 Samuel 26:1 — 28:2; 29:1 — 30:31

"David Returns to Achish" by J. James Tissot. *The Old Testament,* Illustrated. The King of Gath asked David to join his troops in an attack on the Israelites. M. de Buffan & Co.

"Appearance of Samuel's Ghost to Saul" by Rosa. The Louvre, Paris. When the Philistines prepared to attack Israel, Saul was afraid because he no longer had anyone to advise him. In desperation he visited the Witch of En-dor.

Alinari

THE DEATH OF SAUL

SAUL FACED ANOTHER GREAT BATTLE with the Philistines and he was weary, frightened, and lonely. No longer could he consult with Samuel, because the prophet was dead. Nevermore would he hear the soothing tones of David's music, for he was an exile in the land of the Philistines. Even God had forsaken him. When he asked the Lord what he should do, he received no answer.

Achish led his army into Israel and was soon encamped at Shunem. His men were in full battle array and his army would attack the Israelites the next day. Saul's army was camped at the foot of Mount Gilboa. As he gazed across the Jezreel Valley and saw the enemy, Saul became more and more fearful. If only he could have Samuel's advice!

Saul was desperate. Two of his men had volunteered to show him the way to the home of the Witch of En-dor. The king disguised himself and, in the still of the night, he and his men were silently approaching her home. When Saul entered the woman's house, he asked her if she could materialize the spirit of the person he named. On hearing this, the woman was terrified. She knew that such practices had been banned by the king, and she was fearful that the man was laying a trap for her. Saul calmed her fears by assuring her that no harm would come to her for doing what he asked.

The woman then asked Saul, "Whom shall I bring to you?"

"Bring Samuel to me!" Saul's startling answer caused her to be more frightened than ever.

The woman stared into his face and cried out: "Why have you deceived me? You are Saul, the king!"

The story of the Witch of En-dor is a strange one. Nevertheless, Saul certainly thought that he spoke to Samuel and that Samuel spoke to him. However, the news was all bad for the distressed king. Samuel told him that the Israelites would lose the battle on the following day and that Saul and all his sons would be killed.

The Battle of Mount Gilboa was over, and the Philistines had scored a great victory. Disorganized and in panic, the Israelites, including Saul and his three sons, fled from their enemies. The Philistines finally overtook the three princes—Jonathan, Abinadab, and Melchishua—and killed them. Saul, a short distance away, was felled by an enemy arrow. As he lay badly wounded, Saul urged his armor-bearer to kill him, so that he would not be captured alive. When the armor-bearer refused, Saul took his own sword, fell upon it, and killed himself. Thus it was that the royal house of Saul came tumbling down, out on the rolling slope of Mount Gilboa.

Saul might have gone down in history as one of Israel's great kings. Certainly he had all the qualifications. Yet he allowed temper tantrums, jealousy, and periods of depression to start him on the long slide from the pinnacle of popularity to a suicide's death.

Although Saul and his sons were dead, the Philistines had still further degradations in store for them. First, they cut off the king's head, stripped him of his

"Saul Falls upon His Sword" by J. James Tissot. The Old Testament, Illustrated. After the battle of Mount Gilboa, Saul was pursued and wounded by the Philistines. Rather than be captured, he killed himself.

M. de Buffan & Co.

armor, and placed both the head and the armor in an idol temple at nearby Beth-shan. Then they fastened the bodies of Saul and his sons on the walls of the city.

When they heard what had happened to Saul and his sons, the gallant men of Jabesh-gilead were on the march toward Beth-shan. The grateful people would never forget that long-ago day when Saul fought his first battle as king and saved them from being blinded. They reached Beth-shan late at night, took down the bodies of Saul and his sons, and carried them back to Jabesh-gilead. There an impressive funeral was held, and Saul and his sons were buried underneath a sacred tree. Then these courageous friends of Saul mourned and fasted for seven days.

While the battle raged, David was on his way back to Ziklag with the people he had rescued and the spoils he had taken from the desert raiders. They camped outside the burned city and had been there two days when a stranger approached. David asked him who he was and where he came from. The man replied that he was an Amalekite and had come from the camp of the Israelites. Then David asked anxiously how the battle had gone.

The Amalekite replied: "The Israelites fled from the battle and many of them were killed, including Saul and his three sons."

This incredible news stunned David, so he asked, "How do you know for sure that the king is dead?"

Whether he hoped to curry David's favor or whether he wanted to appear as a hero to him, the Amalekite gave an untrue version of how Saul had died. He boasted that it was *his* hand and *his* sword that killed Saul. David became furious when he heard this statement, and he cried out:

"How dared you raise your hand and strike the king of Israel, God's anointed! You shall die this very day because of what you have done."

During the period of mourning, David's heart was filled with sorrow. His respect for the king and his love for Jonathan caused him to compose this great lament:

"Your glory, O Israel, is slain upon your
  high places!
How the mighty have fallen!
Tell it not in Gath,
  Publish it not on the streets of
  Ashkelon,
Because the daughters of the Philistines
  would rejoice.
  O mountains of Gilboa,
Let no dew or rain fall upon you, let
  your fields become arid,
  For there the shield of the mighty was
  defiled,
The shield of Saul, just as though he
  were not God's anointed!
  The bow of Jonathan did not come
  back,
And the sword of Saul did not return.
  Saul and Jonathan, together during
  their lifetime,
Were not divided when they died.
  You daughters of Israel, weep over
  Saul,
Who clothed you in scarlet,
  Who put ornaments of gold upon your
  apparel.
They were swifter than eagles,
  They were stronger than lions.
How the mighty have fallen in battle!
  Jonathan, slain upon the high places!
I long for you, my brother Jonathan;
  Your friendship made me very happy;
Your love for me was wonderful,
  Surpassing the love of women.
How the mighty have fallen,
  And the weapons of war destroyed!"

Based on the story in the Bible:
1 Samuel 28:3 — 29:2, 31:1-13;
2 Samuel 1:1-27

PLACES

in the Story of Saul

MIZPEH (Mizpah)

It was at Mizpeh, a sanctuary and religious center 7 miles northwest of Jerusalem, that the Israelites met and chose Saul to be their king.

GIBEAH

Gibeah was the home town and capital of Israel's first king. It is 4 miles north of Jerusalem, by the side of the main road leading to Samaria. The city has an altitude of 2,750 feet.

JABESH-GILEAD (Jabesh)

It was at this town, 5 miles east of the Jordan and midway between the Armuk and Jabbok Rivers, that Saul had his first opportunity as king to prove his prowess as a warrior. When he learned that King Nahash and his army were besieging the city, Saul summoned his army and scored a decisive victory over the Ammonites.

VALLEY OF MICHMASH

Near a city of the same name lies the Valley of Michmash. It is 7 miles north of Jerusalem and about 3 miles north of Gibeah. Saul's first battle with the Philistines occurred here and Jonathan, his son, struck the first blow against them on the nearby hills. Rout of the Philistines was completed in this valley, and the Israelites pursued them to their own border; but the Philistines continued to hold fortresses in Israel throughout the reign of Saul, resulting in constant warfare.

BETHLEHEM

The little town of Bethlehem is 5 miles south of Jerusalem on the road to Hebron. When God rejected Saul as king, He told Samuel to go to the home of Jesse, in this town, and anoint Israel's second king.

THE WARS OF SAUL

Moabite War

The territory of Moab lies east of the Dead Sea and its northern border is the tribe of Reuben. After defeating the Ammonites at Jabesh, Saul turned his attention to two of

Saul's Kingdom. Saul warred against his neighbors, including the Ammonites and the Amalekites, but particularly against the Philistines, who finally overcame him at Mount Gilboa.

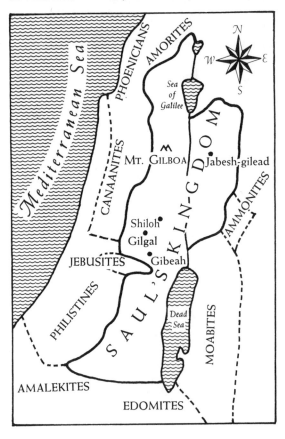

Mount Gilboa rises on the eastern side of the plain of Esdrae-lon. This area is historically important as the site of the final battle that Saul fought with the Philistines, in which he and his three sons were defeated and died. © Matson Photo

their allies. He first fought the Moabites. Although no battle sites are mentioned, it is recorded that the Moabites were soundly defeated.

Edomite War

Saul's next battle was with the other ally, the Edomites. Their northern border was the Dead Sea and the land of Moab, and their western border was the tribe of Judah. Again no battle sites are mentioned, but Saul's victory over them is recorded.

Syrian War

The Aramaean state of Zobah, north of Damascus, had frontiers extending as far as the Euphrates. Located in the Anti-Lebanon range, Zobah was rich in silver. Saul's campaign against Zobah was very likely a defensive one, designed to protect his borders against Aramaean invasions.

Amalekite War

The marauding nomads to the south, the Amalekites, who attacked the Israelites at the time of their migration from Egypt, proved to be Israel's inveterate foes. Saul secured his southern borders by defeating them in a battle, the site of which is not stated.

Valley of Elah

There were doubtless many wars between the Israelites and Philistines during Saul's reign. The second recorded war was notable in that David, who had been anointed privately by Samuel, appeared on the field of battle for the first time. In the Valley of Elah, 15 miles southwest of Jerusalem between the hill-cities of Socoh and Azekah, David met the Philistine giant, Goliath, and killed him. The Israelite victory which followed made David a national hero.

NOB

Nob, "the city of priests," was 2 miles northeast of Jerusalem, and was David's first stopping place as he fled into exile from Gibeah. Ahimelech, a descendant of Eli and leader of the priests of the city, with all the people of Nob, was murdered by Saul for befriending David.

GATH

Gath, one of the five great Philistine cities, was located about 15 miles east of the seacoast city of Ashkelon. After David's escape from Nob, he made his way down the mountains to this city. Known as an enemy of Saul, David was suspected by the Philistines at Gath of being their enemy also, especially when they recalled that he was the man who had killed their town's hero, Goliath. David feigned insanity in order to escape.

ADULLAM

When David returned from Philistia, he took refuge in a cave near Adullam. This city is only a few miles southeast of the Valley of Elah, scene of his first encounter with the Philistines, and midway between Jerusalem and Lachish. Here he was joined by sympathizers, including his parents and brothers. Saul's murder of the priests of Nob doubtless served warning on others friendly to David that their lives were in danger.

MIZPEH OF MOAB

At this unidentified place, David took his parents and left them under the care of the king of Moab.

FOREST OF HARETH (Hereth)

The location of the town of Hareth, from which this forest got its name, is unidentifiable, but it was probably in the mountainous country a few miles southwest of Adullam. On the advice of Gad, the prophet, David and his men moved their headquarters to the forest of Hareth.

Cave of Adullam. David hid in a cave of Adullam after fleeing from Saul and Achish, the King of Gath. He was joined by his family and followers who also were in danger. © Matson Photo

KEILAH

The Philistines attacked Keilah, about a mile southeast of Adullam. David, at his forest headquarters nearby, rallied his men to defend the city. When David learned that the ungrateful people of Keilah were preparing to betray him, he made a hasty departure for the wilderness between Hebron and the Dead Sea.

ZIPH

At Ziph, in the wilderness 4 miles southeast of Hebron, David found a refuge. It was at a nearby cave that David met Jonathan for the last time. When the Ziphites prepared to betray him to Saul, David fled.

MAON

David received his closest escape from Saul at Maon, a hill-city 12 miles due south of Hebron. Saul and his troops had him completely surrounded and were closing in on him. Deliverance came, however, when a Philistine attack forced Saul to leave. Also at Maon, David sought provisions from wealthy Nabal, who contemptuously refused to pay any tribute to David. He and his men were prepared to force the issue when Abigail, Nabal's wife appeared with a generous gift. After Nabal's death a short time later, David married Abigail.

EN-GEDI

Near the center of the western shore of the Dead Sea, about 30 miles southeast of Jerusalem (if the road is followed), was the almost inaccessible town of En-gedi, meaning "well of the wild goat." In one of the numerous caves nearby, David found a place of refuge. When Saul inadvertently entered the cave, David cut off a piece of the king's robe but did not take advantage of the opportunity to kill his persecutor.

ZIKLAG

Despairing of safety in Israel, David fled to the Philistine country. The king of Gath, a city about 10 miles southeast of the seacoast city of Ashkelon, assigned to David the city of Ziklag. This city was about 25 miles southeast of Gaza, near the Philistine and

Israel border. David remained here until after Saul's death.

EN-DOR

Two places were associated with the last hours of Saul's life. En-dor, located about 10 miles northeast of Saul's encampment, was one of them. Fearing for his life, Saul left camp stealthily on the eve of the impending battle with the Philistines for a clandestine interview with a witch at En-dor.

MOUNT GILBOA

The morning after Saul's visit to the Witch of En-dor, a fierce battle was fought between Israel and the Philistines at the foot of Mount Gilboa. Saul and three of his sons, including Jonathan, were killed. The Philistine victory at Gilboa thoroughly humbled Israel but made possible David's rapid rise to power, an event which ushered in the golden age of Israel.

Tell at Beth-shan, which was a Canaanite city in the valley of the Jordan, about 14 miles south of the Sea of Galilee.

After Saul's death, his body was taken by the Philistines and fastened upon the city wall. © Matson Photo

QUESTIONS
on the Story of Saul

1

1 What great event was scheduled to happen soon at Mizpeh?

2 How was Saul chosen?

3 What did Samuel tell the people, after he had anointed Saul as their king?

4 Where did Saul fight his first battle as king? Why and against whom?

2

5 Where was the site of Saul's first battle against the Philistines? How did it start? How did it end?

6 Before starting his pursuit of the Philistines, what was the unwise command that Saul gave to his troops? Who disobeyed it?

7 How was Jonathan's execution averted?

3

8 Name the two things God told Samuel to do. Why was he hesitant to perform these tasks?

9 Where did Samuel go when he arrived in Bethlehem? Why did he go there?

10 What was Saul's reaction when Samuel told him that God had rejected him?

11 Whom did Saul bring to the palace to play soothing music for him?

12 What were the names of the two young men who vowed an inseparable friendship?

4

13 Why was Saul's second war with the Philistines so notable?

14 How did David kill Goliath?

15 What did the Philistines do when they saw their dead champion lying in the dust of the Valley of Elah?

5

16 Why did Saul become increasingly jealous of David?

17 What did Jonathan do when he heard his father order the servants to kill David?

18 Whom did David marry during his temporary reconciliation with Saul? What did the king do late one afternoon that warned David of his father-in-law's bitter hatred for him?

19 How did Michal help David escape her father's ire?

20 How did Jonathan warn David that it was unsafe to return to the palace and that he must flee for his life?

6

21 Why did David stop at Nob when he fled from the palace? What was the tragic aftermath of his visit there?

22 Where did David fight his first war for Israel as an outlaw? Why and against whom was it fought?

23 Where did David and his men go after their hasty departure from Keilah?

24 Why was it necessary for David to leave this city so quickly?

25 What was the unexpected happiness that came to David while he was still in hiding in the mountains?

7

26 Why was David so sure that Nabal would supply him with provisions?

27 What was David's reaction when he heard the reply of the wealthy man? What did David do?

28 What did Abigail, Nabal's wife, do when

she learned that David was approaching Maon?

29 What did David do when he heard that Nabal had died suddenly?

30 What had happened to Michal, David's first wife?

8

31 Where was Samuel buried?

32 What did Saul do when the Ziphites betrayed David's hiding place to him?

33 How did Saul react when he saw David holding the king's spear and water bottle? What did Saul say when he realized that he had been at David's mercy the night before?

34 Why did David decide to go into exile in Philistia? What is the name of the Philistine city that King Achish assigned to David?

35 What did David and his men do when they returned to their city, found it looted and burned, and their wives and children held captive?

9

36 Why did Saul go to see the Witch of En-dor?

37 What was the message that the spirit of Samuel gave to Saul?

38 Where was Saul's encampment when the battle started?

39 Why did the men of Jabesh-gilead retrieve the bodies of Saul and his three sons and give them a respectable burial back at Jabesh?

40 What did David do when he learned of the deaths of his king and of his true friend, Jonathan?

Answers are found on the following pages.

"*David Cuts the Skirt of Saul*" by J. James Tissot. *The Old Testament,* Illustrated. David's men expected him to kill Saul in the cave at Engedi, but David did not harm the king because he knew that Saul was God's anointed. M. de Buffan & Co.

ANSWERS

on the Story of Saul

1

1 The Israelites were soon to assemble at Mizpeh and choose their first king.

2 Saul was chosen as Israel's first king by drawing lots.

3 Samuel's final official act as the last Judge of Israel was to address his people: "I have listened to your request and, with God's guidance, I have anointed a king to rule over you. Now that you have a king, remember my solemn warning: Things will go well with you and your kingdom as long as you obey the Lord and keep His commandments. On the contrary, if you should ever rebel against God and refuse to honor and serve Him, both you and your king shall be destroyed."

4 Saul fought his first battle as king at Jabesh-gilead. All the men in this city were under the threat of being blinded in their right eyes by Nahash, king of the Ammonites.

2

5 The first battle against the Philistines was fought in the Valley of Michmash. It was started prematurely by Jonathan, when he and his aide dislodged a garrison of Philistines up in the highlands overlooking the valley. A sharp earthquake created further confusion in the valley. When defectors to the Israelites saw the tide of battle turn, they rallied behind Jonathan and deserted the people who had befriended them. A great victory was won by the Israelites.

6 Saul commanded that no one eat anything until nightfall and that the penalty for disobedience would be death. Jonathan, Saul's son, unknowingly disobeyed the command.

7 The army rebelled against Saul and protected Jonathan.

3

8 God told Samuel (1) to notify Saul that He had rejected him as king and (2) to anoint a new king. Samuel hesitated, because of his great love for Saul.

9 Samuel went to the home of Jesse. God had told him that one of Jesse's sons was the person He had chosen to be Israel's next king. David, the youngest, was anointed.

10 Saul listened to Samuel's words in shocked disbelief and, soon afterward, began to act so strangely that his servants feared he was losing his mind.

11 Saul brought David to the palace to play music for him.

12 David and Jonathan vowed to remain friends as long as they lived.

4

13 The second war with the Philistines was notable for two reasons: The manner in which it was fought—one combatant from each camp—and the fact that it marked David's appearance on the battlefield for the first time.

14 David stunned Goliath first with a shot from his sling. Then David delivered the finishing blow with the giant's own sword.

15 The Philistines reneged on their pledge to surrender, and they fled in panic to their fortified city of Eglon.

5

16 Saul became increasingly jealous of David because his popularly was rising higher

and higher among the Israelites; conversely, Saul's popularity was dropping lower and lower.

17 Jonathan rushed to his friend, told him of his father's orders, and advised David to stay out of the house and out of sight during the night.

18 David married Saul's youngest daughter, Michal. While David was trying to soothe Saul's troubled mind with music, the king suddenly threw his spear at him.

19 First, Michal lowered David from a window with a rope. Then she placed a dummy on David's bed and covered it so that, if the guards came up unexpectedly, they would think the decoy was David.

20 By a pre-arranged signal with David, Jonathan took an arrow-bearer to a field near the cave in which David was hiding. When Jonathan shot the arrows over the lad's head and shouted out that the arrows were in front of him, David knew that he must flee for his life.

6

21 David stopped at Nob because he needed food and a weapon. When Saul learned that Ahimelech had aided David, he ordered all the priests and all the people in Nob to be killed. Abiathar, son of Ahimelech, was the only priest to escape the massacre.

22 At Keilah. David fought the Philistines, who were waging war on the people of Keilah and were robbing them of their grain.

23 David and his men went to a mountainous wilderness between Hebron and the Dead Sea.

24 Despite the fact that David had just liberated their city, the ungrateful men of Keilah were preparing to turn him over to Saul.

25 Jonathan came to visit his friend, David. This proved to be the last time that they would see each other.

7

26 When Nabal's servants were shearing their flocks near David's camp, the outlaw chieftan and his men had guarded and protected the shearers, the shepherds, and the flocks.

27 David became furiously angry when he heard the wealthy man's scornful reply. Leaving two hundred men behind to guard the camp, David and the other four hundred began a forced march to Maon. He was determined to kill Nabal and all the men in his household because of his actions that day. David vowed that the provisions, which could have been given peacefully, would now be taken by the sword.

28 Abigail quickly gathered a bountiful supply of food and went out to meet David. She gave him the food and pleaded with him not to enter his kingship with bloodstained hands. Abigail's gift and plea caused David to reconsider his plan.

29 After Nabal's sudden death, David asked Abigail to marry him. She accepted his proposal.

30 Saul had dissolved Michal's marriage with David, and she had married another man.

8

31 Samuel was buried in his home town of Ramah.

32 Saul selected three thousand of his finest warriors and set out for David's hiding place.

33 Saul became penitent and asked David to return to the palace with him. Saul promised David that never again would he try to harm him, because he had spared his king's life the night before.

34 David despaired of ever re-establishing rapport with Saul and felt that the king would continue the chase as long as David remained in Israel. David was tired of running so he and his band, along with their families, sought asylum in the land of the Philistines. King Achish assigned the

border city of Ziklag to David and his men.

35 David and his men pursued the Amalekites, caught up with the raiders, and killed all of them except four hundred young men who escaped on camels. All the women and children were rescued, and everything that had been taken was recovered.

9

36 Saul went to the oracle of the Witch of En-dor because he was lonely and alone. He could no longer consult with Samuel, because he was dead. Never again would he hear lilting strains of David's music, for he was an exile in Philistia. Even God had forsaken him. Saul was in desperate need of someone with whom he could consult.

37 The spirit of Samuel told Saul that Israel would be defeated on the morrow and that he and his sons would be killed in the battle.

38 Saul and his army were camped at the foot of Mount Gilboa.

39 The grateful men of Jabesh-gilead retrieved the bodies of Saul and his sons because they remembered that Saul's first battle as a warrior-king had saved their men from being blinded.

40 David composed a great lament for Saul and Jonathan.

"Jesse Presents His Sons to Samuel" by J. James Tissot. *The Old Testament,* Illustrated. Samuel sought the next king of Israel among the Bethlehemites, especially in the family of Jesse, who had many sons. M. de Buffan & Co.

FURTHER FACTS AND OUTLINE
for the Story of Saul

FIRST SAMUEL (continued)

AUTHORSHIP AND DATE

See *Further Facts and Outline for the Story of Samuel.*

DESTINATION

For the Jewish people and posterity.

PURPOSE AND THEME

Saul was chosen as Israel's first king. What a pathetic, mentally disturbed figure he was! He could not distinguish between the material and the spiritual. He was fickle and he did not obey God. At the end of his life he confessed, "I have played the fool," and he committed suicide. (Contrast this statement with the words of another Saul—Saul of Tarsus: "I have fought a good fight.") Out of King Saul's career is brought to light his disobedience of God's command to exterminate the Amalekites (1 Samuel 15:3) and Samuel's words of censure, "... Obedience is better than sacrifice," exemplifying the truth that right ritual is no substitute for a right heart.

OUTLINE

Saul the King
(chapters 8-15, 17-24, 26-28, 31)
Israel's Desire for a King (chapter 8)
Saul Anointed King (chapters 9-10)
Samuel's Retirement Address: "... Serve the Lord with all your heart."
(chapter 12)
Saul's Disobedience of God's Command (chapters 13-15)
Saul and David (chapters 17-24, 26-27)
Saul and the Witch of En-dor (chapter 28)
Saul Defeated and Killed (chapter 31)

"David Goes to the Cave of Adullam" by J. James Tissot. *The Old Testament,* Illustrated. Because of Saul's relentless persecution of him, David took refuge in a cave near the city of Adullam, where he lived for a long time.   M. de Buffan & Co.

Where Courage Begins

by
Richard Tregaskis

Some men start well and end badly. Such, in brief, is the story of Saul, first king of Israel. At the beginning of his career, as recorded in the pages of the Bible, Saul was so filled with the kind of courage depicted here by Richard Tregaskis that he could inspire men to deeds of great valor—a power that he lost when the source of his strength, a refreshing reliance on God, dried up. One of America's best-known war correspondents, Tregaskis has been characterized as our fightingest correspondent by such military leaders as Gen. Matthew B. Ridgway and Gen. Merritt S. "Red Mike" Edson. Tregaskis' first book, *Guadalcanal Diary,* established him as a top-ranking war reporter. Other books include *Invasion Diary, John F. Kennedy and the PT-109, Vietnam Diary,* and *Stronger than Fear,* a novel which resulted from the experience related here. The death of Tregaskis' hero, Ozell Smoot, stands in stark contrast to that of King Saul. ("Where Courage Begins" by Richard Tregaskis, copyright © 1964 by Family Weekly Magazine, Inc. Reprinted by permission of Paul R. Reynolds, Inc., 599 Fifth Avenue, New York, N. Y. 10017.)

THE BATTLE FOR SELF-RESPECT

IT WAS AMONG THE RUINS of Aachen that I met Ozell Smoot, the lean, dark captain who taught me how to grapple with fear and discover courage, military style—or for that matter, any style.

Aachen in the late fall of 1944 was full of the shocks, sounds, and dangers of an embattled city. But its ruination was not yet complete.

Determined German soldiers and Americans of the famous First Division were further reducing it to rubble. Block by block, street by street, room by room, we were battling to drive them out of this, the first sizable German city we had reached since D-Day—and they were resisting bitterly.

I was involved as a correspondent in this clash of armies, writing about the thousands of human beings killed and wounded there. And, if there was any lesson to be learned, it seemed to be that *any spot could suddenly become bloody and mortal.*

I was much aware of this when I met Ozell, a lanky, rawhide son of the Deep South who commanded the company which I was attached to. Ozell had an extra-slow drawl and a good company-commander manner: he was thoughtful enough but decisive; tall enough so you could see him; neat enough but not too neat. If the GIs of E Company, 26th Infantry, First Division, had prepared a list of physical requirements for their commander, they probably couldn't have found a better-looking C.O. than Ozell.

This was all I knew about him at the beginning. I didn't find out till later that I couldn't have found a better man to help me solve the pressing psychological problem which I was facing.

After a year of the Pacific War, I had gone

to Sicily and then from Salerno up to San Pietro in the Italian campaign. I had seen a lot of our people killed and hurt, usually much too close. At last, on the mountain approaches to San Pietro, I was hit by a German mortar. They carried me out with a hole in my skull the size of a soup spoon and bone and steel fragments embedded two inches deep in my brain.

I worked my way toward the States through six Army and Navy hospitals. Finally, a tantalum plate was put into my head at Walter Reed Hospital in Washington—and I went back to the fighting front.

I caught up with our forces in Normandy and went along with them through a good many actions. But I knew I was not the same as I had been. I was aware of a new and dreadful sensitivity to the dangers of war—an acute, nervous state that made the sounds of incoming shells or enemy machine-gun fire crushing and unbearable.

I had a succession of bad "nerve shakes" across France, Belgium, Holland, and into Germany. So I decided to put the whole business to the acid test by plunging into the Aachen battle with a front-line company; I knew that if I survived I would have a new set of nerves—and probably a good story, too.

But now, as I joined up with Ozell Smoot's company in Aachen, I was kicking myself for having made what was very evidently the wrong decision. As I walked cautiously through the rubble-streaked streets, heading for the Second Squad, First Platoon, with whom I would be staying, I already felt waves of terrible apprehension—an awareness that the worst could happen to *me,* that *I* would be the statistic in the casualty list and not someone else.

I knew that for every death in battle there were always four or five terrible injuries. And, thanks to my previous wound, I had a good idea what wounds meant: long sessions of jolting pain, desperate abandonment of hope, the horrible hours of not knowing whether you would ever recover, the contemplation of ways to kill yourself if you became no more than a vegetable.

The second squad was hunkered down for the night in a cellar which had served as an air-raid shelter in roofless Aachen. Checking with the corporal who led the squad, I learned that the 11-man unit had lost three men in the last few days.

We spread out on the cellar floor to wait out the night. It was calm. The only real alarm was the rattling of a German tank a couple of blocks away and a few bursts of artillery shells. One shell hit into our block, and there was a terrible waterfall of smashing glass upstairs in our building. I was sure we were going to get it.

But war ran to its usual form: anticlimax piled on expected catastrophe. No more close hits, no German counterattack that night.

In the morning things really turned bad. After getting orders to clear the blocks ahead of us and reach a new phase line, we dragged ourselves out of the cellar and deployed along the street. Behind us, the 90-mm tank destroyers began a nerve-shattering barrage designed to clear the way for our attack.

The haughty coughing of the 90s, the choirlike sigh of the outgoing shells, the shattering impact of the rounds beyond us and the shaking of the earth as they hit—these were the usual sounds before an attack, yet already my nerves were at the breaking point!

The attack that day and the days after was a blur of terror, a living nightmare: running down streets; faces full of dirt as shells screamed in and you hit the rubble which was the earth; the shock of the cracking bullets that were coming too close (close ones don't whine as they do on tv—if they're dangerous, they crack); the knowing that an unseen enemy rifleman or machine gunner is trying to kill you; the breathless hunt for him among the ruins; the silencing of him, usually with grenades or artillery; the horror on men's faces at the moment you know well—when you have been hit; and the dreadful ignorance of whether or not you are going to die.

This was what it was like for me in the fiery crux of that front line. And it would have been unbearable and maddening except for one thing: the frequent appearance of Ozell. When things were worst, we always saw

Ozell. Darting into our street while the firing was still going on all around, he would stop to talk to the platoon leader as calmly as if we were on maneuvers. He would make sure the wounded were carried out and reached ambulances. And he would spot snipers and Kraut artillery and observation posts with a cool eye and call artillery or mortars down on them.

I was always astounded by his coolness and his effectiveness. He never seemed concerned that he would be killed or wounded. He was just what a company commander should be: a prime mover, a leader, an example of courage.

Then came the moment when I was most nearly distraught. Sprawled in the broken shell of a house, alone as you usually are at the front, I heard the ripping sounds of a German machine gun in the next street. The firing grew heavier; it was a couple of Kraut "paper cutters" close together. Then there was a heavy fusillade of small arms which came like a cascade. It seemed closer; it seemed to be moving in *my* direction. Then it stopped for a moment—and in that moment Ozell came skidding into the broken bricks which formed my hole.

He grinned at me. "A rough day," he said. As usual, I admired his calm—but also a streak of something like jealousy hit me. He wouldn't be so calm if he had once been wounded, as I had! In that moment, he seemed to read my face, or perhaps he had heard from some members of the platoon that I had been running much too scared.

He said quietly, as if he understood my mood completely:

"I got it myself a couple of times. I came in with the Division in North Africa." Ozell must have heard about my being wounded, and he knew exactly how to get to me.

In a lull between spurts of firing, he went on: "It took me a while to figure it. Your chances aren't any worse after you've been hit once. It just seems like it. It takes more guts because you know what can happen."

He didn't look right at me when he was talking, and in a second he was gone, running down the street toward the corner.

The truth of what he said didn't hit me immediately. It actually was months before I had redefined it in my own terms. Yet by the special magic that he commanded as a leader, what he said somehow made me feel more at ease. He wanted me to know that he had long since come to grips with the same problem I faced then.

What he was saying was: when you first go into a war (or anything else mortally dangerous), you think it can never happen to you. It might happen to someone else but not to you—until, unbelievably, it does happen. Then comes the real beginning of courage: when you go on taking chances despite the fact that now you know the realities you couldn't imagine at first. Suddenly, you are a battle-qualified veteran with a new, seasoned kind of courage. Like Ozell's.

After that moment in Aachen, the fighting suddenly seemed less dreadful, and I knew I had gained a new grip on myself. Ozell had restored to me the toughness I needed, a new kind of toughness, the seasoned kind of inner strength that comes after battle scars.

Ozell came through the battle of Aachen unharmed. He kept his company together, he rode his platoons, he led his men, he got the result: at the end of a harrowing week, we had taken our casualties and had pushed the Krauts out of Aachen.

When the battle was over and I was lucky enough to have a rest in the States before going out to the Pacific again with a B-29 crew, I had time to think about Ozell and what he had meant to me.

A fever of wanting to write about the fighting in Aachen seized me, and in a couple of months of frenzied work I wrote a novel about it called *Stronger than Fear*. It was about an imaginary captain named Paul Kreider—not too unlike Ozell Smoot—who fought a battle with fear in a city like Aachen. I called the city Unterbach.

The writing of the book was a hard struggle, but when it was over, I felt I had distilled a central truth of life at war, and perhaps even of life in general. This truth was that when you are faced with a mortal fear which demands the deepest kind of courage, and you can find that courage, you have won life's most important battle, the battle for self-respect.

But this story isn't complete without mention of what happened to Ozell. I lost touch with him when I left Aachen and the First Division, and it was not till after the war was over that I learned his fate.

He had been killed about a month after I left him, in the tough winter fighting among the tall pines of the Hürtgen Forest. He died a soldier's death, leading his troops in battle, taking the chances he had to with his usual calm competence. He died facing the ultimate danger, respected and loved by his men.

I would hope to die as well. But however that may be, I will always be grateful to him for showing me how to face life with the strength that comes when you realize the magnitude of the dangers—and nevertheless tackle them head-on.

David

THE WARRIOR-KING WHO CONQUERED the enemies of Israel in a dark and desperate period of her history; the sagacious statesman who gave unity to the various tribes and formed them into a powerful monarchy; the matchless poet who bequeathed to all the ages a lofty and beautiful psalmnody; the saint who, with all his backsliding and inconsistencies, was a man after God's own heart—David is worthy of our study. As the most illustrious of all the kings of whom the Jewish nation was proud, David is a striking example of a good man occasionally enslaved by sin, yet breaking its bonds and rising above subsequent temptations to a higher plane of goodness. A man so elevated, with almost every virtue that makes a man beloved and yet with defects that will forever stain his memory, cannot easily be portrayed.

What character in history presents such contradictions? What career was ever more varied? What recorded experiences are more interesting and more instructive? He lived a life of heroism and adventure, of triumphs and humiliations, of inner and outer conflicts. Who ever loved or hated with more intensity than David? He was tender yet fierce, brave yet weak, magnanimous yet unrelenting, exultant yet sad, committing heinous crimes yet rising triumphantly after each disgraceful fall by a force of piety so ardent that even his backslidings now appear as but spots upon a sun.

David's varied experiences call out our sympathy and admiration more than those in the life of any secular hero whom poetry and history have immortalized. He was . . . equally great in war and peace, in action and meditation, in creation of an empire and in transmission to posterity of a collection of poems identified forever with the spiritual life of individuals and nations.—John Lord, *Beacon Lights of History*

1
THE STRUGGLE FOR THE THRONE

AFTER DAVID HAD GIVEN VOICE to his beautiful dirge for Saul and Jonathan, he had it written in the Book of Jashar. This book was an anthology of the early poems of Israel. Then David asked God what He wanted him to do next. God's answer was for him to return to Israel. So, after fourteen months in exile, the happy people began their journey back to their native land. When David and his caravan arrived at Hebron, there was great rejoicing throughout all Judah. After giving David a tumultuous welcome, the people met in solemn conclave and anointed him king of Judah.

David's first act as king was to honor the brave men of Jabesh-gilead. He sent his couriers to the city with this message:

"David, king of Judah, sends greetings to the courageous men of your city. God bless you now and always because of your loyalty to Saul, your king. You clearly demonstrated your dedication to him when you removed his body and the bodies of his sons from the walls of Beth-shan and gave them a decent burial. I shall never forget your kindness to God's anointed. Therefore, I now solemnly promise to guard, protect, and befriend you all the days of my reign."

After the disastrous defeat of the Israel-ites at Mount Gilboa, Abner and the remnants of his army retreated across the Jordan to the city of Mahanaim. It was here that Abner proclaimed Ish-bosheth, Saul's youngest son, king of all Israel with the exception of Judah. Poor weak-willed, weak-minded Ish-bosheth! Al-though he was king in name, Captain Abner was the real power behind the throne and he had the secret ambition actually to become the king of Israel.

To further his ambition, Abner knew that he must have an army powerful enough to defeat and destroy David and his army. To that end, he immediately began a feverish recruitment and training program.

Meanwhile, across the Jordan at Hebron, David was not idle. He, too, realized that, before Israel could become

David's First Kingdom. It was many years before Israel was united. After Saul's death, his son Ish-bosheth became king of most of the tribes. David was anointed only as king of Judah.

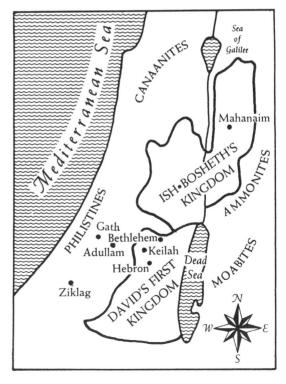

a united nation, either his dynasty or the dynasty of Saul, represented by Ish-bosheth and Abner, must be eliminated. Therefore, a similar flurry of activity was going on there.

The day finally came when the two armies were face to face with each other. Joab, David's captain, stood poised on one side of the Pool of Gibeon; Abner, with his men, was on the other side. The first battle of the first recorded civil war would soon begin. However, before the battle actually started, each captain chose twelve of his men to engage in a tournament to the death. This was done to arouse the emotions and stimulate the passions of hatred among the other soldiers of each army. Then, even as now, an "incident" must occur before nations willingly topple over the brink into war.

Joab and Abner shouted out in unison: "Let the young men come forward!"

These awesome words have come thundering down the centuries, whenever and wherever there have been wars or rumors of wars.

When all of the young men had been killed, a fierce battle ensued. Abner and his men were defeated in the initial skirmish, so he called for his armies to retreat. Asahel, who could run as fast as a wild deer, noticed that Abner had become separated from the main body of the retreating army. What an opportunity to become a hero by capturing and killing the captain of Ish-bosheth's army! Joab would be very proud of his youngest brother Asahel that day. So the race of death was on.

Fleet Asahel gained rapidly on the fleeing captain. Soon the two men were within shouting distance of each other. Abner pleaded with the young runner to return to his brother. The captain had no desire to wage an individual fight with the impetuous youth, because the outcome was certain. Asahel would be no match for the experienced warrior. However, Asahel refused to turn aside; instead, he raced on until he came so close that Abner, in self-defense, thrust his spear at Asahel and killed him.

Joab's men pursued the men of Ish-bosheth until the shades of night began to fall. Abner had managed to regroup his men at the top of a small hill and, in the gathering gloom, shouted down to Joab:

"Must we die by the sword forever? If we continue to fight, the only result will be increasing bitterness and a deeper rift between us. If you will take your army back to Hebron, I will return to Mahanaim with mine."

Joab was magnanimous in victory. He accepted Abner's proposal and blew his trumpet to signalize the beginning of the truce. On the way back to Hebron, Joab and Obishai paused at Bethlehem to bury their brother in the family tomb. After the funeral, the march was resumed and the army reached Hebron just as the sun peeped over the nearby hills. Joab went to the palace and made his report of the battle to David.

The truce lasted for only a few days. A long war between the house of Saul and the house of David followed the initial battle. David became stronger and stronger as his army conquered more and more of Israel; conversely, the house of Saul became weaker and weaker.

As king of Judah, David often dreamed of the day when peace would come to Israel and the people would be united into one nation. Perhaps that day was nearer than he thought, because Abner was nearing the palace for peace talks.

Abner approached the gates of Hebron with mingled emotions—sadness, because he was about to defect from the house of Saul which he had served long and faithfully, and happiness, because the end of an arduous, wearisome, seven-year struggle was in sight. He had seen the handwriting on the wall, and he knew that the sands of time were fast running out for Ish-bosheth and his shrinking kingdom.

After the great feast was over, David and Abner, with their delegates, gathered around the conference table. Abner wasted no time. He arose and addressed David and his advisors.

"I am here to propose an alliance between the house of David and the people of Israel still under my command,"

"*Abner and Asahel*" by J. James Tissot. *The Old Testament*, Illustrated. Asahel, a brother of Joab, was killed in his attempt to murder Captain Abner. M. de Buffan and Co.

he declared. "When I come back, I shall bring the elders of my cities with me. They will anoint you king of all Israel, and I will place my army at the disposal of my king."

Abner's proposal, with no strings attached, surprised and pleased David. He had expected to spend many long hours of negotiation before such an agreement could be worked out. David accepted the offer without hesitation and sent Abner away in peace.

Joab was furious. He had returned from a successful raid to learn that David not only had entertained Abner but had also formed an alliance with him. David's grizzled warrior, who had survived campaign after campaign by being both cautious and suspicious, decided that there was only one thing to do. Accordingly, he sent his fastest messengers after Abner to tell him to return to the palace.

Joab stood silently outside the city gate waiting for Abner to come back. His mind was churning with thoughts and question after unanswered question. How could David have been so gullible? Why hadn't David waited to hold the conference until his reliable old Joab had returned from the raid? Was it possible that David was planning to supplant him and appoint Abner as commanding general of all the armies of Israel? Surely David must have seen through Abner's ruse and realized that he had come to the city only to spy and to deceive. In any event, there would be nothing to worry about in a few minutes, because Joab was fully determined to kill Abner as soon as he arrived at the city gate.

When the news of Abner's assassination reached David, he was shocked and sent for his nephews, Joab and Abishai, immediately. He reprimanded the two brothers severely, and warned them that God would surely punish them for their murderous act. David then issued this proclamation:

"A prince and a great man has fallen this day in Israel. I therefore proclaim a period of public mourning for this brave and gallant soldier, Captain Abner, leader of the armies of Israel. All the people of Judah shall dress in sackcloth and ashes, and I shall lead the funeral procession."

Abner was buried at Hebron. David and all the people of Judah wept as his body was slowly lowered into the grave. Then David composed this sorrowful lament:

"Shall a tried and true warrior like you,
    Abner, die by your own folly?
You were not captured,
    nor were you killed in battle.
As a man falls before treacherous men,
    even so you have fallen!"

Although David did not know it, there was to be one more act of violence and bloodshed before the way would be clear for him to be king of a united Israel.

Panic, instead of Ish-bosheth, reigned when Saul's son and his people learned of the death of Abner. Yet David himself did not wish any harm to befall Saul's son. However, the king was to receive another shock. One day, not long after Abner's death, David was stunned when two men entered his royal chamber carrying the head of Ish-bosheth.

"We went to Ish-bosheth's palace at noon, sneaked into his bed chamber, and killed him," they proclaimed, proudly. "Look! Here is the head of the son of Saul, your enemy. Now you are fully avenged of Saul and his descendants."

The two men, who fully expected high praise and a great reward, were horror-stricken when David, boiling with rage, exclaimed:

"You have killed a righteous man while he slept. For this cowardly deed both of you shall be executed immediately!"

After the execution, David buried with royal honor the head of Ish-bosheth in the grave of Abner.

Based on the story in the Bible:
2 Samuel 1:1 — 4:12

Citadel of Zion. David captured a Jebusite fortress on Zion, one of the four hills of Jerusalem. He set up his capital there, and Zion became known as the City of David.   © Matson Photo

2
DAVID, KING OF ALL ISRAEL

DAVID WAS KING OF JUDAH for seven and one-half years. During this time his reign was marked by violence, civil warfare, and assassinations. However, the turbulence and the civil war ended with the deaths of Abner and Ish-bosheth and, at that very moment, the elders of all the tribes were converging on Hebron to anoint David king of all Israel. Now the elders had come and gone, and David's long cherished dream of a united nation had become a reality.

King David's first decision was to move his royal capital to Jerusalem, a more centralized location. However, there was an obstacle that prevented the immediate establishment of his capital there. The Jebusites still occupied the city.

The Jerusalem that David knew was far different from Jerusalem today. Then the city was spread out over four hills of varying heights, and the valleys surrounding it were deep ravines. Although the principal sites can still be recognized, the topography of Jerusalem today is almost level. Erosion, the hand of man, and debris from battles throughout the centuries have virtually filled in the ravines.

David and his thirty thousand men stood at the foot of Mount Zion, Jerusalem's most important hill, and gazed slowly up its craggy side. No wonder the Jebusites had shouted a taunt to the warriors: "Even our blind and lame can defend the city against you!"

Jerusalem did seem to be impregnable. David felt certain, however, that God would show him a way to capture the city, so he and Joab went off to scout along the base of the hill. Eventually, they came to a large spring and David noted with interest that the Jebusites had carved out a water-shaft, leading from the top of the hill to the spring. He knew that it had been built so that the people could maintain their water supply, even under siege, by lowering buckets down its smooth bottom and sides. Little did the Jebusites dream that this water-shaft would be their Achilles' heel!

Shortly after dark, David assembled his men at the foot of the water-shaft and gave a sharp command. Led by Captain Joab, the soldiers began creeping, one by one, silently up the shaft. Soon it was full of David's fighting men. Joab finally had enough men at the top of the hill to launch an attack, and the startled Jebusites, caught by surprise, offered no resistance. The capture of Jerusalem proved to be one of the truly great things that David did during his reign. It became a very important city, and from that day to this it has been a center of history.

At long last David had a home of his own. His friend, King Hiram of Tyre, sent not only sturdy cedars of Lebanon but also the skilled carpenters and masons needed to help David build a beautiful palace. When he and his wives and children entered the palace, David established a dynasty that was to rule for more than four hundred and fifty years.

The Philistines were on the rampage again. They had watched the growing power of the Israelites with fear and dismay. Finally, the Philistine king decided to invade Israel and crush this young nation once and for all. The Philistines were arrayed in the Valley of Rephaim and David's men were deployed near the Cave of Adullam. The Philistines were resoundingly defeated and were almost driven into the Great Sea. Thus it came about that Israel's chief enemy posed no threat during the reigns of David and Solomon.

Once again David led his thirty thousand men out of Jerusalem. This time, they were not on a mission of war; instead, it was one of peace and happiness. They were on their way to Kerjath-jearim to bring the Ark of the Lord to Jerusalem.

Abinadab and his sons had done their job well. Now they brought the Ark out of their house and lowered it, gently and reverently, to the floor of a new wagon. As David and the people looked at the beautiful, glistening Ark, there was a spontaneous outburst of music, played on all kinds of instruments such as lyres, lutes, drums, rattles, and cymbals. Singing, dancing, and rejoicing were the order of the day as David and his men moved along toward Jerusalem.

The procession paused to rest and, as the wagon drew to a halt, one of the oxen stumbled, causing the Ark to shift its position. Uzzah reached back to steady it but, in his haste, handled the Ark irreverently. The startled people watched in awe as Uzzah stood up, uttered a piercing scream, and toppled from the wagon, dead! The merriment ceased immedi-

"David Dancing before the Ark" by J. James Tissot. *The Old Testament*, Illustrated. Filled with joy that the Ark of the Covenant was on its way to Jerusalem, David and the Israelites rejoiced by dancing, singing, and making music. M. de Buffan & Co.

ately, and even David was perplexed as he cried out in despair to the Lord, "How shall I ever bring the Ark to Jerusalem?"

Because of this turn of events, David ordered the golden Ark to be carried to the home of Obed-edom, where it was to remain for three months. Then the great procession sadly returned to Jerusalem.

Three months later there was great excitement throughout Jerusalem. Soon the golden Ark of God, carried properly this time by four dedicated men, would pass through the gate of the city and be taken to the Lord's Tent.

Michal stood silently by the window and watched the jubilant crowd below. Everyone was singing, dancing, and rejoicing as David himself led the procession which followed the Ark toward the Holy Tent. Ever since he had forced her to break up a happy marriage with Phaltiel, her feelings toward David had completely reversed. Gone was the lovely, loyal young wife who had helped him escape the wrath of her father. In her place was a young woman whose heart was filled with bitterness and hatred toward him. When she noticed that the king had taken off his regal robe and had put on the simple attire of a priest, Michal turned away from the window in disgust and exclaimed, scornfully: "What a spectacle my husband has made of himself this day!"

When the golden Ark was once again in its proper place, David made sacrificial offerings to God and blessed the people in His name. After the religious rites were over, he gave every man and woman in Israel a piece of bread, a piece of the sacrificial meat, and their choice of a flagon of wine or a bunch of raisins.

From the day that the Ark of the Covenant was returned to Jerusalem, David had the burning desire to build a beautiful house of cedar for the Lord, a Temple that would far outshine his own splendid pal-

ace. One day he summoned Nathan the Prophet to the palace, told him of his plans, and sought his advice.

"Look! I live in a magnificent palace of cedar that is trimmed with silver and gold," he began, "but the Ark of God dwells within curtains underneath the Lord's Tent. Do you really believe that God wants me to follow through on this desire of mine?"

Nathan felt so certain of God's wish that he answered without hesitation, "Do whatever is in your heart, for God is with you."

Early the next morning, David was up on the roof of his palace, looking in every direction. He wanted to find the most beautiful spot in all Jerusalem to build God's Temple. Suddenly, there in the distance, he saw a man racing toward the palace. Not only was David surprised to see Nathan return to the palace so soon after their talk, but he was dumbfounded at the message that the prophet gave to him.

"Make no further plans to build a beautiful Temple of gold and cedar," Nathan said. "God revealed to me last night that you are not the person who shall build a Temple for Him. Instead, the next king, one of your sons yet unborn, is the man God has chosen to build it."

Nathan then told David of the many wonderful things God had in store for him and his descendants, if they would only allow Him to live in their hearts forever. After Nathan left, David went to the Lord's Tent and uttered this fervent prayer:

"O Lord God, who am I that You should speak of my descendants for generations to come? May it please You to bless my house, so that my people shall worship and serve the Lord forever."

Little did David realize that he would soon incur God's anger, nor could he then know that his descendants would commit many sins before Israel reached her final destiny.

Before David began his career as an empire builder, there was one other thing that he wanted to do. One day he asked his servants, "Do you know if there is anyone from the house of Saul who is still living?"

The servants found one of Saul's men, Ziba, who came to David and said:

"Jonathan, your great friend, had a son named Mephibosheth who is still living. However, he is lame in both legs because his nurse dropped him while fleeing into seclusion when she learned that Saul and Jonathan had been killed in battle."

Because he had never forgotten his deep friendship with Jonathan, David immediately sent his royal chariot to bring Mephibosheth to the palace. When the lame lad arrived at the palace, David greeted him warmly.

"Welcome to Jerusalem and to the palace!" he said. "For your father's sake I have this day ordered the restoration of your grandfather Saul's property to you. You shall be a member of my court, eat at my table, and live like a prince. Ziba, the man who told me about you, shall be your steward and look after you and your property."

Based on the story in the Bible:
2 Samuel 5:1 — 7:29, 9:1-13

Ark of the Covenant. A relief sculpture, found in the ruins of a synagogue at Capernaum, is thought to be a representation of the golden Ark. It is mounted on wheels, as was the Ark when David brought it to Jerusalem. © Matson Photo

3
DAVID'S SIN

WHEN DAVID BECAME KING OF ISRAEL, its territory embraced about six thousand square miles. During his reign, however, the warrior-king engaged in fierce battles with neighboring enemy nations. They were defeated and, one by one, fell under the control of Israel. So successful was David's "divide and conquer" method of warfare that, when he turned the kingdom over to Solomon, its territory had increased to an area of sixty thousand square miles.

Late one afternoon, far from the hue and cry of the current battle in which his men were engaged, David was strolling on the roof of his palace. He looked over to a neighboring roof and saw a beautiful woman, Bathsheba, taking a bath. His infatuation for her grew from that moment on, and finally he had his heart set on marrying her. But there was a problem. Bathsheba had a husband named Uriah the Hittite, one of David's ablest fighting men.

David's personal life sank to its lowest ebb when he plotted and carried out a wicked plan whereby he might legally marry Bathsheba. His first step was to bring Uriah home from the front on a three-day "rest and recreation" leave. This part of David's plan was doomed to failure, because Uriah stubbornly refused to leave the palace for a visit in his own home.

When Uriah reported back for duty, he delivered a sealed message from David to Joab. The captain must have read the orders with a cynical smile, as he recalled the day when David had severely rebuked him for killing Abner. The command to Joab was simple and direct:

"Place Uriah in the front lines where the battle is raging the hottest, so that he will be certain to be killed."

Joab did as David commanded; so, near a wall outside the city of Rabbath, one of David's bravest soldiers met his death. Uriah was another tragic victim of evil in high places.

When the news of Uriah's death reached

"*Bathsheba Bathing*" by Wolfgang Krodel. Kunsthistorisches Museum, Vienna. David fell in love with Bathsheba and married her after having arranged the death of her husband. She was the mother of his son Solomon.　Kunsthistorisches Museum

the city, Bathsheba went into a period of mourning, and David secluded himself in the palace. It seemed to him, on reflection, that one sin had followed another as he had carried out his plan to make Bathsheba his wife. He had first broken the tenth commandment, and then the seventh. Finally, in order to cover up the unexpected consequences of his second sin, he had resorted to murder—a crime that violated the sixth commandment.

When the mourning period was over, David brought Bathsheba to the palace and married her. Later, a handsome child —a son—was born to them, and the couple appeared to be quite happy. David was even beginning to believe that the Lord God had overlooked the great sin that he had committed. How wrong he was!

"Be not deceived; God is not mocked: for whatsoever a man soweth, that shall he also reap." (Galatians 6:7) Before long, the full meaning of these inspired words, written centuries later, would pierce David's heart and revive the conscience he had allowed to lie dormant. In response to God's command, Nathan returned to the palace, stood before the throne, and spoke to David:

"Once there were two men in a certain city. One of them was very wealthy and the other was exceedingly poor. The rich man had a large number of flocks and herds; the poor man had nothing except one lamb which he had raised and nourished from the day it was born. It fact, this lamb was treated just like a member of his family.

"One day a visitor came to see the rich man and a feast was being prepared for him. You will never guess what the rich

man did! Instead of taking a lamb from his own flock, he took the poor man's lamb and prepared it for the feast."

David listened, his anger mounting against this rich and greedy man. Then he cried out:

"As surely as the Lord lives, that man deserves to die for what he has done. Tell me his name, and I will make him repay fourfold for the lamb he took."

To David's astonishment, Nathan looked at him sternly and said:

"You are the man! God anointed you king over all Israel and saved you from the hand of Saul. Why, then, have you broken the commandments of God and done evil in His sight? You killed Uriah and took his wife for your own."

David fully understood Nathan's story now. He was thoroughly conscience-strickened, as he cried out with tears in his eyes:

"O God, I have sinned against heaven and against You. Have mercy on me, I pray, and blot out this great transgression."

Nathan then spoke to David again:

"God has forgiven your sin, and you will not die because of it. However, through members of your own family, God will punish you for this great iniquity."

After Nathan left, David went into his study and composed Psalm 51, the great song of repentance.

"Through members of your own family, God will punish you." These words of Nathan were to haunt David until the day of his death. Evidence that the first phase of the prophecy was coming true lay in the fact that even now the young son, whom he loved so tenderly, was critically ill. For six days David fasted and prayed for the child's recovery but, on the seventh day, death came.

When David saw the servants whisper-

"Nathan Reproaches David" by J. James Tissot. The Old Testament, Illustrated. The prophet Nathan rebuked David for sinning against Uriah and predicted the king would suffer retribution in his family affairs.   M. de Buffan & Co.

ing among themselves, he knew what had happened but he wanted them to tell him, so he asked:

"Is the child dead?"

"He is dead," they answered sadly, while watching anxiously to observe the king's reaction.

David surprised them. He arose immediately, bathed, changed his clothes, and went into the Lord's Tent to worship God. When he returned to the palace, he ate with relish the food that his servants set before him. During the six days when he had been fasting and praying, he had paid no attention to them when they had tried to get him to eat. Now he was acting like himself again, so they asked him why he had changed so completely. David gave them a simple, majestic explanation:

"While the child was still alive, I thought that perhaps God would be gracious to me and let him live. Now that he is dead, all my fasting and praying will not bring him back. My son is safe in the arms of the Lord and, one day, I shall see him again."

Based on the story in the Bible:
2 Samuel 11:1 — 12:24

"David in Prayer" by Rembrandt. Although David was king of Israel, he was humble before God. In time of trouble he prayed for forgiveness or help; in victory he gave praise and thanks to the Lord.   The Pierpont Morgan Library, New York

4
ABSALOM'S REBELLION

THROUGH MEMBERS OF YOUR OWN FAMILY, God will punish you." So far, Nathan's prophecy had been fulfilled with a vengeance. David's son, Bathsheba's first-born, had become sick and had died. Amnon, another son, had been killed by his half-brother, Absalom, in revenge for a wrong done to Absalom's sister. David was now face to face with his worst punishment yet. He had been shocked and stunned when a messenger reported that Absalom was in open rebellion and that the people of Israel were following him.

Absalom had planned the coup d'état wisely and well. First, the handsome

"Absalom Has His Brother Killed" by Preti. National Museum, Naples. Amnon, one of David's sons, had wronged his half-sister. Absalom, her brother, ordered his servants to kill Amnon at a feast.   Alinari

young prince, with his long hair flowing in the breeze, had made a deep impression on the people as he drove through the streets of Jerusalem with fifty men running in front of the beautiful chariot, shouting his name and praising him. Then, he had started a "whispering campaign" that had succeeded far beyond his expectations. The word that he would be a better king than his aging father had quickly spread throughout the kingdom. Finally, he had requested and received permission to go to Hebron, the very place that his father had begun his reign, for a feast. Little did David know of the treason his son was planning!

After the feast, Absalom startled the two hundred guests by announcing that he was now king of Israel and would rule temporarily at Hebron. His conspiracy against his father reached its climax that night. The people of Israel rallied strongly behind their new self-proclaimed king. Even Ahithophel, grandfather of Bathsheba and one of David's chief advisers, had defected to Absalom's side.

Meanwhile, back in Jerusalem, David made a strange decision. This brave and victorious warrior of many battles might have been expected to stand up and fight for his kingdom. Instead, for reasons known but to him, David decided to abandon his palace and flee across the Jordan. A few hectic hours ensued as David made preparations to leave Jerusalem. He had sent all his wives and children and all but ten of his concubines, who remained to take care of the palace, across the Brook Kidron to the starting point of the march. He had hired and paid Ittai and his six hundred mercenaries, along with other mercenaries from the Cherethites and the Pelethites, and they had already established their positions in the line of march. Subjects who had remained loyal to David had also passed across the brook. The

king's last task had been to send the Golden Ark back to the Lord's Tent. When he had seen Zadok and Abiathar, chief priests of Israel, approach the stream while carrying the Ark, David had stopped them and said:

"Take the Ark of the Lord back to the Tabernacle. If it is God's will, I shall return to Jerusalem. If not, the Ark will be in its proper place. In any event, you and your sons can be of more service to my cause back there. Perhaps you can learn some of Absalom's plans and relay them to me by your sons."

David thus made his first move toward a comeback by establishing a fifth column near the court of the usurper. Surrounded by his personal bodyguard, the six hundred mighty men who had stood by him through thick and thin since the days he was fleeing from Saul, David crossed the Kidron and led his people to the Jordan.

Two events of interest occurred during this march. When David and his group reached the top of Mount Olivet, he paused to worship God. When he had finished, he was surprised and delighted to see Hushai, his other chief adviser, kneeling beside him. Although he wanted to accompany the people, David had a better plan of action for Hushai:

"Go back to the palace and pretend to Absalom that you, too, have deserted me. Then you will be able to countermand any advice that Ahithopel may give. You will also be able to keep a close watch on Absalom. If he should make any plans that you think I should know about, you can pass the word to Zadok and Abiathar, the chief priests who are also working on my side. They will relay the message to me."

"David Flees" by Rochegrosse. *Biblia Sacra*. David was warned that Absalom conspired to overthrow him. He fled from Jerusalem with his servants and crossed the Jordan, but he left spies in the city. Lemercier and Co., Paris

Hushai thought that the plan was a good one and did as suggested. David had taken another step in the right direction. A spy in the palace itself!

A little later Ziba caught up with David and the people. He brought gifts of bread, raisins, fruits, and wine from his master. He also brought the astonishing and unbelievable news that Mephibosheth had elected to remain in Jerusalem because he, too, had ambitions for the throne. He reasoned and hoped that, with the house of David divided and fighting one another, the people of Israel would restore the dynasty of his grandfather, Saul, and anoint him as their king. Ziba then returned to the city.

David and his people finally reached the bank of the Jordan. Since he had received no word from the priests regarding Absalom's plans, David decided to wait on the west side of the river.

Meanwhile, Absalom entered Jerusalem without opposition and rode in triumph to the palace. His four years of plotting and scheming had at last paid off. Even now he was in his council chamber, waiting for Ahithophel and Hushai to appear. How fortunate, Absalom reflected, that two of David's wisest men had defected to him! The three of them would soon plan the strategy to be used in destroying David and his fighting men completely.

Ahithophel wasted no time in telling Absalom what he thought should be done:

"We must pursue David and his men, immediately. Give me twelve thousand men, and I will go after the king's army this very night. I will force them to fight while they are still tired."

This sounded like good advice, but Absalom wanted to hear his other adviser, too. Hushai arose and said:

"The counsel of Ahithophel is not good, right now. You know your father and his mighty men. At this moment they are blazing with anger. Should you pursue them and catch up with them now, you would find them as angry as a mother bear that has just lost her cub. You must not risk defeat until your kingdom is firmly established."

Absalom now had two conflicting pieces of advice. He must choose between them. Finally, he announced that would take Hushai's advice to delay pursuit of the king and his men. David's spy had done his job well. Ahithophel, disappointed and disillusioned on hearing Absalom's decision, went out into the night and hanged himself.

Based on the story in the Bible:
2 Samuel 15:1 — 17:14, 23

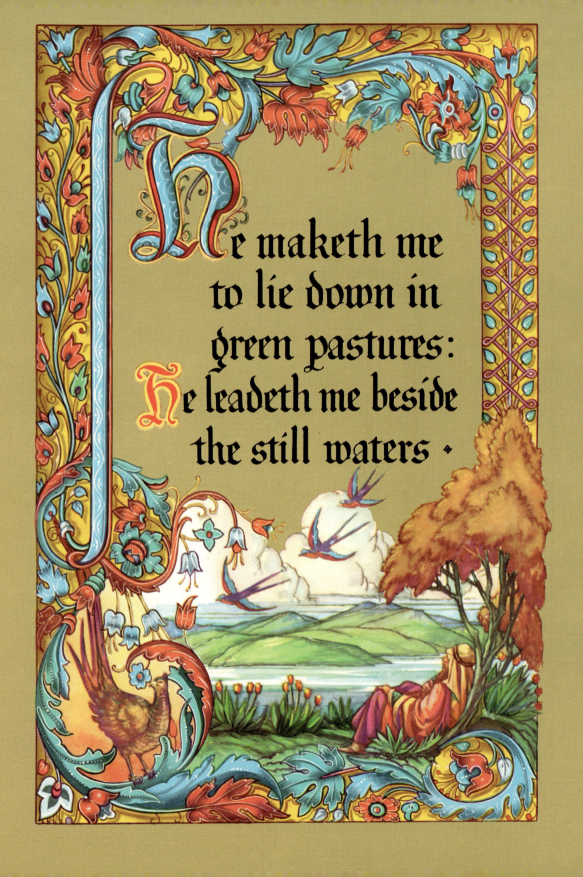

He maketh me
to lie down in
green pastures:
He leadeth me beside
the still waters ·

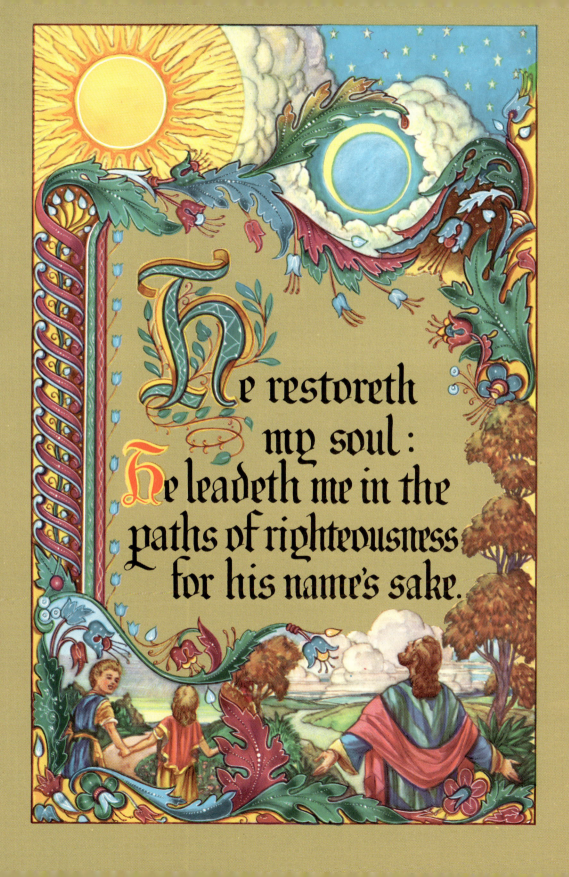

He restoreth my soul : He leadeth me in the paths of righteousness for his name's sake.

Yea, though I walk
through the valley
of the shadow of death,
I will fear no evil:
for thou art with me;

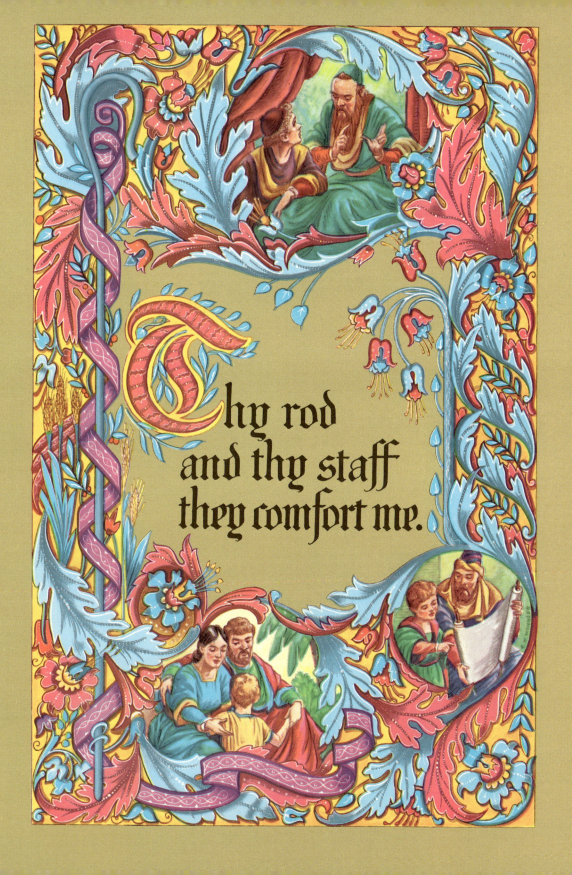

Thy rod and thy staff they comfort me.

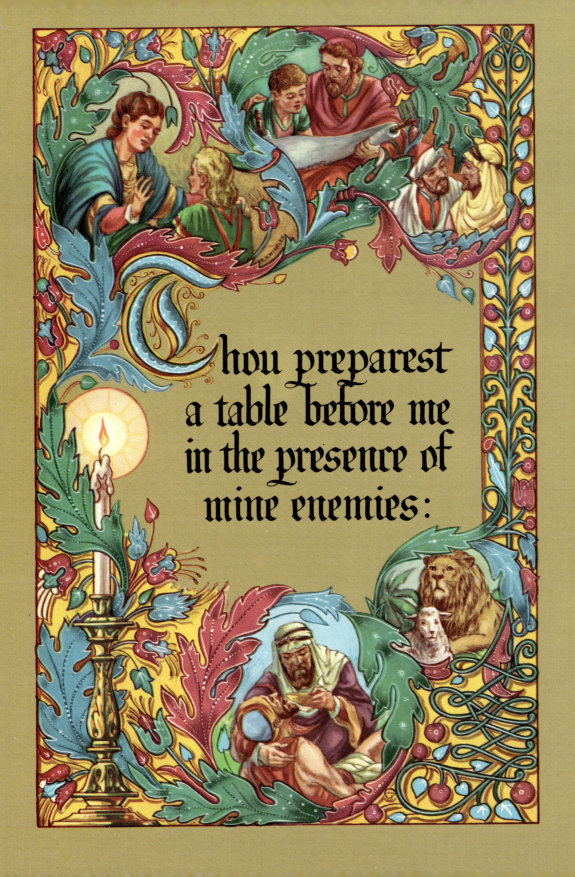

Thou preparest a table before me in the presence of mine enemies:

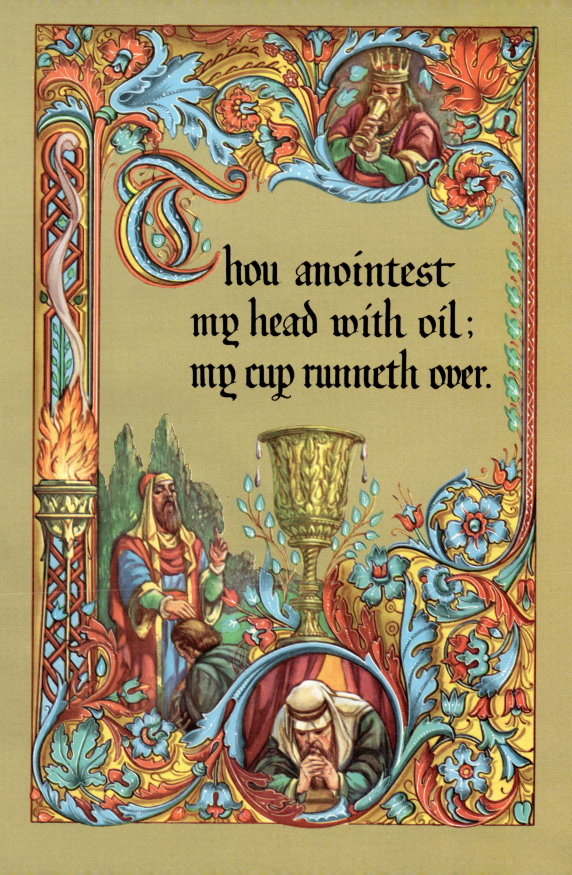

Thou anointest my head with oil; my cup runneth over.

Surely goodness
and mercy shall follow
me all the days of my
life: and I will dwell
in the house of the
Lord forever.

5
DAVID'S ARMY VICTORIOUS

AVID'S FIFTH COLUMN at the palace was functioning well. When Hushai learned of any new plan, he would go straight to the priests and tell them what had happened, and they would relay the message to David by their two sons, Ahimaaz, and Jonathan. Only a short time before, they had carried their last but most important message to David. It was short and to the point:

"Absalom and his soldiers have begun their march. Cross over the Jordan and seek help from your powerful friends there. Follow these instructions immediately."

David's prior generosity to the nations east of the Jordan began to pay off. When he and his people reached Mahanaim, a walled city not far from the Jordan, they were welcomed warmly. The people had not forgotten the kindness David had shown to Ish-bosheth, who had made this city his capital during his two-year reign as king of Israel. The women and children traveling with David were granted the protection of the city for the duration of the war. Barzillai, a rich and powerful Gileadite, supplied the women and children with couches, chairs, dishes, pots, pans, and everything else they needed. He also provided large quantities of food for all the Israelites who accompanied David.

As the word spread that David was at Mahanaim and in trouble, the vassal nations rallied strongly behind him. This was especially true of the Ammonites. Nahash would always remember that day when David had defeated him and his people at Rabbah. Instead of seeking revenge for the rudeness to his ambassadors, David had negotiated a peace treaty with him. In grateful remembrance of this act of mercy, Nahash sent a large contingent of soldiers, led by his son Shobi, to David's aid.

David's army in Gilead had grown by leaps and bounds. He now had a military force of over 10,000 men. In preparation for the imminent battle with his son, David divided his soldiers into three companies which were to be commanded by Joab, Abishai, and the mercenary Ittai. David wanted to lead his men as they marched out of the city but they protested, saying:

"You are worth 10,000 of us! Remain in the city and help us from here."

When the three companies were regrouped outside the walled city, David gave his final order to the men and their commanders:

"For my sake, deal gently with the young man, my son Absalom."

Absalom and his men were deployed near the forest of Ephraim when he saw David's army approaching. What a shock it must have been to the rebel son as he noted how his father's forces had grown! Absalom realized too late that he should have followed the wise counsel of Ahithophel. The expected easy victory appeared likely to become a disastrous defeat.

Shrewd, battle-wise Joab had selected the battle site well, and his battle strategy had come off as he had planned. David's three companies of seasoned, veteran warriors had Absalom's men trapped in a ring of steel. Thousands of the enemy lay

"Absalom's Death" by Rochegrosse. *Biblia Sacra.* For David, one of the saddest events of his life was the ignominious death of Absalom, whom he loved, even though this son had conspired against him.

Lemercier and Co., Paris

dead on the battlefield and, now, those remaining had been slowly but surely pushed back to the edge of the forest. Thoroughly defeated and panic-stricken, Absalom and the remnants of his army plunged into the treacherous, trackless, pit-filled, jungle-like forest. Little did Absalom realize that this forest would claim the lives, his own included, of thousands and thousands of his soldiers!

Now Absalom himself was in serious danger. While fleeing on his mule, his hair became entangled in the branches of an oak tree and he could not free himself. When Joab arrived at the oak tree a short time later and saw Absalom dangling helplessly in mid air, he remembered David's final command. However, he knew that real authority on the throne could not be exerted and that the kingdom could not be reunited if Absalom's life was spared. The ruthless Joab, therefore, went close to Absalom and jabbed his spear into the rebel's heart three times. Joab then had some of his men take the body to a deep pit, throw it in, and cover it with stones.

When David had learned of Absalom's death, he went into a room above the city gate to mourn for his disobedient and traitorous son. He cried out:

"O, my son Absalom! My son, my son Absalom! Would God I had died for you, O Absalom, my son, my son!"

The victory celebration took on an air of disappointment as the soldiers marched back into the city and heard David, in a room above the gate, still mourning loudly and bitterly for Absalom. When Joab passed through the gate and heard David's lamentations, he went to his room and spoke sternly to him:

"This day you have made mockery of your brave men who have saved your life! You have clearly shown that you love your enemies and hate your friends and that, if Absalom had lived and all of us

had died, you would have been well pleased.

"It is now your duty to arise, stand before your soldiers and congratulate them on their victory, praise them for their bravery, and commend them for their exploits. I solemnly warn you that, if you do not do so, you will not have a single soldier standing beside you by nightfall. Then you will be in the worst trouble of your life, because a king without an army is like a chariot without a horse."

David knew in his heart that Joab was right, so he stood before his army and did all the things his captain had suggested. David's men reciprocated by reaffirming their loyalty to him.

As David prepared to return in triumph to Jerusalem, his old friend Barzillai, with his son Chimham, came to David and offered to escort the group to the Jordan. When they neared the Jordan, in appreciation for all the things he had done, David, asked Barzillai to go with him to Jerusalem and live in the palace. Although rich and powerful, Barzillai was also eighty years old, so he replied to the king:

"I am an old man and would only be a burden to you. Besides, I wish to remain in Gilead and to be buried beside my father and mother. However, my son, Chimham, will be glad to go with you and be of service to you."

After wishing David well, Barzillai, the true and loyal friend who had helped simply because he had wanted to, returned to his home alone. Two other people came to David before he crossed over the Jordan.

Shemei, a member of the clan of Saul, who had thrown curses and stones at the fleeing king, knew that he had to do some fence-mending. When he crossed the Jordan and bowed low before the king, he asked David to forgive him. Even as he was bowing, Abishai asked David to let

"David Enters Victoriously into Jerusalem" by Raphael. Loggia di Raffaello, Vatican. After David defeated the rebellious army of Absalom, he and his soldiers again crossed the Jordan and returned to Jerusalem in triumph.

Alinari

him kill the man. David answered calmly:

"There shall be no bloodshed in the land today, because I am again king of all Israel." Then he turned to Shimei and said:

"You are forgiven and, as long as you remain in the city of Jerusalem, you shall not die."

David's other visitor was Mephibosheth, who rode across the Jordan on his mule. He bowed down to David and said:

"My servant Ziba tricked you that night when he brought you the refreshments. I wanted to go with you very badly, and I ordered him to saddle a mule for me. Instead, he slipped away and came alone to see you. When he returned home and told me that you had given him all my property,

that did not worry me. My only concern was that you would return safely. All the time that you were away, I was loyal to you and I rejoiced on learning that you were on your way back to Jerusalem."

David's eyes filled with tears as he listened to this moving speech. He realized now how unjustly he had treated Jonathan's son. He therefore ordered the immediate restitution of one-half the land to Mephibosheth. Thus it came about that artful Ziba's clever plan succeeded, at least partially. With the land problem resolved, David and his people crossed over the Jordan and returned to Jerusalem.

Based on the story in the Bible:
2 Samuel 17:1 — 19:43

DAVID CHOOSES SOLOMON AS KING

MANY YEARS PASSED after David's return in triumph to Jerusalem. Old and feeble now, he knew the time had come for him to choose the new king to rule over the people of Israel. Under normal circumstances this would have presented no problems. Adonijah, his oldest son, would have succeeded him. However, David had made a vow to his wife Bathsheba that her son Solomon would be the next king.

Adonijah, who was determined to secure the throne for himself, knew that he faced an almost impossible task. He must first attract the attention of the public. To do this, he adopted the tactics of his rebellious brother, Absalom. Adonijah, too, rode through the streets of Jerusalem in a beautiful golden chariot with fifty men running in front of him singing, dancing, and shouting.

Adonijah's next step in the plot to succeed his father was far more successful than he had dreamed possible. All of his brothers and many of the royal officials, including Joab and Abiathar, agreed that Solomon was too young and inexperienced to become king, so they switched over to Adonijah's side. It was now time for action. He prepared a great coronation feast, near the sacred spring of En-rogel, and invited all his followers to attend.

Meanwhile, back at the palace, a counterplot was set in motion. As soon as Nathan had learned what was going on, he rushed to the palace and said to Bathsheba:

"Adonijah is plotting to become king! At this very moment, he is at the spring En-rogel awaiting the arrival of his guests for the coronation feast. You must report this matter to David immediately, and be sure to remind him of his vow that Solomon, your son, would be next in the line of succession."

When Bathsheba unfolded the conspiracy and Nathan confirmed it, David was roused to action. He gave Nathan a command:

"Prepare for Solomon's anointment at once! Place him on my mule. Stop by the Lord's Tent for Zadok, the priest, who will carry the sacred oil. Then lead the young prince out of Jerusalem to the nearby spring of Gihon. After Solomon has been anointed, sound your trumpets and shout, 'God save King Solomon!'"

Escorted by Benaiah, Captain of the Royal Guard, and the other guardsmen, the procession soon reached Gihon. This spring is nearer the city than En-rogel and is out of sight of, though not out of sound of, the place where the feast to honor Adonijah was still in progress.

The mighty blast of the trumpets brought all the people of Jerusalem out into the streets. When they saw Solomon riding the king's mule—led by Nathan and Zadok and escorted by Benaiah and his men—re-enter the city, they knew that David had abdicated and that they had a new king.

There was wild excitement throughout the city. Musical instruments of every description seemed to spring out of the ground itself. The sound of music and singing filled the air, interrupted intermittently by shouts of "GOD SAVE KING SOLOMON," as the people danced joyously behind the colorful procession.

The piercing blast of the trumpets was also heard by the people at the feast, and its sound had barely faded away when Jonathan, Abiathar's son, came racing up and shouted:

"King David has made Solomon king! He was anointed by Zadok and Nathan at the spring of Gihon. The noise you hear is the tumultuous ovation he is receiving from the people as he goes down the streets on his inaugural parade."

Poor Adonijah! He sat alone at the banquet table with his dream of becoming king of Israel shattered forever. One by one, his fair-weather friends fled in terror when they learned that Solomon was the new king. Adonijah now must make plans to save his own life. He knew that, if he could make it to the Lord's Tent before the celebration ended, he would be safe. Not even the king could order him to be killed as long as he remained in the Tabernacle, so he hurried back to Jerusalem.

David's sick-bed would soon become his death-bed. His long illness had given him ample time to think over his strange life. He had been a great warrior and had won many victories. He had expanded Israel ten-fold, and there had been peace in the kingdom for many years. He had made Israel the dominant power and most prominent nation in Western Asia. He had established the worship of the one true God, not only at Jerusalem but also throughout the land. He had won the hearts and affection of his people. Yet there had been acts in his past life that appalled him and caused cold chills to run up and down his spine when he remembered them.

One day, shortly after Solomon's coronation, David called the young king to his bedside and said:

"The time for me to die is drawing near. Be strong and prove yourself to be a real

"David Blesses His Son Solomon in the Presence of Nathan, Bathsheba, and Tamar" by De Maere. Museum of Archaeology, Saint Nicholas, Belgium. National Archives, Brussels

man. Walk in the ways of the Lord and keep His commandments and ordinances, as they are written in the law of Moses. If you and your sons follow these instructions, God has promised me that one of my descendants shall always be on the throne of Israel.

"Now for a few practical matters. Show kindness to the sons of Barzillai and let them be among those who eat at your table. I must caution you to keep a wary eye on Joab. Although he has proven to be an able and brave soldier, he is also treacherous. Look what he only recently tried to do to you and me! He is a cold-blooded murderer, too. He ruthlessly killed two great military leaders of Israel during a period of peace. Your wisdom will tell you how to deal with him. Finally, you must keep a close watch on Shimei who cursed me grievously when I went to Mahanaim. Upon my victorious return, he met me at the Jordan and begged forgiveness. I promised him that he would not die as long as he remained in Jerusalem. You are a wise man, and you will know what you ought to do with him."

David was exhausted now, so he turned over and went to sleep with his fathers. The voice of the sweet singer of Israel was stilled forever.

No greater wrong can be done to David than to judge the life of this powerful warrior, wise statesman, and empire-builder on the basis of his human frailties. Despite his sins and mistakes, David, "a man after God's own heart," remained loyal and true to Him throughout his life.

If David had done nothing else during his lifetime, his Psalms will be an eternal monument to this great king. David's beautiful 23rd Psalm is learned early and is long remembered in Christian homes throughout the world.

Based on the story in the Bible:
1 Kings 1:1 — 2:10

"King David Playing the Harp" by Rubens. Stadel Art Institute, Frankfurt. David was an accomplished musician even before he went to Saul's court. Some of the psalms that he wrote are of unsurpassed beauty.   Stadel Art Institute

PLACES
in the Story of David

HEBRON

Twenty miles southwest of Jerusalem, in the hill country of Judah, lies the city of Hebron. David was anointed king of Judah and king of all Israel at this town. It was also here that Absalom began his abortive rebellion against his father.

GIBEON

It was at the pool of Gibeon, a town 6 miles northwest of Jerusalem, that the forces of Joab, David's general, and the army of Abner, Ish-bosheth's commander, met in their first battle of the civil war.

JERUSALEM

This ancient Canaanite city has been known by several different names. Back in the days of Abraham, it was named Salem. The Jebusites, who occupied Jerusalem for many centuries, named it Jebus. In the Amarna Tablets, dated about 1400 B.C., it is called

The Tomb of David. A mosque has been built over the traditional burial place of David on Mount Zion, outside the walls of Jerusalem. It is near the Zion Gate, or Gate of David, located in the southern wall of the city.   © Matson Photo

The Spring of Gihon. David kept his promise to Bathsheba that Solomon would succeed him. When Adonijah usurped the throne, David sent Solomon to Gihon with Zadok and Nathan; there they anointed Solomon as king. © Matson Photo

Urusalim which means "city of peace." Jerusalem, a fortress city high in the Judean mountains, lies on the border of Benjamin and Judah. It is about 105 miles south of Dan and about 45 miles north of Beer-sheba. Joab captured it for his king, and David made it the capital city of Israel. It served as the political and spiritual center of Israel, a position Jerusalem continues to occupy in the hearts of Jews throughout the world.

VALLEY OF REPHAIM

In this valley, about three miles southwest of Jerusalem and running toward Bethlehem, David utterly routed the Philistines. Following up his victory in the valley, he pursued them to the coastal plain, capturing and oc-cupying many important Philistine cities in the process.

KERJATH-JEARIM (Keriath-jearim)

David came to this city, 8 miles west of Jerusalem, to get the golden Ark and return it to his capital.

RABBATH-AMMON (Rabba, Philadelphia, 'Amman)

During the siege of this capital city of the Ammonites, 23 miles east of the Jordan at the headwaters of the Jabbok River, Uriah the Hittite met his death. The city is known today as 'Amman, capital of Jordan.

MAHANAIM

This walled city is located 8 miles east of the Jordan and 2 miles south of the Jabbok

Absalom's Pillar. The traditional tomb of Absalom, the rebellious son of David, is near the southeast corner of the Jerusalem walls, overlooking the Kedron valley. The monument is about 60 feet high. © Matson Photo

river. David and his retinue sought refuge here when they fled from Absalom and his army. It was also Ish-bosheth's capital city during his brief reign as king of Israel.

FOREST OF EPHRAIM

Near and in this forest, not far from Mahanaim, Joab crushed the revolt of Absalom.

EN-ROGEL

At this spring, a short distance south of Jerusalem, Adonijah planned to launch his drive for the throne of Israel.

Modern 'Amman from the Acropolis Hill. This city was once known as Rabbath and was the capital of the Ammonites. The Israelite army, under Joab, conquered these people after their king had insulted David's emissaries. © Matson Photo

GIHON

At the command of David, Solomon was anointed king of Israel at this spring, a few hundred feet from Jerusalem.

DAVID'S FOREIGN CONQUESTS

The reign of David marks, politically speaking, Israel's golden age. Periods of political weakness in both Egypt and Mesopotamia made it possible for the tribes, which had entered Canaan under Joshua a few centuries earlier, to become a mighty nation. The following lands were conquered by David:

Moab

The Moabites were the first victims of David's expansion program. He incorporated

Falls of Boiling Water, Moab. The kingdom of Moab lay east of the Dead Sea. It was one of the lands conquered by David. The Moabites became his servants.   © Matson Photo

this land east of the Dead Sea into his empire shortly after he became king of all Israel.

Zobah

This Aramaean state, far to the north of Jerusalem, extended from Damascus northward to Riblah. In David's time this state was the most powerful in Aram and had considerable wealth in copper. David defeated Hadadezer of Zobah, even though large contingents from other Aramaean states aided in resisting the Israelite power.

Damascus

Damascus, an ally of Zobah, was the largest city in Aram. It is located in a valley about 30 miles long and 10 miles wide and is watered by the Abana river. The defeat of the coali-

tion armies brought the rich, fertile valley of Damascus under the control of the Israelites.

Edom

Edom was defeated by David in the Valley of Salt. This valley is directly south of the Dead Sea.

Ammon

The Ammonite war was the longest in David's career. After peace was concluded with the Aramaeans, David turned his attention to Rabbah, the capital city of Ammon. When its water supply was exhausted, the besieged city was finally forced to surrender. With victory assured, Joab sent for David so that he might supervise the final operations and so receive credit for being the conqueror of Rabbah. With the successful conclusion of the Ammonite war, David was king of an area extending from the River of Egypt to northern Syria (Aram).

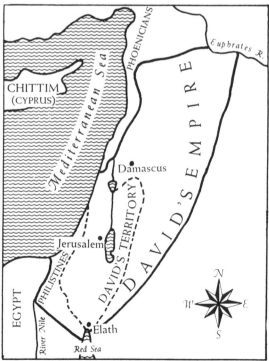

David's Empire. Israel was expanded under the able leadership of David. At the time of his death, united Israel occupied a vast area extending from the Red Sea to the Euphrates River.

QUESTIONS
on the Story of David

1

1 Where was David anointed king of Judah?

2 Who was king of the rest of Israel? Where was his capital city? Who was the real power behind his throne?

3 Where was the first battle of the civil war between Israel and Judah fought? Who won?

4 Why did Captain Abner come to Judah for a conference with David? What was the final result of his visit?

5 What happened to Ish-bosheth? What was David's judgment, when he learned of it?

2

6 Where did David move his capital when he became king of all Israel? What strategy did he use to defeat the Jebusites who occupied the city of his choice?

7 Which was the first enemy nation that a unified Israel had to fight? What was the result of this battle?

8 What great event occurred in Jerusalem soon after the Israelites' first battle?

9 What burning desire did David have? What did Nathan the prophet tell David regarding this desire?

10 Was there anyone from the house of Saul still alive at this time? What action did David take with regard to the house of Saul?

3

11 Who was Uriah? What was his wife's name?

12 Why did David order Joab to place Uriah on the front line, at a spot where the fighting was the fiercest?

13 How was David to be punished for his great sin?

14 What was his first punishment?

4

15 List the steps that Absalom took as he planned the coup d'état against his father.

16 When David learned that Absalom had proclaimed himself king and that the people were following him, what strange decision did he make?

17 What resources for help did David still have in Jerusalem?

18 What was the conflicting advice given to Absalom by his two wise men, Ahithophel and Hushai? Whose advice did he take?

5

19 What was the final message that Hushai relayed to David while the king waited on the west bank of the Jordan?

20 How were David and his people treated when they reached the walled city of Mahanaim? What did Barzillai do to help?

21 Which of the puppet states helped David most when it learned that he was in trouble? Why?

22 Why did Joab feel that it was necessary for him to kill Absalom?

23 What was David's heartbroken lament when he learned of his son's death?

24 Why did Shimei cross the Jordan to meet the victorious David?

25 Why did Mephibosheth ride across the Jordan to meet David?

6

26 Why was Adonijah, David's oldest son,

denied the right to succeed his father as king over Israel?

27 Why did Joab, Abiathar, and many other royal officials switch over to Adonijah's side in his struggle for the throne?

28 What did David do when he learned of Adonijah's treachery?

29 What are some of the things David told Solomon in his farewell talk with the young king?

30 What did David do that stands out in the minds of many people as a permanent monument to his memory?

*Answers are found
on the following pages.*

"*David*" by Michelangelo. Detail. Academy, Florence. David, one of the greatest men in Israelite history, rose from shepherd to king through his many talents as musician, soldier, statesman, and poet, but he never forgot his duty to God. Alinari

ANSWERS
on the Story of David

1

1 David was anointed King of Judah at Hebron.
2 Ish-bosheth. His capital city was Mahanaim. Abner, the military commander, was the real power behind the throne.
3 The first battle of the civil war was fought near the pool of Gibeon. David's army was victorious.
4 Abner came to visit David because he wished to form an alliance with the king. The visit cost Abner his life when Joab, on the pretense of avenging his brother's death at Abner's hands, assassinated him.
5 Ish-bosheth was killed in his sleep by two men, who then cut off his head and took it to David. The king ordered the two men to be executed for their crime.

2

6 David moved his capital to Jerusalem. He found a water-shaft and ordered his men to climb up this shaft, in the darkness, to reach this seemingly impregnable city.
7 Philistia. The Philistines were so thoroughly defeated that they posed no threat to Israel during the reigns of David and Solomon.
8 David brought the golden Ark of the Covenant to Jerusalem and placed it in the Lord's Tent.
9 David had his heart set on building a beautiful Temple to replace the Lord's Tent. At first Nathan told David to proceed with his plans, but the prophet had to reverse this advice when God revealed that David would not be allowed to build the Temple.
10 Mephibosheth, Jonathan's son, was still alive. David brought him to the palace and made him a member of his court. David also restored Saul's property to Mephibosheth, who was his grandson.

3

11 Uriah was one of the bravest of David's mighty men. His wife's name was Bathsheba.
12 David wanted to make certain that Uriah was killed in action, so that he could marry Bathsheba.
13 Nathan told David that God would punish him through members of his own family.
14 His young son whom he adored, Bathsheba's first child, died after an illness of seven days.

4

15 Absalom attracted the attention of the people by riding through the streets of Jerusalem in a beautiful chariot with fifty young men running ahead of it, singing and praising him. He started a whispering campaign that quickly convinced the majority of the Israelites that he would be a much better king than his aging father.
16 David decided not to defend Jerusalem. Instead, he and those who were still loyal to him retreated across the Jordan.
17 David had a spy in the palace itself. One of his wise counselors, Hushai, pretended that he had defected from David's cause. He also had a pipeline from Jerusalem through the two priests and their two sons.
18 Ahithophel wanted Absalom to pursue David at once. Hushai advised him to delay the pursuit until he had built an army so powerful that there would be no risk of defeat. Absalom took the advice of Hushai.

5

19 David was told to cross the Jordan immediately, because Absalom and his army were on the march.

20 David and his people were warmly welcomed by the citizens of Mahanaim. Barzillai, one of the city's inhabitants, provided David and his followers with food, cooking utensils, and furniture.

21 Nahash, king of the Ammonites, sent the largest number of soldiers to David's rapidly expanding army. He remembered the kindness David had shown to him and his city when Ammon was defeated.

22 Joab knew that the throne would never be secure and that the nation would never be united unless the instigator of the rebellion was killed.

23 "O, my son Absalom! My son, my son Absalom! Would God I had died for you, O Absalom, my son, my son!"

24 Shimei crossed over the Jordan to apologize to David for his actions and to ask forgiveness.

25 Mephibosheth came to meet David in order to explain why he did not go with him when the king fled from Jerusalem.

6

26 David had made a vow that Solomon would be the next king.

27 Adonijah convinced them that Solomon was too young and inexperienced to be their king.

28 David commanded Nathan and Zadok to anoint Solomon as king without delay.

29 David told the young king to walk in the ways of the Lord and to keep His commandments. He also told him to be good

"David Sees the Messenger Arrive" by J. James Tissot. *The Old Testament,* Illustrated. David waited in Mahanaim during the battle in the wood of Ephraim. Two runners brought the news that David's army had won; but it was a sad victory for him because his son Absalom was dead.   Lemercier & Co., Paris

to the sons of Barzallai, and warned him to keep a close watch on Joab and Shimei.

30 He composed Psalm 23 and many others.

FURTHER FACTS AND OUTLINES
for the Story of David

SECOND SAMUEL

AUTHORSHIP AND DATE
Same as First Samuel.

DESTINATION
Same as First Samuel.

PURPOSE AND THEME
The book covers almost the entire period of David's reign (forty years, according to 1 Kings 2:11). Thus the purpose is to record the history of the Jews from Saul's death to the beginning of Solomon's reign, and to demonstrate the power of the monarchy during this greatest period in Israel's history.

David did not always obey God, but he was a far more consistent leader of men than Saul had been. David's youthful days as a shepherd gave him a strong body and taught him the wisdom learned in the out-of-doors from nature. He amazed everyone by killing Goliath. (His sling probably carried a one-pound stone, and it is estimated that a skilled marksman could hurl such a stone at a speed of from one hundred to one hundred and fifty miles per hour.) Protecting his sheep, David had learned methods of defense that gave him confidence against a blustering giant. His trust in the Lord gave him this first great victory.

David was to know greater victories—military victories—but these were to come later. His capture of Jerusalem was a high point in Jewish history, because that city was to become the religious center of Israel. His keen sense of the fitness of things religious is seen in his bringing the Ark of the Covenant to Jerusalem (2 Samuel 6:1-23) and in his desire to build a house for the Lord God (7:1-29).

David's artistic temperament, which expressed itself in music and poetry, has always endeared him to aesthetic souls. The related capacity for depth of feeling is expressed in his lament over the death of his son Absalom, as well as in his sorrow over the deaths of Saul and Jonathan.

The tragic truth that even a good and gifted man can yield to temptation is illustrated in David's sin with Bathsheba. Nathan the prophet is to be admired for exposing the sin to the sinner himself (11:1 – 12:14). David's sin was to have tragic results and, among members of his own family, far-reaching by-products.

The story of David has its beginning in First Samuel, as shown in the Outline that follows.

OUTLINE

FIRST SAMUEL
David Enters the Picture (chapters 16-31)
David Anointed To Be Future King
   (chapter 16)
David and Goliath (chapter 17)
David and Jonathan (chapter 18)
David's Life Sought by Saul
   (chapters 19-23)
David Spares Saul's Life (chapter 24)
Samuel's Death, Nabal (chapter 25)
David Spares Saul Again, Saul's Confession (chapter 26)
David Flees Saul (chapter 27)

"Sacrifice of David" by Santolo Cirillo. Church of San Paolo Maggiore, Naples. David built an altar to the Lord and offered burnt offering and peace offerings in order to save his people from a plague, and his prayers were answered. Alinari

PSALMS

AUTHORSHIP AND DATE

Headings suggest the traditional view of authorship as follows:

73 Psalms accredited to David

12 Psalms to Asaph, a musician

11 Psalms to the Sons of Korah, Levites doing Temple service during David's time

2 Psalms to King Solomon

1 Psalm to Ethan, perhaps a musician under David

1 Psalm to Moses

1 Psalm to Heman

49 so-called Orphan Psalms (Psalms without indication of authorship)

The Greek (Septuagint) Version indicates Haggai and Zechariah as authors of five Psalms. The Psalms were written over a long period of time, from Moses to the Exile, but most were done about 1000 B.C. though time should be allowed for additions and revisions.

DESTINATION

Written for Jewish worship experiences, they now serve, and have served, as the basis of private and public worship of Christians and Jews.

PURPOSE AND THEME

The Psalms was the hymnbook of the Temple. As such, it is a guide to prayer and praise (the Hebrew title, *Tehillim,* means "Songs of Praise"). The Psalms contain the moods, doubts, joys, and hopes universal to the human heart. There are Psalms of faith in adversity (90, 91), of praise (Psalm 8, 113-118), godliness (1), penitence (51), and nature (19). There are also royal Psalms to be used at a coronation or royal affair (110, 21). The Messianic Psalms (2, 8, 16, 22, 31, 40, 41, 45, 68, 102, 110, 118) are especially meaningful to Christians, Historical Psalms (78, 81, 105, 106) are especially meaningful to Hebrews, for they tell of God's faithfulness to His covenant. National Psalms (120, 137) also have great meaning for Jews.

Some titles (superscription) refer to musical directions (Psalm 4); others have no known meaning (the term "maskil," Psalm 69). Songs of "ascents" (Psalms 120-134) may be pilgrim hymns sung on the "ascent" to Jerusalem and the Temple. The strange and repeated word "Selah" perhaps indicates the appropriate point for a musical interlude.

OUTLINE

The Book of Psalms is much too long and of too great variety to attempt an outline as such. But it should be noted that the book is divided into five smaller books (perhaps to remind the reader of the five books of the Pentateuch) as follows:

Book I: Psalms 1-41

Book II: Psalms 42-72

Book III: Psalms 73-89

Book IV: Psalms 90-106

Book V: Psalms 107-150

Psalm I is an introduction to the entire book of Psalms; each of the five sections concludes with a doxology, and Psalm 150 is the doxology to the whole book as well as to Book V.

LESSONS FOR TODAY'S LIVING

The Statesmen, David and Churchill

by

James Kelso

In seeking present-day parallels with personalities of the Bible it is often considered sufficient if the two lives possess but one outstanding common characteristic. The lives of the Hebrew king, David, and of the English statesman, Winston Churchill, were parallel at more points than one would think, as pointed out by James Kelso in a chapter from his book, *Archaeology and Our Old Testament Contemporaries* (© 1966, Zondervan Publishing House, Grand Rapids, Michigan).

TWO ARTISTS WHO BECAME HEROES

WHEN WINSTON CHURCHILL died, Great Britain laid to rest one of the greatest figures in all of her long history—a man at home in war and peace, a statesman, an artist, and a champion of the uniqueness of his people. If you will compare Churchill with David you will discover that they had much in common and that the two worlds in which they lived were much the same in essence, although the externalities may seem quite different . . . .

In the military field each of these great men found his nation in a desperate military tragedy, and each pulled his nation back into a place of international power. David was actual commander in chief on the field of battle and, as such, he extended the boundaries of his empire to the title-deed promised to Abraham; that is, from the Euphrates to the Nile. For once, and once only, Israel was the dominant world power in the Levant. David would have doubtless been the first to admit, however, that God's providential action in making Egypt and Assyria third-rate powers was a major factor in Israel's victory. Churchill, on the other hand, was not a general in the field; but, as prime minister, he did dictate the military policy for a British Commonwealth scattered around the world.

David's military conquests had a most unusual turn. His conquest of Syria made him one of the greatest, if not the greatest, "steel magnates" of his day. Iron was then coming into history as a revolutionary new metal which was rapidly replacing copper. Its emergence, however, was not as sudden and spectacular as that of aluminum in our own time. Israel profited so greatly from this versatile new metal, coming out of Anatolia via Syria, that the size of the plowshare which the farmer used was so increased that he could almost double his crops. In those days this meant doubling the population, as well.

David and Churchill each had "personality plus," and each was a natural leader. In statesmanship, Churchill's problem was to preserve the English law and spirit. David had a still greater problem, to reinstate the Mosaic law and make it a vital force in the lives of his people. Preserving faith in God is always more difficult than preserving faith in one's nation. To the ancient Israelites the Davidic kingdom was the climax of their glory. He could have no superior except Messiah, and they called the Messiah the Son of David.

Churchill and David both instinctively did the dramatic. [Churchill's "V for Victory" and his drama-packed speeches are familiar.]

Look at David in the Goliath episode. Read the passage with this emphasis in mind. Note also the dramatic in the following: David's love for Jonathan, although Jonathan was heir apparent to Saul; David's episodes with Saul at En-gedi and Ziph; his behavior before King Achish, and so on. But for sheer drama nothing equals David's lament at Absalom's death, unless it is his 51st Psalm. Who ever heard of a king confessing in public that he had broken the Ten Commandments and pleading with God for mercy! . . .

David and Churchill both were artists. That term is used here in its basic sense of any person proficient in any one of the fine arts. Both men were geniuses with the pen, David in poetry and Churchill in prose. Each used the pen to exalt his beloved land and people, but David concentrated also on the God of Israel—his personal Good Shepherd.

In David's day, songs were of a common authorship; that is, the same man wrote the words and composed the music. Even in his youth David was so exceptional that he was called in to perform before King Saul. A reading of the Psalms shows that David never laid down his harp nor stilled his voice. It used to be popular to deny David the Psalms attributed to him, but the archaeological research in Phoenicia and Qumran have given him back his "copyrights."

The Syrians and the Palestinians were always known internationally as musicians. Even the Greeks learned from them. Many of the Psalms show Canaanite literary forms. Psalm 29 is a striking example of a converted Canaanite Psalm. The psalms composed by Essenes at Qumran are very different in style from the Old Testament Psalms. Furthermore, they are in large part a blending of quotations taken from Scripture. They also have a strong emphasis on mysticism.

Every phase of David's life bursts out into song. The shepherd world lives again. The temple service echoes and re-echoes God's praise. Even war marches to David's music. His songs mark both his victories and his defeats. There are songs of trust and desperate pleas for help. Both the vanity of life and the glories of life form themes for his songs. The finest tribute to the Psalms is their use in connection with the death of Christ. As for ourselves, we use David's 23rd Psalm [for comfort] in death and his 51st Psalm [as an example of repentance] in life. The Psalter [as the Old Testament collection of the Psalms is sometimes called] has always been the song book of the Christian church. Note that the New Testament did not write a new hymnal, although short hymns are scattered through its pages. We cannot overemphasize the fact that David introduced music as an integral part of the church service.

Although David did not write the fine prose that Churchill did, some of the best prose of the Old Testament dates from the days of David and Solomon. The narratives dealing with the lives of Samuel, Saul, David, and Solomon are immortal prose. Sit down and read these narratives through quickly, enjoying them as pure prose. Then reread them to get the timeless spiritual message that speaks to each succeeding generation. We are indebted to the unnamed literary men who wrote of David. They were excellent forerunners of the gifted Churchill and his historic prose.

Churchill was an artist with the brush as well, but David could paint pictures only with words. David's hand was as versatile as Churchill's, but it was the hand of a musician. Even in youth he was already playing before royalty, but we know him best as one whose music was played before his God.

Both men were national heroes and will ever remain so. To us, however, David emerges as the greater because his finest contributions were to the kingdom of God rather than to his nation. The melody of his music still echoes in every church. God said of him, "I have found David the son of Jesse, a man after my own heart, who shall do all my will." (Acts 13:22 ASV) This is, indeed, the supreme tribute.

Solomon

AMONG THE ORNAMENTS of Solomon's reign, not least were his own extraordinary intellectual gifts. He surpassed all his predecessors and successors in those things that strike the imagination as brilliant and imposing, but he has also passed into history as the wisest of ancient kings and one of the most favored of mortals. Although his reign was one of unequalled prosperity and glory, yet he was to be the last king under the Jewish monarchy. After him, the kingdom was to be divided.

This remarkable man grew up amid the evils that saddened the last days of his father David. Solomon's interests were protected by his mother Bathsheba—an intriguing, ambitious, and beautiful woman—and his education was directed by the prophet Nathan. He was ten years old when his elder brother Absalom rebelled; he was only a youth of fifteen to twenty when he was placed upon the throne during the lifetime of his father David, and with his consent.

Solomon's peaceful and prosperous reign of forty years was favorable to the one grand enterprise that David longed to accomplish, but to whom it was denied. This was the building of the Temple, for so long a time identified with the glory of Jerusalem. Common interest in this great project might have bound the twelve tribes together, except for the excessive taxation which the extravagance and ostentation of the monarch had rendered necessary. . . . As the great event in David's reign had been the removal of the Ark to Jerusalem, so the culminating glory of Solomon's was the dedication of the Temple he had built for the worship of the Lord. The ceremony equalled in brilliance the glories of a Roman triumph and, in popular enthusiasm, infinitely surpassed them. . . .

We read of no other king who so belied the promise of his early days, and on whom prosperity produced so fatal an apostasy, as Solomon. With all his wisdom and early piety, he became an egotist, a sensualist, and a tyrant. What vanity he displayed before the Queen of Sheba! What a slave he became to wicked women! How disgraceful was his toleration of the gods of Phoenicia and Egypt! How hard was the bondage to which he subjected his people! How different was his ordinary life from that of his illustrious father —with no repentance, no remorse, no self-abasement! . . . We read of no other illustrious man whose glory passed through so dark an eclipse. The satiated, disenchanted, disappointed monarch— prematurely old and worn out by self-indulgence—passed away without honor or regret on the part of his subjects before reaching the age of sixty.—John Lord, *Beacon Lights of History*

1
SOLOMON'S WISDOM

When David died, Solomon sat upon the throne of his father. Israel had been at peace with neighboring countries for many years, so Solomon inherited a nation that was powerful, prosperous, and peaceful. The young king knew, however, that he could wait no longer to purge the court of the leaders of the recent rebellion. So, one by one, the opportunity came whereby he could justifiably destroy his enemies.

Adonijah was the first to seal his doom. Through the queen mother, he had the audacity to make the unwise and ill-considered request that Solomon permit him to marry Abishag, the Shunamite. Young, strong, and beautiful, Abishag had married David in his old age in order to care for him and minister to his needs. Solomon was stunned when he learned what Adonijah wanted. Surely, he must have known that only one interpretation could be made of such a request: Adonijah had not given up his ambition for the throne. Solomon did the only thing left for him to do. He sent Captain Benaiah, leader of his bodyguard, to execute Adonijah without delay.

Solomon next turned his attention to Abiathar, the chief priest, who had defected. Although the priest deserved to die, Solomon knew that he could not order the execution. But he *could* send him into exile! When Solomon reached the Lord's Tent, he spoke to Abiathar.

"You are no longer welcome in Jerusalem," he said, bluntly. "I have stripped you of your priestly duties, and I have made Zadok chief priest. Here and now, I order you to return to your home at Anathoth."

Joab was third on the list. Once the proud, courageous, and valiant leader of David's army, he now stood in the Lord's Tent, trembling with fear. As soon as he had learned the fate of his erstwhile allies, Joab had raced to the Tent for sanctuary. Someone told Solomon where his enemy was hiding. Joab's flight proved his guilt

"Solomon" by Di Gand. Ducal Palace, Urbino, Italy. Solomon, son of David and Bathsheba, was the third king of Israel. During his rule, Israel was prosperous and at peace.   Alinari

beyond a shadow of doubt, so Solomon sent Benaiah on another execution mission. The intrepid executioner rushed back to the palace with the news that Joab refused to come out of the Tabernacle.

Solomon then gave his captain this stern order: "Kill Joab wherever you find him, and take a burial detail with you so that I may never see him again."

Solomon's orders were carried out; and thus it came about that Joab, a man who had lived by the sword, died by the sword. He was buried at his home out in the wilderness.

Solomon now had only one other problem. He must decide what to do with Shimei. Having made his decision, Solomon called Shimei before him.

"I suppose you have been wondering what is going to happen to you, now that my father is dead," he said. "Long before I was born, he spared your life back there at the Jordan on the condition that you never leave Jerusalem. I have decided to go along with my father's judgment on you. You will remain under 'house arrest' here in the city of Jerusalem. Death shall be your penalty if you ever disobey the condition imposed upon you by King David."

About three years later, Shimei learned that his two run-away slaves had been caught at Gath. He promptly saddled his donkey and went there to bring them back to Jerusalem. Shimei thus became a parole violator, and his punishment was swift and certain. Once again Benaiah became the executioner. Solomon's domestic problems were completely resolved now, and he was firmly established as king over all Israel.

One night, shortly after he became king, Solomon lay sleeping. The Lord appeared to him in a dream and said, "I will give you whatever you ask from Me."

In his dream, Solomon replied: "O

Lord, You have placed a teen-ager on the throne of a great and powerful nation. I know that I shall have endless problems and shall have to make many difficult decisions. My only request, therefore, is that You give me a wise mind and an understanding heart in order that I may govern Your people justly, wisely, and well."

God was so pleased with Solomon's request that He answered promptly: "I have answered your prayer. You will be the wisest person in all the world. So that no king can compare with you, I have also given you some things for which you did not ask—fame, riches, and honor."

Two mothers, who lived in the same house, stood before Solomon one day with a strange story. Each of them had given birth to sons at approximately the same time. During the night, one of the mothers had accidentally smothered her son. She had arisen and stealthily exchanged the dead baby for the one that was alive. Each woman now claimed that she was the real mother of the live child. Solomon listened patiently as the argument increased in intensity. At last, he raised his hand for silence.

"I have reached a decision in this case," he said. "I shall take my sword and divide the child into two parts. Then each of you will have one-half of the baby."

Upon hearing this awesome ruling, one of the women shrugged her shoulders indifferently and said: "Divide the child!"

A far different response came from the other mother as she knelt before the king and, with tears in her eyes, said: "O my lord, give her the living child. I ask only that the baby remain alive."

When he heard this plea, Solomon took the baby and gently placed it in the arms of the mother kneeling at his feet. News of this wise judgment and the way in which it was reached spread far and wide.

"Solomon's Judgment" by Frank Dicksee. *Biblia Sacra.* Two women claimed to be the mother of a baby. Solomon deter- mined the truth by ordering the child to be cut in two. The real mother cried out in protest. Lemercier and Co., Paris

It clearly showed to the people the great wisdom of their new king.

In the days that followed, Solomon's fame as a wise man spread throughout the world. He knew three thousand proverbs, many of which were collected and made into a book which is in the Bible. Although he did not write all the Proverbs, even as his father David did not write all the Psalms, they are known as the *Proverbs of Solomon.* Little wonder that people traveled from faraway places to see this king and to listen to his words of wisdom!

Based on the story in the Bible: 1 Kings 2:12—3:28, 4:29-34

2

SOLOMON BUILDS THE TEMPLE

FOUR HUNDRED AND EIGHTY YEARS after the people of Israel came out of the land of Egypt, Solomon began to build the Lord's Temple. At long last, David's fondest dream was on its way to becoming a reality. There were many things that had to be done before the actual construction of the Temple could start. Building materials had to be secured, labor battalions had to be formed, and skilled artisans had to be found.

Solomon's first step was to send a message to his good friend, King Hiram of Tyre:

"I plan to build a beautiful Temple for the Lord, and I need your help. Please

King Hiram's Sarcophagus at Deir Qanoun, Lebanon. Both David and Solomon were friends of Hiram, the Phoenician king of Tyre. Hiram supplied timber and workmen to build David's house and Solomon's temple and palace. © Matson Photo

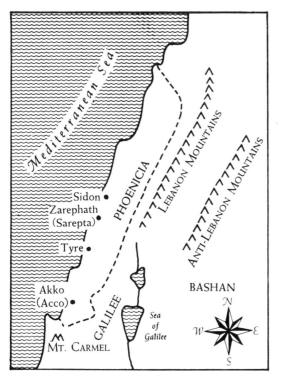

Phoenicia occupied a strip of land between the Lebanon range and the Mediterranean Sea. The Phoenicians were organized in city-states; Tyre and Sidon were the most important of these. Israel was fortunate to have neighbors like Hiram of Tyre.

finest cedars was floating down the Mediterranean toward Joppa. This steady flow of log-rafts would continue as long as Solomon needed lumber.

Because a huge labor corps would be needed to build the Temple, Solomon's next move was to take a census of all the foreigners in Israel. These people were to be the bulk of his labor battalions. The census showed that there were 153,600 foreigners in the land. Solomon assigned 80,000 of this group to the stone quarries up in the mountains. There the stones were to be cut and made ready for use before they were brought to the construction site. Another 70,000 of the men were assigned to such common labor tasks as bringing the prepared stones down from the mountains or bringing the cedars and cypress from Joppa to Mount Moriah. The remaining 3,600 foreigners were appointed supervisors of this gigantic labor force.

Solomon stood on Mount Moriah near the site his father had chosen for the

send me men trained to work with gold, silver, bronze, brass, and iron. Also send me cedar and cypress from Lebanon. In return, I shall send you 10,000 men, rotated each month on the basis of one month's work and two month's rest, to perform the unskilled jobs and to prepare the timber for shipment. I shall also supply you with 130,000 bushels of wheat, 130,000 bushels of barley, 120,000 gallons of wine, and 120,000 gallons of pure oil."

Solomon's request was promptly honored by King Hiram. He sent his most skillful woodsmen, the Sidonians, into the forest of Lebanon. Soon the ring of the axe and the sound of crashing trees echoed throughout the forest. Within a short time, raft after raft of Lebanon's

Floor Plan of Solomon's Temple. Certain details are uncertain, but in general the Temple was patterned after the Tabernacle, although it was more complex. Virtue & Co., Ltd.

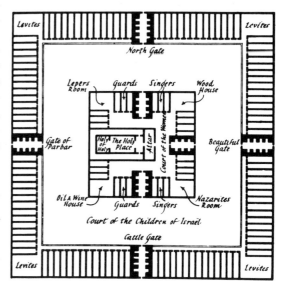

Model of Solomon's Temple (Shick). The House of the Lord was Solomon's greatest achievement. Only the finest materials and most skilled workmen were employed. For detailed description see 1 Kings 6-7 and 2 Chronicles 3-4. © Matson Photo

erection of the Temple. He looked around and saw the skilled workmen that King Hiram had sent. He also saw the large stockpiles of building materials which were increasing daily. Solomon decided that the time had come for the construction to start, so he issued a sharp command: "Proceed with the building of the Temple!"

After seven years of back-breaking toil by the forced laborers, the Temple was ready for Solomon's final inspection prior to its dedication, scheduled for the following day. The young monarch passed between the two large bronze pillars, glistening in the sunlight, toward the porch which was built of polished, gleaming white stones. He crossed the porch and entered the vestibule which had cypress-paneled walls and ceiling, overlaid with gold. Then he walked slowly toward the Holy Place.

When Solomon went inside the Holy Place, he gazed in wonder at its breathtaking beauty. The walls and ceiling were paneled with cedar, overlaid with gold and studded with precious jewels. All the furnishings in the room were made of pure gold: the golden altar with its burning incense, the golden table for the show-bread, and the golden candlestick holders. The skilled artisans from Tyre had done their jobs exceedingly well.

Solomon next turned his attention to the Holy of Holies. The inner sanctuary was majestic and awe-inspiring. Its walls and ceiling had received the same treatment as those in the Holy Place. The only piece of furniture in the room was a golden table, covered with a beautiful purple cloth, upon which the Ark was to rest. Behind the table, two golden cherubs had been attached to the wall. The inspection tour was over and Solomon left the Temple, pleased and proud that the one great mission of his life had been accomplished.

There was an air of excitement throughout the land. All the roads leading toward Jerusalem were swarming with people, as the elders and the chiefs of the tribes, together with the rest of the Israelites, responded to Solomon's call:

"Come to Jerusalem for the dedication of the Temple of the Lord! After seven days of dedication, meditation, and prayer, a great feast will be held for seven more days."

A deep silence fell upon the vast throng. The priests had returned from Mount Zion, bringing with them the Ark of the Covenant, the Lord's Tent, and other sacred articles that David had dedicated and placed inside the Tent. The hushed crowd watched the priestly procession disappear into the Temple. Once inside, the priests moved silently and swiftly to perform their assignments: The folded Tent of the Lord, outmoded and unused, still commanded the respect of the people and was stored in a specially prepared place. The sacred articles were placed in their depositories. Then the golden Ark of the Covenant was gently and reverently set upon the golden, purple-draped table, beneath the outstretched wings of the golden angels. When the priests emerged from the Holy Place, a very dark cloud filled the Temple. The glory of the Lord also filled the Sanctuary, and God's presence was felt by all the people.

Again the crowd was silent, as all eyes were turned to the speaker's platform and the rostrum toward which Solomon was solemnly approaching. Upon his arrival there, Solomon gave a brief dedication address:

"At long last, the golden Ark of the Covenant, containing only the two tablets of stone and the Laws of the Covenant which were placed there by Moses centuries ago, now has a beautiful, permanent home. As all of you know, my father David had his heart set upon building such a home as this for the Lord. But the Lord said to my father: 'You did well to have it in your heart to build a house in My name. Nevertheless, you shall not build this house for Me. Your son Solomon shall build My Temple.'

"The Lord's promise to my father has been fulfilled this day. The next seven days shall be spent in prayer, meditation, and the dedication of this resplendent Temple to the Lord our God."

At the conclusion of these words, Solomon lifted his arms toward the heavens and began the first dedicatory prayer:

"O, Lord God of Israel! There is no other God in the heavens above or on the

earth below as great as You. You have kept Your covenant and shown mercy to Your people. Instill in their hearts a deep desire to walk in Your ways and obey Your commandments. Hear and forgive, O Lord, not only Your people but strangers within our gates when they come to Your Temple with prayers and petitions. Only You know what is really in the hearts of all men."

Solomon closed his beautiful, powerful, and eloquent prayer by reminding the Lord of the covenant that He had made with the Israelites when He, with Moses as the human leader, had led their forefathers out of the land of Egypt. (This prayer in its entirety can be found in 1 Kings 8:22-53.)

While the dedication of the Temple was in progress, the forced laborers were preparing 22,000 oxen and 120,000 sheep for the great feast which was to follow. During the feast, there would be singing, music, dancing, and rejoicing throughout the vast assembly. How proud and happy the people were that their great and wise king had built such a dazzling Temple for the Lord, their God!

On the eighth day Solomon called the people into a solemn conclave to bestow his final blessing upon them:

"Blessed be the Lord who has given peace to His people Israel. May the Lord our God be with us even as He was with our forefathers. May He not leave us or forsake us. May He give us a strong desire in our hearts to follow Him and to obey all of His commandments, statutes, and ordinances. May we remain true to the Lord our God with all our minds and with all our hearts. May the Lord bless us and keep us safe and free all the days of our lives."

At the conclusion of the blessing, the people of Israel left Jerusalem and returned to their homes, confident, happy, and secure in the knowledge that there was no other king in all the world who could compare with their own King Solomon.

Based on the story in the Bible:
1 Kings 5:1 — 8:66

"Solomon Dedicates the Temple at Jerusalem" by J. James Tissot. *The Old Testament,* Illustrated. King Solomon's eloquent prayer during the dedication ceremonies at the Temple was an inspiration to the Israelites. Lemercier and Co., Paris

3
SOLOMON IN ALL HIS GLORY

ISRAEL WAS AT THE PINNACLE of her most shining hour. Her treasure houses were bulging with gold, silver, copper, brass, bronze, and with diamonds, rubies, and other kinds of precious stones. The building of the Temple of the Lord had been completed in seven years and now, after thirteen more years of strenuous labor, workmen were putting the finishing touches on the king's magnificent palace. Solomon in all his glory would soon enter the palace to await the arrival of the Queen of Sheba.

When Solomon went into the throne-room and looked at the throne, even he was amazed at its beauty and brilliance. It was made of ivory and was overlaid with gold. Precious jewels, partially embedded in the throne, gave it even more lustre. Solomon walked slowly up the six steps leading to the throne, passing a brass lion on both the right and left side of each step. As he sat upon the throne, Solomon thought, "Surely there is no other throne in all the world that can compare with mine."

While waiting for his royal visitor from faraway Arabia to arrive, Solomon thought back on some of the events that had occurred during the first twenty-four years of his reign. Early in his kingship, he had made a marriage alliance with Pharaoh, king of Egypt. This alliance had been necessary because Egypt was his nearest and most powerful neighbor. The result of this alliance was that he not only had made the southern section of Israel secure but that he had married his first wife, the Princess of Egypt. His next important act had been to negotiate a trade agreement with his father's old friend, King Hiram of Tyre.

Solomon recalled that the commercial interests of Israel had not been neglected. He had built a great fleet and, from its base in the harbor of one of Israel's port cities, Ezion-geber, his ships had plied the trade routes of the world and had brought back great treasures from foreign nations. He had also established two copper mining centers. One was located near Ezion-geber and the other was in the Jordan valley near the Jabbok river. These mines had quickly become thriving and prosperous.

Solomon remembered that, in the fourth year and second month of his reign, construction work had begun on a beautiful Temple for the Lord. King Hiram had responded immediately when Solomon called for assistance in his great building projects. After seven years the Temple had been built and dedicated to the Lord. Now, thirteen years later, the king's own majestic palace – the last of his massive building projects—was ready for occupancy.

Solomon was roused from his thoughts of the past when one of his servants came to the door and announced that the Queen of Sheba, with her great caravan, had just entered the city.

Solomon welcomed the lovely Arabian queen with all the pomp, ceremony, and courtesy due to visiting royalty. As she alighted from her camel, twenty-one shrill blasts from the trumpeteers echoed and re-echoed through the nearby hills. Solomon then conducted the Queen on a

"The Embarkation of the Queen of Sheba" by Lorrain. National Gallery, London. The Queen visited Solomon to test his reputed wisdom. She brought questions posed by her wise men, and she marveled at the King's knowledge.   National Gallery

personally escorted tour of the Temple grounds, the Temple, the palace court, and the palace. Never had the Queen seen such magnificence and luxury!

Before leaving Arabia, the Queen of Sheba had asked the wisest of her wise men to give her a list of the most difficult questions known to them. She was determined to test thoroughly the wisdom of Solomon. The king and the visiting queen were sitting on one of the luxurious couches near the throne room. The Queen asked Solomon question after difficult question, and his answers were always prompt, thorough, and satisfactory. The Queen gasped in amazement at the wisdom and knowledge displayed by Solomon.

According to the custom of the times, there was then an exchange of gifts between the two rulers. For her part, the Queen gave Solomon an almost unbelievably large amount of gold, precious jewels, and spices. Solomon, in turn, proved that no one could equal his capacity for giving. He offered the Queen of Sheba anything her heart might desire, as presents to take back to her kingdom.

"The Queen of Sheba Brings Gifts to Solomon" by Bonifazio. Academy of Fine Arts, Venice. When the Queen was ready to return home, she gave Solomon gifts of gold and precious stones and brought special spices from her country.   Alinari

As she prepared to mount her camel, the Queen turned to Solomon and said: "Before leaving home, I thought that the report of your wisdom and prosperity was exaggerated. Now that I have seen with my own eyes and heard with my own ears, I must admit that the tale was only half-told. How happy your people must be! They can listen constantly to your words of wisdom. Blessed be the Lord your God, Who has delighted in you and has set you upon the throne of Israel, to judge your people wisely and justly."

This was truly the Golden Age of the Israelites. Gold continued to pour into Solomon's storehouses in vast quantities. In addition to what he received from the traders, merchants, and tribute paid by all the kings of Assyria, every year Solomon's ships brought back 666 talents of gold ($16,250,000). Hundreds of shields were handcrafted of beaten gold. Even the dinnerware, cups, and glasses were made of solid gold.

Jesus Himself, nearly ten centuries later, spoke of this glittering era in Israel's history: "Consider the lilies in the field .... I tell you, Solomon in all his glory was not arrayed like one of these."

Again He said: "The Queen of the South came to hear the wisdom of Solomon, but One greater than Solomon is now here."

Based on the story in the Bible: 1 Kings 3:1, 5:1, 7:1, 9:26-28, 10:1-23

4
THE LATER YEARS OF SOLOMON

SOLOMON'S GLORY DID NOT DIE suddenly; it just faded away. Although the people of Israel were proud of the splendor and fame that Solomon had brought to their land, there were rumblings of discontent and anger directed at the throne long before the end of his reign. The people of Israel had a tax problem. Solomon had found it necessary, in order to maintain the luxury and magnificence of the royal court, to levy continual tax increases upon his subjects. Eventually they were suffering under such an unbearable burden that they found it difficult to provide for themselves even the bare necessities of life. This heavy tax oppression was but one of

"Worship of Idols by Solomon" by Conte. Prado, Madrid. Among Solomon's wives were foreign women. As time went on, he allowed them to influence him, and he built altars for their gods. Solomon even worshiped with them.　Prado

the things that started Solomon's decline.

During his years on the throne Solomon married seven hundred wives, many of whom were foreign women. He also had three hundred concubines, or women of secondary position, in his household. It was not the number of Solomon's wives that displeased God because, in those days, it was considered a mark of prestige for a great monarch to have many wives. What really made God angry with Solomon was the fact that he not only built altars for the gods of his foreign wives but that he actually worshiped at them.

As the Israelites began to follow the example set by their king, and idol worship spread throughout the land, God's patience with Solomon was exhausted. Finally, it became necessary for the Lord to speak sharply and sternly to the king who had begun his reign with such great promise.

"Solomon, you have not loved Me with all your heart like your father David did," He said. "You have not kept My covenants and My commandments as I told you to do. Because of your sins, I will surely take your kingdom away from you and give it to one of your servants. However, for the sake of your father David, I will not do this during your lifetime. Instead, I will take your kingdom away from your son, with the exception of one tribe which I will give to him, both for the sake of your father David and for the sake of Jerusalem, my chosen city."

Who was this person to whom God planned to make king of ten of the tribes of Israel? His name was Jeroboam, one of Solomon's most important and most trusted officials. One day while Jeroboam was walking outside the walls of Jerusalem, he met the prophet Ahijah, who did a startling thing. Taking off his new cloak, he tore it into twelve pieces and gave ten of them to Jeroboam, along with the reason for this action.

"Because the people of Israel and their king have begun to worship false gods, the Lord is planning to divide the kingdom after Solomon dies," he said. "God has chosen you to reign over ten of the tribes. The tribe of Judah, which has absorbed the decimated tribe of Benjamin, will be given to Solomon's son. God will punish the descendants of David a long time, but not forever."

Ahijah's prophecy soon became known throughout the land. Jeroboam, remembering the fate of Solomon's enemies early in his reign, fled for his life into the land of Egypt.

Solomon ruled Israel for forty years. During that time he had brought the kingdom to its greatest heights and now, in his later years, was destined to drag it to its lowest depths. Solomon's religious apostasies had dulled his mind, and his over-indulgences had weakened his body. Old before his time and amid gathering storms of political revolution that would soon shatter his kingdom, Solomon died near the comparatively young age of sixty and was buried in the city of David.

Rehoboam, Solomon's son, was crowned king of Israel, but his reign over all the tribes was to be short-lived. For all practical purposes, his father Solomon was the last king to rule over a united Israel.

Based on the story in the Bible: 1 Kings 11:1-13, 26-40, 42-43

PLACES
in the Story of Solomon

ANATHOTH

Two and one-half miles northeast of Jerusalem is found Anathoth, the home town of Abiathar, chief priest of Israel during David's reign. It was to this place that Solomon exiled the priest because of the part he played in the abortive attempt to seize the throne for Adonijah.

SHUNEM

Located in the territory of Issachar, 5 miles north of Mount Gilboa and 3 1/2 miles northeast of the Jezreel valley, is the home town

of David's last wife, Abishag. Adonijah's request to marry her cost him his life.

GATH

Recklessly disobeying Solomon's order that he never leave Jerusalem, Shimei paid with his life for coming to this important Philistine city to retrieve his two run-away slaves. Gath is located about 15 miles southeast of the coastal city of Ashkelon (Ascalon).

GIBEON

This hill city, 6 miles north of Jerusalem, is the place where God came to Solomon in a dream and promised him wisdom.

Modern Tyre (Sur) in Lebanon. During Solomon's time, the Phoenician city of Tyre was an important Mediterranean seaport and a world center for trading and seafaring. Its king, Hiram, was friendly to the Israelites. © Matson Photo

TYRE

This Phoenician maritime Mediterranean coastal city, 20 miles south of Sidon, was ruled by King Hiram, who supplied Solomon with materials for the Temple and the palace.

MOUNT MORIAH

One of the four hills comprising the city of Jerusalem is Mount Moriah. It was on this hill that Solomon built the Lord's Temple.

EGYPT

This great and powerful nation, occupying the northeastern portion of Africa, was Israel's nearest neighbor. Solomon made a marriage alliance with Pharaoh in order to protect the southern sector of Israel.

EZION-GEBER (Elath, modern Eilat)

Israel's provincial city, located on the north end of the Gulf of Aqabah (Aqaba), became an important Red Sea port in Solomon's time. It was in the harbor of Ezion-geber that Solomon based his great fleet of trading ships.

JABBOK RIVER

This river is an eastern tributary of the Jordan, into which it enters about 23 miles north of the Dead Sea. In the Jordan valley near the Jabbok, Solomon established one of his copper mining centers.

SHEBA

This city is located in southwest Arabia and, on a direct route, is approximately 1,200 miles southwest of Jerusalem. The Queen of Sheba made this long journey to verify the truth of reports she had received of the wisdom of Solomon and the prosperity of Israel.

JOPPA

This city on the Mediterranean coast was assigned to the tribe of Dan, but the Danites were never successful in wresting its control from the Philistines. Joppa is about 34 miles northwest of Jerusalem. It was to this seaport that King Hiram of Tyre floated his raft-logs for Solomon's use.

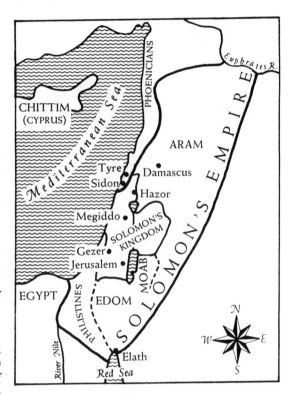

Solomon's Empire. King Solomon ruled over a united Israel that had been achieved by his father, David. His territory extended from the Euphrates River as far south as the Red Sea.

QUESTIONS
on the Story of Solomon

1

1 Why did Adonijah become the first victim of Solomon's purge of his enemies?

2 What did Solomon do in the case of Abiathar, the chief priest, who had joined Adonijah in his rebellion?

3 Why did Solomon order the execution of Joab, Israel's greatest military leader?

4 What was the condition on which both David and Solomon spared the life of Shemei? What was the ultimate fate of Solomon's last enemy? Why?

5 What was Solomon's request when God told him that He would give the young king anything his heart desired?

6 What did Solomon say to two women, in a judicial case, that enabled him to decide which of them was the real mother of the child and should have sole custody of it?

2

7 How long had the Israelites been out of Egypt when Solomon began the construction of the Lord's Temple?

8 How many foreigners living in Israel were affected by Solomon's forced labor policy? Give the number from this group who were in each of Solomon's assigned work forces.

9 Who supplied Solomon with materials and skilled workmen needed for the building of the Temple?

10 Describe briefly the interior of the completed Temple.

11 What important event occurred just prior to the dedication of the Temple?

12 What happened when the priests emerged from the Temple?

13 How long did the dedication ceremonies last? How many days did the people feast and rejoice?

3

14 What was the economic situation in Israel as Solomon began the silver anniversary of his reign?

15 What commercial interests did Solomon develop?

16 Why did the Queen of Sheba come to visit Solomon in Jerusalem? Was she impressed by what she saw and heard?

4

17 Why did God become angry with Solomon?

18 What did God tell him?

19 Whom had God chosen to reign over ten tribes of the divided kingdom?

20 How long did Solomon rule over Israel? Who succeeded him on the throne?

*Answers are found
on the following pages.*

ANSWERS

on the Story of Solomon

1

1 Adonijah made the mistake of requesting permission to marry Abishag, David's last wife. This indicated to Solomon that his oldest half-brother still had high hopes of occupying the throne.

2 Solomon sent the treacherous chief priest into exile.

3 Joab was the military leader of the rebellious group. When he heard of the fate of his partners-in-crime, Joab fled to the Lord's Tent for sanctuary. The old general's flight to the Tabernacle proved to Solomon that Joab could never again be trusted.

4 Both David and Solomon ordered Shimei never to leave Jerusalem. Shimei made his fatal mistake when he went to Gath to retrieve his two run-away slaves. When he returned to Jerusalem, Shimei paid with his life for his heedless disregard of Solomon's command.

5 Solomon asked the Lord to give him a wise mind and an understanding heart.

6 Solomon told the two women that he had decided to divide the baby into two parts so that each of them could have a share. One of the women shrugged indifferently, but the other pleaded for the life of the child, even offering to surrender her claim.

2

7 The people of Israel had been in the land of Canaan 480 years.

8 A census revealed that there were 153,600 foreigners in Israel. Solomon assigned 80,000 to the stone quarries; another 70,000 were given the menial, hard labor jobs; and the remaining 3,600 were appointed supervisors of the two groups.

9 Solomon's friend, King Hiram of Tyre, supplied the materials and skilled men.

10 All the walls and ceilings in the Temple were overlaid with gold and studded with precious jewels. All the furnishings in the Holy Place were made of pure gold: the altar, the table, and the candlestick holders. In the Holy of Holies, two golden angels were attached to a wall and, beneath their outstretched wings was a golden table, covered with a beautiful purple cloth, upon which the golden Ark was to rest.

11 The priests went to Mount Zion and brought the Ark, the Lord's Tent, and other dedicated articles to Jerusalem. When the priests arrived at Mount Moriah, they solemnly and reverently placed everything in the Lord's Temple.

12 A very dark cloud filled the Tabernacle, and God's presence was felt by all the people.

13 The dedication program lasted for seven days. The feasting and rejoicing also lasted for seven days.

3

14 Israel's economy was booming. Her treasure houses were bulging with gold, silver, copper, brass, bronze, diamonds, rubies, pearls, and many other types of precious jewels.

15 Solomon built a great fleet of trading ships, based at the Red Sea port of Ezion-geber. He also established two copper mining centers.

16 The Queen of Sheba came to Jerusalem to satisfy her curiosity concerning the

rumors she had heard of Solomon's great wisdom and untold riches. The Queen gasped in amazement at the beauty, luxury, and magnificence of the Temple and the palace. The sight of the great wealth in the treasure houses almost took her breath away. Solomon's great wisdom and vast store of knowledge made a lasting impression on her.

4

17 God became angry with Solomon because he not only built altars for the gods of his foreign wives; he actually worshiped at these altars.

18 The Lord told Solomon that, because of his sins and failure to love Him with all his heart, the kingdom would be taken away from him. For David's sake and the sake of Jerusalem, God said that He would not take away the ten tribes until after the death of Solomon.

19 God had chosen Jeroboam to rule over the ten tribes. When the news spread that he was the heir-apparent to the throne of the ten tribes, he fled for his life into Egypt. He fled because he remembered the fate of Solomon's enemies early in his reign.

20 Solomon ruled over Israel for forty years. His son Rehoboam then sat on the throne of his father.

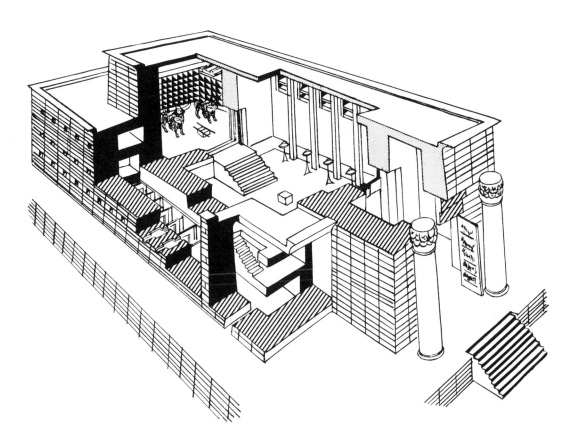

Diagram of Solomon's Temple. An artist's concept of the Temple of Jerusalem depicts the stairway leading to the entrance and the two pillars (right), the Holy Place (center), and the Holy of Holies (left), with the Ark guarded by two cherubim.

FURTHER FACTS
AND OUTLINES
for the Story of Solomon

FIRST KINGS

AUTHORSHIP AND DATE

The author is unknown. Jewish tradition says that Jeremiah wrote both First and Second Kings. Some scholars have held to this view in modern times. It is interesting that 2 Kings 24:18 – 25:30 resembles closely Jeremiah 52. But there are enough problems in this view of authorship to make it improbable. Sources were used—examples: the "Book of the Deeds of Solomon" (1 Kings 11:41), the "Book of the Chronicles of the Kings of Judah" (1 Kings 14:29 and elsewhere), the "Book of the Chronicles of the Kings of Israel" (1 Kings 14:19 and elsewhere). It is thought that these were official documents, and other sources may have been employed, too. There has emerged the view that a contemporary or near-contemporary of Jeremiah did the Books of Kings in the first half of the sixth century B.C. (1 and 2 Kings are one book in the Hebrew Bible; in the Septuagint, Samuel and Kings are 1, 2, 3, 4 Books of the Kingdoms, and 1, 2, 3, 4 Books of the Kings in the Vulgate.)

DESTINATION

The People of Israel and posterity.

PURPOSE AND THEME

The purpose of 1 Kings is to trace Israel's history from David's death to Ahab's death, and to show that most of the kings turned their backs upon God in spite of the Covenant. God's promise to David (2 Samuel 7:12-16) is the basis for judging Judah's kings; indeed the kings in 1 and 2 Kings are compared with David himself who, for the most part, kept the Covenant, and King Jeroboam who did not keep it. Most of the kings were evil, like Jeroboam; a few were good, like David: Asa (1 Kings 15), Jehoshaphat (1 Kings 22), Hezekiah (2 Kings 18-20), Josiah (2 Kings 22-23). But even these good kings had, like David, their defects. David's parting words to Solomon make clear the way of a righteous rule (1 Kings 2:1ff). Solomon's greatness and kingly reign, the division of the kingdoms into North ("Israel") and South ("Judah") through the reigns of Ahab in the North and Jehoshaphat in the South—all are told in 1 Kings. Elijah enters the picture (as Elisha does in 2 Kings) as a kind of bridge between the earlier era and the period of the prophets.

OUTLINE

Solomon's Reign (chapters 1-11)
  In His Last Days, David Chooses Solomon To Succeed Him (1:1 – 2:11)
  Solomon's Reign Begun (2:12-46)
  Solomon's Prayer for Understanding (chapter 3)
  Solomon's Wise Judgment and Administration (chapter 4)
  The Building of the Temple (chapters 5-7) (The Temple was arranged like the Tabernacle.)
  The Dedication of the Temple, Solomon's Sermon and Prayer (chapter 8)
  God's Promise to Solomon (chapter 9)
  Solomon Visited by the Queen of Sheba (chapter 10)
  Solomon's Sins, His Punishment, and His Death (chapter 11)

Cedars of Lebanon. These stately coniferous trees, native to Lebanon, were popular for building because of their durabil- ity. Hiram of Tyre shipped cedars from the Phoenician forests for use in Solomon's Temple and palace.   © Matson Photo

PROVERBS

AUTHORSHIP AND DATE

Ancient tradition says that not one person but several wrote the Proverbs. In the text titles of Proverbs it is recorded that Solomon (1:1, 10:1, 25:1), Agur (30:1), and Lemuel (31:1) all wrote sections of the book. These titles also indicate that certain "wise men" wrote other sections (22:17, 24:23). Probably some of these Proverbs emerged from oral tradition and were eventually written down.

The date of Proverbs, in the book's final form, is impossible to fix. Solomon lived in the 10th century B.C., yet some of the Proverbs were copied down or written in the time of Hezekiah (25:1), who lived in the 8th century B.C. The collection of Proverbs given in the book grew over a long period of Jewish history, and the final form of the book was fixed at an unknown date.

DESTINATION

Apparently, to Solomon's son (Rehoboam, presumably: 1:8, 2:1); to all Jewish people (4:1); applicable to the whole human race.

PURPOSE AND THEME

The Proverbs is an intensely practical book. The nearest thing to it in the New Tes-

111

tament is the book of James. The proverb form cuts deep into the thinking of man and elicits responses. Every area of human life is treated; moral and ethical implications are drawn. Evil associates, immorality, intemperance, bickering, falsifying, shady business ethics, sloth, selfishness—all are handled with an incisiveness unmatched elsewhere in the world's literature. Generosity, reverence for God, careful child-rearing, the power of influence (both of men and of women), young manhood—these are the areas of positive instruction. All in all, the Book of Proverbs constitutes a genuinely helpful manual of everyday living. *Wisdom* (knowledge plus the ability to use it meaningfully) is exalted throughout and is a key word of the book. Note that in Proverbs wisdom begins with, and centers in, God.

OUTLINE

Like the Book of Psalms, the Book of Proverbs is too large and composed of too many dissimilar parts to permit a detailed outline. The following division of material gives an outline in general terms.

Wisdom Versus Folly (chapters 1-9)
Miscellaneous Proverbs of Solomon (10:1—22:16)
Miscellaneous Proverbs Dealing with Human Responsibility and Rules for Righteous Living (22:17—24:34)
Miscellaneous Proverbs of Solomon. Copied by Hezekiah's Scribes—25:1 (chapters 25-29)
Proverbs of Agur (chapter 30)
Proverbs of Lemuel (31:1-9)
The Virtuous Woman: An Acrostic (31:10-31)

ECCLESIASTES

AUTHORSHIP AND DATE

An old tradition says that Solomon wrote Ecclesiastes, but many scholars do not consider this well-founded and so list the authorship as unknown.

DESTINATION

Although unclear from the text, it was probably written to young Jewish men (11:9, 12:12).

PURPOSE AND THEME

The word "Ecclesiastes" means "preacher" or "assemblyman" (Hebrew *Qoheleth*) and is the title of his office. It is the preacher's aim to make clear that the things of this world are mere vanity, they are unrewarding in the depth dimension. Satisfaction of the human heart is achieved in terms of wisdom, not folly. The conclusion to the book indicates its Gospel thrust: ". . . Fear God, and keep His commandments; for this is the whole duty of man. For God will bring every deed into judgment, with every secret thing, whether good or evil" (12:13-14). There is no meaning in life and creation apart from God. In Him is meaning and satisfaction, apart from Him is

meaninglessness and intense dissatisfaction. This is the considered conclusion of a man who has tried now this, now that—indeed everything—in an attempt to come to a sound philosophy of life and living.

OUTLINE

The Prologue (1:1-11)
The Heading (1:1)
The Theme of the Book Introduced: the Vanity of all Worldly Things (1:2-11)

The Vanity of all Worldly Things (1:12—6:12)
The Vanity of Searching after Purely Human Wisdom (1:12-18)
The Vanity of Pleasures (2:1-11)
The Vanity of Human Wisdom and Riches (2:12-23)
The Vanity of Human Effort (2:24—3:15)
The Vanity of the Wicked and the Oppressors (3:16—4:6)
The Vanity of One Attempting a Task by Himself, Work Is more easily Done by Two People (4:7-12)
The Vanity of Folly and Riches as over against Wisdom and Poverty (4:13-16)

The Vanity of Empty Words (5:1-7)
The Vanity of Riches (5:8 — 6:12)

Observations on Wisdom and Folly
   (7:1 — 12:8)
  The Well-Ordered Life as over against the
  Mass of Mankind Which is Sinful
  (chapter 7)
  In Actuality the Wicked Do not Fare Better

than the Righteous—It Only Looks that
Way (chapters 8-9)
The Excellence of Wisdom
  (chapters 10-11)
Remember God in Youth (12:1-8)

Epilogue: Respect God, Keep His Commandments (12:9-14)

SONG OF SOLOMON

AUTHORSHIP AND DATE

There is an old tradition supporting the view that Solomon wrote this book (1:1) in the 10th century B.C.

PURPOSE AND THEME

This ancient oriental song or poem communicates the sacredness and purity of human love. As such, the book describes the love and marriage of King Solomon ("the beloved") and a peasant girl ("the Shulamite"). Genuine love is true and noble, as expressed in a series of talks or speeches primarily by Solomon and the country girl. While the poem celebrates the beauties of human love, it also suggests the intensity of the love of God for His children. It is a parable of Divine love which is the source of human love. The book may also be viewed as symbolic of the love of Christ for His Bride, the Church.

OUTLINE

The Meeting of the Bride and Bridegroom,
  Their Delight in One Another (1:1 — 3:5)
The Espousal (3:6 — 4:16)
Temporary Separation, the Bride Longs for
  Her Bridegroom (5:1 — 6:3)
Love to One Another Expressed
  (6:4 — 8:14)

"Desidirium" by Morelli. *Biblia Sacra.* "Song of Solomon," thought to have been written by him in the 10th century B.C., tells the story of the king's love for a peasant girl. It has been interpreted in various ways.   Lemercier and Co. Paris

Solomon, King and Scholar

by

James Kelso

In a chapter from his book, *Archaeology and Our Old Testament Contemporaries* (© 1966, Zondervan Publishing House, Grand Rapids, Michigan), Author James Kelso describes Solomon as "the king with many a Ph.D." and makes a good case for this claim. He also shows that, despite the king's wisdom and scholarly attributes, the zest for living departs when God is relegated to a place of little or no importance in a man's life...an important lesson for today.

KNOWLEDGE IN MANY FIELDS

SOLOMON'S WISDOM is best appreciated in the Near East, where today anything super-gigantic, distinctly unique, or unfathomably difficult is always attributed to Solomon or Alexander the Great. In the logic of the Near East, only these two geniuses could have done the impossible.

BOTANY AND BIOLOGY

Solomon's wisdom was indeed versatile. To begin with his less publicized scholarship, he was a botanist and a biologist (1 Kings 4:33). In the former field he was at home with all plant life, from the tiny "hyssop that grows in the wall" to the greatest tree the ancients knew, the cedar of Lebanon. Palestine and Syria are said to have the greatest variety of flowers per square mile of any area on earth. Their flora reaches from the sub-tropics of the Dead Sea area (deepest spot on the globe) to the Lebanon Range, over 10,000 feet high, with its deep winter snow.

While excavating New Testament Jericho, I commuted daily between Jerusalem and Jericho. The spring flowers along that road are simply impossible to describe, for variety, color, and profusion. It seems impossible that God did invent so many varieties. The biologist, of course, had a parallel of animal life in those days, but many of these species have been depleted today. . . .

LITERATURE AND ARCHITECTURE

In the fine arts Solomon specialized in two fields, literature and architecture. He should be entitled to degrees in both fields.

Solomon's proverbs have been preserved in the book of that name. Among the Semites of antiquity and the Arabs of today the proverb constitutes a major form of literature. The proverb is a substantial truth, dramatically phrased and condensed for quick and permanent memory, usually only two to four lines long. It was the child's schoolbook, the phraseology of business and politics, and the epigram by which you finally clinched your argument in court. The more subtle factors in the use of Proverbs are listed in the first six verses of the book.

The English translation of Proverbs 1:7 is too thin. The play on words here is saying that the fear of the Lord (that is, obeying God) is the first thing and *always* the most important thing in knowledge (that is, the experience of godly living). The Book of Proverbs was Solomon's brochure on how to live the godly life. Its phraseology made it easier for the common man to understand and practice his faith. In its most common denominator, wisdom is godliness and foolishness is sin. The Pentateuch was the lawyer's book, but the common man kept out of the law's clutches by practicing the precepts of the Proverbs. The modern Arab says, "A proverb is to speech as salt is to food." A Christian missionary to an Arab country must have a minimum of a thousand keen proverbs at the tip of his tongue for use on all occasions.

Solomon's interest in architecture was occasioned by the necessity of his building a central sanctuary in Jerusalem where all Israel could worship the Lord. This Temple was simply a modification of the mobile Tabernacle of Moses' day put into a permanent stone sanctuary. The basic pattern of the court, the Holy Place, and the Holy of Holies (or inner sanctuary) remained, but the decorative features differed greatly from those of the Tabernacle. (God did not give specific plans and specifications to Solomon as He had done to Moses). A related ground plan is seen in the Syrian Temple of Tell Tainat. The Judaean city of Arad copied the Jerusalem pattern for its local sanctuary. Solomon's builders were Phoenicians, and they apparently suggested most of the decorative changes.

These Phoenicians introduced into Palestine for the first time the structural wall built with headers [bricks or stones with their ends toward the face of the wall] and stretchers [bricks or stones laid with their length parallel to the face of the wall] and using quoin [solid exterior angle] construction on the corners with proto-Aeolic [primitive Greek] capitals [tops of columns, bearing the weight of the wall or story]. They improved the quarrying and dressing of stone over any earlier Israelite work. The quarry which produced the stone for Solomon's Temple can be seen in an enormous cave underneath what is now the northern section of a Turkish walled city.

The Syrian custom of lining a temple with cedar panels was another new feature introduced into Solomon's Temple. The use of the columns, Jachin and Boaz, in his Temple was also a carry-over from Near East temple architecture. Their exact structural nature is disputed by scholars, but these columns seem to have been used by Solomon to symbolize the pillars of cloud and fire that led the Israel-ites in their desert wanderings. Not only did Solomon double the size of the Tabernacle when he erected his Temple, but he also surrounded it with a new structure that had three floors of rooms on all sides of the Temple except the front. These rooms were for the use of Temple personnel and for storage of materials used in the Temple service. The new addition was built directly against the Temple proper but not incorporated into its walls. The Temple remained a completely separate and distinct unit, as the Tabernacle had been.

The wide use of copper and bronze in this Temple should be noted. Hebrew has only one word for both metals, but the metallurgists of that day were so excellent that the use to which the metals were put tells whether it was copper or one of the various tin alloys of copper. It was never brass, for that alloy was not discovered until centuries later. The Bible gives us details of this copper industry from the mines and smelters of the Arabah to Arabian markets via the port city of Ezion-geber. The skilled fashioning of the metal by hammering or casting, along with the special technique used for the most delicate work, was done in the Jordan near the place where the Jabbok River enters the Jordan (1 Kings 7:13-51).

Solomon did not neglect his own royal buildings, such as the palace with its throne room, the armory, and so on. Too, his twelve new administrative capitals throughout the nation had to have their own public buildings. Even his chariot depots used the clearstory [the part of a building that rises clear of the roofs of the other parts and whose walls contain windows for lighting the interior] in their stables.

One of the by-products of Solomon's Temple palace complex was a new type of house architecture among the common people. The government's prodigious demand for large drafted stones [stone with a narrow border along its edge or across its face as guide to the stonecutter] required thousands of skilled stone masons. When the government contracts closed down, craftsmen returned to their homes in all sections of Palestine and introduced the stone column into house architecture, making a building unlike anything found in earlier periods.

POLITICS

Politics was another field of study in which Solomon excelled. His reign began with a theophany [visible manifestation of God] as had the administrations of Moses and Joshua. God said, "Ask what I shall give you," and Solomon replied, "Thank You for all that You did for my father, David." Then, confessing his own inability to rule without God's help, he pleaded, "Give therefore Thy servant an understanding heart to judge Thy people, that I may discern between good and bad: for who is able to judge this Thy so great a people?" (1 Kings 3:9) This prayer differed strikingly from the common pagan prayers we see in archaeological inscriptions and other records. The latter are excellently condensed [in the summary of things Solomon did not ask for] in 1 Kings 3:11-12: "And God said unto him, Because thou hast asked this thing, and hast not asked for thyself long life; neither has thou asked riches for thyself, nor hast asked the lives of thine enemies; but hast asked for thyself understanding to discern judgment; behold, I have done according to thy words...."

Solomon's emphasis on peace is seen in that he permitted the fringes of the new empire which David had created to slip away without a struggle. Although he was a man of peace, he still believed in military preparedness for Palestine proper and he added the chariot to the nation's military equipment. Excavations at Megiddo have uncovered the remodeling of his chariot depots with stalls for four hundred and fifty horses plus parade grounds. . . . David, for some reason unknown to us, did not emphasize chariot warfare. Solomon also rebuilt the fortresses of Hazor, Megiddo, and Gezer. Since Solomon's reign was essentially an epoch of peace, Israel reached her peak of material culture at that time.

Solomon remodeled the federal government by replacing the original tribal unit with twelve new geographical areas, directly responsible to Solomon alone. Some of the new units

followed the old boundary lines, others did not. . . .

In international affairs, too, Solomon did well. He intermarried into Egypt, which is an ancient diplomatic term for an alliance. Hiram of Tyre was his business partner. Even the Queen of Sheba came from the farthest corner of Arabia to Jerusalem. Business was always an important part of international politics, and she had great riches in gold and incense, which were the rarest items in the commerce of that day. At Bethel we found a pottery stamp used by the merchants of the Queen of Sheba to stamp their signatures on the bags of incense. It dates to about a century after the visit of the Queen of Sheba to Solomon.

Solomon controlled all the caravan trade on the eastern desert's edge from Palmyra to Aqabah. . . . Hiram of Tyre dominated commerce of the Mediterranean Sea, but Solomon had him join Israel in a maritime venture down the Red Sea and around the shoulder of Africa. Egypt, which was a major manufacturing center, had to pay taxes to Solomon on her goods that had to go north through his kingdom to reach Anatolian and Mesopotamian markets. The Hittites from Asia Minor sold Solomon horses, which he in turn sold at a profit to Egypt.

His proverbs often refer to business matters. Here is a variety of themes in that field. "A false balance is abomination to the Lord: but a just weight is His delight." (Proverbs 11:1) "He that is surety for a stranger shall smart for it: and he that hateth suretyship is sure." (11:15) "The liberal soul shall be made fat: and he that watereth shall be watered also himself." (11:25) "Whoso mocketh the poor reproacheth his Maker: and he that is glad at calamities shall not be unpunished." (17:5) "He also that is slack in his work is brother to him that is a destroyer." (18:9 ASV) "The rich ruleth over the poor, and the borrower is servant to the lender." (22:7) Some of the most significant of these proverbs on the ancient and modern problems of poverty are: "He that oppresseth the poor reproacheth his Maker: but he that hath mercy on the needy honoreth Him." (14:31 ASV) "He that hath pity upon the poor lendeth unto the Lord: and his good deed will He pay him again." (19:17 ASV) "The rich and the poor meet together: the Lord is the maker of them all." (22:2) Unfortunately, in his later years Solomon repudiated many of his own proverbs.

PSYCHOLOGY

Just as politics and business cannot be separated, so neither can good government and psychology. Solomon was certainly an expert in this field, a psychologist par excellence. Read 1 Kings 3:16-28 for his first court decision, remembering that an Israelite judge did not simply pass judgment on the evidence presented by the opposing parties in a case; the judge himself had to ask questions in such a way that one of the litigants would demonstrate his innocence and the other would demonstrate his guilt. This was where Solomon was a genius. Since Solomon was king, he was the final court of appeals.

Most of the Book of Proverbs shows a good appreciation of psychology at its best. Here is [presented] a variety of striking verses: "Walk with wise men and thou shalt be wise; but the companion of fools shall smart for it." (13:20 ASV) "A rebuke entereth deeper into one that hath understanding than a hundred stripes into a fool." (17:10 ASV) "Even a fool, when he holdeth his peace, is counted wise; when he shutteth his lips, he is esteemed as prudent." (17:28 ASV) "Whoso findeth a wife findeth a good thing, and obtaineth favor of the Lord." (18:22 ASV) "Bread of falsehood is sweet to a man; but afterwards his mouth shall be filled with gravel." (20:17 ASV) "Buy the truth and sell it not; yea, wisdom, and instruction, and understanding." (23:23 ASV) "Rejoice not when thine enemy falleth, and let not thy heart be glad when he is overthrown." (24:17 ASV)

THEOLOGY

Solomon was also at home in the field of theology. He offered one of the most significant prayers found in all of Scripture when he dedicated the Temple (1 Kings 8). Seven times he used such phrases as "... when they shall pray toward this place." This was the Old

Testament equivalent of praying in the name of Christ in New Testament times. It was looking toward Jerusalem, as under Moses the children of Israel looked toward the brazen serpent and as Christians now look toward the crucified [and risen] Christ. The ancient Israelites were justified by faith in the promised Messiah (typified in this Temple and its ritual). Remember how Daniel prayed thus toward Jerusalem.

In spite of all his "Ph.D. degrees," Solomon "flunked" one of the most important courses in the Old Testament University; namely, "Israelite Homelife." (His father David has also "flunked" this course.) "And he [Solomon] had seven hundred wives, princesses, and three hundred concubines; and his wives turned away his heart. For it came to pass, when Solomon was old, that his wives turned away his heart after other gods; and his heart was not perfect with the Lord his God, as was the heart of David his father. For Solomon went after Ashtoreth the goddess of the Sidonians, and after Milcom the abomination of the Ammonites.... Wherefore the Lord said unto Solomon, Forasmuch as this is done of thee, and thou hast not kept My covenant and My statutes, which I have commanded thee, I will surely rend the kingdom from thee, and will give it to thy servant." (1 Kings 11:3-5, 11)

Unfortunately, Solomon is typical of too many modern Christians in that he failed to practice what he preached. He outlived his faith. Mammon replaced God, and Solomon was no sooner dead than his kingdom was rent asunder. Still more tragic, he lost his first love and asked the Lord to share a place with the heathen gods of his harem. And these pagan temples were built on the Mount of Olives, directly across the Kidron Valley from Solomon's Temple to the Lord.

Nevertheless, Christ Himself put such a high value on Solomon's Book of Proverbs that it is reflected everywhere in the Gospels. If you knew your Proverbs by heart and your Gospels equally well, you would have a new appreciation of Solomon. Since Solomon's book was modern enough for Christ, it is modern enough for us.

THE Divided Kingdom

**N**ATIONAL BREAK-UP AND DEGRADATION are depicted in appalling detail in four chapters of the First Book of Kings. The entire story covers a period of sixty years, from the disruption after the death of Solomon to the corruption under Ahab and the coming of Elijah. The seeds of strife had long been growing. The occasion of the actual division arose with the accession of Rehoboam and the rebellion of Jeroboam. Both of these men were unworthy, as the folly of the one and the sin of the other prove.

Jeroboam led a popular movement of protest against the burdens which had been imposed upon the people under the reign of Solomon. He was later to lead his people into the sin of idolatry.

Rehoboam was so proud and despotic that he answered the people in these foolish and empty words: "My father made your yoke heavy, but I will add to your yoke; my father chastised you with whips, but I will chastise you with scorpions." (1 Kings 12:14) Rehoboam had no right to reign so despotically. The rending of the kingdom into two parts was the result.

This story illustrates graphically the fact that despotic power is not hereditary. Solomon had gained such a position that his rule had actually become despotic. Rehoboam's wish and will aimed at increasing the power and severity of his father's rule. He could not do so. The people will strangely submit to tyranny for a long time, if the tyrant has managed by some means to gain a personal influence over them. But there are limits.

Stooping humanity has the persistent habit of lifting itself up after a time. Then kings are swept aside and revolutions result. Such revolutions are often wrong in method; but, in asserting the greatness of humanity, they all contribute to the onward march of God.—G. Campbell Morgan, *Searchlights from the Word*

1

BREAK-UP: REHOBOAM VS. JEROBOAM

"UNEASY LIES THE HEAD that wears the crown." Two days earlier all Israel had come to Shechem to make Rehoboam king. Swift messengers had been sent to Egypt to bring Jeroboam out of exile so that he could act as spokesman for the depressed, unhappy people. Rehoboam now sat restlessly upon his throne, reviewing events of the past few days.

After the coronation ceremony, the king had been surprised when Jeroboam had stood boldly before him and had spoken in plain terms.

"Your people are groaning under the grinding taxes and the forced labor policy instituted by your father, Solomon," he said. "Lighten our burdens, and we will serve you faithfully and well."

Rehoboam replied, "Give me three days to think the matter over. Come back then, and I will announce my decision."

Rehoboam had only one day left to decide on his reply to the people, so he first consulted with the older members of the court who had been close to his father. Their counsel was not to his liking: "If

"Rehoboam and His Counsellors" by J. A. Adams and J. G. Chapman. *The Illuminated Bible* (1846). Ignoring the elders, Rehoboam took the advice of his peers and added new burdens upon the people, who rebelled.   Harper & Brothers

you listen to the pleas of your people and speak kindly to them now, they will serve you as long as you live."

Rehoboam turned from the older men, who understood only too well the deep undercurrent of discontent that was rising among the subject people, and asked a group of his young companions what he should do. He received the foolish answer for which he was looking. His decision was made.

As he stood before the people at Shechem, Rehoboam had a golden opportunity to win them back, but he missed it completely. He looked at their tired, strained, anxious faces and then spoke sharply.

"So you think my father made your burden heavy!" he began, in a voice tinged with sarcasm. "Well, I tell you here and now that they will seem like a bundle of straw compared to the ones I plan to impose on you!"

At first the stunned people stared at one another in amazed disbelief when they heard their king's cruel words. Then the angry, maddened crowd shouted:

"What can we hope for, and what redress can we expect, from the throne of David? Return to your homes, O Israel! As for you, Rehoboam, take a long, new look at the throne of David!"

Their cry was a clear and open declaration of rebellion. There was nothing left for Rehoboam to do but to escape to Jerusalem as fast as his chariot horses could gallop. As soon as he reached the palace, he hastily recruited a powerful army of 180,000 men, in the hope that he could defeat Jeroboam and the ten rebellious tribes to win back his kingdom. This hope was shattered, however, and the proposed civil war was nipped in the bud, when a prophet named Shemaiah came to him with a message from God:

"Thus says the Lord, 'You shall not go out to fight with brothers. Let your soldiers return to their homes. The breakup of your kingdom is the result of My plan and My action.' "

When Rehoboam heard these words, he knew that it was useless to continue preparing for the struggle. He released his men, who returned to their homes in Judah, and he went back to his palace in Jerusalem. What a staggering blow for Rehoboam! Only Judah and the priestly Levites had remained loyal to him. Solomon had "sown the wind," and his son

The People of Israel finally rebelled after a long period of oppression, and the country was divided into the Kingdom of Israel in the North and the Kingdom of Judah in the South.

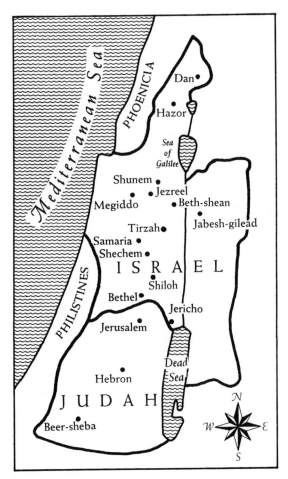

122

Rehoboam was "reaping the whirlwind."

God's warning to Solomon had reached its fruition. There were now two kingdoms in tiny Israel. The Kingdom of Judah, as it was to be known henceforth, was ruled from Jerusalem by Rehoboam and would continue to be ruled by descendants of David. The Kingdom of Israel was ruled from Shechem by Jeroboam.

Almost immediately after being made king of Israel, Jeroboam did something evil in the Lord's sight. He led his people on their first step toward becoming a nation of idolaters. In order to keep his people away from Jerusalem for their religious feasts and sacrifices, he set up two religious centers in his own territory. He did this because he was afraid that, after going to Jerusalem and making friends with the people there, some of his followers might decide to switch their allegiance to Judah. He, therefore, made two golden calves and placed one of them in Bethel. He put the other calf in Dan, far to the north. Because the Levites had remained loyal to Rehoboam and the Temple, Jeroboam chose some makeshift priests and sent them to the two cities. When everything was ready at both altars, he called his people together and said:

"It is too much trouble for you to go to Jerusalem every time you want to make sacrifices. Look at the gods I have made for you! Now you can worship near your own homes. I have this day issued a proclamation forbidding you to go to Jerusalem."

Thus the chasm between the two parts of the divided kingdom became wider and wider. Following the example of their leader, the people of Israel plunged into idol worship with wild abandon.

Meanwhile, back in Jerusalem and matching Jeroboam step for step, Rehoboam led his own people into idolatry. He established altars to false gods on all the hills of Judah and encouraged his people to set up altars to their own homes. Time after time, God warned the two kings to stop their evil ways, but neither of them paid any attention to Him. Finally, God lost His patience with Rehoboam and Jeroboam. He decided to punish both kings.

In the fifth year of Rehoboam's reign, God turned Judah over to Pharaoh of Egypt for chastisement. Shishak's vast army plundered and looted the kingdom of Judah, paying particular attention to Jerusalem. There they took away all the golden treasures of the Lord's Temple, the golden shields, and all the jewels and golden objects in the palace. The invasion of Judah was highly successful, and the kingdom lost all its riches in the twinkling of an eye. Gone was the glitter of gold. Brass became its substitute.

While an exile in Egypt, Jeroboam had married Ano, sister of Pharaoh's wife. This marriage alliance spared him and his people from the ravages of the Egyptian army. His loss, however, was to be far greater than the loss of Judah's wealth. Jeroboam was to lose his son. Back in Egypt, he and Ano had become the proud parents of a handsome son whom they had named Abijah. As he grew older, he became not only the idol of his father's heart but also a favorite of the court. As a final warning to Jeroboam, God decided to remove Abijah, a lad He loved, from the wicked household of Jeroboam.

Abijah lay desperately ill and Jeroboam, in his anxiety, told his wife to disguise herself as an ordinary woman and go to Shiloh, about twenty miles away, and consult with Ahijah, a prophet of God, regarding the fate of their son. The queen did as directed and set out on her journey.

Blind and aged, Ahijah sat in his room. His head was bowed in prayer as he meditated on the things of the Lord. Quietly the voice of God came to Ahijah and told him that the Queen of Israel, disguised as a commoner, was approaching his house. A knock sounded on Ahijah's door, and he called out:

"Come in, Queen Ano, wife of Jeroboam. Why did you pretend to be another woman? Sit down, because I have some bad news for you."

The queen remained silent as she sat down, with a heavy heart. There was no doubt in her mind as to what the dreaded message would be.

Ahijah spoke bluntly to his visitor:

"Tell Jeroboam that he has angered God by his fickleness and disobedience. God will abandon Israel because of your husband, who has sinned and has made Israel sin. Arise, now, and return to your home. When you arrive, however, your son Abijah will be dead. All Israel will mourn him, and he will be buried with the honors befitting the son of a king."

Despite God's warning to the two kings, and the punishment He meted out to them, both continued their idolatrous ways until the end of their reigns.

Rehoboam, after ruling Judah for seventeen years, died and was buried in the city of David.

Jeroboam ruled over the people of Israel for twenty-two years before he died and slept with his fathers.

Based on the story in the Bible:
1 Kings 12:1-33, 14:1-31

Historical Reliefs and Inscriptions of King Shishak in the temple at Karnak, Egypt, show the king commemorating his victory over Rehoboam, King of Judah.   © Matson Photo

2
SUCCESSORS TO THE TWO THRONES

THE KINGDOM OF JUDAH lasted almost four hundred years and, during this long period, was ruled by nineteen kings and one queen. Some of them were good, some were apathetic, and some were wicked. There was only one dynasty in the Southern Kingdom—the Davidic. The Kingdom of Israel had a shorter life of about two hundred and sixty years. Nineteen kings, all of whom were bad, reigned during this period. By the time of its collapse, nine dynasties had served the Northern Kingdom.

Abijam was ready for action. In response to his call, 400,000 of Judah's finest men rallied behind him as he prepared to fight the Kingdom of Israel. God did not intervene this time as He had done when Abijam's father, Rehoboam, had planned a similar campaign. During the eighteenth year of Jeroboam's reign, Abijam declared war on him.

The fifteen-mile march from Jerusalem to the border dividing the two kingdoms was made in rapid time. Abijam and his army crossed the frontier and had penetrated Jeroboam's territory for about a mile before they arrived at the town of Zemaraim. Seeing Jeroboam and his mighty army in battle formation not far from the town, Abijam climbed a nearby hill and began to harangue the opposing army with withering words:

"Listen to me, O Jeroboam and all Israel! Have you forgotten so soon that the Lord God promised all Israel to the descendants of Abraham? The people of Judah have the Temple, the Golden Ark, and the priestly Levites. We serve the Lord! Who do you have as priests and what do you worship? Your priests are picked up from the street. You consecrate any man who makes a sacrifice to the golden calves that you worship.

"God is at the head of our army, and His priests are standing by with their trumpets, ready to sound the call to battle. O men of Israel, do not fight against the Lord, the God of your fathers! You cannot win!"

Abijam's oratory fell on deaf ears. Even as he spoke, Jeroboam maneuvered part of his vast army of 800,000 men behind the troops of Abijam. When the priests signalled the start of the battle, Jeroboam was ready to spring the trap. But God *was* with Judah that day, because 500,000 of Israel's best soldiers died on the field of battle and Jeroboam, with the remainder of his shattered army, fled back to Shechem. Abijam hurried in hot pursuit of the panic-stricken Israelites and took city after city from Jeroboam. This was the first and almost successful attempt to conquer the Northern Kingdom.

Jeroboam never recovered from his crushing defeat and the loss of more than half of his army. Four years later he died, and his son Nadab ruled in his stead.

After his great victory at the Battle of Zemaraim, Abijam returned to Jerusalem in triumph. The memory of the part God had played in that victory soon faded from his mind. Abijam followed in the footsteps of his wicked father by permitting and encouraging his people to worship strange

The Temple Area of Jerusalem, capital of old Judah and modern Israel, is seen at upper left. The Hill of Ophel slopes up to the southeast corner of the city to the Temple area. Old city walls appear on the hillside. © Matson Photo

gods. After a short reign of only three years Abijam died, and his son Asa became king of Judah.

Good King Asa! His first official act was to launch a great religious reformation in the land of Judah. He and his men roamed the hills and high places, pulling down altars and destroying false gods. Finally, all the public places were eliminated. Then he issued a proclamation:

"Idolatry is strictly prohibited throughout the kingdom. Anyone found contin-uing this practice in private will be severely punished."

Asa played no favorites as he enforced his decree. Even the queen mother was banished from the court when it was discovered that she had made a grotesque caricature of the goddess Asherah. How unlikely it was that such a good man should have emerged from such an evil household!

During the first ten years of Asa's reign no wars were waged against his kingdom.

Asa took full advantage of these peaceful times by shoring up his defenses. He recruited an army of 580,000 valiant men. Three hundred thousand of his soldiers were skilled in the use of spears and wore bucklers to protect themselves. The other 280,000, who carried shields for their protection, were experts with the bow and arrow.

Asa's next step during these years of peace was to build fortified cities all over Judah. With these completed and with his vast army standing by, Asa felt that he was prepared for any eventuality. Little did he know that the first test of Judah's military prowess was fast approaching.

The era of peace for Judah was over. King Zerah of Ethiopia, with a million men and three hundred chariots, invaded the land and advanced as far as the fortified city of Mareshah. King Asa and his army met the invaders in the Valley of Zephathah, located near Mareshah. When the battle lines were drawn, and Asa saw that he was outnumbered almost two to one, he lifted up his voice in prayer:

"O Lord our God, You alone can protect the weak from the mighty. Have mercy on Your servants this day, O Lord God, and help us as we prepare to fight for Your people. Our lives are now in Your hands, as we acknowledge our complete dependence upon You."

God showed his approval of Asa's reign by striking terror into the hearts and minds of the Ethiopians. Their king paid dearly for his vain attempt to conquer Judah. The Lord and His army, led by Asa, soon had Zerah and his desperate, disorganized troops fleeing toward their homeland. By the time Asa and his pursuing forces reached Gerar, every Ethiopian agressor had been killed.

With the enemy completely annihilated, city after city in Ethiopia was raided and plundered by the soldiers of Judah. Asa and his men returned to Jerusalem with vast stores of gold, silver, and precious jewels, as well as uncounted thousands of sheep and camels. The treasure houses, emptied by the disastrous visit from the Pharaoh of Egypt during Rehoboam's reign, were beginning to be refilled.

During the third year of Asa's reign, King Nadab of Israel and his army began a siege of the Philistine city, Gibbethon. While the siege was under way, Baasha plotted against Nadab, staged a successful coup d'état, and assassinated him. After proclaiming himself the third king of Israel, Baasha of the house of Issachar consolidated his hold on the throne by killing all the house of Jeroboam. Thus the first dynasty of Israel was ended, and the prophetic words of Ahijah to Jeroboam I were fulfilled.

Baasha proved true to his name, which literally means "wicked." He sinned and caused his people to sin. During his reign Baasha waged unrelenting warfare against Asa and gradually encroached on the territory of Judah. When Baasha reached Ramah and captured it, he began to fortify this city lying two miles inside Judah's borders.

Asa was in trouble. If Baasha were successful in fortifying Ramah, he could control all traffic to and from Jerusalem. Asa needed a friend—and he needed him *now!* Suddenly he remembered his father's old friend, King Ben-hadad of Syria. Perhaps he could bribe Ben-hadad to break his treaty with Baasha and make a friendship with Judah. Quickly the treasure houses were emptied of their gold and silver. Swift messengers sped with the treasure to Damascus, capital of Syria.

Ben-hadad's greed outweighed his scruples as he eyed the gold and silver that King Asa offered to him in exchange for his help in fighting Baasha and the people of Israel. Within a short time the captains

127

of Syrian armies were marching against cities in northern Israel.

Baasha was confronted with the one thing he wished to avoid: a two-front war. When he found out about Syria's treachery, he abandoned his plans to fortify Ramah and returned to Tirzah, now the capital city of Israel, to map the strategy of battle against his two-faced ally.

In the twenty-sixth year of the reign of Asa, Baasha died and was buried in Tirzah. Elah, his son, became the fourth king of Israel. His short reign of two years was marked by drunkenness and debauchery. One day Zimri, his ambitious military commander, conspired against the king and killed him as he lay in a drunken stupor. Although Zimri ruled Israel for only seven days, he found time to destroy

completely the house of Baasha. Jehu's prophecy to Baasha was fulfilled as Israel's second dynasty, which began with murder and closed with murder, reached its tragic end.

When the people learned that Zimri had murdered their king, they rose up against him and crowned Omri king of all Israel. He and his army then proceeded to Tirzah and besieged the capital city. When the city fell, panic-stricken Zimri raced to the palace, set fire to it, and died in its ashes.

For four years after the death of Zimri, Israel itself became a divided kingdom. Half the people followed the usurper, Tibni the son of Ginath, and made him their king; the other half followed the legal sovereign, King Omri. The civil war ended with the death of Tibni and his

"Death of Zimri" by J. A. Adams and J. G. Chapman. *The Illuminated Bible* (1846). After murdering Elah, Zimri became king of Israel, but he ruled only seven days. He perished at Tirzah after Omri conquered the city.

Harper & Brothers

Samaria was built by Omri and became capital of the Northern Kingdom of Israel. Excavations during the 20th century revealed remains of the city, including fortifications and the palace of Omri, shown above.

© Matson Photo

brother, and Omri became king of a united Israel.

Little is recorded of the twelve-year reign of Omri except that he, like his predecessors, walked in the footsteps of Jeroboam and that he built the fortified city of Samaria. Because of its strategic location, Omri made Samaria the new capital city of Israel.

In the thirty-eighth year of Asa's reign Omri, who did worse than any of the kings who had preceded him, died and was buried in Samaria. His son Ahab became his successor.

After a reign of forty-one years Asa, the third king of Judah, died. All Judah mourned for him and paid high tribute to him. He was buried in a sepulchre that he himself had made, in the city of David. Jehoshaphat, his son, mounted the throne and ruled in his place.

Based on the story in the Bible:
1 Kings 15:1 — 16:28;
2 Chronicles 13:1 — 16:14

129

PLACES

in the Story of the Divided Kingdom

SHECHEM

This ancient city is located about 30 miles due north of Jerusalem. It was at Shechem that Rehoboam announced the unwise decision that tore his kingdom apart. Shechem was also the capital city of the Northern Kingdom during part of Jeroboam's reign.

BETHEL

At the southern tip of Israel, about 12 miles north of Jerusalem, is Bethel, another ancient city, which Jeroboam chose as one of his two shrine cities.

DAN

In the extreme northern part of Israel, at the foot of Mount Hermon, lies Dan. This became Israel's other shrine city when Jeroboam placed a golden calf there.

SHILOH

A few miles east of the highway connecting Bethel and Shechem, and almost equidistant from the two cities, stands the former religious center of the Israelites, Shiloh. It was to Shiloh that Jeroboam sent his wife to consult with Ahijah, the prophet.

MARESHAH

Located some 22 miles southwest of Jerusalem lies the fortified city of Mareshah, and near by is its valley, Zephathah. King Zerah of Ethiopia invaded Judah and advanced as far as Mareshah before being confronted and defeated by the defending king, Asa.

RAMAH

About 5 miles north of Jerusalem and 2 miles south of Israel's border is the hill town of Ramah. Baasha's capture of this town and his plan to fortify it caused Asa to look for help from a foreign nation.

DAMASCUS

It was to this capital city of Syria that King Asa of Judah sent gold and silver as a bribe to King Ben-hadad in a successful effort to get the Syrian king to break his alliance with Israel and attack her northern cities.

SAMARIA

Fortress capital of Judah, Samaria was built by Omri, sixth king of Judah. This strategic city is about 6 miles northwest of Shechem and approximately 6 miles due west of Tirzah, two former capitals of the Northern Kingdom.

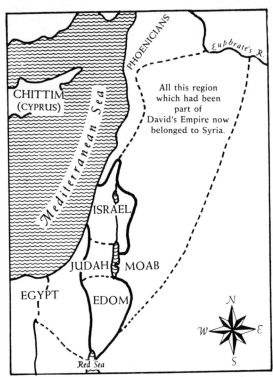

The Divided Kingdom. Wars between Judah and Israel allowed stronger foreign nations to encroach upon their territory.

QUESTIONS

on the Story of the Divided Kingdom

1

1 What request did Jeroboam, as spokesman for the ten Northern Tribes, make of King Rehoboam?

2 How did Rehoboam reply? What was the result of his answer?

3 What did God's messenger, the prophet Shemaiah, tell Rehoboam as the king prepared to make war on the Northern Kingdom?

4 Why did Jeroboam decide to set up two religious centers in his own territory? Where were these centers located?

5 What did Rehoboam do that kindled God's anger against him?

6 How did God punish Rehoboam and the Kingdom of Judah for their sins?

7 Whom did Jeroboam marry while he was an exile in Egypt? Give their son's name.

8 How did God punish Jeroboam for his wicked ways?

9 What did the aged blind prophet Ahijah tell Queen Ano when she went to consult with him about the outcome of her son's illness?

10 How long did Jeroboam, Israel's first king, rule over his people? How many years did Rehoboam, Judah's first king, reign?

2

11 How many years did the Kingdom of Judah stand? Tell the number of rulers and dynasties the kingdom had.

12 How long did the Kingdom of Israel last? How many rulers and dynasties did it have?

13 Who succeeded Rehoboam as king of Judah? What was one of the first things that he did? What resulted from this action?

14 Name Jeroboam's successor on the throne of Israel. How did Israel's first dynasty come to an end?

15 What did the third king of Judah do, upon his accession to the throne, to earn for himself the name, "Good King Asa"?

16 Name the foreign nation that invaded Judah at this time. What was the result of this invasion?

17 Who succeeded Baasha, to become Israel's fourth king? How was Israel's second dynasty brought to its tragic end?

18 How long did Zimri rule? Tell the circumstances of his death and what happened as its aftermath.

19 What was Omri's chief accomplishment as king of Israel? Who became Israel's seventh king?

20 How long did Asa reign over Judah? Where was he buried? Who was crowned as the fourth king of Judah?

*Answers are found
on the following pages.*

ANSWERS

on the Story of the Divided Kingdom

1

1 Jeroboam asked Rehoboam to reduce taxes and abolish the forced labor policy.

2 After three days' consultation with his advisers, Rehoboam made it clear to the people of Israel that, instead of becoming better, conditions would be worse than ever. The Northern Tribes rebelled and the nation became a Divided Kingdom.

3 Shemaiah warned Rehoboam not to wage war on the people of Israel because the break-up of the kingdom was the result of the Lord's plan and action.

4 Jeroboam set up religious centers in Israel to keep his people from going to the Temple in Jerusalem to worship. He feared that continued close contact with the people there might cause some of his people to defect. The centers were located in Bethel and Dan.

5 Rehoboam led the people of Judah into idolatry. He set up altars and idols on all the hills and high places throughout the land.

6 Pharaoh Shishak of Egypt was permitted to loot and plunder Jerusalem and all Judah during the fifth year of Rehoboam's reign.

7 Jeroboam married Ano, sister of Pharaoh's wife. Their son was named Abijah.

8 God decided to remove Abijah, Jeroboam's adored son, from the wicked environment of his father's household.

9 Ahijah told Queen Ano that God was displeased with her husband because of fickleness and disobedience and that He would abandon all Israel because of the king's sin. He also told her that when she reached home, her son would be dead.

10 King Jeroboam ruled Israel twenty-two years, five years longer than the reign of his contemporary, King Rehoboam of Judah, whose wicked rule lasted for seventeen years.

2

11 The Kingdom of Judah stood for almost four hundred years. Nineteen kings and one queen ruled during this long period. There was only one dynasty, that of David's line.

12 The Kingdom of Israel lasted for almost two hundred and sixty years. This kingdom had nineteen kings, all of them bad, and nine dynasties.

13 Abijam (Abijah) succeeded his father on the throne of Judah. He declared war on Jeroboam and the Northern Kingdom. Jeroboam's army was routed, 500,000 of his best soldiers were killed, and Abijam established a beachhead in Israel by capturing many of her cities.

14 Nadab succeeded his father on the throne of Israel. While he and his army laid siege to the Philistine town of Gibbethon, Baasha plotted against King Nadab and assassinated him. He then killed all the household of Jeroboam.

15 "Good King Asa" earned that title by starting a religious reformation throughout Judah. Altars were pulled down, idols were destroyed, and anyone caught practicing idolatry in secret was severely punished.

16 King Zerah of Ethiopia invaded Judah. King Asa met the invaders at the fortified city of Mareshah and, with God's help, advanced against the enemy and destroyed the 1,000,000-man army—to the very last

man. Vast quantities of gold and silver, as well as uncounted thousands of sheep and camels, were taken back to Jerusalem.

17 Baasha's son Elah became the fourth king of Israel. After a short reign of two years Elah was killed, as he lay in a drunken stupor, by Zimri, one of his ambitious military leaders.

18 Zimri's reign lasted only seven days, but during this brief period he eliminated all the house of Baasha. After his capital fell to Omri, Zimri ran to the palace, set fire to it, and died in its ashes. Omri had been crowned on the battlefield as Israel's sixth king but Tibni, a usurper, conspired against him and won the loyalty of one-half of Israel. On Tibni's death, after four years, Omri ruled over a united Israel.

19 Omri built the beautiful, strategic, fortified city of Samaria and made it the capital of Israel. Ahab, Omri's son, was crowned as the seventh king of Israel.

20 Asa ruled over Judah for forty-one years. He was buried in the City of David. Then his son Jehoshaphat, the fourth king of Judah, sat upon the throne.

FURTHER FACTS AND OUTLINE
for the Story of the Divided Kingdom

FIRST KINGS (continued)

AUTHORSHIP AND DATE
See *Further Facts and Outline for the Story of Solomon.*

DESTINATION
The people of Israel and posterity.

PURPOSE AND THEME
See *Further Facts and Outline for the Story of Solomon.*

OUTLINE
Hostility and the Divided Kingdom: From Rehoboam and Jeroboam* through the reign of Omri (12:1-16:28)
*In a note on page 415 *The Amplified Bible* gives Ano as the name of Jeroboam's wife, based on an insertion in the Greek Septuagint text (285 B.C.).

The Ten Tribes Revolt, the Kingdom Divided North and South, Rehoboam Reigns in the South, Jeroboam in the North (chapters 12-14)

Abijah and Asa Reign over Judah (15:1-24)

Nadab Reigns over Israel (15:25-32)

Baasha Reigns over Israel (15:33-16:7)

Elah Reigns over Israel (16:8-14)

Zimri Reigns over Israel (16:15-22)

Omri Reigns over Israel, Omri Establishes Capital at Samaria (16:23-28)

The Thin Line between Success and Failure

by

Bobby Richardson

The All-Star second baseman of the New York Yankees received, before his career as a big league baseball player began, a set of well thought out rules which spelled the difference between success or failure for him in baseball, the game that is won or lost by inches. Many centuries earlier another young man, Rehoboam, needed the guidance of a good set of rules as he started his career. He took the wrong kind of advice, which marked him for failure and divided his kingdom, permanently. Bobby Richardson talks about the thin line separating success and failure in an article for *Guideposts Magazine* (© 1965 by Guideposts Associates, Inc., Carmel, N.Y.).

PLAY BY THE RULES

MINE has been an unusual baseball career of ups-and-downs ... from defeat to victory, from periods when I could do nothing wrong to periods when I could do nothing right. This covers 20 years of baseball—beginning at age ten when I was a catcher for a Salvation Army team in Sumter, South Carolina, and up to my present career with the New York Yankees.

I have discovered that the difference between winning and losing can be a matter of inches. Perhaps you have heard the expression "baseball is a game of inches?"

Here is an illustration of what I mean:

During a game with Baltimore several years ago we were behind by one run. It was the last inning; I was at bat with one man on base. I hit one high and deep into the left field stands. The crowd roared, thinking we had won.

"Foul!" cried the umpire. My hit had just missed being a home run. On the next pitch, I flied out. So we lost—by inches.

My ups-and-downs in baseball have taught me how important it is to have a balanced mental approach to the game. For me, this means having a solid religious philosophy. Let me tell you of three experiences in which I was given a spiritual lift at important times.

When I was 14, I was playing in the American Legion League and our team from Sumter was competing with a team from Richmond for the Sectional championship. The winner was to go on to the National Tournament.

There were some 5,000 people in the stands ... mothers, fathers, brothers, sisters ... and the excitement was intense. Before the game our coach, H. N. Hutchinson, called us together for a pep talk. He read us the League's rules of conduct.

Now, boys are always having regulations read to them, and often their inclination is to only half listen. Yet these rules were well thought out:

- Keep faith with your teammates.
- Keep a stout heart in defeat.
- Keep your pride under in victory.

• Keep a sound soul, a clean mind and a healthy body.

On this particular day, one of these rules was to become especially pertinent to me. For we lost the game by one run. What was worse, the winning run scored when the umpire ruled that I did not touch second base while pivoting on a double play. I was sick at heart. And the next day when I read the newspaper, I felt even worse.

"Bobby Richardson was the goat of the game," said the story.

At 14, it is pretty devastating to be a "goat" before 5,000 people—and to over 100,000 newspaper readers. My parents tried to have me take a philosophic point of view. I would have none of this.

Yet after brooding for a while, I knew that my dream was still to be a Major League player. *Keep a stout heart in defeat . . . keep a sound soul, a clean mind . . .* I began growing up the hard way.

Today, I find that I still repeat these rules subconsciously before each Yankee game.

A second turning point came after I signed a contract with the Yankees. Just out of high school, I was assigned to play with their farm club at Norfolk, Virginia, in a "B" league. Nervous, in competition with older players, I did miserably . . . booted easy grounders . . . struck out time after time.

After a month of this, the Yankee organization reassigned me to a team in a slower league. And so I faced a decision. Did I belong in baseball?

Several years previous to this, I had given myself to the Lord. At the time I considered going into the ministry. But then, it was pointed out to me that perhaps the Lord wanted me to serve Him in baseball. The offer from the New York Yankees seemed to be my answer.

But now I was in doubt again. I wrestled with the problem during lonely nights in hotel rooms and while taking long walks in unfamiliar cities. My playing continued poor.

Then came a letter from my first coach in junior high school, Conley Alexander. It was an encouraging letter. "Just remember, Bobby, that Jesus gave us the only real answer to discouragement when He said *Seek ye first the kingdom of God, and His righteousness and all these things shall be added unto you.*" (Matthew 6:33)

This was great advice just when I needed it. *Seek ye first the kingdom.* As long as I made God first in my life, kept in touch with Him through prayer, and didn't violate His laws, then somehow my questions would be answered.

Thus, freed from confusion, I gave myself completely to baseball. And at once there was an improvement. Within a few years I made it to the Big Leagues.

And, of course, my wife Betsy is wonderful at helping me ride out depressing periods. When I get home after a game in which I'd missed a homer by inches, we talk for a while, drink some coffee, then meet this whole matter of defeat through the devotions which Betsy and I have whenever we can before bed.

In the prayer we tell God how grateful we are for our love, for our healthy children, and for all the friends and experiences that have come through baseball.

Finally, I repeat the words of a verse that has come to mean a great deal to us. It was sent to us by Betsy's aunt, Jenny Alderman, who is a missionary to Formosa. Somehow, this verse always helps us to see difficulties in proper perspective and to realize again that our goal is always to *seek ye first the kingdom:*

He giveth more grace
  when the burdens grow greater;
He sendeth more strength
  when the labors increase.
To added affliction He addeth His mercies;
  To multiplied trials, His multiplied peace.
When we have exhausted
  our store of endurance;
When our strength has failed
  ere the day is half done;
When we reach the end
  of our hoarded resources;
Our Father's full giving has only begun.
  His love has no limit,
His power no boundary known unto men,
  For out of His infinite riches in Jesus
He giveth and giveth and giveth again.

Elijah

THE SUDDEN INTRODUCTION OF ELIJAH into the Bible story is in itself suggestive of the startling and dramatic way in which he broke in on the national life of the kingdom of Israel. He came like a bolt from the blue; or, more accurately, he flamed like a lightning flash upon the prevailing darkness. His coming was the initiation of a new method in the Divine government, that of prophetic authority.

There had been prophets before, but with the appearance of Elijah the office was elevated to one of supreme national importance. From that point onward the prophet was superior to the king. Certain kings arose whose hearts were set upon reform, but their work was directed by the prophets of God, through whom the Divine will was made known.

The very first words of Elijah declared his authority. He affirmed that the Lord God of Israel lived; and he announced the fact that, in the message he was about to deliver, he spoke as the messenger of the enthroned Lord. God's action in thus sending Elijah brought him immediately to the attention of king and people alike.

All earthly authority and protection were swept aside as unnecessary. In simplest ways God protected His messenger and provided for him. Thus does God break in upon human affairs and assert Himself, from time to time, by some messenger.

Men may refuse the message and persecute the messenger, but the word he speaks is the word of the Lord. This is the word by which men live or die, according to their response to it.—G. Campbell Morgan, *Searchlights from the Word*

1
ELIJAH, AHAB, AND JEZEBEL

FROM EAST OF THE JORDAN, out of the land of Gilead, there suddenly strode on to the world's stage the long-haired, bushy-browed, shaggy-cloaked Elijah the Tishbite to play his role in the history of Israel. What a short introduction to one of the truly great men of the Bible! Centuries later, he and Moses were to meet with Jesus atop the Mount of Transfiguration.

Ahab has maintained his reputation through the centuries as one of Israel's most wicked kings; his wife Jezebel, whose name even today is used to desig- nate an evil woman, was far more infa- mous. She was a devoted worshiper of her father's deity, Baal, the Phoenician rain- god who (his followers believed) con- trolled the weather. Jezebel's burning desire was soon realized. She easily persuaded Ahab, already steeped in sin

"Elijah by the Brook Cherith" by Rembrandt. Kupferstich- kabinett, Berlin. Elijah is one of the most revered and re- spected men of the Bible. He called the Israelites back to God. Ravens fed him at Brook Cherith.   Kupferstichkabinett

and idolatry, to establish the worship of Baal as the national religion of Israel.

Elijah loved the people of Israel, and he was grieved when he learned what Ahab had done. The rugged old prophet's heart was stirred to righteous indignation as he watched the rapidly growing strength of Baal-worship throughout the land. The king had actually built a temple for Baal in the capital city. Elijah knew that the time had come for him to go to Samaria.

Elijah stood before Ahab and spoke sternly: "Just as surely as God is in His heaven, you and your people will be punished for your wicked ways. There shall be neither dew nor rain upon your land until such time as the Lord God of Israel causes the drought and famine to end."

King Ahab and Queen Jezebel were furious when they heard this prophecy. How dare this stranger to disparage and show contempt for their own great rain-god, Baal! He would soon find out how powerful their god was! But the drought *did* come, and Elijah found that his life was in danger.

One night the Lord came to him and said: "Go back across the Jordan to the brook Cherith. I have commanded the ravens to feed you, and there will be plenty of water for you to drink."

Elijah found himself in distinguished company as, once again, God sent one of His servants to a lonely spot for prayer and meditation. The ravens came each morning and each night, bringing him meat and bread. Everything went smoothly for Elijah until, finally, the drought became so severe that the brook dried up. He wondered what he should do. The Lord answered his unspoken question.

"Arise now and go to Zarephath, in Sidon," He said. "I have put it into the heart of a widow there to feed you and give you shelter."

Elijah arose and began his long journey to the north, a fugitive from his beloved Israel.

Based on the story in the Bible:
1 Kings 17:1-10

2

ELIJAH AND THE WIDOW IN SIDON

ELIJAH TRUDGED SLOWLY northward along the shore of the Mediterranean. Soon now, he would be a refugee in the homeland of his archenemy, Jezebel. He paused momentarily as he approached the town of Zarephath and sat down on the sand for a short rest. The ebb and flow of the tide and the sound of the lapping waves cascading onto the beach soon lulled him to sleep.

Elijah awoke refreshed. The arduous trek up the east bank of the Jordan, the slow walk westward to the Mediterranean, and the signs of famine that were all around him soon faded from his memory. Near the gate of Zarephath Elijah noticed a woman, who later proved to be the

Sidon (Modern Saida). Sidon on the Mediterranean Sea was an important Phoenician city during Elijah's time. Although Queen Jezebel's father was King of Sidon, Elijah found refuge here from the wrath of Ahab. © Matson Photo

"*Elijah and the Widow's Son*" by V. De Brožick. *Biblia Sacra.* While in Sidon, Elijah was befriended by a widow. When her son died, Elijah prayed to God to restore the boy to life, and his prayer was answered.

Lemercier & Co., Paris

142

widow the Lord had mentioned, picking up sticks. He approached her and said politely, "Please bring me some water. I have traveled all the way from the land of Israel and I am thirsty."

As the woman turned toward the town to get the water, Elijah added: "Bring me a piece of bread, please, for I am hungry, too."

The woman paused and looked intently at this stranger from Israel. Then she replied: "The Lord your God knows that I have only a handful of meal in my barrel and just a little oil in my bottle. As you can see, I am gathering some sticks so that I can prepare a final meal for my son and myself. Then we shall starve to death."

The prophet answered her gently: "Have no fear about using your meal and oil. Go and prepare some bread for me; and after that, make some for you and your son. The Lord God of Israel has told me that, no matter how much you use, there will always be meal in your barrel and oil in your bottle."

The widow did as Elijah requested, and everything happened just as he had said it would. After he had eaten, Elijah went home with the widow and lived there for about three years.

One day the widow's son became ill and died. The distraught mother came to Elijah and told him what had happened. Then she cried out: "O man of God, what have I done to deserve this great affliction? Did you come here only to bring back to me memories of my past sins, and to cause my son to die?"

Elijah's heart was filled with compassion for the grief-stricken woman. He spoke to her kindly: "Give me your son."

As he carried the body of the young boy to the upper room, Elijah, too, was puzzled by the turn of events. He placed the lad upon the bed and began a passionate and somewhat reproachful prayer:

"O Lord my God, have You brought such great sorrow even upon the woman in whose house I am staying, by letting her son die? Didn't You lead me to this home and to this widow?"

Elijah then got upon the bed, leaned over the boy, and uttered this prayer three times: "O Lord, my God, I beseech you to let this child come back to life."

God heard the voice of His prophet, and the child was revived. The cold, still body became warm, his eyes opened, and he gazed into the friendly face of the prophet who was bending over him. Elijah tenderly lifted the lad with his strong arms, carried him downstairs, and placed him in the arms of his mother. Then he said: "Look! Your son is alive!"

Tears of happiness streamed down the widow's face as she joyously exclaimed: "Truly you are a man of God, and His words are revealed by you!"

Based on the story in the Bible:
1 Kings 17:10-24

3

BAAL—OR THE LORD?

IN THE THIRD YEAR of Elijah's sojourn in the land of Sidon, the Lord came to him with news that the drought would soon be ended and that he should return to Israel for a meeting with Ahab. Elijah wasted no time in preparing for the return journey to his native land. Before leaving Sidon he said goodbye to the widow and her son—who was again a healthy, robust lad—and thanked her for the hospitality shown him.

Meanwhile, things were not going well at the palace in Samaria. The prolonged drought had spared neither the king nor his people. Ahab now faced a serious problem. There was no grass in the royal stables, and all his valuable chariot horses were in danger of starvation. Quick action had to be taken if the horses were to survive, so the king called in Obadiah, his chief steward, for consultation. Ahab told Obadiah what he planned to do.

"We will divide the land into two parts and will go to all the springs, brooks, and valleys in search for grass," he said. "Perhaps we shall find enough to keep the horses alive."

The land was divided, and Ahab went one way while Obadiah went the other way. Although Obadiah held a high position in the wicked court, he had remained faithful to the one true God of Israel. Even when Jezebel was killing the faithful priests, he had managed to hide one hundred of them in a cave and had fed them with bread and water. As he walked over the hard, burned land, he suddenly came face to face with Elijah. Overcome by surprise, Obadiah fell to his face.

"Are you really Elijah, the Lord's prophet?" he asked.

Elijah replied: "I am. Go tell your king that Elijah is here and wants to talk with him!"

Obadiah was dismayed when he heard these words, so he answered quickly: "What have I done to you that you should place me in such a dire predicament? Since your disappearance from Samaria three years ago, the king has staged a massive manhunt for you in all kingdoms and nations. If I go and tell him that you are here and, when he comes back with me, you have vanished again, he will surely kill me."

Elijah solemnly promised Obadiah that he would remain where he was until the king came. With that assurance, Obadiah hurried off to tell Ahab the news. The king was delighted. At long last he would soon have Elijah in his clutches! Ahab and Obadiah rushed to the place where Elijah was patiently waiting for them. Little did the king dream that this encounter would prove disastrous for him, for Jezebel his wife, and for Baal!

When Ahab came near to Elijah, he stormed out: "So, you trouble-maker! You have finally returned to Israel!"

Elijah replied, calmly but sternly, "It is not I who have troubled Israel. You and your father's house are the ones! You have forsaken God and followed Baal. Go now and tell your people to come to Mount Carmel. There they shall see who is more powerful, Baal or the Lord!"

"*The Prophets of Baal*" by J. James Tissot. *The Old Testament,* Illustrated. Elijah challenged the prophets to a contest to determine the true God. When Baal failed them, the prophets leaped upon their altar.   M. de Buffan & Co.

Word spread quickly throughout the famished land that Elijah had returned and that the king had ordered all Israel to assemble at Mount Carmel. The move was on! All the people of Israel, including the four hundred and fifty prophets of Baal and the four hundred prophets of Asherah, began streaming from town and city toward the appointed place. When everyone reached the foot of the mountain, the fearless prophet Elijah took charge. His booming voice rang out as he first rebuked the Israelites and then issued his startling challenge to the prophets of Baal.

"How long, O Israel, will you continue to dilly-dally?" he asked. "Make a firm decision and stick to it. If the Lord is God, follow Him; if Baal, follow him.

"And hear me, you prophets of Baal! The moment of truth has come. You stand four hundred and fifty strong on the side of Baal while I, only I, stand as a prophet of the Lord. In spite of this, I challenge you here and now to a contest to determine who is the real God of Israel."

Preparations for the contest were simple. Two altars were set up, one for Baal and one for the Lord. Wood was placed on each altar, and the sacrifice was laid upon the wood. The agreement was clear. Whichever "god" personally ignited the wood on the altar would be acclaimed as the one true God of Israel.

145

From dawn until noon the prophets of Baal danced, chanted, and prayed to their god. But nothing happened! There was no voice or other answer from Baal. As Elijah stood watching the frenzied efforts of the prophets, he called out in derision:

"Cry louder to your god, Baal! He *is* a god, isn't he? Maybe he is talking to someone just now, or perhaps he is thinking, or has gone off on a short trip. Possibly he is asleep and needs to awakened."

Elijah's merciless taunts served only to increase the tempo of the frenzied activity the prophets of Baal were engaged in: they cried louder, they danced faster and, in their frenzy, they even cut themselves with knives. Still no fire came, no voice of Baal was heard, nor was there any sign that he was listening. Late in the afternoon Baal's altar and sacrifice still stood on the side of the mountain, intact and untouched; so his prophets gave up their efforts.

The time had come for the prophet of the Lord to enter the competition. Elijah startled the people with his very first act. He dug a trench around the altar. Then asked for four barrels of water to be

"Elijah and the Prophets" by V. De Brožick. *Biblia Sacra.* After Elijah rebuilt the altar and offered a sacrifice, he prayed to God for a sign by fire. The altar burst into flames and consumed the offering.
Lemercier and Co., Paris

RUBENS: *The Ascension of Elijah*

The Ascension of Elijah

by PETER PAUL RUBENS (1577-1640) *Flemish School*

Private Collection

Behold, there appeared a chariot of fire, and horses of fire, and parted them both asunder; and Elijah went up by a whirlwind into heaven. 2 KINGS 2:11

THIS SMALL CANVAS is so filled with thunderous motion that it almost seems as though it would burst its frame. Intended as only a sketch for a larger painting, the grand sweep of its composition could comfortably fill a whole wall. The extraordinary freedom of Rubens' brushwork is at its freshest here, as is his spontaneous vigor. Both skill and conviction are needed to persuade us that horses and a chariot as solid as these could be skyward bound.

poured over the altar and the sacrifice—not once, but three times! Everything was soaking wet; even the trench was filled with water. Now Elijah was ready for the test. He approached the altar, knelt down, and then calmly prayed:

"O Lord, God of Abraham, Isaac, and Jacob! Let it be known this day that You *are* God in Israel, and that I *am* Your servant, who has done all that You commanded. Hear me, O Lord! Show these people that You are the omnipotent God of Israel and, once again, win back their hearts."

Just as Elijah completed his prayer a mass of flames engulfed the altar, burning up the sacrifice and the wood and the stones, as well. Even the water in the trench was dried up. When the people saw all these things, they fell to their knees and cried in unison: "The Lord, He is God! The Lord, He is God!"

The dauntless, grizzled old prophet Elijah, by this manifestation from the Lord, had brought an idolatrous nation to its knees. For however brief a time, the Israelites had again turned their faces to God. Elijah, however, could not rest on his laurels. There was still much to be done. The repentant people obeyed the prophet instantly when he issued the sharp command:

"Arrest all the false prophets of Baal! Don't let even one of them escape! When all have been captured, take them down to the River Kishon. There I shall execute them."

King Ahab watched the proceedings in dazed and helpless bewilderment. Questions ran through his mind. Should he interfere? Should he try to save the prophets of Baal? What would Jezebel say and do when he told her all that had happened? The present mood of his people convinced him that there was nothing he could do at Mount Carmel.

"Elijah from Mt. Carmel Sees a Cloud Afar Off" by J. James Tissot. *The Old Testament,* Illustrated. Heavy rains relieved the drought after the Israelites returned to their God and Elijah executed the prophets. M. de Buffan & Co.

After the executions Elijah climbed to the top of Mount Carmel to watch for signs of rain. His servant had looked toward the sea six times in a vain search for clouds. The seventh time, however, he saw a small cloud about the size of a man's hand, far in the distance. He rushed back and told his master. Elijah sprang to his feet, and he and his servant rushed down the mountain to warn the king and all the people gathered there to leave at once for their homes.

There was no time to lose, because the skies were already dark with heavy

"Elijah before the Chariot of Ahab" by J. James Tissot. *The Old Testament,* Illustrated. Elijah warned Ahab to go to Jezreel because a storm was brewing. He ran in front of Ahab's chariot all the way to the city. M. de Buffan & Co.

clouds. Loud claps of thunder reverberated through the valley, and brilliant streaks of lightning flashed across the sky. Elijah went to the king and said:

"Prepare at once to leave for your summer palace at Jezreel. The plains of Jezreel will soon be impassable."

As the wind increased in intensity and the first drops of the torrential rain began to fall, the people saw a strange sight. Elijah had tightened his girdle and cloak and was racing across the plain in front of Ahab's fast moving chariot! God gave Elijah the strength to maintain this pace throughout the seventeen-mile marathon run to the entrance of the city of Jezreel.

Rain! Blessed, life-giving rain. Rain in the cities, rain on the countryside. The wells, the streams, and the rivers were filling up. Happy, God-loving people everywhere lifted up their voices in praise and thanksgiving to the God of Abraham, Isaac, and Jacob.

Based on the story in the Bible:
1 Kings 18:1-46

148

4

ELIJAH ON MOUNT HOREB

DESPITE THE DROUGHT-BREAKING RAIN, there was no joy in the summer palace at Jezreel. Ahab had just told Jezebel about the fate of the prophets of Baal. At first, the cruel queen sat stunned and aghast at the incredible news. Then her eyes flashed with anger and her face became distorted with hatred and rage. She was determined that Elijah should be punished for his affront against her god.

Elijah sat outside the city, resting from his long run. He looked up and saw the queen's messenger coming toward him with a hastily written message: "About this time tomorrow, you shall pay with your life for the execution of my prophets. Nothing can save you!"

When he read the awesome words from the queen, Elijah lost his nerve and fled for his life. The intrepid old prophet had once again become a fearful fugitive from the wrath of Jezebel. Elijah and his servant raced through Judah toward Beersheba. When they reached this border town of Judah, he left his servant there and proceeded southward another day's journey. Toward evening, he saw a juniper tree and decided to rest beneath its branches.

Gone was the elation, faith, and confidence of just a few days ago at Mount Carmel! Hopelessness and despair had taken their place in his mind and heart. Elijah reached the depths of despondency when he cried out to the Lord: "Enough! Enough, O Lord! I give up. Let me die now for I am no better than my ancestors."

Tired, hungry, and grievously disappointed at the way things had turned out, Elijah lay down and tried to sleep. While he was dozing, an angel of the Lord touched him and said: "Elijah, arise and eat!"

Startled and wide-awake again, the forlorn prophet sprang to his feet. No one was there but, nearby, he saw some bread baking on hot stones, and a jug of water. After he ate and drank, Elijah lay down once more and was about to fall asleep when the angel touched him a second time and said: "Arise and eat some more, for you have a long journey ahead of you!"

Elijah arose and did as the angel commanded. When he finished eating and drinking, he felt a surge of God-given strength and power flow through his body. The mysterious food kept him alive for the forty days and forty nights that it took him to reach Mount Horeb (Sinai).

Elijah arrived, just in time, at the mountain where Moses received the Ten Commandments from God. As he approached the base of the Mount, a sudden and violent storm erupted, and he hurriedly sought the shelter of a cave. Gale winds tore at the mountain and sent huge rocks crashing down its sides. After the winds, there came an earthquake; and, after the earthquake, there came a fire. Then a deathlike silence prevailed, and Elijah heard a still small voice speaking: "What are you doing here, Elijah? There are many things that you should be doing for Me back in Israel."

The discouraged prophet answered: "I

"Elijah Dwelleth in a Cave" by J. James Tissot. *The Old Testament,* Illustrated. Elijah fled to Mount Horeb (Sinai) after he was threatened by Jezebel.   M. de Buffan & Co.

have been very zealous in my work for You, O Lord God of hosts, because the people have forsaken Your covenant. They have destroyed Your altars and killed Your prophets. I, even I, am now the only one left and they are trying to kill me."

The Lord reminded Elijah of the one hundred prophets whom Obadiah had hidden in a cave, and that He knew of seven thousand people in the Northern Kingdom who had not bowed down to Baal or kissed his image. Then, in order to quickly lift Elijah from the slough of self-pity into which he had fallen, the Lord gave him some definite job assignments.

"Return now to the world of action," He said. "First, go to Damascus and anoint Hazael king of Syria. Next, you must go to Abel-meholah in the territory of Manasseh and anoint Elisha as your successor."

Elijah found Elisha, the son of Shaphat, plowing in his father's field. Elijah walked up to him and threw his mantle across Elisha's shoulders. He realized that it was his destiny to take the place of the owner of the mantle.

Elisha stopped plowing and asked Elijah's permission to go home and tell his mother and father goodbye. When he reached home, two oxen were killed and a farewell feast was prepared. After the feast was over, Elisha returned to Elijah, followed him, and became his pupil.

Based on the story in the Bible:
1 Kings 19:1-21

5
JEZEBEL TAKES NABOTH'S VINEYARD

KING AHAB STOOD by an open window of his summer palace at Jezreel and gazed enviously at a beautiful vineyard near the palace grounds. The longer he looked at this plush, well-cultivated, and well-tended property, the more determined he became to possess it. He would make a deal for it.

Naboth, the owner of the vineyard, was startled and alarmed when he saw the king walking slowly toward him. When Ahab came near, Naboth bowed low and waited respectfully for the king to speak. Ahab minced no words as he demanded:

"Give me your vineyard so that I may make a beautiful garden on its land! It is near my palace and should certainly be included with the other land around it."

The king noticed the determined look on Naboth's face, so he became more conciliatory: "If you will let me have the vineyard, I will give you a larger and better one. Or, if you prefer, I will pay you cash for it." Naboth could not yield to the king's pressure, so his reply was polite yet firm: "I cannot let you have this property, my lord. This land is not wholly mine. It has belonged to my family since the Israelites first came to Canaan and it will be handed down to generations yet unborn."

Although Ahab knew that Naboth was within his rights to refuse to part with his ancestral property, the king acted like a spoiled child as he stalked angrily back to the palace and flung himself upon a luxurious couch. When Jezebel came into the room and saw her husband, she asked mockingly: "Why is the great king of Israel lying sullen and sulky upon his couch?"

Ahab explained that he had tried to purchase the vineyard from Naboth and that he had refused to sell it. The diabolical Jezebel became indignant when she heard the explanation. Her eyes blazed as she cried out:

"What can this lowly Israelite hope to gain by disregarding the wishes of his king? Arise and eat, drink, and be merry. And don't worry! I will get Naboth's vineyard for you."

Vicious Jezebel's satanic plans worked

"Jezebel Advises Ahab" by J. James Tissot. *The Old Testament,* Illustrated. Jezebel plotted the death of Naboth so that Ahab could have his vineyard.   M. de Buffan & Co.

151

to perfection. Using the king's name and his great seal, she instructed the elders and chief priests of Jezreel to arrest Naboth and charge him with committing blasphemy against the king of Israel and the Lord God of Israel. How strange that such an ardent Baal-worshiper should bring this accusation of blasphemy against God!

Poor Naboth! He was probably the first man in recorded history to stand trial on trumped-up charges for a crime he did not commit. Court was in session. In vain, Naboth pleaded that he was innocent. Disreputable and corrupt witnesses paraded before the jury and perjured themselves when they swore that they had heard Naboth commit blasphemy. The verdict was a foregone conclusion. Naboth and his sons were rushed out of the city and stoned to death.

When heartless Jezebel heard that Naboth and his sons were dead, she said to Ahab: "Go now and take possession of the vineyard. Naboth has paid with his life for his refusal to sell it to you."

God watched the sin of Ahab and Jezebel from the beginning to the end. Then He sent Elijah to Jezreel with a message for the guilty king. Ahab was in the vineyard admiring his newly acquired property when Elijah suddenly confronted him. The king shrank back in consternation when he saw the prophet.

"So my enemy has found me!" he exclaimed.

Elijah answered sternly: "Yes, I have found you—and it wasn't hard to do. You left a bloody trail from your throne to this very spot. How cheaply you have sold out to wickedness! Your wrongdoing has provoked the Lord to anger and He has told me to tell you that in the same place where the dogs licked up the blood of Naboth, so shall they lick your blood. As for Queen Jezebel, she shall die a terrible death and the dogs shall eat her."

These grim words and gruesome prophecy made a deep impression on Ahab. He tore his clothes, put on sackcloth, covered his head with ashes, fasted, and humbled himself before the Lord.

The Lord came to Elijah again and said, "See how Ahab has humbled himself before Me! Because he has shown genuine repentance for his iniquity, I will not bring down evil upon his house during his reign. Instead, I shall bring it down during the reign of his son."

"The sins of the father...."

Based on the story in the Bible: 1 Kings 21:1-29; 2 Kings 9:26

6
AHAB AND JEHOSHAPHAT

T WAS TRUE, almost incredibly true! Two *great* kings in succession reigned over the land of Judah. When Jehoshaphat succeeded his father Asa, he not only continued the good king's policies but he also enlarged, expanded, and improved them. During the twenty-five-year reign of the pious sovereign, Judah became prosperous and powerful.

Although the saintly king walked in the footsteps of his godly father, Jehoshaphat's occasional errors proved that he was also human. When he permitted his son Jehoram to marry Athaliah, the daughter of Ahab and Jezebel, Jehoshaphat made the greatest mistake of his life. This unholy alliance provided the crack through which Baal-worship eventually re-entered Judah, and it almost cost him his life.

One day, not long after his son's marriage, Jehoshaphat decided to pay a state visit to the king of Israel. Upon his arrival in Samaria, Ahab gave him a royal reception and prepared a great banquet in honor of the visiting king. When the feast was over, the two kings withdrew from the other guests for private talks about the state of their kingdoms.

The conference had barely started when Ahab made a surprising proposal to his visitor: "As you know, the Syrians have constantly invaded my land. After their crushing defeat three years ago, King Ben-hadad, in exchange for his life, agreed to return all the cities that he had captured. However, he did not fully keep that promise. He still occupies Ramoth-gilead and I want that strategic city! And, as my ally, I call upon you to join forces with me in the attempt to recapture the city."

Jehoshaphat found himself in a difficult position. In his heart he knew that God did not approve of his alliance with the wicked king of Israel, and he was certain that the Lord would be even more displeased if he acceded to Ahab's request. On the other hand, his honor was at stake, and he felt duty-bound to keep his pledged word. After much thought, Jehoshaphat reluctantly agreed for his army to join Ahab's in the forthcoming battle. However, he made one stipulation: "Before we take any action, let's find out what the Lord has to say."

Wearing their royal robes, Ahab and Jehoshaphat sat on hastily constructed thrones near the gate of Samaria. They were waiting for the arrival of the 400 prophets whom Ahab had summoned. When all of them were assembled in front of the kings, Ahab arose and asked: "Should I lead my armies in battle against the Syrians at Ramoth-gilead, or should I remain here?"

The prophets were unanimous in their declaration to their king: "Go! The Lord will give you a great victory at Ramoth-gilead."

These were exactly the words that Ahab wanted to hear. However, Jehoshaphat felt that their answer had come too quickly and too easily so he asked Ahab: "Are there any more prophets here whom we may question?"

Ahab admitted that there was one other whose name was Micaiah, the son of Imlah. The king then added: "I did not send for him because I hate him. He never prophesies anything good concerning me —only evil things."

Jehoshaphat said somewhat sharply: "Send for him!"

While waiting for the messenger to return with Micaiah, the false prophets continued their optimistic predictions of an easy victory for Israel.

As they came within sight of the gate to the city, the messenger turned to Micaiah and gave him a friendly warning: "All the other prophets have approved the king's proposed battle. It will be best for you to follow their example."

Micaiah was quick to reply: "Whatever the Lord says to me, *that* will I tell the king."

The prophet stood before the two kings and Ahab asked: "Micaiah, shall we go to Ramoth-gilead and fight the Syrians, or shall we postpone the battle?"

Micaiah answered ironically: "Why ask me? Haven't your prophets already advised you? Sure! Go on and fight the Syrians. The Lord will be with you, and give you a great victory."

Ahab sensed the ridicule in the prophet's reply, so he spoke sternly to Micaiah: "How many times must I warn you to speak nothing but the truth when you give me messages from the Lord?"

The crowd watched and waited silently for the prophet to speak. Finally, in a trance-like tone, Micaiah said: "I see all Israel scattered upon the mountains, like sheep that have no shepherd. And the Lord said to me, 'These people have no leader. Tell them to return to their homes in peace.'"

Ahab was so angered at such a dire prediction that he commanded his guards: "Take this fellow back to prison and tell my son Joash to feed him bread and water until I return in triumph."

Micaiah, however, had the last word. As he was being led away, he turned and shouted to the king: "If you come back in peace, or at all, it will surprise me!"

Meanwhile, the king of Syria was making preparations for the defense of Ramoth-gilead. He had no intention of giving up this frontier town without a struggle. Since he had already been defeated twice by King Ahab, he knew that he faced a dangerous enemy. He therefore issued strict orders to the thirty-two captains of his charioteers.

"Fight only against the king of Israel," he commanded. "If you can quickly kill him, perhaps his leaderless army will retreat in panic."

On the way to Ramoth-gilead, the ominous words of the prisoner-prophet kept ringing through Ahab's mind. Shortly before reaching the battle area, he turned to his ally and said: "I am going to disguise myself and fight as a common soldier. I want you, however, to continue to wear your regal robes and to fight in your royal chariot."

Jehoshaphat saw through his wily partner's ruse immediately: Ahab was setting him up as a decoy and prime target of the Syrian army. He also realized how foolish he had been in forming an alliance with the wicked king, but it was too late to back out now. The Syrian captains had already spotted Jehoshaphat and were charging toward him, shouting: "There is the king of Israel!"

When the onrushing charioteers drew near, Jehoshaphat cried out and the Lord helped him. The spirit of God moved the soldiers' hearts and caused them to halt their charge. Then the Syrians saw that

"Death of Ahab" by V. De Brožick. *Biblia Sacra.* Even though Ahab disguised himself in order to deceive the soldiers of Ben-hadad, an arrow from an unknown archer killed him. The prophecy of Micaiah was fulfilled.   Lemercier and Co., Paris

this man was not the king of Israel, so they turned away and continued their search for King Ahab; but their search was in vain.

The king of Israel had already left the battlefield and sat propped up in his chariot, mortally wounded. He watched the battle rage until sunset; then he died. How strange it was that an unaimed arrow from the bow of an unnamed archer should bring about the fulfillment of Micaiah's prophecy! The word spread quickly through the army that their king was dead. His death marked the end of the battle and the soldiers of Israel returned to their cities and to their homes.

The king's body was brought back to Samaria, where he was buried in full honor. His servants took his chariot to the pool of Samaria to wash out the blood and, just as Elijah predicted, the dogs came and licked up Ahab's blood.

Jehoshaphat and his army returned safely to Jerusalem, but not before the king had received a well-deserved rebuke from Jehu, one of God's prophets.

"Why did you make an alliance with the wicked and help those who hate the Lord?" Jehu asked. "Because you did this, God is angry with you. Nevertheless, He has found much good in you and will permit you and your kingdom to continue to prosper."

Upon hearing these words, Jehoshaphat became his pious old self again and firmly resolved to never make another alliance with the enemies of the Lord.

In the seventeenth year of the reign of Jehoshaphat, Ahab's son Ahaziah became king of Israel. He reigned for two years.

Based on the story in the Bible:
1 Kings 22:1-53; 2 Chronicles
17:1 — 19:3

ELIJAH'S LAST WALK WITH ELISHA

MANY YEARS PASSED after that day when Elijah found Elisha plowing in a field and chose him to be his successor. During that time a deep friendship developed between the two men, and each of them admired and respected the other. Elisha knew that one day his wise old leader would leave him and that Elijah's mantle would fall upon his shoulders.

Early one morning Elijah arose from his bed in Gilgal seminary and went quietly to Elisha's room to tell him the good news. The younger prophet was already awake, and was not surprised at part of Elijah's message:

"The Lord came to me last night and told me that this is my last day on earth. I want you to remain here because I must first go to Bethel, come back by Jericho, and then cross over the Jordan."

Elisha jumped out of bed, dressed hurriedly, and firmly declared his intention to stay with his friend and master to the very last moment. Twice more during their circuitous journey, Elijah tried to persuade his faithful follower to remain behind.

Each time, Elisha's reply was the same: "I will not leave you!"

The young men from the school for prophets in nearby Gilgal stood on a hill overlooking the Jordan and witnessed a strange sight. They saw the two prophets standing on the west bank of the river. Then they saw Elijah take off his mantle, roll it up, and touch the water with it. They watched in amazement as the waters divided and the two men walked across on dry land. They soon disappeared from the young men's sight.

As the two prophets walked quietly across the valley, Elijah broke the solemn silence when he spoke to his young protege: "Tell me what you want me to do for you before I leave you."

Elisha answered promptly, "Please give me a double portion of your prophetic spirit."

Elijah replied: "You have asked something from me that is not within my power to give. Only the Lord can grant your divine request. However, if you see me when I leave you, you can be certain that your request has been granted."

The two friends had walked only a short distance further when, suddenly, they were separated by a chariot of fire and horses of fire. Then Elisha looked up and saw his master, teacher, and friend for the last time. Elijah, escorted by the flaming chariot, was sucked up by a whirlwind and carried into Heaven. After tearing his clothes in mourning, Elisha picked up Elijah's mantle and started back to the Jordan.

Fifty young prophets had remained on the hill, watching and waiting. Finally, far in the distance, a solitary figure appeared on the horizon and walked slowly toward the Jordan. When he drew closer, they saw that it was Elisha. When he reached the water's edge, they saw him repeat Elijah's performance and cross back over on dry land. They hurried down the hill to greet their new master and, when they reached him, they bowed

"Elijah Taken Up in a Chariot of Fire" by Piazzetta. National Gallery of Art, Washington. Elisha watched in awe as Elijah was carried into heaven by the horses and a fiery chariot. National Gallery of Art, Washington (Samuel H. Kress Collection)

themselves respectfully to Elisha and said:

"The spirit of the Lord and of Elijah now rests on you."

While Elisha was resting at the seminary, one of the student-prophets came to him and said:

"Let us send fifty of our strongest young men across the Jordan to search for Elijah. Perhaps the whirlwind picked him up and then set him down on the top of some mountain or in some valley."

Elisha assured them that it would be a waste of time because he had seen Elijah ascend into Heaven. However, the young men begged so hard that Elisha finally consented for them to go.

After three days of diligent search, the search party returned to Gilgal and reported their failure to Elisha. He replied quietly: "Didn't I tell you not to go?"

Based on the story in the Bible:
2 Kings 2:1-18

PLACES

in the Story of Elijah

TISHBE (not shown on the map)

Elijah's home town is in the land of Gilead, several miles east of the Jordan, and is near the city of Jabesh (Jabesh-gilead).

SAMARIA

The capital of the Northern Kingdom is 6 miles northwest of Shechem and 6 miles due west of Tirzah, two former capitals. Elijah came to Samaria and warned the king of an approaching drought.

BROOK CHERITH

This brook is east of the Jordan and flows into that river. Elijah fled to this place to escape the wrath of Ahab and Jezebel.

ZAREPHATH

Elijah spent about three years at this Phoenician seacoast town. It is located 8 miles south of the city of Sidon and is 14 miles north of Tyre.

MOUNT CARMEL

A range of hills about 15 miles long, Mount Carmel terminates in a promontory that juts into the Mediterranean and forms the southern boundary of the Bay of Accho (Acre). The Carmel range also comprises the southwest boundary of the Plain of Jezreel. Elijah challenged the prophets of Baal here.

RIVER KISHON

At the foot of Mount Carmel, the River Kishon flows. It was at this river that Elijah executed the prophets of Baal.

JEZREEL

About 17 miles southeast of Mount Carmel, on the edge of the Plain of Jezreel, lies the city of Jezreel. King Ahab's summer palace was here and much of his court's activity centered here. Naboth's vineyard was adjacent to the palace grounds, and Elijah fled from the gates of this city to the wilderness around Mount Horeb (Sinai).

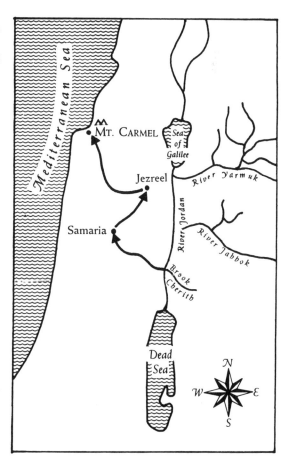

Elijah's Journey. To Brook Cherith he fled after foretelling the drought in Samaria. From Mt. Carmel he raced ahead of Ahab to Jezreel after defeating and slaying prophets of Baal.

BEERSHEBA

Approximately 100 miles slightly southwest of Jezreel is the southernmost city of Judah. Elijah paused briefly here in his frantic flight to escape the jurisdiction of Queen Jezebel.

MOUNT SINAI (Horeb)

This sacred mountain, located in the southern part of the Sinai peninsula, was the scene of many great experiences of the people of Israel. Elijah's mad dash from Jezreel ended at the foot of this mountain. It was here that he heard God's still small voice tell him what he should do.

DAMASCUS

This city-state in southern Aram (Syria) is located about 40 miles northeast of Dan, Israel's northernmost city. God instructed Elijah to come here and anoint Hazael king of Aram (Syria).

ABEL-MEHOLAH

Located about half way between the Sea of Galilee and the Dead Sea, this city is 5 miles west of the Jordan. It was in the lush Jordan valley near here that Elijah found Elisha plowing on one of his father's farms.

RAMOTH-GILEAD

Twenty miles east of the Jordan in the territory assigned to Gad lies this strategic city. While trying to recapture it from the Arameans (Syrians), King Ahab was fatally wounded.

GILGAL

This ancient city is 2 miles west of the Jordan and about 6 miles northeast of Jericho. Elijah and Elisha began their last walk together from this town.

BETHEL

Steeped in Israelite history, this city is about 12 miles north of Jerusalem and 15 miles west of the Jordan. It is one of the places visited by the two prophets before crossing over the Jordan.

JERICHO

This old and once fortified city is about 17 miles northeast of Jerusalem and 5 miles west of the Jordan. Elijah and Elisha made their final stop west of the Jordan at this historic city.

PLAIN EAST OF THE JORDAN

On a rolling plain, perhaps near his old home town, Elijah became the second person to depart from his earthly life and enter into the life of the hereafter without dying.

Mount Carmel, the Place of Sacrifice. The site where Elijah challenged the prophets of Baal is alleged to be on this rocky promontory. © Matson Photo

QUESTIONS
on the Story of Elijah

1

1 Where was Elijah's native land? Briefly describe his appearance.
2 What was King Ahab's reputation in Israel? What does his wife Jezebel's name symbolize, even today?
3 Why did Elijah decide to go to the city of Samaria?
4 What was his warning to the king and his people?
5 Why did Elijah flee across the Jordan to the brook Cherith? How was he fed while there?
6 Where was Elijah next directed to go? Who would feed and shelter him there?

2

7 What was Elijah's first request to the widow of Zarephath? His second?
8 What was the widow's response to these requests? What did Elijah tell her would happen to her meal and oil?
9 What tragedy came to the widow's house? What did Elijah do when the widow told him of her sorrow?

3

10 How long did Elijah stay in Sidon? Why did he return to Israel?
11 Who was Obadiah? What did he do when Jezebel began her purge of the Lord's prophets?
12 Why was Obadiah hesitant to go and tell Ahab that Elijah wanted to see him?
13 What did Elijah tell Ahab to do?
14 Why was the showdown between Baal and the Lord necessary at this time?

15 What preparations were made for the contest?
16 What happened to the prophets of Baal after their god was soundly defeated?
17 How were the people of Israel rewarded for acknowledging that the Lord was the one true God of Israel?
18 What was the significance of Elijah's 17-mile run in front of Ahab's chariot?

4

19 What did Jezebel do when she learned of the fate of her prophets?
20 How did Elijah react to Jezebel's ultimatum?
21 What was Elijah's state of mind as he lay under the juniper tree? What did he ask the Lord to let him do?
22 Where did Elijah go after he had eaten the food that the Lord had provided? How long did it take him to get there?
23 What did the still small voice tell Elijah to do?
24 Where did Elijah find Elisha? What was he doing?
25 What did Elisha do before he joined with Elijah?

5

26 Why did Ahab covet Naboth's vineyard?
27 Why did Naboth refuse to sell, swap, or give his vineyard to the king?
28 What was Jezebel's nefarious plot against Naboth?
29 What did Ahab do when he learned that Naboth and his sons had been stoned to death?
30 What did Elijah tell Ahab that God's

punishment for him and Jezebel would be? Why did the Lord grant a reprieve to Ahab?

6

31 What was the greatest mistake of King Jehoshaphat's life? What was its effect later on the people of Judah?

32 What startling proposal did Ahab make to his regal visitor? What was Jehoshaphat's response?

33 What did Prophet Micaiah, the lone dissenter, predict would be the outcome of the battle between Israel and Syria?

34 When King Ahab was killed in action, what did the army of Israel do? What did Jehoshaphat and his army do?

35 Who succeeded Ahab as king of Israel? How long did he reign?

7

36 How many cities did Elijah and Elisha visit during their last walk together? Name them.

37 What was Elijah's last miracle?

38 What was Elisha's last request? How did he know that God had granted it?

39 What did young prophets say to Elisha when they saw him repeat Elijah's miracle and cross over the Jordan on dry land?

40 Why did the young men want to search for Elijah's body? What was the result of their search?

Answers are found in the following pages.

Ruins of Ahab's Palace, Samaria. Today, only ruins remain of Ahab's "ivory house." Samaria was besieged in Ahab's time by Ben-hadad; later it was conquered by the Assyrians, and from then on it was under foreign rule.   ©Matson Photo

RUBENS: *Jonah Cast into the Sea*

Jonah Cast into the Sea

by RUBENS? (1577-1640) *Flemish School*

Museum, Nancy

So they took up Jonah, and cast him forth into the sea:
and the sea ceased from her raging. JONAH 1:15

A DRAMATIC EPISODE in the life of Jonah provided Rubens with
exciting subject matter for a picture that demonstrates his genius.
The sturdy sailors swing Jonah into the maw of a sea monster
during a raging storm. The force of the painting is achieved by
the dynamic diagonal that the related figures form, from the
sailor (top left) to the outstretched arms of Jonah. The motion of
the waves and the lights in the sky repeat and accent this movement. Further tension is created by the contrast of the warm
fleshtones of the sailors and the red coat of Jonah against the
darkened sea and overcast sky.

ANSWERS

on the Story of Elijah

1

1 Elijah's home town was Tishbe, in the land of Gilead. He was long-haired, bushy-browed and wore a shaggy cloak when he first appeared on the scene.

2 Ahab was known as one of Israel's most wicked kings. The name Jezebel has stood the test of time as a symbol of "an evil woman."

3 Elijah went to the capital city because King Ahab, at the behest of Queen Jezebel, had established Baal-worship as the national religion of Israel.

4 Elijah warned the king that God would punish him and his people by withholding both rain and dew from the land.

5 Elijah fled across the Jordan to the Cherith because his prophecy came true and his life was endangered. Ravens brought him bread and meat each morning and each evening.

6 The Lord told Elijah to go into exile at a town named Zarephath in the land of Sidon. A widow would feed and shelter him during his stay there.

2

7 Elijah first asked the widow for a drink of water. Then he asked her for a piece of bread.

8 The widow told Elijah that she had only a handful of meal in her barrel and only a few drops of oil in her bottle. He told the widow to have no fear about using the oil and the meal because the Lord had assured him that, no matter how much she used, neither the oil nor the meal would ever run out.

9 The widow's son became ill and died. Because of Elijah's faith and prayers, God restored the young boy's life.

3

10 Elijah was a refugee in Sidon for almost three years. The Lord told him that the time had come for him to have another talk with Ahab.

11 Although Obadiah was one of the top officials in Ahab's wicked court, he had remained faithful to the one true God of Israel. During Jezebel's relentless pursuit and extermination of the Lord's prophets, Obadiah had saved 100 of them and had hidden them in caves.

12 Obadiah feared that Elijah would have again disappeared when he returned with the king.

13 Elijah told the king to assemble all his people at the foot of Mount Carmel.

14 The people of Israel had wandered so far away from God that words alone were ineffective now. Only a physical demonstration of God's might and power could halt their downward plunge and turn their faces once more toward the Lord.

15 Two altars were set up, one for Baal and one for the Lord. Wood was placed on each altar, and the sacrificial meat was laid upon the wood. Whichever "god" personally ignited the wood on the altar would be acclaimed the one true God of Israel.

16 The four hundred and fifty prophets of Baal were taken to the River Kishon, where they were summarily executed.

17 The Lord gave them a refreshing, drought-ending rain.

18 Elijah's seventeen-mile marathon run in front of Ahab's chariot demonstrated effectively that the prophet was not only spiritually great but also physically strong.

4

19 Jezebel pronounced the death penalty on Elijah for the massacre of her prophets.

20 Elijah lost his nerve and fled for his life. He made the hundred-mile (as the crow flies) journey from Jezreel to Beersheba in record time. Although he was at the southern tip of Judah, he still didn't feel safe so he proceeded another day's march southward.

21 Elijah was despondent, discouraged, and grievously disappointed at the turn of events. In fact, his spirit was so low that he asked the Lord to let him die.

22 Elijah continued his southward journey until he reached Mount Horeb (Sinai). Forty days.

23 The still small voice told Elijah to snap out of his feeling of self-pity and return to action. He was instructed to go to Damascus and anoint Hazael as king of Syria. Then he was to go to Abel-meholah in the territory of Manasseh and choose Elisha as his successor.

24 Elijah found Elisha plowing in a field.

25 Elisha went home to tell his family and friends goodbye. While there he gave a farewell party and then departed to follow Elijah.

5

26 The king wanted Naboth's vineyard because it was adjacent to the palace grounds and could be transformed into a beautiful garden.

27 Naboth refused to part with his vineyard because it was ancestral property and had belonged to his family since the Israelites first came to Canaan.

28 Jezebel planned to have Naboth accused of blasphemy against the king and against the Lord. Witnesses were hired to falsely swear that they had heard Naboth blaspheme the king and the Lord. This frame-up resulted in the death of Naboth and his sons.

29 Ahab confiscated Naboth's vineyard.

30 Elijah told Ahab that the dogs would lick up his blood at the very spot that they licked up the blood of Naboth and his sons. He also told the king that Jezebel would die a terrible death and that the dogs would eat her body. God granted a reprieve to Ahab because he sincerely repented of his sin.

6

31 King Jehoshaphat permitted his son to marry Athaliah, the daughter of Ahab and Jezebel. This alliance caused the eventual return of Baal-worship to Judah.

32 Ahab proposed an alliance against Syria. Jehoshaphat asked to seek God's answer.

33 Micaiah predicted that Israel would be defeated and King Ahab would be killed.

34 Leaderless, the men of Israel returned to their cities and homes. King Jehoshaphat and his army returned to Jerusalem.

35 Ahaziah succeeded his father as king of Israel and reigned for two years.

7

36 During their last walk together, Elijah and Elisha visited two cities. Their names were Bethel and Jericho.

37 Elijah rolled up his mantle in the shape of a rod and touched the water of the Jordan. The water parted and he and Elisha crossed over on dry land.

38 Elisha asked for a double portion of Elijah's prophetic spirit. When he saw Elijah ascend into Heaven, he knew that the Lord had granted his request.

39 The young prophets told Elisha that they knew the spirit of the Lord and of Elijah was with him.

40 The young men felt that perhaps the whirlwind had picked Elijah up and then set him down upon some mountain top or in some valley. After a diligent search, the young men failed to find any trace of Elijah.

FURTHER FACTS AND OUTLINE
for the Story of Elijah

FIRST KINGS (continued)

AUTHORSHIP AND DATE

See *Further Facts and Outline for the Story of Solomon.*

DESTINATION

The people of Israel and posterity.

PURPOSE AND THEME

See *Further Facts and Outline for the Story of Solomon.*

OUTLINE

Elijah the Prophet and the Reign of Ahab
(16:29 – 22:53)
   Elijah Foretells Three Years' Drought, He Is Fed at the Brook Cherith; He Raises the Widow's Son from the Dead (16:29 – 17:24)
Contest: Elijah vs. Prophets of Baal and the Ensuing Rain (chapter 18)
Elijah Encouraged, "A Still Small Voice" (chapter 19)
Ahab's Victory over Ben-hadad, Ahab's Sin (chapter 20)
Ahab and Jezebel kill Naboth To Get His Vineyard (chapter 21)
Ahab Killed in Battle (chapter 22)
Elijah's Last Days, His Translation to Heaven (2 Kings, chapters 1 and 2)

Ahab's Well on the Plain of Jezreel (Esdraelon). This large and beautiful valley is still famous for its fertile land. Naboth's coveted vineyard was located at the city of Jezreel on the southeastern edge of the Plain. © Matson Photo

Elijah, the Abraham Lincoln of the Israelites

by
James Kelso

Both Elijah and Lincoln appeared at a watershed in the history of their respective nations, Dr. James Kelso points out in a chapter from his book, *Archaeology and Our Old Testament Contemporaries* (© 1966, Zondervan Publishing House, Grand Rapids, Michigan). After noting the other ways in which these two rugged men were alike, Dr. Kelso finds one major difference: No one was great enough to fill Lincoln's shoes, while Elijah's successor had been in training under "the old master" for many years and was ready for his enlarged responsibilities. There is a lesson here for trusted leaders as well as for the average man of our own day.

WHAT MAKES A LEADER?

WHEN TALKING to young people, I often speak of Moses as the George Washington of the Jews and of Elijah as their Abraham Lincoln. The Book of Kings in Hebrew was written on a single scroll, for the Hebrew [language] was written with consonants only. When it was translated into Greek, which specializes in vowels, two scrolls were necessary, and that is why the English Bible contains 1 and 2 Kings. If you were using the original Hebrew scroll of Kings, you would find that approximately the center third of the book concentrates on two men, Elijah and Elisha! This shows their importance. A still better test is to check every feature of the lives and work of these two men against the life of Christ, and note the parallel.

From Abraham to the Babylonian Captivity represents about thirteen centuries of Israelite history, all of which can be summarized in a single question put by Elijah to the Israelites on Mt. Carmel: "How long go ye limping between the two sides? If Jehovah be God, follow Him; but if Baal, then follow him. . . ." (1 Kings 18:21 ASV) The local settings change, the characters come and go, nations rise and fall; but the theme of Israel's history remains the same—Jehovah or Baal—just as since New Testament times it has been Jesus or Athena.

The Israel of Elijah's day was in many ways quite similar to the United States about the time of the Civil War, if you eliminate manufacturing from Israel. (That did not come in for more than another century.) The Northern Kingdom was the breadbasket for Phoenicia, which had only a minimum of farm land but specialized in manufacturing and shipping. She was the Great Britain of her day.

Omri was the first strong king in Israel [after the kingdom was divided], and he was able to make himself stronger through alliances with both Phoenicia and Judah. From his time onward the Assyrian records refer to Israel as "the house of Omri," although that dynasty was quickly gone. Omri moved the capital to Samaria, and when the work [on the new capital] was completed, it became one of the best fortified cities of Palestine. The Assyrians captured it only after a three-year siege.

Two extensive campaigns of excavations have been carried on here, and they have uncovered many details of the city's history. Samaria occupied an isolated hilltop easy of defense. At least some of the Israelite city walls were of the casemate type, a military importation from the Hittites. Two fairly thin walls were joined together by cross walls every few meters, and this gives the appearance of a long series of small rooms. Each room was probably filled with earth. Much of the wall was the twelve-foot Palestinian wall, but at one place it was thirty-two feet wide.

Sections of the Omri-Ahab palace and its later remodeling by Jeroboam II have been found. The palace area was just a little over three hundred feet long. It followed the common plan of Near Eastern palaces; that is, a series of two-story buildings erected around open courts. At the side of one courtyard is an excellently constructed rectangular pool, thirty-three by seventeen feet in area. One naturally conjectures that this may have been the pool near [the spot] where the dogs licked up the blood from the chariot that carried the dead Ahab home (1 Kings 22:35-38).

Many ivory inlays were found in the palace complex. They came from the inlaid wall paneling of wood and from inlaid furniture and toilet articles (1 Kings 22:39, Amos 6:4). This work was doubtless done by Phoenician craftsmen who patterned their work after Egyptian and Syrian originals. Writing of any type is a rare find in Palestine, but Samaria yielded sixty-three ostraca. These inscribed potsherds [pieces of broken earthen pots] from the royal archives served as tax receipts and business documents. They show that the old federal districts created by Solomon were still intact in the Northern Kingdom.

Sargon II, the conqueror of Samaria, rebuilt the city and made it the capital of an Assyrian province. Persia continued it as a district capital, and at that time even Jerusalem was under its control. The city was captured by Alexander the Great and converted into a Greek city. Samaria was again destroyed, this time by the Maccabees, but it became strong again under the Romans.

Samaria was embellished by Herod the Great, who erected there a magnificent temple to his political patron, Augustus Caesar. Herod renamed the city Sebaste, after Caesar. (*Sebaste* is the Greek equivalent for the Latin *Augustus*.) Here the Greek population of Samaria worshiped Augustus Caesar as a god! This temple was provided by the same Herod who built the great Jerusalem Temple in which Christ worshiped. . . .

Now, to return to Omri. His son (Ahab) married Jezebel, the fanatical Baal worshiper, who insisted that the Israelites worship her gods, as well as Jehovah.

Into this crisis came Elijah. The drought referred to in this episode was so critical that it is actually mentioned by writers from the Phoenician capital at Tyre. Elijah chose Mt. Carmel as the perfect setting for his work [of demonstrating the superiority of Jehovah over other gods]. Carmel literally means "the garden spot," and this mountain is a great headland jutting out into the sea. Here both the Canaanites and the Phoenicians worshiped Baal, the giver of fertile farm lands, and Asherah, goddess of the sea. The story of the Lord's victory here is so condensed in the Scripture that it must be read *in toto*. (See 1 Kings 18:16-46.) Elijah is king for a day! Little Ahab cringed before him and could only do the prophet's bidding.

As Jehovah justified Himself against Baal in Joshua's day, so [He did] at Carmel. It is Jehovah's lightning, not Baal's; it is Jehovah's rain, not Baal's. "The wages of sin is death": the four hundred and fifty prophets of Baal and the four hundred prophets of Asherah are slaughtered at the base of Carmel beside the River Kishon—the same stream which, swollen by Jehovah's cloudbursts, drowned the hosts of Sisera [in the days of the Judges]. From a map of the area (see page 159) can be seen the distance of Elijah's marathon run, before the chariot of Ahab from Carmel to Jezreel. What a blend of the physical and the spiritual in Elijah! . . .

The Naboth episode illustrates [the fact]

that, even in the Northern Kingdom, the old Mosaic land laws were still valid in all real estate transactions. According to these laws, farm land could not be sold outside the family circle. Naboth, the commoner, refused to sell his ancestral property to King Ahab, but the pagan Jezebel solved the dilemma for her husband by having Naboth killed and his land confiscated by the crown. God, however, always makes the last move. He promised Jezebel that the dogs would eat her body near this very field, and they did. Contrast her death with Elijah's chariot ride to heaven!

Elijah and Lincoln appeared at a watershed in the history of their respective nations. Each had to make a choice involving the whole concept of national life—to follow the [tried and true] old path or to cater to selfish partisan interests. With Elijah, the choice involved both church and state; with Lincoln, the state alone. Baalism went down with Jezebel—or, more accurately, it phased off from sensualism into secularism and finally into political death. Both Elijah and Lincoln held to a theory of state where all men are equal and where the state must be kept intact to preserve that equality.

Neither man fitted the ecclesiastical pattern of his day. Elijah completely ignored Jerusalem and its sanctuary. No clergy pattern fitted him. He used only his Bible [the Scriptures]. There was no other like him until John the Baptist. The world was Elijah's parish, but God seemed to be his only intimate friend. Lincoln, too, was completely outside the church pattern of his day, although he was on good terms with God—and he certainly knew and practiced [the teachings of] the Book. Outside of the United States today Lincoln is not only the most respected American in history; he has no close competitor. Christ's evaluation of Elijah is seen in Elijah's presence at the Transfiguration.

In their successors, however, Elijah and Lincoln part company. No one was big enough to step into Lincoln's shoes, and the nation suffered greatly from that absence. Elisha, however, wore Elijah's sandals, and they were an excellent fit. Elijah and Elisha provide a perfect demonstration of the fact that the Church needs different human temperaments for the same time and the same task.... The ministry of the pulpit and the pew must always be both timely and timeless.

Elisha

POISED AND CALM, ELISHA had a ministry that stands, in many respects, in striking contrast to that of Elijah. There is a gentleness about it that inevitably reminds us of the ministry of Jesus. Instead of suddenly appearing at a critical moment, like thunder and flame, Elisha seems to have moved about among people, doing good wherever he went.... In the fourth chapter of Second Kings there are four instances in Elisha's ministry where he is seen carrying on his beneficent work among the people: his provision for the widow whose creditors were threatening her; his kindness to the Shunammite woman who had shown him hospitality; his curing of the poisoned pottage at Gilgal; and his feeding of a hundred men with twenty loaves of bread....

The ministry of Elisha was wholly a ministry of the word of the Lord. Everything he did was in obedience to that word and in interpretation of that word in the life of the nation. In his every activity Elisha was demonstrating, to those who had the spiritual capacity to understand it, how beneficent were the thoughts and intentions of God concerning His people.

During all this time Elisha was at the head of the schools for prophets and, as he journeyed from place to place, was known as the messenger of God. His deeds were the expositions of his message. His life was that of the utmost simplicity. This is evident from the provision made for his entertainment by the wealthy Shunammite woman. His apartment was a room on the wall, containing a bed, a table, a stool, and a candlestick.

Yet Elisha's life was full of dignity, as the attitude of the people toward him testifies. A ministry "according to the word of the Lord," interpreting the will of God and illustrating it by deeds of goodness, is independent of all except the simplest ways of life. But it is always full of sublime influence.—G. Campbell Morgan, *Searchlights from the Word*

1

SUNSTROKE IN THE HARVEST FIELD

ELISHA'S MINISTRY as spokesman for the Lord lasted about fifty years. During that time five kings reigned over the Northern Kingdom and three of them were his personal friends. What a study in contrasts between the pupil and his teacher! Yet, despite their differences in appearance, environment, manners, and method of operation, Elisha and Elijah were close friends.

Early in his ministry, Elisha had two interesting experiences with women. One of them was a widow of a prophet. She came to Elisha one day and told him her sad story.

"Your servant, my husband, is dead," she began. "You know that he feared the Lord and always dealt fairly and honestly with people. Shortly before his death, he borrowed some money and did not have the opportunity to repay it. Now I am in real trouble. To satisfy the debt, his creditor has come to take away my two sons and sell them into slavery."

Elisha listened with compassion to the widow. Then he asked, "Do you have anything of value in your house?"

"I have nothing except a pot of oil," she replied.

The kindly prophet spoke to her again.

"Listen closely and follow my instructions," he said. "You and your two sons are about to enter into the oil business. Go among your neighbors and borrow as many empty pots and other empty vessels as you can. After this you and your sons return home, close the door, and start pouring oil into the empty vessels. As long as there is one empty vessel remaining, the oil in the original pot will not run out. After all the pots and vessels are filled, take the oil to the market place, sell it, and pay your debt. You and your sons can live off the money that is left."

The grateful woman did as directed, and her two sons were spared from a life of slavery.

Up the hills and through the valleys, Elisha went about doing good. One day his wandering brought him to the little village of Shunem. It was north of the

"The Prophet Elisha." Anonymous. Museum of Fine Arts, Bruges. By following the direction of Elisha, a poor widow was able to pay her creditor and save her sons from being sold into slavery.　　　　National Archives, Brussels

Jezreel Valley and nestled high among the hills. He had a particularly warm spot in his heart for this town because of the close friendship he had formed with a wealthy farmer and his wife. As Elisha and his servant Gehazi approached the farmer's house, the prophet was surprised to note that something new had been added to it. An upper room, with an outside entrance, had been built upon the roof of the house.

The farmer's wife greeted Elisha politely and invited him to have lunch with her. After they had finished eating, she turned to him and said: "I have a surprise for you! You and your servant come and follow me."

She led them outside the house and up the stairs to the new room. When the three of them were inside, the lady from Shunem handed the key to Elisha.

"My husband and I want you to have this room as your very own," she said. "We know that you are a holy man of God. Your visits to our home and your wise words have meant a great deal to us. This private, furnished room is just a token of our appreciation and friendship."

Elisha sat on the edge of his bed, puzzled and perplexed. What could he do to repay the farmer and his wife for their kindness to him? He had asked his hostess if she would like for him to speak to the king on behalf of her husband. She had told him that she had no desire for life at the royal court and that she was quite content to dwell quietly among her own

Villagers of Shunem (Sulem). This town was located on the border of Issachar. Elisha often visited Shunem, where he was welcomed in the home of a wealthy farmer and his wife, who provided a room for his comfort. © Matson Photo

"Elisha and the Woman from Shunem" by van den Eeckhout. Budapest Museum. Elisha was grateful to the woman of Shunem and her husband for their goodness to him. He repaid their kindness in a number of ways. Budapest Museum

people. Suddenly, in the stillness of the room, God revealed to Elisha that this childless couple were to be proud parents of a son.

The good woman of Shunem could hardly believe her ears. Elisha had just told her that God would give her and her husband a son. How miraculous that her greatest wish and fondest dream would be realized!

The farmer and his wife were very proud of their young son. They watched him as he grew and developed into a strong, healthy lad who liked nothing

173

better than to romp and play in his father's harvest fields. Little did they know that tragedy was soon to strike their happy home!

On one intensely hot day, the child accompanied his father to the corn field and was racing between the stalks when suddenly he toppled to the ground and cried out, "Father! My head! Oh, my head!"

Although the father did not think anything was seriously wrong, he took the precaution of having a servant take their son back to his mother. She nursed him tenderly until noon, and then he died.

Her son was dead! His gay laughter was stilled forever, his bright eyes were closed in death. The broken-hearted mother carried him to Elisha's room and laid him on the bed. Then she had her donkey saddled. She and one of her servants hurried toward Mount Carmel to try to find her friend, the prophet.

Elisha sat beneath a tree on a hill overlooking Jezreel Valley, seeking relief from the blazing, searing sun. As he looked far down the valley, he saw a woman speeding toward him. He turned quickly to his servant, Gehazi.

"Look!" he exclaimed. "Here comes my Shunammite friend. Quick! Rush down to meet her and ask if all goes well with her husband, herself, and her son."

"All is well," she told the servant. Then she kept going up the hill toward Elisha. When she reached him, she dismounted, fell at his feet, and poured out her tale of grief and anguish.

Elisha was stunned. It was hard for him to realize that his vivacious young friend now lay dead upon the bed where they had talked so often. Realizing the necessity for speed, he again spoke to his swift young servant.

"Here!" he cried. "Take my staff and go ahead of us to my room. When you get there, lay the staff upon the face of the child. Be sure not to let anything or anyone deter you as you hurry on your way."

When Elisha and his friend reached her house, Gehazi came downstairs to report that nothing happened when he laid the staff on the child's face.

Elisha entered the room and closed the door. Then, emulating Elijah, his teacher of old, he knelt down beside the bed and prayed fervently that the Lord would restore the life of the child. After completing his prayer, he leaned over the lad and did what is known today as mouth-to-mouth resuscitation. The flesh of the child was growing warm once more. Suddenly he sneezed seven times and opened his eyes.

Elisha's heart beat high with joy as he called the boy's mother to the room and said: "Pick up your son and take him with you. He is alive!"

With deep gratitude, the happy mother bowed low before the noble prophet. Then she picked up her son and left the room.

Based on the story in the Bible: 2 Kings 4:1-37

2
NAAMAN, THE LEPER

NAAMAN, THE GREAT COMMANDER of the Syrian army, "was a mighty man of valor, but he was a leper." Leprosy was and is a terrible disease and, in those days, it was so infectious that lepers were not allowed to mix and mingle with

healthy people. There was no known cure and, as Naaman's condition grew worse, he would certainly have to leave his home, his wife, and the king's court.

In Naaman's household there was a charming young Hebrew girl who served as his wife's maid. This little maid had lived near Samaria and had been captured by the Syrians during one of their raids on Israel. She had often seen Elisha and had heard of the many wonderful things he did through the power of the Lord.

The young girl had become fond of her master and mistress, and it grieved her to see the sadness that was creeping into the home as Naaman's illness became increasingly worse. One day she spoke to her mistress about it.

"There is a man of God in Samaria who has performed many miracles," she said. "His name is Elisha, the prophet, and perhaps he could heal your lord."

Naaman's wife hurried to her husband and told him what her little maid had said. Naaman rushed to the king and repeated his wife's message. The king agreed that perhaps there was a gleam of hope from the Lord God of Israel. Clearly the Syrian gods had done nothing to cure his commander.

Naaman and his retinue departed for Samaria, carrying with them a letter to the king of Israel, about $80,000 worth of gold, and 10 beautiful suits. A fabulous treasure, indeed, but it would be well worth it to be cured of this terrible disease.

The king of Israel was startled at the unexpected appearance of the Syrian commander, his chariots, and his cortege. Why, there was peace between his people and Syria at that time! What could be the meaning of this procession?

The king of Israel was not kept in the dark for long. Naaman descended from his chariot, approached the king respectfully, and handed him the letter. The king was alarmed and puzzled as he read the letter: "I am sending Naaman my servant to you so that you may cure him of his leprosy."

The king threw down the letter, rose up, and cried out in despair to Naaman: "Who does your king think I am? A God Who can cause men to live or die? This is merely a trick on his part to find an excuse to wage war against me."

The news of the Syrian commander's visit and its purpose soon reached Elisha. He hastened to send a message to his king: "Have no fear! Tell the Syrian to come to my house and he shall know that there is a prophet of the Lord God in Israel."

The king was relieved and happy to shift this problem to Elisha, so he gave Naaman the message. Soon Naaman, his chariots, and his followers reached Elisha's house. Everyone expected that the prophet would consider it an honor to be visited by such a great man and that he would welcome the Syrian with all due respect. Imagine their shock and surprise when Elisha made no appearance at all! He merely sent his

Ruins of the House of Naaman in Damascus. Naaman was commander in chief of the Syrian king, Ben-hadad. After Elisha cured him of leprosy, Naaman rejected all other gods and worshiped the God of Israel.

© Matson Photo

servant with a message for Naaman: "Go to the River Jordan and bathe in it seven times. Then your flesh shall be healed and you shall be cured."

At first, Naaman was indignant at what he considered the disrespectful treatment he had received at the hands of the prophet, so he refused even to consider going to the Jordan. Finally, however, he became convinced that this was his one last opportunity to be cured of his dreadful disease, so he ordered his chariot to be turned to the east and the River Jordan.

When he reached the river, Naaman descended from his chariot, undressed, and bathed seven times in the Jordan. When he had finished for the seventh time, he looked in vain for the hideous sores. They were gone! His skin was soft and wholesome, like the skin of a little child.

Full of joy and gratitude, he and his company hurried back to Samaria to thank the prophet. This time Elisha came out to greet him. Naaman leaped from his chariot and bowed low before this man of God.

"Now I know that there is no real God in all the earth except in Israel," he said. "Never again shall I offer sacrifices to any god except the Lord God of Israel."

Before returning to Syria, Naaman had things to do. First, he asked Elisha for as much soil belonging to Israel as two mules could carry. The reason for this strange request was that, in those days, people believed that each land had its own particular god or gods. Since Naaman had resolved to worship the Lord God of Israel, he thought it necessary to build an altar on genuine soil of Israel.

Then the Syrian commander led Elisha and his servant, Gehazi, to the pack animals bearing the bags of gold and the ten suits. The servant had never seen such a vast amount of wealth, and he listened in annoyance and disbelief as he heard his master repeatedly refuse to accept the gifts offered by the Syrian.

How sad that the story of Naaman must end with a report of the greed, deceit, and punishment of a faithful servant! As soon as Elisha entered the house, Gehazi raced after Naaman's chariot. He was determined to secure some of the wealth that had dazzled his eyes and dimmed his conscience.

When Gehazi reached the chariot, he cried out: "My master has sent me after you, because two young prophets have just arrived at his house. He is now willing to accept a gift of a talent of silver and two suits from you."

Naaman was so delighted to have this opportunity to do something for Elisha that he gave the servant the two suits of clothes and twice the amount of money he had requested.

Gehazi was back in his master's house, silently performing routine chores just as though nothing had happened. Suddenly Elisha broke the silence: "Where have you been, Gehazi?"

At first the trembling servant thought of trying to bluff it out by telling Elisha that he had been nowhere. But he knew in his heart that there was no use pretending. His heart sank as he heard the next stern words of his master.

"You have tried to make a profit out of a wonderful manifestation of the power of God," Elisha said. "Because of your wicked act, the leprosy of Naaman shall be transferred to you and your descendants forever."

Gehazi's punishment was swift and severe. He walked out of Elisha's house for the last time, a leper as white as snow.

Based on the story in the Bible:
2 Kings 5:1-27

TWO EXPERIENCES WITH THE SYRIANS

TWICE DURING HIS LONG CAREER Elisha, as an agent of the Lord, played an important role in Israel's conquest of the Syrians. These two occasions again proved that whenever and wherever he was needed, this holy man of God was always there. In the first instance, he actually made prisoners of the entire Syrian army.

The king of Syria was at his wit's end. Time after time he had laid clever traps for the Israelites, but they had always managed to avoid them. He was firmly convinced that there was a spy in his army, so he called for a meeting of his military experts.

When they were assembled, the king asked them bluntly: "Who is the traitor in our midst? Who is reporting our every move to the king of Israel?"

One of his men spoke up: "None of us are guilty of treason, O king! Elisha the prophet is the advisor of the king of Israel. He knows every word you speak, even in the privacy of your bedroom, and tells his king what you plan to do."

When he heard these words, the king issued this sharp command: "Go and find out where this man is, so that I can send out an army and capture him."

One of his officers said, "I know where he is! This is the week that he visits Dothan."

Elisha and his servant arose early one morning and saw that a large Syrian army had surrounded the town during the night.

"Alas, my master!" The servant exclaimed. "What shall we do?"

"Have no fear," replied Elisha. "Those who are with us are more than those who are with them." Then he prayed that the Lord would open the eyes of his servant —Gehazi's replacement—so that he could look to the hills and mountains and also see that they were full of horses and flaming chariots.

As the Syrians advanced on Dothan, Elisha asked the Lord to strike the whole army with blindness. When this was done, the prophet proceeded from the town toward the blinded men.

"You have gone the wrong way," he said to them. "This is not the city for which you are looking. Follow me and I will guide you to the man whom you seek."

The king of Israel was astounded when he saw Elisha calmly directing the Syrian prisoners into the fortified capital city of Samaria. When God removed the blindness from the men, they were very dejected. One innocent-appearing man had tricked them, and they were now in the hands of the Israelites! The king rushed out to meet Elisha and shouted eagerly: "Shall I have them all killed? Shall I have them all killed?"

Elisha scorned this proposal, as he reprimanded his king: "Would you kill those whom you did not capture? Instead, prepare a great feast for these men so that they may eat and drink. Then you must guarantee safe conduct for these soldiers as they return to their camp and to their king."

When the men reported what had happened in Samaria, the Syrian king withdrew his armies and there was peace throughout the land of Israel.

The truce did not last long. Soon forgotten was Elisha's merciful treatment of the Syrian captives! King Ben-hadad and his huge army had again violated Israel's borders and had penetrated into the land to the capital city itself. They promptly laid siege to Samaria, and this strategy was so effective that it was impossible for any food to be brought into the city.

From the king on down, the people of Samaria were in a terrible predicament. The cruel siege had lasted so long that food supplies were completely exhausted, and the wretched people were eating anything they could find—horses, donkeys, and other animals. The king's patience was exhausted. He was convinced that Elisha was at the bottom of all the trouble, so he began a massive manhunt for the prophet. He was determined that Elisha should not live another day.

Strangely enough, Elisha was not in hiding but was in his own house talking with some of the elders. When the king found him, he stormed out:

"You are the cause of all our trouble! Many of the very men you persuaded me to treat mercifully are out there now besieging our city. Before the sun goes down you shall pay for that mistake with your life."

Elisha replied calmly to this outburst.

"Hear the word of the Lord," he said. "Tomorrow, about this time, there will be an abundance of food in the city. Consequently, the high cost of living will drop sharply."

Upon hearing these words, an officer with the king laughed mockingly and said. "This could only happen if the Lord your God put windows in heaven and gave us food."

Elisha strongly rebuked the officer: "Just wait! Tomorrow you shall see the food with your own eyes, but you will die before you have a chance to eat any of it."

As night began to fall, four lepers sat outside the city gate bemoaning their fate.

"Why do we sit here until we die?" one

"King Ben-hadad of Syria" by J. James Tissot. *The Old Testament,* Illustrated. Ben-hadad was king of Syria during the time of Elijah and Elisha. Israel and Syria were frequently at war during these years. M. de Buffan & Co.

of them asked. "Even if we were permitted in the city, we would die there because of the famine. There is only one hope for us. Come! Let's go to the camp of the Syrians. If they save us, well and good. If not, we will be no worse off than we are now."

When the sun sank beneath the western horizon and darkness covered the land, four lonely lepers slowly went their way to the Syrian camp. Imagine their surprise when they arrived at the outskirts of the camp! The place was deserted. Just about twilight, God had caused the Syrians to hear horses and chariots, and the noise of a great host of marching feet. Their imagination had done the rest, as they had said to one another: "Listen! The king of Israel has hired the kings of the Hittites and the kings of the Egyptians to fight against us. Let's drop everything and flee for our lives!"

When the four lepers entered the silent, deserted camp, they were amazed. There was no sign of life except for the horses, mules, and donkeys that the panic-stricken Syrians had left behind. The four men entered a tent and ate and drank to their heart's content. Then they emptied the tent of all the gold, silver, and clothing. Tent after tent received the same treatment.

"Wait!" one of the looters suddenly exclaimed. "We are not handling this situation right. This is a night of good tidings for the people of Samaria. Yet here we are gathering treasures. Let's hurry back to the city and spread the good news right now. If we wait until morning, we shall surely be punished."

When they reached the gate of the city,

the lepers shouted to the guard: "We have just come from the camp of the Syrians, and there is no one there! Quick! Hurry to the king and tell him the good news!"

The guards rushed off and made their report to king. They were astounded to note that the king showed no jubilation. Instead, he called his ministers of war together.

"This report is just another trick of the Syrians," he said, gloomily. "Let *me* tell you what they have done. They know that we are starving and would do anything to get some food. They have left their camp and have hidden in the nearby woods. When we come rushing out to look for food, they will capture us and the city, as well."

The ministers finally persuaded the king to send out two men on two of the horses remaining in the city to check the report. The two men followed the trail of the terrified Syrians as far as Jordan. The way of their retreat was scattered with clothing and other valuables which they had thrown away during their hasty flight.

The messengers returned and made their report to the king. When the people learned that the Syrians had departed and left vast quantities of food at their camp, there was a mad stampede. The mocking officer who had scorned Elisha the day before was knocked down in the milling crowd and trampled to death.

Based on the stories in the Bible:
2 Kings 6:8 — 7:20

4

ELISHA'S SWAN SONG

ELISHA LAY ON HIS DEATHBED, deep in thought. As he reflected on his past experiences, it seemed that his had been a ministry of miracles, performed to portray the power of the Lord to the sinful, defiant Israelites. . . . His first miracle had been performed at Jericho shortly after his last walk with Elijah. The people had complained that the water in the springs was bad and that nothing would grow on the land surrounding them. He had purified the water by throwing salt into the springs.

He had left Jericho and was on his way to Bethel when he had heard the taunts and jeers of the young boys who were rude to him because he was bald. He shuddered even now as he remembered the terrible consequences of their disrespectful, malicious act.

He vividly recalled the battle with the Moabites. Despite his firm resolve never again to form an entangling alliance, King Jehoshaphat of Judah had joined with the armies of Israel and Edom to wage war on the encroaching army from Moab. After marching for seven days, the three kings had sent for the prophet because all the streams were dry and there had been no water for the men or the animals. Upon his arrival, the streams had miraculously filled and the reflecting rays of the setting sun had caused the enemy to think the waters had turned to blood. The Moabites had thought that the three kings had fought among themselves and that the blood of the dying soldiers had trickled into streams, creating this phenomenon. When the enemy had rushed down to finish the job, the coalition of kings had completely annihilated the Moabites.

Elisha was roused from his reverie by the appearance of his friend, King Joash of Israel, who had come to pay his respects to the aged prophet. The king wept over his ailing friend and exclaimed: "O my father, my father! The chariot of Israel and its horsemen!"

Elisha now spoke to the king for the first time since his arrival: "Take your bow and arrows, open the east window, and shoot an arrow into the air."

Joash did as directed.

"Look!" the prophet cried out. "That is the Lord's arrow of victory! Yes, the arrow of victory over the Syrians. You shall fight them in Aphek until they are utterly destroyed."

Elisha had still more instructions for his king. He told him to take an arrow and strike the floor with it. Joash struck one time . . . two times . . . three times. Then he stopped. Elisha, annoyed because he had stopped striking the floor so soon, made his final prophecy.

"You should have struck at least five or six times," he declared. "Then you would have completely defeated the Syrians. Now you will only win three battles from them."

After speaking those words, the tired old man sank upon his pillows, closed his eyes, and went quietly to the God Whom he loved so well and had served so faithfully. Elisha was buried in his family burial ground at Abel-meholah.

Based on the stories in the Bible: 2 Kings 2:19-22, 23-25; 3:1-27, 13:14-20

"*Joash Readies His Arrow*" by Frank Dicksee. *Biblia Sacra.*
Shortly before Elisha died, King Joash visited him. Following a test with arrows, Elisha prophesied that Joash would defeat the Syrians three times.

Lemercier and Co., Paris

PLACES
in the Story of Elisha

SHUNEM

Nestled in the hills, about 5 miles north of Mount Gilboa and 3½ miles northwest of the city of Jezreel, lies the town of Shunem. It was here that Elisha restored to life the son of a Shunammite woman.

MOUNT CARMEL

A range of hills about 15 miles long, Mount Carmel terminates in a headland that juts into the Mediterranean. It forms the southern boundary of the Bay of Accho (Acre) and is the southwest boundary of the Plain of Jezreel. It was here that the farmer's wife from Shunem found Elisha and told him of the death of her son.

SAMARIA

The capital city of Israel is located 6 miles northwest of Shechem and 6 miles due west

A Stream near Jericho flows from a source known as Elisha's Fountain. It is thought that in this area Elisha caused the water to be purified and the land to become fertile. The Mount of Temptation is in the distance. © Matson Photo

of Tirzah, two former capitals. Much of Elisha's life revolves around this city. He was granted the privileges of the royal court by three of the reigning kings, and he had a home here. It was also here that he correctly prophesied the miraculous lifting of the Syrian siege of the capital.

DOTHAN

This centuries-old, tradition-steeped city is about 10 miles due north of Samaria. Elisha and his servant were visiting this town when a large number of Syrian soldiers appeared on the scene. They were under strict orders of their king to capture the prophet and take him to Damascus. When God, at Elisha's request, struck all the soldiers with blindness, the situation was reversed. Elisha, the hunted, became Elisha, the hunter. He captured the blinded men and led them to Samaria.

RIVER JORDAN

This is the largest river in Palestine. It rises at the foot of Mount Hermon, flows through the Sea of Galilee, and empties into the Dead Sea. Its total length is 104 miles. Elisha sent Naaman, the leper, to this river. He bathed in it seven times and was miraculously healed.

SOMEWHERE EAST OF THE JORDAN

After a seven-day march toward Moab, the Triple Alliance of Israel, Judah, and Edom was face to face with the enemy. They were also face to face with trouble. All the streams were dry! Elisha was called for and once more a miracle was performed. The stream-beds silently filled with water. An optical illusion caused the Moabites to attack the coalition prematurely, and the armies of the three kings won a decisive victory.

APHEK

This town is in the territory of Geshur and was occupied by the Aramaean (Syrian) kingdom during Elisha's time. It is about 2 miles east of the Sea of Galilee. The dying prophet told his friend King Joash that he would be victorious over the Aramean (Syrian) army three times at Aphek.

Jordan River, at its source at the foot of Mount Hermon, near Dan. Although Naaman was repelled by the river's muddy waters, he obeyed Elisha and bathed in it seven times and was cured of leprosy.   © Matson Photo

QUESTIONS
on the Story of Elisha

1

1 How long did Elisha's ministry as a prophet last? How many kings ruled over Israel during that time?

2 Why was the widow of a prophet in trouble?

3 What did Elisha tell her to do?

4 What did the rich farmer and his wife do to make Elisha's visits to Shunem more enjoyable?

5 Why did the farmer's wife go to Mount Carmel, seeking Elisha?

6 What did Elisha do to restore happiness in his friends' home?

2

7 Who was Naaman? What was his affliction?

8 What did Elisha tell Naaman to do in order to be healed?

9 What was Gehazi's great sin? How was he punished?

3

10 Why did the king of Syria wish to capture Elisha?

11 What happened to the Syrian army as it approached Dothan?

12 How were the prisoners treated when Elisha led them into Samaria?

13 What was the effect on the people of Ben-hadad's long siege of Samaria?

14 Why was the king of Israel so angry with Elisha?

15 What did the four lepers find when they reached the Syrian camp?

16 Why did the Syrians abandon everything and retreat in panic to their homeland?

4

17 Against whom was the coalition of kings fighting? Why did the three kings send for Elisha?

18 Who came to visit Elisha as he lay on his deathbed?

19 What did Elisha first tell his visitor to do? What were his next instructions?

20 What was Elisha's last prophecy?

*Answers are found
on the following page.*

ANSWERS

on the Story of Elisha

1

1 Elisha's ministry lasted about fifty years. There were five kings over Israel during this time.

2 The widow's husband died owing some money. To satisfy the debt, his creditor came to take away her two sons and sell them as slaves.

3 Elisha told the widow to borrow all the empty pots, jars, and other vessels that she could find, and to pour oil from her own jar of oil into the empty vessels until all were full. He told her to take the oil then to the market place, sell it, and pay off her debt.

4 The rich farmer and his wife built and furnished a private room for Elisha on the roof of their house.

5 Her son had suffered a sunstroke and had died.

6 Through the power of the Lord, Elisha restored the life of her young son.

2

7 Naaman, the commander of the Syrian army, "was a mighty man of valor, but he was a leper."

8 Elisha told Naaman to bathe seven times in the River Jordan.

9 When Naaman came back from the Jordan to thank Elisha, Gehazi saw the fabulous treasure that Elisha refused to accept. The servant then devised a plan whereby he could capitalize on the miraculous manifestation of God's power. Gehazi's punishment for this plot was that he and his descendants were doomed to be lepers.

3

10 The king was told that Elisha was giving away Syrian military secrets to the king of Israel.

11 All of the soldiers involved in this action against Elisha were struck with blindness.

12 At first the king of Israel wanted to kill all the Syrian prisoners. However, Elisha persuaded him to feed them and let them return to their king.

13 King Ben-hadad's long siege of Samaria had caused near-starvation there.

14 The king was furious with Elisha because the prophet had persuaded him to show mercy to a large group of Syrian prisoners. His anger grew by leaps and bounds when he saw these same men patrolling the walls of Samaria, helping to maintain the tight siege against his capital city.

15 The four lepers found the Syrian camp silent and deserted.

16 God had caused the Syrians to hear horses and chariots, and the noise of a great host marching. These sounds led them to believe that reinforcements from other kingdoms had arrived to help Israel. Hence, they fled in panic, leaving all their possessions behind them.

4

17 The kings of Israel, Judah, and Edom were fighting the Moabites. The three kings sent for Elisha because, when they reached the battlefield, there was no water in the stream-beds nearby.

18 King Joash of Israel came to visit Elisha.

19 Elisha first told the king to shoot an arrow out the east window. He then told him to strike the floor with an arrow.

20 Elisha told Joash that he would be victorious over the Syrians only three times because he had stopped striking the floor after the third time.

FURTHER FACTS
AND OUTLINE
for the Story of Elisha

SECOND KINGS

AUTHORSHIP AND DATE

See above under *Further Facts and Outline for the Story of Solomon:* First Kings.

DESTINATION

The Jews and posterity.

PURPOSE AND THEME

The aim of 2 Kings is to record the history of the Jewish people from the deaths of Ahab and Jehoshaphat to the Babylonian Captivity and a few years beyond the Captivity. The story at the outset of 2 Kings commences about the ninth century B.C. and it carries on through and beyond the Captivity of 586 B.C. The great cry of the Old Testament—that those who obey God and His Covenant (Exodus 19:5, 24:3-8) have His blessing and those who disobey have His wrath—is clearly seen in 2 Kings, especially in chapters 17-23. This principle is dramatically and historically illustrated in the fall of Israel at the hands of Assyria (2 Kings 17) and of Judah at the hands of Babylon (2 Kings 25). Thus 1 and 2 Kings convey the same message, that man's rebellious act results in God's punishing act.

OUTLINE

Elisha the Prophet Succeeds Elijah
(chapters 1-13)
   Elisha succeeds Elijah after His Translation to Heaven (chapters 1-2)
   Elisha Predicts Victory over Moab
(chapter 3)
   Elisha Performs Miracles: Widow's Oil, Son of the Shunammite Raised from the

Dead, Naaman's Leprosy Cured, Axe Head Floats on Water (chapters 4:1-6:7)
Ben-hadad Besieges Samaria (chapter 6)
Syrian Army Flees (chapter 7)
Hazael Becomes King of Syria (chapter 8)
Jehu Made King of Israel, Kills Jezebel and Others (chapter 9)
Jehu Executes the Sons of Ahab and Wipes Out the Worship of Baal (chapter 10)
Elisha's Death (chapter 13)

"Elisha Makes an Axe Head Float" by Rembrandt. Bredius Museum, The Hague. Elisha recovered a borrowed axe for a woodsman by causing it to rise to the water's surface.

John Fletcher's Miracle-filled Life

by
Anna Talbot McPherson

The life of John Fletcher, like that of the prophet Elisha, was miracle-filled. Their careers were similar from the time each man entered upon his ministry; indeed, each of these stalwarts experienced many elements of the miraculous before his full-fledged ministry began. Thereafter, it can be said of Fletcher and Elisha as it was of Jesus, "He went about doing good." Their lives were spent for others, with little or no regard for their own personal comfort or convenience. Anna Talbot McPherson tells the story of John Fletcher's life in "More Like an Angel than a Man," a chapter from her book, *Spiritual Secrets of Famous Christians* (© 1964 by Zondervan Publishing House, Grand Rapids, Michigan). It has vital meaning for today.

A PILGRIM IN THIS WORLD

JOHN FLETCHER laid down the letter, and pulled his chair up to the breakfast table. Then he addressed the maid.

"My tea, please," he said.

Tapping his fingers nervously on the cloth-covered board, he immediately lost himself in pondering this disconcerting missive from his home town in Switzerland, which the postman had just delivered. For disconcerting it was!

He was well aware that his parents disapproved of his going into the army. But this venture of his was not "going into the army" in the strict sense of the word. He merely had accepted a captain's commission and had engaged to serve the King of Portugal on board a man-of-war which was at that moment making ready with all speed to sail out of Lisbon's harbor to Brazil. The money he had asked his parents to send he had not intended merely for himself. He had felt sure he could invest it to "vast advantage" in this new country to which he was going, and his parents as well as he would profit greatly thereby.

But they had refused.

Well, he would proceed anyway. He had no doubt that his parents' objection was based on their belief that he ought to give himself to the ministry. He had believed the same thing intermittently since he was seven years old. But though he would never so much as entertain the thought of fighting against a call of God, he felt now that the prospect of preaching the Gospel could never be his. Why, he was miserably lacking in the state of heart commensurate to the minister of the Gospel! Definitely unqualified for so high and holy a calling!

At this moment the maid approached with the teakettle, and John was recalled from his disturbing reflection. She was hurrying. He was glad of that. If he did not soon betake himself to the wharf, the boat would be off without him!

"Here," he offered politely, holding his cup so that the pouring could be more quickly dispatched.

But just at that instant the teakettle slipped from the servant's hands, and a seething swash of boiling hot water scalded the young man's leg from his hip to his toe!

Just as quickly as that were the plans of the

youth dashed to pieces, and he was in bed days on end bemoaning his lot. But when, in due time, he learned that the ship on which he was to have sailed perished at sea, his thoughts took a different turn. Why, just why, had his life thus been mercifully saved again?

For this was not the first time John Fletcher had been miraculously preserved from almost certain death. While fencing with his brother when just a lad, he had received an abdominal wound so deep that he carried the scar to his grave; again he fell from a wall so high that death would have been his certain plight had he not providentially landed in a quantity of freshly-mixed mortar; three times he had nearly drowned, once having been pinned under a building for twenty minutes. Of this latter experience, John Wesley remarked later, "Some will say, 'Why this was a miracle!' Undoubtedly it was. It was not a natural event, but a work wrought above the power of nature, probably by the ministry of angels."

Baffled as he now was in every attempt to become a soldier, John gave up his aspirations in that field. Having then no business to engage him, he made his way to London, here to study the English language. Later he was to serve as tutor in the houshold of a Mr. Hill at Ternhall, Shropshire.

All this time, John had the fear of God deeply rooted in his heart, but there was no one to take him by the hand and lead him forward in the things of the Spirit. Indeed, being naturally one of genteel behavior, and eminently sweet-tempered, he had never become aware of his own inward heart need until one Sunday evening when a servant entered his room to replenish his fire. John was writing music in preparation for the next day's duties in the classroom

"Sir," said the servant with kindly but serious concern, "I am sorry to see you so employed on the Lord's Day."

John made no answer, though at first his pride had risen in indignation and resentment that he should have been reprimanded by a servant. Then upon reflection he realized that the reproof had been just. So he immediately put away his music, to become a strict observer of the Lord's Day from that very hour.

He was ever known to aspire after rectitude, and as being anxious to possess every moral perfection. Such a soul God did not leave to grope in darkness very long. When Mr. Hill went to London to attend the Parliament, he took his family and the young tutor with him. While they stopped at St. Albans, John walked out into the town and did not return until the others had set out again for London. A horse had been left for him, however, and he overtook the party in the evening.

"We waited for you as long as we dared," apologized Mr. Hill. "Was it anything serious that detained you?"

"Nothing serious, no," John returned, "and I regret my causing you concern. But as I was walking, I met with a poor woman, who talked so sweetly of Jesus Christ, that I knew not how the time passed away."

"So?" queried Mrs. Hill pleasantly, then continued, "I shall wonder if our tutor does not turn Methodist by and by."

"Methodist, madam?" questioned John vaguely. "What is that?"

"Why," replied she, "the Methodists are a people that do nothing but pray; they are praying all day and all night."

"Are they?" exclaimed John. "Then by the help of God, I will find them, if they be above ground."

He did find them not long afterward, and was admitted into the society. Encouraged and inspired by these people of God, John entered into the experimental knowledge of salvation for which his heart had so long hungered. From this time his hopes and fears, his desires and pursuits, were totally changed. He walked cheerfully as well as valiantly in the ways of God, taking up his cross daily.

It was not long after John Fletcher "felt the powers of the world to come" that he found within his being an earnest longing

"To pluck poor brands out of the fire,
To snatch them from the verge of hell."

Thus, even a considerable time before he was admitted into holy orders, he began exhorting sinners to righteousness with such unspeakably tender affection that multitudes were drawn to hear him. And by the blessing of God his words made so deep an impression on their hearts that very few went away empty.

In 1757 John Fletcher dedicated himself to the work of the holy ministry.

He continued in London, assisting John and Charles Wesley and preaching wherever he had a call; then, in 1760, he was given the vicarage of Madeley. Here he was to stand forth as a preacher of righteousness and as a burning and shining light for the next twenty-five years.

Entering upon his ministry with an extraordinary degree of earnestness and zeal, he instructed the ignorant, reasoned with gainsayers, exhorted the immoral, and rebuked the obstinate. He had a most resolute courage in reproving evil. It is well known that, to daring sinners, he was a "son of thunder." In season, out of season, he diligently performed the work of an evangelist. He spoke as in the presence of God, and taught as one having "Divine authority." Said one, "Without aiming at sublimity, he was truly sublime; his . . . word soared on eagles' flight above humanity. In short, his preaching was apostolic."

Like the vigilant pastor he was, he daily acquainted himself with the needs of the people, anxiously watching over their households, and diligently teaching them from family to family. Esteeming no man too mean, too ignorant, or too profane to merit his affectionate attention, he condescended to the lowest and most unworthy of his flock, cheerfully becoming the servant of all.

If a knock came at his door, though in the depth of the coldest winter night, his window was thrown open in a moment. As soon as he learned that someone had been hurt in a mine pit or that a neighbor was near death, he hastened to the suffering one without any thought for the darkness of the night or the sharpness of the cold.

When some excused themselves from attending the services by saying that they could not awaken early enough to get their families ready, John Fletcher himself took a bell in his hand and set out at five o'clock every Sunday morning. On foot he made his rounds, even to the most distant points of his parish, in-

viting all the inhabitants to the house of God.

His heart went out to other sheep also. To a little society which he had gathered about six miles from Madeley, he preached two or three times a week, beginning at five in the morning. For many years he preached regularly at places eight, ten, or sixteen miles away, returning the same night, though he seldom reached home before one or two in the morning.

The parish of Madeley being of some size, it abounded with people who, either through infirmity or misfortune, were reduced to a state of poverty and distress. Over this despised and destitute part of his flock Fletcher watched with unusual solicitude. Not content with offering them the consolations of the Gospel, he contributed largely to the relief of their temporal needs, and divided among them the greater part of his income. The profusion of his charity constantly emptied his purse, frequently unfurnished his house, and sometimes left him destitute of the most common essentials of life.

Once a poor, God-fearing man fell into great difficulty. Fletcher's heart went out to him at once. He took down all the pewter from the kitchen shelves and thrust it into the man's arms. "Here, take this," he insisted. "It will help you, and I can do without it; a wooden trencher will serve me just as well."

It was no wonder then that Fletcher's selfless ministry, to which he gave himself early and late, in foul weather and fair, in heat and cold, rain and snow aggravated his tendency toward a consumptive disorder which he had battled for some time. His weakened constitution was still more seriously impaired by his intense and uninterrupted studies and writing, over which he pored at times for fourteen, fifteen or sixteen hours a day, almost without intermission, allowing himself only a little bread and cheese or fruit, two or three times in twenty-four hours. Then sometimes, being too absorbed in his work to stop even long enough for these light refreshments, he would merely take a drink of milk and write on again.

From Fletcher's pen came many valuable works on controversial and spiritual subjects, but the toll was paid in a complete breakdown of health which kept him on the brink of eternity for his remaining fourteen years.

When he began to realize the precariousness of his physical condition, he said "O how life goes! I walked, now I gallop into eternity. The bowl of life goes rapidly down the steep hill of time. Let us be wise: embrace we Jesus and the resurrection. Let us trim our lamps and continue to give ourselves to Him that bought us, till we can do it without reserve."

In the latter end of this same year, he said to Charles Wesley, "Old age comes faster upon me than upon you. I am already so grayheaded that I wrote to my brother to know if I am not fifty-six instead of forty-six."

Thinking that a change of air and climate might benefit his health, Fletcher made several excursions to the continent. On one occasion, as he was passing through southern France, he expressed a longing desire to visit the Protestants in the Sevennes Mountains, whose fathers had suffered so greatly in the cause of godliness. Though the journey proved long and difficult, yet he could not be prevailed upon to give up his resolution to try it on foot.

He said to a friend, "Shall I make a visit on horseback and at ease, to those poor cottagers, whose fathers were hunted along yonder rocks like partridges along the mountains? No. In order to secure a more friendly reception among them, I will visit them under the plainest appearance, and with my staff in my hand."

So thoroughly did he make himself a blessing and inspiration to one family under whose roof he spent the night, that the villager told the story to his neighbor the next day. "And to think," he concluded almost fearfully, "I nearly refused to take a stranger into my house—a stranger more like an angel than a man!"

While traveling through a part of Italy, Fletcher directed the driver to stop before he entered upon the Appian Way. He then ordered the chaise door to be opened, assuring his fellow-traveler that his heart would not permit him to ride over that ground upon which the Apostle Paul had formerly walked, chained to a soldier because he had preached the everlasting Gospel.

As soon then as Fletcher set his foot upon this old Roman road, he took off his hat, and walking on with his eyes lifted up to heaven, returned thanks to God in a most fervent manner for that light, those truths, and that influence of the Holy Spirit which had continued to that time because of the apostle's faithfulness.

In his home town of Nyon, Switzerland, Fletcher preached many times to multitudes who flocked from all quarters to hear him. Among others, a good old minister past seventy years of age heard him gladly and earnestly entreated him to lengthen out his visit to their village that they might hear more of the glorious Gospel from his lips. When the old man found that his desire could not conveniently be granted, he wept unashamedly. Turning to Fletcher's fellow-traveler, he exclaimed, "O sir, how unfortunate for this country! During my day it has produced but one angel of a man, and it is our lot to be deprived of *him!*"

Recovering his health to some degree while in Switzerland, Fletcher used his strength as fast as he gained it, and the stronger he became the oftener he preached. His ministry, however, was not confined to the churches. Upon one of his morning walks, he saw a great crowd gathered at the door of a house.

"What does this mean?" he asked a bystander.

"Why," was the reply, "a poor woman and her babe lie dying within."

Fletcher made his way through the curious number to the bedside of the stricken. Death, indeed, appeared to be very near. The minister of God addressed the people standing about concerning the imminence of eternity, the need of a Savior, and His sufficiency for the soul's need. Said he, "He is able to save you all from sin, as well as to save this mother and infant from death. Come, let us ask Him to save both us and them."

While Fletcher prayed as only he could pray, the child's convulsions ceased, and the mother received healing and strength. The people were utterly amazed. They stood speechless, almost senseless! When they finally came to themselves, the man of God was gone.

"Who could it have been?" they asked one another, increduously.

There was a general shaking of heads. No one knew. Then a voice ventured, hushed and reverent, "Certainly, my friends, it was no man. Certainly . . . it was an angel!"

In all his travels, including several itineraries in company with John Wesley, Fletcher missed no opportunity of buying up proper occasions to speak of heavenly things.

Visiting at times Lady Huntingdon's Seminary at Trevecca, to whose superintendency the Countess had appointed him, his challenges to holy living so inspired the students that he was loved and revered like Elijah in the schools of the prophets. His whole conversation was in heaven. The result was that his listeners seldom listened long before they were all in tears, and every heart had caught fire from the flame that burned in his soul.

He was indeed a pilgrim in this world, so much so that he was unallured by its smiles, unmoved by its frowns. While thousands and ten thousands were contending around him for the advantages and honors of the present life, he desired to pass unnoticed through its "idle hurry," without being entangled in its concerns or encumbered with its gifts. . . .

As death approached in his fifty-sixth year, Fletcher's silent meditations were frequently accompanied with so much visible delight. Such an ecstatic glow diffused itself over his whole countenance, and his eye was directed upward with a look of such inexpressible sweetness, that one would almost have supposed him to be conversing with angelic spirits about his approaching entrance into heaven and the glory that should follow.

Once in particular the man of God was so filled with the love of the Most High that he could contain no more, but cried out, "O my God, withhold Thy hand, or the vessel will burst." But he afterward told a friend he was afraid he had grieved the Spirit of God, and that he ought rather to have "prayed that the Lord would have enlarged the vessel, or have suffered it to break, that the soul might have had no further bar or interruption to its enjoyment of the Supreme Good."

Perhaps remembering this, he continually admonished his brethren at Madeley to seek the fullness of the pure love of God in their hearts. Said he, "Let not a drop satisfy you: *desire an ocean!*"

It was just such an ocean that from the heart of John Fletcher overflowed to water the thirsty ground wherever he went and made him the seraphic minister of Jesus Christ he was. It must have been for this that God had miraculously pulled him from the jaws of death so many times, and to make of him a man after His own heart—yet indeed, as the French peasant had aptly said, "more like an angel than a man!"

A King, A Prophet, A People

THE LAD JEHOASH WAS MADE KING when he was seven years old, and he occupied the throne of Judah for forty years. In the early days he was the symbol of the restoration of the true order, and the government of the people was really in the hands of the priest Jehoiada. As the years passed on, the responsibility necessarily devolved upon the king himself, but he had the great advantage of the friendship and guidance of the priest of God. So long as this continued, he did that which was right. . . .

During this period the Temple was rebuilt. In order to accomplish this, there was first the correction of official abuses and then the institution of a voluntary system of giving. These reforms, however, were not complete. . . . The story of the good in this reign is the story of the power behind the throne.

The king himself was not a strong personality, but under the influence of a good man his actions were right. When that influence was removed, the weakness of the man was manifested in the craven cowardice which, in an hour of threatened invasion by Hazael, gave up all the vessels and treasures of the House of God to secure safety.

Men naturally weak prove their wisdom when they consent to be guided by some other person of a stronger personality. The trouble, too often, is that weak men are too proud to do anything of the kind. Perhaps we can pray no more important prayer than that God will teach us our weakness and make us willing to seek the help of those who are stronger. . . .

Amos, by contrast, was a naturally strong personality. He was a man of Judah whom God sent to prophesy in Israel. Although he was no prophet, in the technical sense, nor the son of a prophet—that is, he had no training in the schools of the prophets—Amos, nevertheless, was a veritable prophet of God.

His outlook upon the the Divine government was of the widest. He saw God judging, not Judah and Israel only, but all the nations. . . . The truth thus emphasized with reference to all the nations is that of the Divine patience and justice. . . . —G. Campbell Morgan, *Searchlights from the Word*

1

JEHOASH, THE BOY KING

THE SHADOW OF JEZEBEL fell across the land of Judah when her daughter Athaliah usurped the throne and reigned over the people for six years. She had seen three generations of kings come and go since marrying Jehoram, son of King Jehoshaphat. After the death of her husband, her son, Ahaziah, ruled over the land.

When Ahaziah died, Athaliah saw a golden opportunity for herself to become queen of Judah. However, there were obstacles in the path to the fulfillment of her aspirations: her son's young princes! Cruel, brutal, vicious Athaliah proved to be even more wicked than her infamous mother, Jezebel. Word of Athaliah's decision to murder all of her grandchildren spread quickly throughout Jerusalem. When the news of this planned atrocity reached the ears of Jehosheba, the children's aunt, she was determined to try to thwart the inhuman plan.

Alas! Poor Jehosheba reached the palace too late. Athaliah had already begun the gruesome massacre of her grandchildren. However, in her feverish haste to finish her cold-blooded, heartless task, she failed to see Jehosheba pick up the youngest prince and take him and his nurse to the safety of the Temple. Jehoiada, Jehosheba's husband and High Priest of the Temple, joined with her in rejoicing because the life of one of the princes had been saved.

Athaliah took her place as reigning queen of Judah. Because of her power and the merciless manner by which she seized the throne, many of the people rallied behind her. The queen's burning desire to establish Baal-worship in the land was crowned with success. Idols of Baal were placed in all the cities; a temple of Baal was built in the heart of Jerusalem. Audacious Athaliah then actually took some of the treasures from the Lord's Temple and put them in Baal's temple.

Prince Jehoash (Joash) remained hidden in the Temple chambers for six years. His presence there was a well-kept and well-guarded secret. During these years, the young prince was carefully tutored by his uncle Jehoiada about the Lord God of Abraham, Isaac, and Jacob. He was taught the meaning of the Mosaic laws and the laws of the Ark of the Covenant. The High Priest had done everything possible to prepare Jehoash for the day when he would take his rightful place on the throne of Judah.

Jehoiada had laid his plans well for the overthrow of Athaliah. After gaining the support of the palace and Temple guards, he had secretly organized the growing number of malcontents who were opposed to the queen and her policies. They were prepared to swoop down on Jerusalem at a moment's notice. With no assigned territory of their own, the Levites had increasingly infiltrated Jerusalem and had gone to the Temple to offer their support in the revolt against the queen. Jehoiada promptly accepted their offer and armed them with weapons that David had stored in the Temple centuries before.

Jehoash was seven years old, and the time for action had come. The palace guards silently left their posts, leaving the queen defenseless, and converged on the

Temple and its grounds. When everyone was in his place, Jehoiada brought out Jehoash, anointed him, and crowned him king.

Queen Athaliah was startled when she heard the tumult, the shouting, and the blaring of the trumpets. She called for her guards—but no one came! She rushed out of the palace toward the scene of action. As she drew nearer, she could make out the words of the exuberant, shouting crowd: "Long live the king! Long live King Jehoash!"

Athaliah's heart skipped a beat when she heard those awesome words. Determined to brazen through this unexpected development, she came to the Temple court and screamed out: "Treason! Treason! All of you have committed treason!"

Jehoiada, speaking for the defiant crowd, turned to the ex-queen and said: "No, Athaliah. It is not the people who have committed treason, it is you. The real treason against the throne of David took place that day when you killed your innocent grandchildren. As you have lived, so now shall you die."

Two guards escorted Athaliah from the Temple and, as they neared the palace grounds, executed her with their swords. When that wicked woman died, the fall of the House of Ahab was completed.

The guards returned to the Temple and a procession was formed. Then the young king was taken to the palace and set upon the throne. Jehoash's uncle Jehoiada, his guardian and regent for the kingdom, sat beside him.

Throughout the lifetime of Jehoiada, Jehoash did what was right in the sight of the Lord. Immediately after his corona-

tion, a covenant was made between the king, the High Priest, and the people that all Judah would belong to the one true God of Israel. The next right thing that Jehoash did was to order the house of Baal destroyed, the priest of Baal executed, and the treasures taken by Athaliah restored to the Lord's Temple.

The third right thing that required the immediate attention of Jehoash and Jehoiada was the restoration of the Lord's Temple. How sadly different the run-down Temple was now from what it had been in the glorious days of King Solomon! Even worse than the neglect of the Temple was the people's neglect to bring in their tithes and offerings. The pressing need was for money to pay the carpenters, masons, and iron and brass workers, so Jehoash called the priests and the Levites to the palace.

"The Lord's Temple badly needs to be repaired, but the treasury is empty," he told them. "Therefore, you must conduct a building fund campaign. Go the length and breadth of Judah and urge the people to obey the commandment of Moses and bring their tithes and offerings to the Temple."

The young king soon realized that his voluntary contribution method would be unsuccessful. So he called the princes of all the cities to the palace and spoke to them.

"Money for the repair of the Temple is not coming in fast enough," he said. "I have, therefore, this day issued a royal decree that all the people bring their tithes and offerings to Jerusalem and put the money in a chest that I have placed near the entrance to the Temple. I shall hold each of you responsible for the obedience of this decree by those under your jurisdiction."

The money poured in! There were many days when Jehoash and Jehoiada had to empty the chest several times. Work on

"Athaliah's Arrest" by V. De Brožick. *Biblia Sacra.* Athaliah went to Jehoiada and the newly-crowned king, Jehoash, crying, "Treason." She received no support from her guards, and was led away to be executed.   Lemercier and Co. Paris

the restoration of the Temple proceeded rapidly. Soon, it was ready to be rededicated to the Lord.

During all the days of Jehoiada, the people came to the Temple regularly and offered burnt sacrifices to the Lord. But the High Priest was growing old, and his days on earth would soon end. When Jehoiada died, he was buried in Jerusalem among the kings, because of his good works for the Lord and for His house.

After the loss of his staunch friend and loyal advisor, King Jehoash changed completely. Some of the princes of Judah, who at heart had remained loyal worshipers of Baal, persuaded the king to leave the Lord God of his fathers and to re-establish the worship of Baal throughout the land. Poor weak, unstable Jehoash! How quickly he had yielded to the subtle flattery of the princes!

Baal-worship again ran rampant in Judah. The Lord sent prophet after prophet to warn the king and his people of the consequences of their evil acts, but they paid no attention.

Conditions finally became so bad that the High Priest himself—Jehoiada's son, Zechariah—stood boldly before the king and cried out: "Why do you sin against the Lord and break His commandment? Because you have forsaken the Lord, He has forsaken you!"

The people rose against the brave prophet and demanded that the king order him to be put to death. What an ingrate Jehoash turned out to be! The king, who owed his own life to the house of Jehoiada, yielded to the pressure of the mob and ordered Zechariah to be stoned to death.

Following this wicked deed, troubles came thick and fast to the king and his people. The Syrians invaded Judah and killed the princes of all the cities. Then they looted and plundered the land and sent great riches and treasure to Damascus. When the Syrians departed, they left the king seriously ill and the people in great distress. The nation no longer loved and respected Jehoash, so a conspiracy was formed against him. His own servants assassinated him as he lay upon his bed.

Jehoash, who reigned over Judah for forty years, was buried in the city of David but not among the kings, because he had the blood of the son of Jehoiada on his hands.

Amaziah was twenty-five years old when he succeeded his father, and he reigned for twenty-nine years.

Based on the story in the Bible:
2 Kings 11:1—12:21,
2 Chronicles 22:10—24:27

2

AMOS, THE HERDSMAN OF TEKOA

IN OBEDIENCE TO THE COMMAND of the Lord, Amos, with his blazing eyes and powerful voice, came striding out of the wilderness of Tekoa to warn the people of Israel of their impending doom. King Jeroboam II sat on the throne of Israel when this rugged herdsman from Judah made his appearance in the Northern Kingdom.

Amos wasted no time when he arrived at Samaria. He began to proclaim his messages, and large crowds gathered around him and listened with eager interest. At first the people were pleased at the fierce predictions that he made, because all his words were in condemnation of the wickedness of their enemies, the people of Syria, Philistia, Tyre, Edom, and Moab. It was good to hear woes pronounced against these nations.

The people of Israel soon were stunned and startled. Amos was directing his words to them, their sins, and their punishment.

"Listen, O people of Israel," he called out, "to this word that the Lord has spoken against you: 'I brought you up from the land of Egypt and only you have I known among all the nations of the earth. I shall therefore punish you for all your sins.'"

Again and again Amos cried out his message of warning and the Lord's verdict of doom to the land of Israel.

"Woe to those who live a life of ease and luxury in Zion!" he proclaimed. "Woe to those who lie upon beds of ivory and stretch out upon couches of silk; to those who sing and dance and listen to soft music; to those who eat the best food and drink the finest wine from goblets of gold! Woe and double woe to you, because the Lord has declared that you will be the

"Amos" by J. James Tissot. The Old Testament, Illustrated. The herdsman Amos prophesied the conquest of Israel because of the wickedness of her people.   M. de Buffan and Co.

first of those who will be taken into captivity!"

One day while he was in Bethel, the clarion voice of Amos once more rang out across the land: "Listen to the word of the Lord! Jeroboam shall be killed by a sword, and Israel shall be conquered and taken into captivity far beyond the borders of Damascus."

When Amaziah heard this prophecy, he hurriedly sent a message to Jeroboam: "Amos is here and has conspired against you. He is foretelling your death and the conquest of Israel. The people are becoming restless and cannot bear his dire predictions much longer."

Jeroboam must have given Amaziah authority to order Amos out of the country, because the priest of the golden calf of Bethel went to the herdsman from Tekoa and said, "Go back to Judah and prophesy there! You must never again prophesy at Bethel, because it is one of the temple cities of the kingdom."

Amos answered calmly, "I am neither a prophet nor the son of a prophet. I am a herdsman and a fruitpicker. But one day the voice of the Lord came to me as I followed my flock and said to me, 'Go to My people in Israel and prophesy to them the things I shall reveal to you.'"

Amos was growing old now and his voice was no longer vociferous, but he had another fiery message for the people:

"The wrath of the Lord is upon you because you have not heeded His words. Your cities will destroyed and you will be carried to far away places and scattered over the face of the earth. None shall escape the anger of the Lord. He will search you out on the highest mountain and in the deepest pit and will slay you. Even those who are carried into exile will be killed; but the Lord God will not completely destroy His people. The purge will continue until all the sinners among His people have been utterly destroyed.

"When the day comes that His people no longer do evil, the Lord will lead them out of exile. Cities will be rebuilt and the Temple will be restored. Gardens and vineyards will be planted and they will enjoy the fruits of their labors. Israel will again be firmly established on the land that the Lord promised Abraham, Isaac, and Jacob, and never again will it be taken away from His people."

On that hopeful note, Amos left Israel to its certain fate and returned to Tekoa to live the remainder of his life in peace and quiet.

Based on the story in the Bible:
Amos 1:1 — 9:15

3
ISRAEL FALLS TO THE ASSYRIANS

URING THE LATTER YEARS of the reign of Jeroboam II, another prophet rose up to warn the king and the people that time was running out for Israel. His name was Hosea, and the Northern Kingdom was his native land. Unlike Amos, with his thunderous voice of doom, Hosea faithfully reported the words of the Lord in a pleading, compassionate voice.

During the reign of King Pekah, Israel was invaded by Tiglath-pileser, king of Assyria and, just as Amos had predicted, the idle and the wealthy were the first to be captured and carried into captivity. In addition to the loss of his people, Pekah was forced to pay yearly tribute to the Assyrian king.

King Hoshea now sat upon the throne of Israel and he was faced with many problems. Shortly after his successful revolution and the slaughter of Pekah and his followers, the reigning king of Assyria, Shalmaneser, had promptly notified Hoshea, that despite a change in the regime, the agreement between Israel and his country must continue to be honored.

In spite of the fact that Assyria had grown into a powerful, warlike nation, Hoshea decided to stop paying the burdensome, humiliating tribute and to try to form an alliance with the king of Egypt. When the king of Assyria learned of Hoshea's treachery, he had him arrested and thrown into prison. He then invaded Israel in force and laid siege to its capital city.

Although their king was gone, the people of the Northern Kingdom put up a terrific fight to keep their nation free. For three long years, the Israelites withstood the siege of Samaria. However, they had no prophet like Elisha with them this

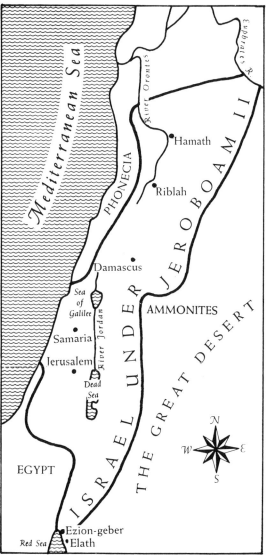

Israel under Jeroboam II (786-746 B.C.). Jeroboam recovered territory, as well as cities, from the Syrians for Israel.

time, and the Lord had plainly spoken when He told them: "I am no longer your God, and you are no longer My people."

Eventually the day came when the soldiers and the people realized that the siege could not be broken. A white flag was run up and the gates of Samaria, closed so long, were creakingly opened. Sargon, who had succeeded Shalmaneser as king of Assyria during the siege, led his victorious army through the gates and accepted the surrender of Israel.

Panic and despair filled the land when the people learned that deportation to foreign lands was to be their fate. The ringing words of Amos flooded their memories when King Sargon separated them into small groups and led them across the Jordan for the last time. Upon their arrival in Assyria, the king would send them far away from one another and they would soon be assimilated by the cities and districts where they lived.

The Kingdom of Israel, set up by Jeroboam I, faded into history and the Ten Tribes of the Northern Kingdom are never heard of again.

Based on the story in the Bible: Hosea 1:1; 2 Kings 15:27-31, 17:1-6

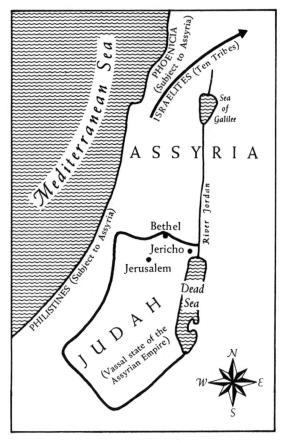

Israel Falls to the Assyrians. In 722 B.C., after the fall of Samaria, the Kingdom of Israel surrendered to the Assyrian king, Sargon II, and her people were carried into captivity. These events had been foretold by the prophets, Amos and Hosea.

PLACES
in Stories of A King, A Prophet, A People

TEKOA

Six miles southeast of Bethlehem and about 12 miles south of Jerusalem is the town of Tekoa. Amos was born here.

SAMARIA

Amos spent much of his time in and about this capital city prophesying to the king and to the people. The fall of this city to the As-syrians in 722 B.C. marked the end of the Kingdom of Israel.

BETHEL

Near the southern border of Israel is Bethel, one of the temple cities that Jeroboam I established early in his reign. Amos and Amaziah met here and the high priest of the golden calf told the prophet to go back to Judah.

Ruins at Tekoa. Amos, the prophet, was born at Tekoa. The town was located in the stony Tekoa wilderness, which is a few miles southeast of Bethlehem. A many-sided baptismal font may still be seen at the site. ©Matson Photo

The Prophets Appear. Hosea and Amos prophesied the punishment of the people and the end of the Kingdom of Israel.

ASSYRIA

This country is east of the middle Tigris, and is bounded on the north by the mountains of Armenia, on the east by the Median mountain ranges, and on the south by the environs of Nineveh. During the period of the Assyrian Empire, this city was its capital, and its territory was extended to reach the Persian Gulf on the south and the Mediterranean on the west. Nineveh was destroyed by the Babylonians and Medes in 612 B.C. and Assyrian power was forever broken.

ASSYRIAN DEPORTATION POLICY

The Assyrian policy to deport captive peoples from their homeland to various new areas was done in order to eliminate the possibility of any future uprising. The Israelites from the Northern Kingdom were taken to the districts of *Halah* and *Gozan* on the banks of the *River Khabur (Harbor),* in faraway northern Mesopotamia.

Ruins of Samaria. Samaria, the capital city of the Kingdom of Israel, withstood many attacks after the time of its founding by Omri. At last, after three years of siege, it yielded to the Assyrians in 722 B.C.   ©Matson Photo

QUESTIONS
on Stories of A King, A Prophet, A People

1

1 What wicked act was it necessary for Athaliah to perform before she could become Queen of Judah? How long did she reign?

2 Who saved the life of Jehoash, the youngest prince? What was her husband Jehoiada's occupation?

3 What did Athaliah do when she learned that Jehoash had been crowned king? What was the former queen's fate?

4 Name three good things that Jehoash did during the early years of his reign.

5 What evil action did Jehoash take after the death of Jehoida, the High Priest?

6 Why did Jehoash order Zechariah, Jehoiada's son, to be stoned to death?

7 How did Jehoash die? Why wasn't he permitted to be buried among the kings?

8 Who was the next king of Judah? How long did he reign?

2

9 Who was king of Israel when Amos appeared on the scene?

10 Why did the people of Samaria listen eagerly at first to the words of Amos?

11 What startling change took place in the prophecies of Amos?

12 What was the main theme of Amos' predictions?

13 Whom did Amos say would be the first to be taken into captivity?

14 What was the message of hope that Amos gave to some of the people of Canaan?

3

15 What was the name of Amos' contemporaneous prophet? Where was his native land?

16 Who was on the throne when Assyria first invaded Israel? What was the result of this invasion?

17 Who was the last king of Israel? What happened to him?

18 How long did Assyria besiege Samaria? Who was king of Assyria when the Northern Kingdom finally surrendered?

19 What was the reaction of the people when they learned that they were to be deported to foreign lands?

20 What eventually happened to the Ten Tribes of the Northern Kingdom?

*Answers are found
on the following pages.*

ANSWERS

on Stories of A King, A Prophet, A People

1

1 It was necessary for Athaliah to eliminate all the rightful heirs to the throne, her son's young princes, before she could become queen. This she did by murdering them. She ruled Judah for six years.

2 Jehosheba, the child's aunt, saved the life of Jehoash. Her husband Jehoiada was the High Priest at the Temple.

3 Athaliah rushed to the Temple Court and accused the people of treason when she learned that Jehoash was king. Two guards led the wicked woman away from the Temple grounds and executed her with their swords.

4 (a) A covenant was made between the king, the High Priest, and the people that all Judah would belong to the one true God of Israel.

(b) Jehoash ordered the house of Baal destroyed, the priest of Baal executed, and the treasures stolen by Athaliah returned to the Lord's Temple.

(c) Jehoash restored the run-down Temple of the Lord to its former brilliance and beauty.

5 Jehoash turned away from the one true God and re-established Baal-worship in Judah.

6 Zechariah criticized the king because he had forsaken the Lord, and warned him that God had forsaken him.

7 Jehoash was murdered in his sleep by his own servants. He was not permitted to be buried among the kings because he had blood from the house of Jehoiada on his hands.

8 Amaziah, the son of Joash, was the next king of Judah. He reigned for twenty-nine years.

2

9 Jeroboam II, the thirteenth king of Israel, was on the throne when Amos came up from Judah.

10 The people of Samaria listened eagerly to Amos because they liked what they heard. It was good to hear woes pronounced against their enemies.

11 Amos suddenly made the people of Israel his target. He condemned them for their sins, and warned them of their impending doom.

12 Amos' main theme was God's certain punishment of His people because of their apostasy.

13 Amos said that the idle and wealthy would be the first to go into captivity.

14 Amos told the Israelites that the Lord would not utterly destroy His people. When the day comes that all the evil ones are eliminated and only the just and righteous remain, the Lord will lead them back to the land that He promised to Abraham, Isaac, and Jacob.

3

15 Amos' contemporary was named Hosea. He prophesied to his own people in his own country, Israel.

16 King Pekah was on the throne of Israel when Assyria first invaded the land. Many idle and wealthy people were taken into captivity.

17 Hoshea was the last king of Israel. He was arrested and thrown into prison because

206

of his treachery against the king of Assyria.

18 Samaria was besieged for three years. Sargon was king of Assyria when Israel finally surrendered.

19 The people of Israel were panic-stricken and in despair when they learned their fate.

20 The Ten Tribes were soon absorbed by the nations into which they were transplanted, and they were never heard of again.

The Wilderness of Tekoa was a rugged, stony, desert area. The town of Tekoa became a fortress, but was reduced to ruins, even though it had a strategic position at the top of a hill. It was the home of Amos.

©Matson Photo

FURTHER FACTS AND OUTLINES

for A King, A Prophet, A People

SECOND KINGS (continued)

AUTHORSHIP AND DATE

See above under *Further Facts and Outline for the Story of Solomon:* First Kings.

DESTINATION

The Jews and posterity.

PURPOSE AND THEME

See above under *Further Facts and Outline for the Story of Elisha:* Second Kings.

OUTLINE

Jehoash Becomes King of Judah, after Seizure of Throne from Athaliah Who Had Usurped It as Queen for Six Years (2 Kings 11 and 2 Chronicles 22:10—23:15)

The Good Reign of Jehoash under Jehoiada's Tutelage: He Destroys Baal-worship, Re-establishes Worship of the Lord, Repairs and Refurnishes the Lord's Temple (2 Kings 12:1-17 and 2 Chronicles 23:16—24:16)

The Downfall of Jehoash: After Jehoiada's Death He Re-establishes Baal-worship and Permits Execution of the High Priest Who Protested, Pays King Hazael of Syria for Protection by Giving Him the Vessels and Treasures from the Lord's House, Then Suffers Defeat by Syria and Death at the Hands of His Own Servants (2 Kings 12 and 2 Chronicles 24:17-27)

The Reign of Amaziah over Judah; The Reigns of Joash and Jeroboam II over Israel (2 Kings 14)

The Reigns of Zachariah, Shallum, Menahem, Pekahiah, and Pekah over Israel (2 Kings 15:3-31)

Assyria Carries the Ten Northern Tribes into Captivity (2 Kings 17:1-6)

"Athaliah and Jehoash" by J. James Tissot. *The Old Testament,* Illustrated. Queen Athaliah was dethroned by Jehoiada and Jehoash, her sole surviving grandson.   M. de Buffan & Co.

AMOS

AUTHORSHIP AND DATE

Amos ("burden")—not to be confused with Isaiah's father Amoz (or Amotz)—lived in the town of Tekoa which was located six miles southeast of Bethlehem and about twelve miles south of Jerusalem. Amos was a sheepherder (1:1) and dresser of sycamore fruit trees (7:14). Sycamore fruit was something like figs and is said to have been eaten only by poor people. Out of this ordinary and everyday work, God called him to be a prophet: ". . . The Lord took me from following the flock, and the Lord said to me, 'Go, prophesy to my people, Israel' " (7:15). He prophesied in the North (Israel) for a short time during the reign of Jeroboam II (785-740 B.C.), and during the time of Uzziah (780-740 B.C.).

DESTINATION

To North Israel, also to Judah in which territory he lived.

PURPOSE AND THEME

God chose Amos to speak a forthright word to Israel. Israel was enjoying a period of prosperity, had forgotten her Covenant relationship with God—indeed had broken her Covenant in awful sinning—and was generally irreligious (5:12). To be sure, there was a lip service kind of worship, but the pattern of daily living made it perfectly clear that worship was quite unconnected with practice (5:21-24). Selfishness, greed, immorality, idolatry, oppression of the poor through extortion, bribery, and injustice (2:6-8)—all these sins and more were committed. Amos cried out for repentance (5:14-15) in the light of the coming doom, and though Assyria is not mentioned specifically, it is clear that the Exile is predicted. But Israel is not grieved, not ready to repent (6:6) and disaster is the inevitable consequence (9:1-8).

Thus one of Amos' purposes is to warn the people. But there is a second purpose—that is, to tell of God's readiness to deliver. Chapter nine speaks of deliverance and in reality includes a promise of Messianic blessing. Ever the theme of the Old Testament prophets, they declare that though people are unfaithful to the Covenant, God remains faithful. Note the emphasis on justice throughout the book.

OUTLINE

Proclamation of Judgment against the Nations (chapters 1-2)
    Superscription (1:1)
    Against Foreign Nations: Damascus, Philistia, Phoenica (Tyre), Edom, Ammon, Moab (1:2-2:3)
    Against the Chosen People: Judah and Israel (2:4-16)
Judgment against Israel (chapters 3-6)
    Israel To Be Punished (chapter 3)
    Israel Has Not Profited from Past Punishments (chapter 4)
    God Laments over Israel, Life Comes from Seeking the Lord (chapter 5)
    Woe to the Unjust (chapter 6)
Five Visions of Coming Judgment (7:1—9:10)
    Vision of Plague of Locusts (7:1-3)
    Vision of Fire (7:4-6)
    Vision of the Plumbline, Historical Materials (7:7-17)
    Vision of the Basket of Summer Fruit (chapter 8)
    Vision of the Destruction of the Temple (9:1-10)
Promise of Messianic Blessing (9:11-15)

Amos: Salvation Army Preacher

by

James Kelso

Amos, the herdsman-prophet, is compared with the Salvation Army preacher by Dr. James Kelso in a chapter from his book, *Archaeology and Our Old Testament Contemporaries* (© 1966 by Zondervan Publishing House, Grand Rapids, Michigan). Dr. Kelso's keen analysis of Amos, and the part he played in warning Israel of the fate awaiting her because of unfaithfulness to God, deserves careful consideration by nations and individuals in today's complex but wonderful world.

THE SHEPHERD HEART

THE SALVATION ARMY is over a hundred years old and still going strong, for it is the one Christian denomination that all the unfortunate of earth can best understand and love. Such a Salvation Army preacher was Amos some 2,700 years ago. He repudiated any prophetic title and thought of himself as an ordinary layman, whose chief business was to work for God. He earned a living by shepherding. Thus he fits the Salvation Army pattern perfectly.

He left us only one sermon, but that one was magnificent and immortal. Seldom will you ever hear as perfect a twenty-minute sermon as this one; and remember that he preached it in poetry, not prose! Although Amos was dealing with the social problems of the mid-eighth century B.C. in Palestine, his presentation of the problem and its solution is far superior to that of most modern speakers. He, like ourselves, was caught in an industrial revolution that all too often ignored God. But, in Amos, God found a spokesman for the new manufacturing age and for ours also.

Some scholars see his book as snatches of various sermonettes blended together, but it is far more reasonable to take the whole book as one single sermon and its political aftermath. This Salvation Army preacher is inseparable from his message. He was a shepherd, and that vocabulary appears everywhere in his preaching. The great out-of-doors was both his home and his vocabulary. He raised a special breed of sheep famous for its wool; this product he sold to the highest bidder.

Bethel was a luxury city which appreciated fine wool and, on this occasion, the city served both as a market for his wool and a pulpit for his sermon. Bethel was located on the great north and south ridge road of western Palestine, which was one of the trade routes that handled commerce between Africa and Asia Minor. Here Amos picked up world news from international traveling men, who are always some of the best judges of political movements. Amos was still better in conversations with God, and God is always the best center for all information.

I spent four summers in the excavations of Bethel and worked in the period of Amos each season. Jeroboam's temple was, of course, the first thing we looked for; and we were still searching for it when we quit work. It eluded us. Most likely it is under the houses of the modern town of Beitin, just north of the two big springs which are the reason for the existence of Bethel. Ancient temples are often built beside springs. Unfortunately, city property is too expensive for excavations.

We did, however, find a mountain top open-air high place where the Canaanite god El was worshipped at least as early as 3500 B.C. It was this god who gave his name to the city. The white limestone ledge was stained in many places with the blood of the animals sacrificed here, preserved by the wet clay in the debris above it. The F.B.I. test for blood was positive on all these dark stains, but the plain white limestone gave no reaction. In the debris above the high place were fragments of many animal bones and hundreds of flints used in butchering these animals. Surgeons at Jerusalem examined these bones but found no sign of human sacrifice here. The debris also contained a great amount of broken pottery from the vessels used to cook the sacrifices and, at one place, the limestone ledge had been calcined [made powdery by action of heat] where they had built their sacrificial fires. It is the Canaanite theology from this old high place that Jeroboam I blended into the Jehovah worship at his Bethel sanctuary.

The great city wall which surrounded the city and was used throughout its history was built shortly after the time of Joseph. It averaged about twelve feet in width and was constructed of massive stones interlocked together. This section of the wall was originally about twenty feet high, and above that rose another ten feet of mud-dried brick. The base of the wall was protected from battering rams by a wide sloping revetment [a facing of concrete or stone].

The only city gate preserved from Amos' time was the north gate. Inside of it was an open area which could be used as a meeting place for the law court. Amos more likely spoke at the west or the south gate. The former is destroyed, down into Canaanite times; but, in the debris outside the gate, was found an inscription from the merchants from the Queen of Sheba. We could not find the south gate dating to the time of Amos, but we did locate the south gate which Christ would have used as He traveled north from Jerusalem to Galilee.

The city was desperately poor in the days of the Judges, but it quickly turned prosperous under David and Solomon and remained so until its destruction by the Assyrians at the time of Samaria's downfall. Some houses, however, lived through that destruction. The most interesting of these had been used and re-used for about three centuries. When its walls were cleared down to the original floor level, they stood about eighteen feet high. Here and there one found a slum dwelling and, at other times, there even appeared something like the header and stretcher walls of the Phoenicians. Most of the homes were built of ordinary field stone. Occasionally, a house wall had been toppled by an earthquake and left just as it fell; a new wall was built beside it.

The normal house plan did not change much after the time of David, except for the tall stone columns used after the days of Solomon. The average room was small and rectangular in shape. The floors were often beaten earth mixed with powdered lime. The same type of floor is common today in poor homes and country school houses. The best houses had flagstone floors.

We found only a few signs of manufacturing, so commerce and cult must have been the secret of the city's wealth. Bethel was the royal shrine, and that insured prosperity. This is the city that Elijah and Elisha and Amos all knew personally. Bethel's history reached from 3500 B.C. to A.D. 800. It is mentioned more often in the Old Testament than any other city except Jerusalem.

In ancient Israel the law court was often held at the city gate or the market place; and, standing at the city gate of Bethel, Amos used the legal pattern of the courtroom as the outline for his sermon. . . .

Amos was a born psychologist. His first problem was to get Israel to condemn herself: "A man convinced against his will is of the same opinion still." So Amos began his message with the theme that God is now ready to judge the Gentile nations. He condemned those nations surrounding Israel: Damascus, for atrocities in war; Gaza, for slave-trading; Tyre, for the same, plus violation of treaty; Edom, for bloody violation of racial ties; Ammon, for crimes against womanhood in war, and Moab, for desecration of the dead. Note the good TV pattern he used—a flash against Damascus to the northeast, then one on Gaza to the southwest. Tyre due north, Edom to the southeast, Ammon to the east and Moab to the southeast. Each flash portrayed an atrocity where Israel had been the victim. Meanwhile, the audience would all be *thinking* "Amen," if not vocalizing it.

Seven is the key item for super-emphasis in Hebrew, so Amos' audience would watch for his climax in the seventh news flash. It was Judah—her sister nation, a people so wicked in the eyes of the northerners that they had been forced to revolt from Jerusalem and establish their own state. In the eyes of Amos, however, Judah's crime was still more heinous for she had violated not only the laws of conscience as had the six Gentile nations but, far more serious, she had blasphemed God. To the audience this was a perfect climax for the first part of a sermon, and they relaxed to get ready for point two.

But Amos startled them with a super-climax, an eighth criminal. That was Israel itself! Amos said to Israel, as Nathan had said to David, "Thou art the man!"

Then quickly, before the audience could recover itself, Amos reviewed how God had wiped out the original Amorite population of Palestine for sins involving the violation of conscience. How much greater would be the doom of Israel which had violated not only the laws of conscience but also the Lord's revelation.

After such a surprising and annihilating attack on church members as Amos had made, his next remarks must of necessity be a compelling indictment of Israel's sin. . . .

"You only have I known of all the families of the earth; therefore I will visit upon you all your iniquities" (Amos 3:2). "The greater the blessing, the greater the guilt." Verses 3-8 that follow are the shepherd's own vivid experiences. Even the trumpet blast in the city was the air-raid siren for the people working in the fields and the desert.

Tekoa, the home town of Amos, literally meant "the alarm trumpet." His literary climax is the "lion's roar." To the shepherd who had intimate experience with the lions, this meant that the king of beasts had already caught his prey and killed it. He was now ready to devour it. Tragic words, indeed, that Israel heard that day in this figure of speech! With God, Israel was already as good as dead, nationally. It only remained for lionhearted Assyria to devour her at his political leisure.

The crimes that had brought Israel her death sentence were:

Violence and robbery in the palaces—sins against conscience.

False worship in the sanctuaries—sins against revelation.

A degenerate womanhood—sins against conscience.

A corrupt church—sins against revelation.

Note the Hebrew climax in a dual repetition: conscience and revelation, conscience and revelation. These were the final steps that had taken Israel down the road to perdition. Violence and robbery in the palaces would correspond to a modern supreme court composed of gangsters. Womanhood was so degenerate that it was actually leading the man into deeper sin. . . .

Quickly, before the audience can reply to this second theme of his sermon, Amos plunges into the third point. First he sings one verse of a funeral song. Next he gives the casualty list from the war. Nine out of every ten of Israel are dead! Then Amos, like a true Salvation Army preacher, makes one last call for repentance. This is not for the doomed nation, as a unit, but for any individuals out of that nation who will return to their Lord and Savior. . . .

Almost in the same breath, Amos concludes his sermon by pronouncing God's judgment upon a guilty and unrepenting Israel:

The day of the Lord, which Israel would expect to bring blessing to her, shall bring inescapable doom.

The Israel of Palestine shall suffer the same judgment as the Israel of the Wilderness, for each worshiped the Lord *and* other gods. . . .

This 2,700-year-old sermon is so modern that it needs no further comment. "Let him that hath ears to hear, hear." In American phraseology this means, "He that hears, let him obey!" Obedience is the mark of God's child in all generations.

212

Jonah

NO OTHER PROPHET IN BIBLICAL HISTORY sought so blatantly to thwart the will of God for his ministry. Jonah actually resigned his office as a prophet of the Lord. He had served in that office with good effect while Jeroboam II was king of Israel. Now he determined not to continue in that office any longer. He had received a direct command to go to Nineveh, which lay over land to the northeast. He left his country by water, setting his face west, to a port at the far end of the Great Sea.

What was the reason for his strange conduct? Jonah himself tells it: ". . . For I knew that Thou art a gracious God, and merciful, slow to anger, and of great kindness, and repentest Thee of the evil." (Jonah 4:2) Let these words be most carefully pondered. Jonah fled because he knew God so well. His resignation was not due to ignorance of God, but rather to accurate understanding.

Jonah was commissioned to proceed to Nineveh and to cry out against it because of its great wickedness. He knew that if he did this, and Nineveh should repent, God would spare the city. This was what he did not want God to do. The cruelties of Nineveh had been brutal, and in the heart of Jonah there was no pity for her. He was in complete sympathy with the righteousness of God proceeding to punish the wicked; but he had no sympathy for the Divine compassions. Therefore he fled.

This is a story of breakdown on a high level, but it is breakdown, nonetheless. A passion for righteousness which makes us vindictive and incapable of forgiveness, even in the case of those as cruel as Nineveh, puts us out of fellowship with God. Jonah had the courage of his convictions —and the decency to pay the fare when he ran away!—G. Campbell Morgan, *Searchlights from the Word*

1

JONAH'S FOREIGN MISSION

THE BOOK OF JONAH is a great missionary story. It portrays, vividly and dramatically, some of the leading events in the life of one of God's servants. Jonah, son of Amittai, was born at Gath-hepher in the territory of Zebulun. He lived during the reign of Jeroboam II of Israel, and was the first prophet to be given a foreign assignment.

King Jeroboam of Israel and King Amaziah of Judah watched with increasing concern the growing strength of the mighty Assyrian Empire. Nineveh, its capital city, had expanded so much that it took a person three days to walk from one end of it to the other. The city's increase in size was matched by its increase in sin. Notorious Nineveh soon became widely known as one of the sinful cities of the world.

One night the Lord came to Jonah and said: "Arise, Jonah, and go to Nineveh, that great city, and speak out against it. Its great wickedness needs My special attention."

From the time he received that strange command from the Lord, Jonah's mind was filled with questions. Why should the Lord God of Israel be concerned about people of another land? How could a stranger, especially one from Israel, suddenly appear in a strange city and have the nerve to speak out against it? What if the people *did* repent and God forgave them and did not destroy the city? The prophet and his predictions would then be the laughing-stock of the entire population.

Jonah was on the run—but not northeastward toward Nineveh, as the Lord had commanded. Instead, he hurried westward to the Mediterranean seaport town of Joppa. Jonah had decided not to go to Nineveh and, to make that mission impossible, he planned to board a ship and sail to faraway places.

Jonah's plans went well. When he reached Joppa, a trading vessel was preparing to leave for Tarshish, a Phoenician

Sea Front of Joppa (Jaffa) in Palestine. This ancient city, assigned to the tribe of Dan (Joshua 19:46), was the seaport at which Jonah embarked on a ship for Tarshish in an attempt to escape God's command to go to Nineveh. © Matson Photo

colony in distant Spain. Jonah arranged for his passage aboard the ship and, when it weighed anchor and was sailing on the high seas, he drew a breath of relief and congratulated himself on his success.

Jonah's folly in attempting to escape from the Lord is expressed in some lines taken from a beautiful psalm (Psalm 139:7-12):

"Where shall I hide from Your presence,
    And where shall I flee from Your Spirit?
If I ascend up into heaven, You are there;
    And if I make my bed in Sheol,
    You are there.
If I should take the wings of the morning
    And dwell in the uttermost parts
    of the sea,
Even there Your hand shall lead me

"Jonah Cast into the Sea" by Bartolomeo Bellano. Basilica of St. Anthony, Padua. This sculpture, one of twelve bronze reliefs of Old Testament scenes, dramatically shows Jonah tossed overboard by the sailors to calm the sea. Alinari

And your right hand shall hold me.
If I say, 'Surely darkness shall cover me,
Even the night shall be light
about me'. . . .
The darkness and light are alike to You."

Despite his stubbornness, Jonah was soon to learn that he had no place to hide. Exhausted from the rigors of his hastily prepared journey to Joppa, he went to his cabin and fell fast asleep. Shortly after Jonah went to sleep, the Lord sent a terrible storm upon the sea. Heavy waves crashed against the ship, gale-force winds whistled across its decks, the thunder rolled, the lightning flashed across the sky, and rain came down in torrents.

When the storm grew worse, the ship's captain rushed to Jonah's cabin and in frenzied tones, shouted to his passenger:

"Wake up! A terrible storm has suddenly come upon us. Arise and call upon your God for help. Perhaps He will hear your voice and save our lives."

Jonah arose, but in his heart he knew that it would be futile for him to ask the Lord for help at this time. Despite the prayers and supplications of all aboard the ship to their heathen gods, the storm raged on unabated. Finally the sailors decided to cast lots to determine who was responsible for their predicament. As

Jonah knew it would, the lot fell upon him!

The sailors turned to Jonah and said, "Tell us, please, why this violent storm has come upon us. What shall we do to cause the sea to become calm?"

Jonah answered courageously, "I have offended the Lord my God by disobeying him. You must throw me overboard, and then the sea will become calm."

The sailors, heathen though they were, at first refused to do what Jonah asked. As the storm increased in volume and power, however, they found no alternative to carrying out Jonah's wishes. As soon as Jonah touched the water the storm ceased raging and the angry sea became calm. The astonished sailors hurriedly made a sacrifice to Jonah's God and vowed to worship and serve Him the rest of their lives.

Jonah had ample time for meditation and prayer after he was cast off the ship. The entire second chapter of the Book of Jonah is devoted to a prayer the prophet made while he was inside the great fish that God had prepared to swallow him. After three days and three nights the Lord spoke to the fish, and it threw Jonah up on dry ground.

Based on the story in the Bible:
Jonah 1:1 — 2:10; 2 Kings 14:25

2

JONAH'S SECOND CHANCE

ONAH WAS ON HIS WAY BACK to his home city. His experiences had done nothing to change his mind and heart. He was still the same selfish, nationalistic isolationist. Jonah still did not want to share the Lord God of Israel with any other nation. However, one thing was made crystal clear to him: There was no way to escape the pursuit of the Lord.

A few days after his return to Israel, the Lord came to Jonah a second time and said, "Arise and go to Nineveh, that great city, and preach the words that I shall tell you."

Jonah was obedient this time, but he was far from happy about his mission. When he finally reached the outskirts of Nineveh, the reluctant prophet walked a day's journey into the city. Then he cried out this strange and alarming message: "Within forty days Nineveh shall be destroyed!"

Just as Jonah had feared, instead of being furious at him, the people believed his message. Even the king of Nineveh put aside his royal robes, dressed in sackcloth, and sat in ashes. The king then issued a proclamation:

"Neither man nor beast shall eat any food or drink any water. Every person shall put on sackcloth, sit in ashes, and repent for his wickedness. Let all people turn away from their evil ways and pray earnestly to God. Who knows? Perhaps the Lord God will change His mind and turn His fierce anger away from us!"

Jonah sat outside Nineveh, underneath a small shelter that he had built, watching and waiting. Despite the complete reformation of the people, he was still hopeful that God would destroy the city. As time passed and Nineveh remained standing, Jonah became sulky and angry. Finally he directed these angry words to the Lord:

"O Lord, isn't this what I dreaded from the beginning? Isn't this why I tried to flee to Tarshish? I knew that you are a gracious God, merciful, forgiving, and slow to anger. Now I beg You to take away my

Mounds Covering Ancient Nineveh. In Jonah's time this city on the Tigris River was the capital of the Assyrian Empire. Jonah went there to prophesy its destruction, but the king and the people reformed their ways and were saved.   © Matson Photo

life, for it is better for me to die than to live."

The Lord then asked Jonah, "Is it right for you to be angry because the people have repented and turned away from their wicked ways?"

Jonah did not answer. He remained in his shelter, sullen and surly. That night the Lord caused a gourd vine to spring up to provide additional shelter for His angry prophet. That did not change Jonah's bitter mood, so the Lord sent an insect to injure the vine. It soon withered and died.

The blazing sun and the blistering east wind bore down on Jonah's shelter so strongly that it soon became like a hot oven. Finally the heat was so oppressive that Jonah fainted. When he revived, he again implored God to let him die. Instead of granting this request, the Lord asked Jonah: "Was it right for you to be angry and concerned because the vine withered and died?"

Jonah replied: "Yes, it was right for me to be angry, even as long as I live!"

The Lord then spoke to Jonah for the last time.

"You have shown pity," He said, "for a vine that you neither planted nor helped to grow. It came up in a night and died in a night. Should not I, therefore, show even greater mercy and compassion for these people whom I created? Should not I spare Nineveh, that great city, with over one hundred and twenty thousand children in it who are too young to know their right hand from their left? Should I destroy the cattle and other animals there, beasts that have committed no sin?"

The story of Jonah ends abruptly at this point, and Jonah fades into history. Whatever became of this reluctant prophet is unknown, but the message from his story is known and has come ringing down the centuries. The Lord wants it clearly understood that He is not the God of only

"The Prophet Jonah" by Michelangelo. Sistine Chapel, Rome. Michelangelo used the vaults of the ceiling of this chapel to portray the Prophets and Sibyls. The fresco of Jonah is considered by many to be the finest of these figures.   Alinari

one nation and only one race, but that He is the Lord God of all nations and all races, and that it is the responsibility and duty of those who know and serve the one true God to spread that knowledge and His message throughout the world.

Based on the story in the Bible:
Jonah 3:1 — 4:11

PLACES
in the Story of Jonah

GATH-HEPHER
Located near the eastern border of Zebulun and about 14 miles west of the Sea of Galilee is the city of Gath-hepher, the birthplace of Jonah.

JOPPA
Joppa is a Mediterranean seacoast town in the territory assigned to, but never controlled by, the Tribe of Dan. From this seaport Jonah boarded a ship in his abortive flight from the Lord.

TARSHISH
Near the Rock of Gibraltar on the southern coast of Spain, some 2,000 miles from Joppa, is found the Phoenician colony of Tarshish. It was in this far distant land that Jonah hoped to find a hiding place.

NINEVEH
The great capital of the Assyrian Empire was located on the east bank of the Tigris River. On a direct route, it was between 500 and 600 miles northeast of the capital city of Israel. This was the city to which the Lord sent Jonah to warn the people of their impending doom.

Reputed Tomb of Jonah. About a mile from the modern city of Mosal, Iraq, are the ruins of Nineveh. Among the remains of the city is the Tell Nabi Yunis, on top of which stands a mosque. Inside is the reputed tomb of Jonah.   © Matson Photo

QUESTIONS
on the Story of Jonah

1

1 Where was Jonah born? Who was king of Israel during Jonah's lifetime?

2 What did the Lord tell Jonah to do?

3 Why did Jonah run away from this assignment? Where did he go?

4 What did Jonah do when he reached the Mediterranean seaport town?

5 What happened when the ship that Jonah was on reached the high seas?

6 How was it discovered that Jonah was the man responsible for the storm?

7 What did Jonah tell the sailors to do in order to calm the sea?

8 What did the sailors do when the storm ceased?

9 How was Jonah saved from drowning?

10 How long did Jonah remain inside the great fish?

2

11 What change, if any, came over Jonah as a result of his three-day experience?

12 What lesson did Jonah learn from this experience?

13 How did God give Jonah a second chance?

14 How large a city was Nineveh? How far into the city did Jonah go before he began to proclaim the words of the Lord? What was his message?

15 How did the people of Nineveh react to Jonah's warning? What did the king do when he heard of it?

16 Why was Jonah sitting outside the city underneath a small shelter that he had built?

17 Why did the Lord destroy the vine that He had caused to spring up and furnish more shelter for Jonah?

18 Aside from the repentance of the people, what was one of the main factors that caused the Lord to abandon His plans to destroy Nineveh?

19 What great message comes from the story of Jonah?

20 What is the duty and responsibility of all who know and serve the Lord?

Answers are found on the following page.

ANSWERS

on the Story of Jonah

1

1 Jonah was born at Gath-hepher in the territory of Zebulun. Jeroboam II was the reigning king of Israel during Jonah's lifetime.

2 The Lord told Jonah to go to Nineveh and speak out against the city because of its wickedness.

3 Jonah did not believe that the Lord God of Israel should be concerned about the actions of heathen nations. Jonah fled to Joppa.

4 Jonah arranged for his passage aboard a trading ship that was preparing to sail for Tarshish, in far away Spain.

5 The ship was caught in a gigantic storm.

6 Lots were cast, and the lot fell upon Jonah.

7 Jonah told the sailors to throw him overboard and the sea would then become calm.

8 The sailors made a sacrifice to Jonah's God and vowed to worship and serve Him.

9 God prepared a great fish that swallowed Jonah.

10 Jonah was inside the great fish for three days and three nights.

2

11 No change came over Jonah. He was still the same selfish nationalist.

12 Jonah learned that there was no way to escape from the pursuit of the Lord.

13 God again came to Jonah and told him to go to Nineveh and preach the words that He would tell him.

14 Nineveh was so large that it took a man three days to walk from one side of it to the other. Jonah went about a day's journey inside the city before he began preaching the words of the Lord. His message was that Nineveh would be destroyed in forty days.

15 To Jonah's horror, the people believed his message. They put on sackcloth, sat in ashes, fasted, and repented. The king himself put aside his royal robes, dressed in sackcloth, sat in ashes, and proclaimed a period of national prayer and repentance.

16 Jonah sat outside the city, watching and waiting. He was still hoping that the Lord would destroy this heathen Assyrian city.

17 The additional shelter that the vine provided failed to change Jonah's angry mood.

18 One of the factors that caused the Lord to abandon plans to destroy Nineveh was that there were in the city more than one hundred and twenty thousand innocent children, not old enough to know their right hand from their left.

19 The great message that comes from the story of Jonah is that the Lord is not the God of only one nation and one race, but that He is the Lord God of all nations and all races.

20 The duty and responsibility of all who know and serve the Lord is to help spread His word throughout the world.

FURTHER FACTS AND OUTLINE
for the Story of Jonah

JONAH

AUTHORSHIP AND DATE

Jonah ("a dove"), son of Amittai (1:1), from Gath-hepher in Galilee. The only Old Testament reference to Jonah, outside of the Book of Jonah itself, is in 2 Kings 14:25, which connects him with the days of King Jeroboam II (reigned 785-740 B.C.).

DESTINATION

This is not specifically indicated, but the missionary objective is the city of Nineveh, capital of Assyria.

PURPOSE AND THEME

Jonah is the outstanding missionary book of the Old Testament. It demonstrates God's love for the Gentiles (4:11), a message always difficult for Jews to comprehend, and especially so hundreds of years before Paul, the missionary to the Gentiles. The character of this prophecy is entirely different from the other books of the Prophets; this gives a personal life story with emphasis upon God's dealings with the man, Jonah. The lessons of the book are manifold: when God speaks, answer and follow Him in faith; God wants to show His mercy upon *all* peoples, Gentiles as well as Jews; people—indeed, a great city—can repent when God's appointed servants obey Him. It is of further significance that Jonah's stubbornness characterized the stubbornness of the Israelite nation as a whole. . . . Also note that Jesus referred to the story of Jonah as a figure of His own death and resurrection (Matthew 12:40-41).

OUTLINE

Jonah's Disobedience and Its Results (chapter 1)
Jonah's Prayer in the Fish's Belly (chapter 2)
Jonah's Obedience Results in Deliverance of Thousands from Destruction (chapter 3)
Jonah's Further Chastisement for His Lack of Love for Souls (chapter 4)

"The Prophet Jonah." The Church of Santa Maria del Popolo, Rome. This is the only example in Rome of a sculpture designed by Raphael, who also designed the Chigi Chapel where it is located. Lorenzetto executed the work.   Alinari

223

Jonah: Reluctant Foreign Missionary

by

James Kelso

Prejudice against people of other nationalities and races is not a new trait among men, as Dr. James Kelso clearly illustrates in his vivid portrayal of the life and times of Jonah in a chapter from his book, *Archaeology and Our Old Testament Contemporaries* (© 1966 by Zondervan Publishing House, Grand Rapids, Michigan). The prophet's reluctance to go as a missionary to a hated nation has parallels in today's world. As in Jonah's day, the answer lies in our being willing to love as God loves.

ARCHAEOLOGIST READS BOOK AS FACT

THE BOOK OF JONAH is often interpreted today as if it were fiction, but the archaeologist finds it much easier to read the book as fact. Jonah's home town was Gath-hepher on the hills near Nazareth in Galilee; so, when Jesus refers to Jonah, remember that He had this common geographical missionary homeland.

Ahab, Jezebel, and Elijah formed the dramatic background for Jonah. Ahab was at Ramoth-gilead where every prophet had promised him victory except Micaiah, who predicted the king's death. Ahab was worried by Micaiah's message, so he went into battle in disguise. A chance arrow, however, brought his death as the prophet had promised. Jezebel had an equally dramatic end. She was thrown out of the palace window and trampled to death by Jehu's horses.

The usurper, Jehu, however, was powerless before the great Shalmaneser III, king of Assyria, and he was only too glad to pay the Assyrian tribute and escape with his life. In this invasion, Shalmaneser had come down from Damascus through the Bashan district, plundering, burning, and destroying its "countless cities." He then crossed over the Jordan River at Beth-shean and marched to the Mediterranean, via the plains of Jezreel and Esdraelon.

On the hills above the latter plain, Jonah looked down on the Assyrian soldiers slaughtering the Israelite population and plundering everything in sight. Since Gath-hepher and the other hill cities were on the flanks of the army, they also probably suffered equally with those of the plains. Then Shalmaneser came to Mt. Carmel and carved his inscription of victory on that mountain—the very same Mt. Carmel where the Lord had triumphed over Baal and Jezebel only a few years before!

If you take the book as fact, Jonah's actions are perfectly plain. He himself had been an eyewitness to the horror of an Assyrian invasion. Here are some of the Assyrian inscriptions:

"I crushed the corpses of their warriors in the battle that caused their overthrow. I made their blood to flow over all the ravines and high places of mountains. I cut off their heads and piled them up at the walls of their cities like heaps of grain.

"A pyramid of heads in front of his city I erected. Their young men and women I burned in the bonfire.

"I hung their corpses on gibbets, stripped

off their skins, and therewith covered the wall of the city."

Doubtless some of Jonah's relatives were killed or made prisoners. All the foodstuffs which would keep the remaining Israelite families alive for the next year had been drained off by the enemy. And all this had been done in sight of that very Mt. Carmel where God had justified Elijah!

When God asked Jonah to preach destruction to Nineveh, a key city of Assyria, he refused to go, for he knew only too well that God usually preaches destruction and salvation in the same sermon.

Jonah, therefore, went down to Joppa and set sail for Tarshish, probably on the Atlantic coast of Spain near the mouth of the Guadalquivir River. The length of the voyage, plus the technical Hebrew term for a "decked-over ship" that is used here, means that Jonah was traveling on a large, well-built ship. She may have been powered by sail only; but, on important business, auxiliary oar power was used in calm weather. The ship would carry a large mainmast and small foremast, both using square sails. Great oars mounted over the stern served as rudders.

We can only conjecture the size of Jonah's ship, but the best geographers estimate it to have been about 250 tons. The flagship of Columbus was only 100 tons, and Magellan's was only slightly larger. Vasco de Gama used a ship of 200 tons. A day's sail in antiquity would probably be about 55 nautical miles. The ships of those times were well-built, and they could stand the severe Mediterranean storms, as is shown by the experience of the ship in which Paul sailed. Ezekiel 27:3-9 gives an excellent description of a ship used by the royalty of Tyre. Phoenician cargoes are listed in verses 12-25 of the same chapter.

Almost 250 years after Jonah, the Phoenicians probably circumnavigated Africa. This cannot be demonstrated but, if they sailed from east to west, there were no special oceanography problems working against them. An old dry-dock 130 feet long at Athens demonstrates the size of the Greek war vessels, which were smaller than cargo ships. Lucian mentions a large Alexandrian grain ship 180 feet long. It would have had a capacity of about 1200 tons. Paul's ship was also Alexandrian, and it carried 276 in its crew and passenger list.

Josephus was in a shipwreck when there were 600 persons on board. Underwater archaeology is a fascinating new field of research. French divers have studied the old stone docks now all under water at the city of Tyre. A Mycenaean ship loaded with copper has been studied in detail on the ocean floor off the coast of Turkey. One of the ships found off the Mediterranean coast of France of New Testament times was probably 100 feet long.

When Jonah sailed for Tarshish, this was exactly the opposite of God's orders, geographically. Jonah soon found himself caught in a cyclonic storm similar to the one described in Paul's shipwreck. (To appreciate Jonah's storm, reread Acts 27:14-41.) The ship's crew was of many nationalities, and each sailor prayed to his own god, but there was no answer. In desperation the sailors took the last resort; that is, they cast lots. Jonah was found to be the guilty party and, at his own request, he was thrown into the sea. The sailors were typical pagans, for in talking with Jonah they had said, "What shall we do to you that the sea may be calm to us?" And speaking to God they said, "We beseech thee, let us not perish for this man's life, and lay not upon us innocent blood; for thou, O Lord, hast done as it pleased thee." (Jonah 1:14) Notice that their gods had no more ethics than the sailors themselves. . . .

To the man of little faith "the fish story" is too much; but, if you have ever known God personally in great and awful crises, you will have no trouble with miracles. If you have not had these experiences, then no one can reason you into believing in miracles. The big miracle, anyway, is Jonah's prayer inside the sea monster, not that animal itself. Read that prayer carefully. In its conclusion, Jonah expresses his thanksgiving to God, vowing that he would actually offer sacrifices; that is, he would yet get ashore somehow and, by God's grace, go to church! His faith triumphed, and God spared his life. Jonah found himself ashore, only to be ordered to Nineveh in the identical words of the first summons.

Nineveh was the second largest of the

Bedouin Encampment at the Ruins of Nineveh. This Assyrian capital was destroyed by the union of the Medes and the Baby-lonians in 612 B.C. Its ancient palaces remain buried beneath Tell Kuyunjik and Tell Nabi Yunis. © Matson Photo

ancient Mesopotamian cities; only Babylon was larger. Nineveh had not yet reached its peak in Jonah's day, but the city's walls were about eight miles in circumference. Suburbs, however, reached as far as the large city of Calah, about fifteen miles away. This expanded Nineveh is the probable city of Jonah's day, where the city is spoken of as a three days' journey. The idiom, "three days," however, may simply mean a big city. Aristotle refers to a statement which mentioned that, at the time of Babylon's capture, three days passed before all the city had the news. The reference to 120,000 children—that is, persons that could not distinguish the left hand from the right—would mean about 600,000 population, a reasonable number for greater Nineveh.

Sennacherib made Nineveh the capital of the Assyrian empire at the end of the 8th century B.C. Note that the king in the book of Jonah is king only of Nineveh, not the king of Assyria. Ashurbanipal, the last great Assyrian king, collected the finest library in the ancient Near East at Nineveh; it is a major source of our knowledge of ancient Mesopotamia. This was the forerunner of the still more famous library at Alexandria in Egypt. The archaeologists know the details of about two thousand years of Nineveh's history, but the city was founded much earlier. Its cult of Ishtar, goddess of love and war, was famous

as far away as Egypt long before the time of Moses.

Jonah's message was annihilation: "Forty days and Nineveh will be destroyed." This message he preached with such enthusiastic sincerity that the whole city, from slave to king, repented. They even dressed their animals in the black sackcloth of mourning. So sincere was the king that he ordered the populace to "cry mightily unto God; yea, let them turn everyone from his evil way, and from the violence that is in his hands." God accepted the repentance of the city.

But what about Jonah? Let us paraphrase a little of the last chapter in the book into modern English: "And Jonah was so angry that he was burnt up and he said to God, 'Isn't this just what I told you in my home town? That's why I left for Tarshish, because I knew that you would spare them. Please God, kill me. I would rather be dead than alive!' And God said, 'Come on now, Jonah, does this red-hot anger do you any good?'"

Jonah refused to answer God. Instead he walked over to the east of the city to watch Nineveh go up in smoke, like Sodom and Gomorrah did. The only burning, however, was the hot sun on Jonah's head. Beginning to swoon, he said, "I would rather be dead than alive. Yes, it does me good to be angry, even if it kills me!"

God reminded Jonah, however, that He

does indeed love the Gentiles just as truly as the Jews and He will instantly pardon any sinner, be he person or nation—be he Jonah or Nineveh! The Ninevites brought forth works worthy of repentance; but Jonah, even after God had twice saved him from death, refused to be a partner in foreign missions. Jonah saw only the sinners in *Nineveh,* forgetting that the vast percentage of *Israel's* population for the past century had been almost as ungodly as Assyria!

Jonah's descendants are probably the most numerous group that you can find in every Christian Church today. They may give a pittance to missions, but essentially Christianity is for middle-class Americans only. In Jonah's day, God was for Jews only, as Christ is for us only today. We see the wickedness in Communism today—but not the wickedness of our own nation, which God has blessed more than any other nation, with the possible exception of ancient Israel.

At the turn of the century, the various boards of foreign missions pleaded for missionaries for Japan and China. American Christians would not give their sons to missions, so a new Assyria arose whose name was Japan. Then American Christians had to give their sons by the tens of thousands to their nation. And China—unevangelized China—who knows her future, and ours? Unless we pray in dead earnest, "Thy kingdom come, Thy will be done," tragedy awaits both countries.

But Jonah was not the only sinner; Assyria's repentance was but for a day. As the drug addict returns to his heroin, so Assyria soon returned to her sins. A new prophet spoke to them. Nahum was God's new agent, not of grace but for doom; Assyria was to pass from the face of the earth, with none to mourn her. "Thy shepherds slumber, O king of Assyria; thy nobles are at rest; thy people are scattered upon the mountains, and there is none to gather them. There is no assuaging of thy hurt; thy wound is grievous: all that hear the report to thee clap their hands over thee; for upon whom hath not thy wickedness passed continually?" (Nahum 3:18-19).

We might rethink Matthew 7:21-23: "Not everyone that says to me, 'Lord, Lord,' shall enter into the kingdom of heaven; but he that does the will of my Father who is in heaven. Many will say to me in that day, 'Lord, did we not prophesy by your name, and by your name cast out demons, and by your name do many mighty works?' And then will I profess unto them, 'I never knew you: depart from me, you workers of iniquity.'"

After these words, the Church should not make sport of Jonah until we can evangelize Russia. And even then God will have to be as gracious to *us* as He is to *Russia!* Why should Christ have to wait more than nineteen hundred years to see the Church appreciate His Gospel enough to take that Gospel to all mankind? Remember that today there are more lost souls than ever before in the world's history.

Any doctor who would discover a cure for cancer and then refuse to share it with his patients and his fellow doctors would be the most hated man in the world. Jesus Christ is the cure for the world's ills. It is the duty of Christians to apply His remedy, love, to the sin-cancer of the world, so that all nations and individuals may have the more abundant life that Christ wants all mankind to enjoy.

"Job and His Friends" by Johann Liss (Lys). Habertak Collection, Berlin. Job experienced a series of misfortunes and was visited by friends who tried to comfort him. They debated the reason for his afflictions.

Alinari

Job

THE SOUL OF JOB, the perfect and upright man, was a battleground between heaven and hell. In the first two chapters of the book the account of Satan's questions and God's answers are given. Job was bereft of all the things Satan said were necessary to his loyalty to God. He passed through great mental strain; but he emerged, vindicating his faith and giving the lie to Satan. Thus we are taught that experiences through which loyal souls pass may have their explanation in some far-reaching purpose of God.

Job's friends came to see him. They desired to comfort him. For a long period neither he nor his friends understood the deepest meaning of his experiences. Their mistake was that of trying to find a solution. It was born of their satisfaction with their philosophy, the whole of which was true, but which was not *all* the truth.

The Divine voice spoke to Job and called him away from discussion with man. God gave Job no explanation of the mystery of his suffering. He unveiled His glory before Job, leading him to more perfect confidence in Him with regard to experiences which were not yet explained. Job was brought to the consciousness of his comparative insignificance in the midst of a universe so wondrously governed.

This very sense of insignificance was also one of comfort, for it came connected with recognition of the fact of God's interest in the smallest things. It spoke to Job about God's understanding of His suffering saint and all his circumstances. Job said, "I had heard of Thee by the hearing of the ear, but now mine eye seeth Thee; wherefore I abhor myself, and repent in dust and ashes." (Job 42:5, 6)

In Job's words of surrender the greatness of the man is revealed. He had found himself in relationship with God, and in so doing he had found rest.—G. Campbell Morgan, *Searchlights from the Word*.

1
GOD'S GOOD AND PROSPEROUS MAN

JOB, WHOSE VERY NAME conjures up the word "patience," lived in the land of Uz. He was a saintly, devout, faultless man who feared God and scorned evil. He and his wife had ten happy, loving children. Each of his seven sons was in the habit of giving a banquet to celebrate his own birthday. To this festive event each invited his brothers and sisters.

Following each banquet Job offered a burnt offering to the Lord for each son because he feared that, during their gaiety and revelry, his sons might inadvertently have sinned against God.

Job was not only a good man but he was also a very wealthy one. His assets included a home for each of his sons, seven thousand sheep, three thousand camels, five hundred yoke of oxen, five hundred donkeys, and many servants. He was known all over the land as the richest man in the East.

There came the day when a celestial

"Job and His Family" by J. James Tissot. *The Old Testament, Illustrated.* Job was a wealthy man who lived happily with his family in Uz. His trust in God was sorely tried when he lost his possessions and his children.   M. de Buffan & Co.

council was to be held in heaven. The sons of God were present and Satan, the Adversary, was also there.

When the Lord saw Satan, He asked, "Where have you been?"

Satan answered, superciliously, "Oh, here and there, all over the face of the earth, watching people and their actions."

The Lord then said, "During your wanderings, you must surely have noticed My servant, Job. There *is* a man—a perfect man! He is honest, faithful, upright, and God-fearing."

Satan replied, cynically, "Little wonder he is all the things You say about him! Look at what You have done for him. Take away all his possessions, and You will see what kind of a man he is. He will curse You to Your face."

God decided to accept Satan's challenge, so He said, "All right, I will permit you to test Job. I place all that he has in your power. Only do not harm him personally."

Job's sons and daughters were gathered one day at their oldest brother's house, celebrating his birthday—but little dreaming that this was to be their last day alive. Meanwhile, back at his home, Job was making preparations for his next burnt offering. The sacrifice would never be offered, though, because Satan's testing time for him was at hand. He was to learn of tragedy after tragedy in rapid succession. The first came soon.

One of Job's servants came racing up to him, gasping the words, "The oxen were at the plows and the donkeys were grazing nearby when the Sabeans attacked your servants, killed them, and took away all the animals. I alone escaped to let you know."

While this servant was still talking, another arrived and stood panting. He said, "Fire fell from the sky and burned up all your sheep and shepherds. Only I escaped

"Sabeans Carry off Job's Flocks" by Bernard van Orley. Royal Museums, Brussels. This painting illustrates the capture of Job's oxen and donkeys by Sabeans.   National Archives, Brussels

to tell you about it." He then collapsed.

Still another rushed up and exclaimed, "The Chaldeans attacked from three directions, killed your men, and carried away all your camels! I alone escaped to bring you this message."

While he was yet talking, still another of Job's servants came to his master and stood silently waiting. Then he spoke sadly, "All of your sons and your daughters are dead. They were having a banquet at their oldest brother's house when, suddenly, a great wind came roaring out of the wilderness, destroyed the house, and killed everyone inside. I alone escaped to let you know."

When Job heard the tragic news about his children, he arose, put on sackcloth and ashes, bowed down, and said, "I had nothing when I came into this world, and I shall take nothing with me when I leave it. The Lord gives, and the Lord takes away. Blessed be the name of the Lord!"

Satan stood nearby, bewildered and amazed. Despite the successful completion of his satanic mission, Job had not cursed the Lord; instead, he had blessed His name.

Based on the story in the Bible:
Job 1:1-22

"Job Hears Bad Tidings" by J. James Tissot. *The Old Testament,* Illustrated. After Job learned of the loss of his livestock and his servants, a messenger arrived and told him that his sons and daughters had perished.   M. de Buffan & Co.

2
JOB'S VICTORY

JOB SAT OUTSIDE THE GATE of the city, covered from head to toe with painful boils. Wracked with pain and grief-stricken at the loss of his sons and daughters, Job cursed the day he was born and—like the prophet Elijah—wished that he might die.

Job's present affliction was the result of another celestial assembly, again attended by the sons of God and by Satan. The Lord reminded Satan that Job had remained upright and loyal in spite of losing all his possessions. Satan conceded defeat in the first encounter, but he had another plan.

"Job's possessions were not as important to him as I had believed," he said. "However, let me take away his health. Then You will see how quickly he will forsake You and curse You to Your face."

The Lord replied, "He is in your hands. Only spare his life."

One day Job's wife made a brief appearance on the scene. She came to him, as he lay in misery, with two pointed questions.

"Do you still believe that you are God's perfect man?" she asked. "Don't you realize that this chain of tragedies proves beyond a shadow of doubt that you have committed some great sin? Curse God and die!"

Job answered his wife, patiently, "You talk like a foolish woman. Is it right for us to accept good things from the Lord and refuse to accept the bad things?"

When three of Job's friends heard of his misfortunes, they decided to visit him and try to comfort him. Their names were Eliphaz, Bildad, and Zophar. In due time, the three comforters arrived and, when they actually saw Job, they hardly recognized him because he had changed so much. Surely this man could not be the

healthy, robust, contented Job they had known. When they finally were convinced that this skeleton of a man was Job, they

"*Job Ridiculed by His Wife*" by A. Van Den Heuvel. Church of St. Job, Belsele, Belgium. Job turned away from his wife's admonition to renounce God.   National Archives, Brussels

234

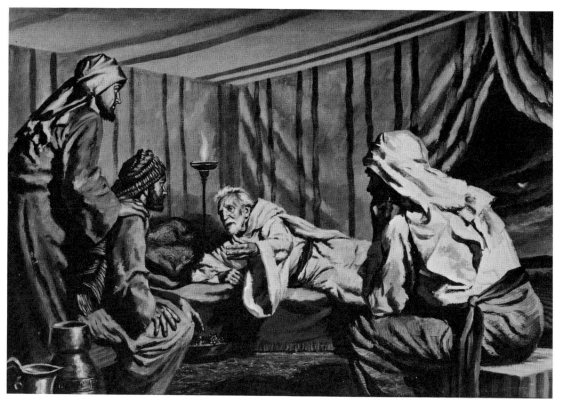

"Three Friends Visit Job." Eliphaz, Bildad, and Zophar visited Job when they heard of his troubles. Sympathizing with his pain, his three friends did not speak until he broke the silence by lamenting his birth and even wishing that he might die.

tore their clothes, put sand on their heads, and mourned for him as though he were dead.

For seven days and seven nights Job's three friends sat on the ground with him, but none of them spoke a word because they saw that he was in great pain. Job finally broke the silence by lamenting the fact that he had ever been born. During this lament, Job expressed a longing for death so that he could rest in peace.

With the silence broken, the three friends began a long series of discussions with Job. Schooled in the stern Mosaic law, they felt certain that their friend had committed some very great sin and that these afflictions were God's punishment for him; but they tried in vain to convince the sufferer that this was true. At one point in their discourses, Job spoke the faith-filled words that have been set to music by Handel:

"I know that my Redeemer lives,
  And that at last He shall stand
Upon the earth;
  And, though my body is destroyed,
I shall see God!" (Job 19:25-26)

Job's testing time was almost over. One of the most beautiful parts of this great poem tells about the Lord's arrival on the scene in a whirlwind. He clearly showed Job and his friends, by a continuous stream of questions, how insignificant man is when compared with the Lord God:

"Where were you," He asked,
    "When I created heaven and earth? . . .
When the morning stars sang together,
    And all the angels shouted for joy?
Who determined the size of the earth?
    And Who made the oceans?
Since your days began,
    Have you caused the dawn to break,
Or the darkness to fall?
    Can you cause the lightning to flash,
The thunder to roll,
    Or the hail and snow to fall?
Does the hawk fly at your bidding?
    Does the eagle soar at your command
And make a nest high in the mountains?"
(Job 38:4–39:27, abridged paraphrase)

The Lord continued to hurl countless questions, similar to these, at Job and his three friends. Finally, Job cried out to the Lord:

"I realize now how unimportant I am and how omnipotent You are! I hate myself for the things I said about You. Then I had heard about You only by ear; but now I have seen You with my eyes. Forgive me, O Lord, as I repent in sackcloth and ashes."

The Lord forgave Job. Then He turned to the three friends.

"I am very angry with you because you have not spoken the truth about Me," He said. "Now, therefore, take seven bulls

Camels Being Watered. Among the possessions Job lost were his many sheep, oxen, donkeys, and camels. The latter were important because of their hardiness. After regaining his wealth, Job owned six thousand camels. © Matson Photo

and seven rams and offer up burnt offerings for yourselves. My servant Job will pray for you, and I will heed his prayer and not deal with you as your folly deserves."

After Job had prayed for his friends, the Lord healed him and restored all his material possessions two-fold. Job returned to his house and prepared for a great banquet. His brothers and sisters and all who knew him came to the feast. Everyone brought him a present and congratulated him on the survival of the ordeals that he had endured.

Job lived for one hundred and forty years after his afflictions. During these years he was more affluent than he had been in the beginning. He owned fourteen thousand sheep, six thousand camels, a thousand yoke of oxen, and a thousand donkeys, with enough servants to look after all these animals. Best of all, he had seven sons and three daughters. And the daughters of Job were the fairest women in all the land.

Based on the story in the Bible:
Job 2:1 — 42:17

"*Job Joins His Family in Happiness*" by J. James Tissot. *The Old Testament*, Illustrated. When Job's trials were over, his family and friends celebrated with him.　M. de Buffan & Co.

PLACES

in the Story of Job

THE LAND OF UZ

The exact location of Job's country is obscure. Job is referred to as the greatest man in the East, and this is generally understood to mean east of Palestine. Modern tradition, which can be traced back almost two thousand years, locates Uz in the Hauran, a rich, fertile land south of Damascus and stretching to Gilead. The German explorer, J. G. Wetzstein, found a monastery of Job in this territory. Another German explorer, Glaser, locates Uz near the western edge of Arabia. All that can be said is that the name points to the east and southeast of Palestine, and that the Book of Job appears to represent its hero as living in the neighborhood of Arabia.

SABEA

This south Arabian country, with settlements to the north, is where the Sabeans launched their attack on Job's servants and took away all his oxen and donkeys.

TEMAN

One of Job's friends, Eliphaz the Temanite, came from this town. It lay in the land of Edom, which also contained the important city of Bozrah, located about 25 miles southeast of the Dead Sea.

Waters of El Azraq. Descriptions of Job's wealth indicate that he owned fertile and well-watered areas, like those shown, suitable for raising domestic animals, and that Uz was east or southeast of Palestine, probably in Arabia.   © Matson Photo

QUESTIONS
on the Story of Job

1

1 Where did Job live? Describe his character.

2 How many sons and daughters were in Job's household? What did they do on their birthdays?

3 What was Job's financial situation?

4 Where did Satan tell the Lord he had been?

5 What was Satan's response when the Lord pointed out Job as a perfect, God-fearing man?

6 What did the Lord agree to let Satan do?

7 What was Job's first test? his second? his third?

8 What was Job's ultimate and sternest test?

9 What did Job do when he realized that all was lost?

10 Why was Satan bewildered?

2

11 How was Job affected by the second heavenly meeting?

12 What did Job do as he sat outside the city gate? Whose experience was similar?

13 What did Job's wife say to him? What was his reply?

14 What were the names of Job's three friends? What did they decide to do?

15 Why did Job's three friends sit in silence for seven days and nights?

16 What did the three men try to convince Job was the cause of all his suffering?

17 What did the Lord do first when He visited Job?

18 What was Job's answer to the Lord?

19 What did the Lord tell the three men?

20 What happened to Job after he had prayed for his three friends?

Answers are found on the following page.

ANSWERS

on the Story of Job

1

1 Job lived in the land of Uz. He was a saintly, devout, faultless, God-fearing man who hated evil.

2 Job had seven sons and three daughters. The brothers and sisters had a party at the home of the one whose birthday was being celebrated.

3 Job was the wealthiest man in the East.

4 Satan told the Lord he had been roaming back and forth across the face of the earth.

5 Satan told the Lord that Job would curse Him to His face if He took away all his possessions.

6 The Lord agreed to let Satan have control of all that Job had, and to do with it as he desired, in order to prove that Job would remain faithful.

7 In rapid succession, Job lost all of his servants, his oxen, his donkeys, his camels, and his sheep.

8 Job's hardest test came when he was told that all of his sons and daughters had been killed as a tornado struck the home of his oldest son.

9 Job arose, put on sackcloth and ashes, bowed down, and said that the Lord gives and the Lord takes away. Then he blessed the name of the Lord.

10 Satan had been certain that Job would curse the Lord when he lost his children and all of his property.

2

11 Job found himself covered with boils, as the Lord permitted Satan to attack His servant physically in order to test him further.

12 Job cursed the day he was born and wished that he might die. In doing so, he had an experience similar to that of the prophet Elijah.

13 Job's wife asked him if he still thought he was such a great and perfect man. She also asked him if he didn't realize that the Lord was punishing him for some great sin that he had committed. She then told him to curse God and die. Job told his wife that they should accept the bad along with the good.

14 Eliphaz, Bildad, and Zophar. Job's friends decided to visit Job and try to cheer him up.

15 The three men sat around Job in silence for seven days and nights and grieved for their friend, who was in such great pain that he looked as if he might die any minute.

16 The three friends tried to convince Job that God was punishing him for some great sin that he had committed.

17 The Lord hurled a series of questions at Job to remind him that God had created the heavens and the earth and to point out that He still controlled the action of every living creature.

18 Job recanted his words, repented in sackcloth and ashes, and asked the Lord to forgive him.

19 The Lord told the three men that He was angry with them and that they must sacrifice burnt offerings for themselves. Then, after Job had prayed for them, He would not punish them.

20 The Lord forgave Job, healed him, and gave him back twice as many servants and animals as he had before his afflictions. Best of all, He also gave him seven sons and three daughters. Job lived one hundred and forty years after his ordeals and saw four generations of his children and grandchildren.

FURTHER FACTS AND OUTLINE

for the Story of Job

JOB

AUTHORSHIP AND DATE

The book gives no very definite clues. Suggestions on date vary from Post-Exilic times (as late as 3rd century B.C.) to Patriarchal times (16th century B.C.). Some have placed it in the age of Solomon (10th century B.C.)

DESTINATION

Unstated. It has been and is a magnificent story for posterity.

PURPOSE AND THEME

The book of Job, largely a poem, grapples with the age-old problem of why the righteous suffer. Job himself is a righteous person, but he suffers almost the gamut of misfortune, losing his health, family, and material possessions. His so-called "friends"—three of them—counsel him on the reasons for his suffering. Sin, hypocrisy, lying, pride, and general wickedness are suggested as causes. The Lord Himself does not accuse Job of any wrongdoing as the cause of his suffering; rather, He says that finite man cannot know or understand the ways of infinite God. The book concludes by observing that Job, even through his terrible affliction, enters into a new, richer, and deeper experience of God. The trial has been a testing, not a punishment.

OUTLINE

The Prologue (chapter 1-2)
  Job, a Godly Man, Suffers Destruction of His Material Possessions and Family with the Lord's Permission (chapter 1)

Job's Health Is Now Destroyed; Job Refuses To Curse God; His Three Friends Observe a Seven-Day Silence out of Respect for His Great Suffering (chapter 2)

Job and His Three Friends Discuss and Grapple with the Problem of His Suffering (chapters 3-41)

  First Discussion Cycle (chapters 3-14)
    Job Complains, Wishes He Had Never Been Born and that He Would Now Die (chapter 3)
    Eliphaz' First Speech: Job Suffers Because He Has Sinned and God Is Punishing Him.
    Job's Reply to Eliphaz: Just Where Is the Sin in My Life To Be Found? (chapters 6-7)
    Bildad's First Speech: Job Suffers Because He Is a Hypocrite (chapter 8)
    Job's Reply to Bildad: Job Is Bewildered —How Can He Approach God with Effectiveness and Declare His Innocence? (chapters 9-10)
    Zophar's First Speech: Job's Pretense of Innocence Only Heaps Sin upon Sin and He Should Be Suffering Even More than This (chapter 11)
    Job's Reply to Zophar: Job's Friends Are Really Giving Him No Comfort; He Cannot Understand His Suffering; Nonetheless, He Places His Trust in God (chapters 12-14)

Second Discussion Cycle (chapters 15-21)

Eliphaz' Second Speech: Reiterates that Job Suffers Because He Is Unrighteous, He Ought to Confess (chapter 15)

Job's Reply to Eliphaz: His So-called Friends Are No Comfort, They Are "Miserable," He Has the Feeling that Both Man and God Have Deserted Him (chapters 16-17)

Bildad's Second Speech: Not Only God but Nature Itself Is Opposed to Wrongdoing, hence, Job's Suffering—It Is Inherent in the Nature of Things that the Wicked Suffer (chapter 18)

Job's Reply to Bildad: Though All Criticize—Even Make Sport of—Job, His Faith Rises To Cry, "I know that my Redeemer liveth . . ." (chapter 19)

Zophar's Second Speech: Are You Accusing *God* of Wronging You? The Wicked Come to a Terrible End (chapter 20)

Job's Reply to Zophar: Your "Reasoning" Is Not Borne Out in Experience, because Frequently the Wicked *Prosper* (chapter 21)

Third Discussion Cycle (chapters 22-41)

Eliphaz' Third Speech: Suffering Cannot Be Due to Piety, so It Must Be Due to Sin; Recommends Repentance (chapter 22)

Job's Reply to Eliphaz: Oh, Where Can I Find God? The Wicked Sometimes Escape Suffering! (chapters 23-24)

Bildad's Third Speech: No Matter What Experience Seems To Reveal, Job Is Arrogant; He Must Have Sinned! (chapter 25)

Job's Reply to Bildad: He Holds Unyieldingly to His Original Statement that He In Fact Has Not Sinned (chapters 26-31)

Elihu, Not Zophar, Speaks this Time (really a series of speeches): Suffering Is Not Always the Result of Sin; God Chastens the Righteous Sometimes; God Does Not Always Explain His Ways (chapters 32-37)

Jehovah, Not Job, Replies this Time: Man Is Finite and therefore Cannot Explain the Mysteries of the Infinite God and His Providence (chapters 38-41)

Epilogue: New Religious Experiences and Resultant Blessing Through Suffering (chapter 42)

Lessons from the Book of Job:

1. The purposes and causes of suffering are not always clear.
2. Suffering may be beneficial. It can strengthen character and enrich personality.
3. Finite man cannot understand fully the justice of God; justice will be completed and perfected in eternity.
4. The righteous who suffer may suffer misunderstanding, but not God's misunderstanding.
5. God provides sustaining grace for trying times—and He does it quite literally.

Faith: The Prize Worth Polishing

by
Justin Fisher

Like a modern-day Job, the father of Justin Fisher suffered financial reverses and loss of health, all with an unswerving faith in God, as shown in the following story that appeared in *Guideposts* (© 1967, Guideposts Associates, Inc., Carmel, N.Y.). The happy ending unrecorded in the story itself is that the elder Fisher, according to his son, "has now recovered and is back at work, although he must rest a great deal." This story has valuable lessons for all who wonder at the "patience of Job."

RIGHT RESPONSE TO REVERSES

I HAD ALWAYS FELT that my father was a religious man. He went to church each Sunday, sang every hymn, and was a good example of a truly successful man. But until two tragic incidents came into my father's life several winters ago, I had never fully understood what it is to be a truly religious man. The faith he gave me was the greatest gift a father can give a son.

February is a cold month in Indiana, and last February was no exception. One school night as I studied my chemistry, I heard the fire alarm blow loudly. In a rural community like ours there is only a volunteer fire department. I hurried outside to join the others who were watching the firemen rush to the blaze. As I glanced upward, I realized that the billows of smoke filling the darkening night were coming from the direction of my father's furniture store.

Minutes later I stood beside my parents and watched one of Indiana's most fashionable furniture stores go up in flames. As hundreds of community residents rushed to save the furniture from the fire, I studied my parents' faces carefully. The yellowish light from the blaze reflected the grief in their faces. They did not shed a tear; they looked straight ahead and held their heads high.

Later that evening we returned home. The damage already had been estimated at $250,000, and the fire was still blazing. We gathered in the den and quietly thought about the evening. Finally Father spoke. I had expected him to just give up. He and his brother had worked for eighteen years to build an ideal furniture outlet, one that was awarded a national prize. Now that proud store was a pile of black ashes.

To my surprise, Father gave thanks to God in those quiet moments. He thanked God for a wonderful family, many wonderful friends, and above all, an undying faith. I couldn't believe my ears! How could he be so thankful? How could God do such a thing to us? How would we survive?

I didn't sleep well that night. I kept thinking about my father. His whole life has been destroyed, and yet he was willing to strike out again, to rebuild his loss because of a faith! Where was mine?

The very next day Father began rebuilding his dream. Along with his brother he worked long and hard each day, and there were many problems.

Finally in May, the store was reopened, more beautiful than before, all because Father never gave up.

And then the second tragedy struck. We found out that Father had active tuberculosis.

He was immediately put to bed, isolated, and confined to his room for a period of six to eight months. I was stunned. For a while, I hated God. Then I began to notice Father. He never blinked an eye when told of his illness. He went to bed. I heard him say again how thankful he was that he had a faith to live by.

I learned a great deal that summer by watching over Father. He didn't complain once. He learned Spanish as a hobby and never let us become discouraged, even when things seemed as if they could never be made right again. As I tried to make him happy and comfortable, I began to look at myself. Could I ever have as much faith as he had? How could I develop it?

As I tried to help him, I found myself being helped. Each day a little of his belief began to take root in me. I began to realize that true faith never hides behind weak men. It is a prized possession that must be cleaned and polished regularly. It is a smile on a sick man's face, a kind word to a forgotten man, an unfailing witness to a changing world. Faith, I discovered, is life itself.

Father is much better now. The doctors are amazed at his progress and we are all waiting the day when he can return to a normal life. He is, for me, a truly great man, and even though his tragedies have been crushing ones, the faith of each one of us has been strengthened greatly through these past months.

I have always felt that my father was a religious man. Now I know it for a fact. The faith he has shown to me will always be my most prized possession.

Hezekiah

THE KING OF JUDAH who approximated most nearly to the Divine ideal of kingship was Hezekiah. The secret of his greatness was that he "trusted in the Lord, the God of Israel; so that after him was none like him among all the kings of Judah, nor among them that were before him." (2 Kings 18:5) This is high praise, and there is no doubt that it was justified. In that trust Hezekiah lived, doing right in the sight of the Lord in all actions. In that same trust he instituted reforms, more widespread and thorough than any that had been attempted by his predecessors. A revealing illustration is that of his behavior in the presence of the invasion of the Assyrian army under Sennacherib. Through Hezekiah's obedience to the prophetic words he received from Isaiah and based upon his trust in the Lord, the nation was delivered. The swift judgment of God passed upon the hosts of Assyria.

The prayer of Hezekiah, when confronted by the threats of Sennacherib, closed with these words: "Save Thou us, I beseech Thee, out of his hand, that all the kingdoms of the earth may know that thou art the Lord God, even Thou only." (2 Kings 19:19) They reveal the deepest fact in his life. He was anxious that his people should be delivered from the oppressor, but the deeper concern of his heart was that of a zeal for the honor of the Lord Whom he served.

God is ever glorified in serving and saving such as put their trust in Him, and seek first His kingdom. Here is the law of fellowship between man and God: man is ever and only to seek the glory of God; God is ever and only seeking the blessing of man.—G. Campbell Morgan, *Searchlights from the Word*

1

REFORMATION UNDER HEZEKIAH

SANDWICHED BETWEEN TWO of the most evil kings of Judah, his father Ahaz and his son Manasseh, Hezekiah stands tall as one of his country's best rulers. He inherited a wicked, corrupt, and idol-worshiping nation that was trembling with fear because the great Assyrian army was gradually encroaching on Judah's territory.

Abi (Abijah), the righteous mother of the young king, had trained her son well. From the first day of the first year of his reign, his foremost thought and one great desire was to bring his people back to the worship of the one true God. Hezekiah began this mission immediately and pursued it diligently and relentlessly. A great religious reformation was soon sweeping the country. Altars and false gods, that the king's idolatrous father had set up all over the land, were sought out and destroyed. Even the brass serpent that Moses had made, years earlier in the wilderness, was crushed into pieces because some of the people had made sacrifices to it.

The Temple, long neglected and even closed during the reign of Ahaz, was

Illustrated Pages from a 14th-century Haggada, the book used during Passover. Hezekiah renewed the celebration of this feast that commemorates delivery of the Israelites when the firstborn in Egypt were slain (Exodus 13).   The British Museum

247

opened and restored to its original brilliance and beauty. Priests and Levites were called back to duty. Everything was in readiness for the consecration service that would soon be held at the Temple.

In response to the king's proclamation, great crowds of people from all over Judah poured into Jerusalem and surrounded the Temple. They listened with pleasure to the singing of the beautiful songs that once again could be heard coming from the Temple courts. When the singing ended, the people consecrated themselves to the service of the Lord and vowed that they would remain true and faithful to Him as long as they lived. How quickly the people had come back to the worship of God! All they had needed was a great and good man to lead them.

Hezekiah was always searching for new ways to further the worship of the Lord. As the day approached for the Feast of the Passover, he had a brilliant idea. He would invite all Israel, both North and South, to come to Jerusalem for a joint celebration of the Passover Feast, an event that had not occurred since the reign of King Solomon. Hezekiah sent his couriers over Israel from Dan in the North to Beer-sheba in the South. In addition to the invitation, he sent an inspiring message to the people in the Northern Kingdom:

"O people of Israel! Come back to the Lord God of Abraham, Isaac, and Jacob, and He will come back to you. Don't be like your forefathers. Instead, surrender to the Lord, enter into His Sanctuary, and serve Him so that the fierceness of His wrath may turn away from you. God is gracious and merciful, and He will not turn His face away from you if you will return to Him."

Poor, sinful people of Israel! They had traveled too long and too far down the wicked trail of idolatry for this stirring message to have any effect on them. Everywhere the messengers went they were greeted with boos, taunts, mockery, and laughter. Nevertheless, small groups from Asher, Manasseh, and Zebulun accepted Hezekiah's invitation and went to Jerusalem.

The response to the invitation was far different in Judah. The couriers were greeted warmly and politely, and preparations for the pilgrimage to Jerusalem were begun immediately. Within a few days, the people were swarming toward their capital city for the celebration of the Feast of the Passover.

King Hezekiah sat upon his throne, pleased and happy. The great Passover Feast had been a tremendous success. In fact, it had been so successful that he had extended it from seven days to fourteen. He had seen the priests and Levites go among the people and bless them. He had watched them as they made sacrifices and offerings to the Lord. He had listened to their beautiful songs and wonderful music. The last visitor had returned to his city and home, and the king's only regret was that most of the people from the North had spurned his invitation.

Based on the story in the Bible:
2 Kings 18:1-6;
2 Chronicles 30:1 — 31:21

"The Prophet Isaiah" by Fra Bartolomeo. Uffizi Gallery, Florence. King Hezekiah was greatly influenced by Isaiah, whose wise counsel and encouragement helped him save his country and bring Judah back to the worship of God.   Alinari

ECCE DE
VS SAL
VATOR
EVS

SAIAS

2

HEZEKIAH AND THE PROPHET ISAIAH

ISAIAH, SON OF AMOZ, received his divine call during the last year of King Uzziah's rule over Judah. This great man of God continued his work in the days of King Jotham and King Ahaz. However, Isaiah went into semi-retirement during the last nineteen years of the reign of King Ahaz because that wicked man, instead of heeding the word of the Lord, had appealed to the King of Assyria for help when he was confronted by the coalition of Syria and Ephraim. Isaiah did not appear on the scene again until Ahaz had died and good King Hezekiah was sitting on the throne of Judah.

Hezekiah owed much to the inspiration of his friend and counselor, the prophet Isaiah. Prophet and king had many experiences together during Hezekiah's reign of twenty-nine years. Perhaps the one that lingered longest in the king's memory was that day, shortly after the miraculous victory over Sennacherib, when he himself suddenly became critically ill. Isaiah had hurried to his bedside.

"Put your house in order, O King!" the prophet had sadly said to him. "The Lord has told me that you shall not recover from this illness."

When Hezekiah heard these words, he turned his face to the wall and wept copiously. Then he prayed earnestly to the Lord: "I beseech You, O Lord, remember now how I have always walked before you in truth and faith and that I have always done that which is good in Your sight."

The Lord listened to the king's prayer and, before Isaiah had left the courtyard, gave him another message for Hezekiah. Isaiah hurried back to his friend's sickbed.

"Good news, O King!" the prophet said.

"The Lord has heard your prayer and has seen your tears. He told me that you will live fifteen additional years and that, three days from now, you will be well enough to go to the Temple and worship."

Although extremely happy to hear these words, the king was still doubtful, so he said to Isaiah: "Prove to me that I really will recover." Isaiah replied, a little impatiently: "What kind of proof do you want?" Hezekiah thought for a moment and then answered: "Look! The shadow of the palace is almost at the bottom step. Let the shadow move back ten steps." The Lord caused the shadow to move backward ten steps, and the king was satisfied.

One of the events that occurred during the king's extended life span appeared, for a long time, to be a tragedy for the people of Judah. This was the birth of his son Manasseh, who would one day succeed him on the throne.

The lilting and picturesque words found in the Book of Isaiah reveal clearly the character and greatness of this man of God. Isaiah proved to be a pillar of strength to Hezekiah during his darkest hour—the invasion of his kingdom by the Assyrians, under the leadership of Sennacherib. One of Isaiah's best known prophecies foretold the birth of the Lord Jesus, almost eight hundred years before the event occurred: "Behold, a virgin shall conceive, and shall bear a son, and shall call his name Immanuel." (Isaiah 7:14)

250

"Isaiah Predicts that Hezekiah Will Recover" by Jacob Backer. Museum of Fine Arts, Ghent. Hezekiah's prayer for a longer life was answered.　　　　　National Archives, Brussels

Here are some other excerpts from the writings of Isaiah:

"If you are willing and obedient
　You shall eat the good of the land;
But if you refuse and rebel
　You shall perish by the sword.
Thus says the Lord God." (1:19-20)

"Woe unto those who call evil, good,
　And good, evil;
Who substitute darkness for light
　And light for darkness.
Woe unto those who are wise
　　in their own eyes
　And clever in their own sight!
Woe unto those who drink wine
　　and strong drink
　Until it inflames them!
Woe unto those who accept bribes

To free the wicked,
And who take away the rights
　Of the innocent!
They have renounced the law of the Lord
　And have hated the word of
　　the Holy One of Israel." (5:20-24)

"For unto us a child is born,
　Unto us a son is given;
And the government shall be
　　on his shoulder,
　And his name will be called
Wonderful Counselor, Mighty God,
　Everlasting Father, Prince
　　of Peace." (9:6)

"The wolf shall dwell with the lamb,
　And the leopard shall lie down
　　with the goat;
The calf and the lion shall be together,
　And a little child
　　shall lead them." (11:6)

"The voice of one crying
　　In the wilderness,
'Prepare the way of the Lord,
　Cut straight through the desert
A highway for our God.
　Every valley shall be built up,
Every mountain and hill made low;
　The crooked shall be made straight
And the rough places shall be leveled.
　The glory of the Lord shall be
　　revealed,
And all people shall see it together.'
　These are the Lord's words." (40:3-5)

"Who has believed our report?
　To whom is the Lord's arm revealed?
For he shall grow up before him
　Like a tender plant,
Just as a root grows out of dry ground.
　He has no beauty of face or form,
No comeliness when we see him
　To cause us to want his company.
He is despised and rejected of men,

251

A man of sorrows, acquainted with grief.
We hid, as it were, our faces from him.
  He was despised and we esteemed
    him not.
Surely, he has borne our griefs
  And carried our sorrows;
But we considered him stricken,
  Smitten by the Lord and afflicted.
Yet he was wounded for our
    transgressions,
  He was bruised for our iniquities;
The chastisement of our peace was on him
  And with his stripes we are healed.
All we like sheep have gone astray,
  We have turned, everyone, to his
    own way;
And the Lord has laid on him
  The iniquity of us all.
He was oppressed, he was afflicted,
  Yet he opened not his mouth.
He is brought as a lamb
  To the slaughter and,
As a sheep before her shearers is dumb,
  He opens not his mouth.

       . . . .

He made his grave with the wicked
  And with the rich in his death;
He had done no violence,
  Nor was there deceit in his mouth.
Yet it pleased the Lord to bruise him;
  He has put him to grief. . . .
'Seeing the suffering of his soul
  Shall satisfy Me,' says the Lord;
'By his knowledge My righteous servant

Shall justify many;
For he shall bear their iniquities.
  Therefore, I will give him
A place among the great;
  The spoils of victory
He shall divide with the strong;
  Because he poured out his soul
    unto death;
He was numbered with the transgressors,
  He bore the sins of many,
And interceded for the sinners.' "
(53:1-7, 9-12)

"Ho, everyone who is thirsty,
  Come to the water and take it!
Even the man without money,
  Come, buy, and eat!
Yes, come and buy wine and milk
  Without money and without price!
Why do you spend money
  For what is not bread?
Why do you expend labor
  For what does not satisfy?
Pay careful attention to me,
  And eat of the fat of the land!
Lend me your ears and come to me,
  And I will make with you
An everlasting covenant, just as sure
  As were My mercy and kindness
    toward David." (55:1-3)

Based on the story in the Bible:
2 Kings 20:1-11; Isaiah 38:1-22

3
VICTORY OVER SENNACHERIB

THE SANDS OF TIME had run out for the Kingdom of Israel. About three years after the haughty refusal of its people to come to Jerusalem, the mighty Assyrians began their conquest of the Northern Kingdom. Three years later their capital city fell, and King Sargon carried the people into captivity.

Hezekiah watched the events in the Kingdom of Israel with growing concern and anxiety. After its collapse and the involuntary departure of its people, Sargon began to repopulate the land with people from other nations. Hezekiah knew that the greedy, roving eye of Assyria would soon fall upon his own kingdom, and that he must hasten his plans for its defense. Three things demanded immediate action.

The king hastened to put all three defense projects into full operation. Men were scattered throughout the land, polluting the water in most of the brooks and streams, so that the Assyrians would find very little drinking water. Another group was busily engaged in rebuilding the walls of Jerusalem and making them stronger. The third group was working around-the-clock to dig a tunnel through the solid rock of Ophel so that the king could divert the flow of water from the outside Spring Gihon to the Pool of Siloam inside the city.

Hezekiah's great engineering feat was nearing completion. Stone cutters from both ends of the rock would soon join each other near the middle of the tunnel. After their juncture, the outside entrance to the spring was covered so that the Assyrians could not find it. This amazing device for supplying water was seventeen hundred and seventy-seven feet long.

Siloam Tunnel. Hezekiah built this tunnel that brought water into Jerusalem from Spring Gihon, outside. He thereby defended the city against an Assyrian siege. © Matson Photo

The Siloam Inscription was found in 1880 by archaeologists. This priceless discovery was about nineteen feet from the Siloam entrance to the tunnel. The six-line inscription, beautifully carved on the

The *Siloam Inscription*, preserved in the Istanbul Museum, Turkey, was found near the lower opening of the Siloam Tunnel. Written in Hebrew, it describes the meeting of the excavators on completion of the tunnel.   © Matson Photo

wall in classical Hebrew, has been translated in English:

"While yet they plied the drill, each toward his fellow, and while yet there were three cubits to be bored through, there was heard the voice of one calling to another, for there was a crevice in the rock on the right hand, and on the day of the boring-through the stone-cutters struck, each to meet his fellow, drill upon drill; and the water flowed from the source to the pool for twelve hundred cubits, and a hundred cubits was the height of the rock, above the heads of the stone-cutters."

Visitors to Jerusalem today can walk through this famous tunnel. Their usual entrance is from the inner end at the pool of Siloam, and they wade through to the Spring Gihon. There is immediate evidence that the tunnel was dug hastily and crudely. The walls are jagged and uneven, and the height of the tunnel varies. Sometimes there is ample room above their heads, while at other places they have to bend so low that their faces almost touch the water. At the place where the two shafts were brought together, the workmen made no effort to conceal the unequal levels of the walls and ceiling.

And now the Assyrians were coming! The thing that Hezekiah and his people had long feared was about to happen. Sennacherib and his vast armies had blazed a trail of victory from Nineveh to the Philistine town of Lachish, and he was preparing to launch an attack on Jerusalem. Despite his defense plans, Hezekiah decided to try making a peaceful settlement with Sennacherib.

The envoys sitting around the conference table with Sennacherib were astounded to hear the king demand a tribute of three hundred talents of silver and thirty talents of gold, a total of $2,500,000. Although they knew that this tremendous amount of money would be difficult to raise, the peace delegation agreed to

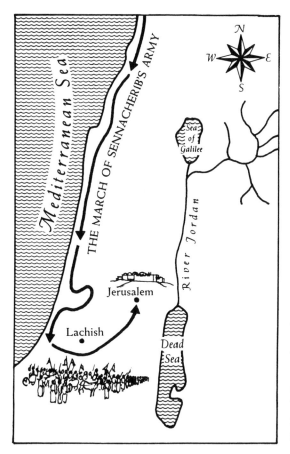

The Assyrian Camp. Sennacherib took the city of Lachish, the stronghold of Judah, and there quartered his troops. He intended to advance on Jerusalem from this vantage point.

The people of Jerusalem were terrified when they saw the mighty Assyrian army advancing upon their beloved city. Isaiah the great prophet, however, moved among the people and spoke words of encouragement and faith.

"Be strong!" he urged them. "Have no fear of the king of Assyria or of the vast army that is with him. He has only physical strength on his side, but the Lord our God is on our side and He will help us fight our battles."

Considering Hezekiah's meek submission in paying tribute, Sennacherib was surprised to find that the king and his people were prepared to defend their city strongly. Even with no opposition, the Assyrian king knew that Jerusalem would be a most difficult city to capture, so he decided first to try undermining the people's loyalty and lowering their morale with threats, taunts, mockery, and promises.

Carrying a white flag, Sennacherib's official spokesman slowly approached the wall of the city. When Rab-shakeh was near enough for those inside to hear, he called out in a loud voice:

"Upon what is your confidence based and upon whom do you trust that causes you to dare fight against the great king of Assyria? Hezekiah will lead you to your death by famine and thirst if you listen to his vain promises. Don't let Hezekiah deceive you! He cannot save you from the might of the Assyrians. And don't let your king cause you to put trust in your Lord."

When this approach failed to arouse any response from the people, Rab-shakeh tried to entice them with wild promises. First, he attempted to bribe two thousand of the men to desert by offering each of them a horse. After this offer was refused, he spoke again, loudly but in an alluring tone:

"Come out of Jerusalem, and I will guarantee you safe passage to your own

report the harsh ultimatum to their king.

Hezekiah gathered all the treasures from the Temple and the palace, as well as the gold from the Temple doors, in order to buy immunity from attack by Sennacherib. This appeasement effort was to be short-lived! As soon as Sennacherib received the tribute, he called a conference with his officials—Tartan, Rabsaris, and Rab-shakeh—and stated, bluntly:

"I am determined that all this territory shall become part of my Empire. I am, therefore, sending you and this great army to Jerusalem to demand unconditional surrender."

opportunity, I give you this serious advice and stern warning: Don't listen to Hezekiah when he tries to persuade you that your God can save you. Where are the gods of other nations that Sennecherib has conquered and destroyed?"

The people did not answer him.

Eliakim, Shebna, and Joah stood before Hezekiah, their clothes torn. They mournfully reported what Rab-shakeh had said. Before entering the Temple, the king—now dressed in sackcloth—sent Eliakim and the other aides to find Isaiah and consult with him. The prophet had a wonderful message of hope for them:

"Return to your king and tell him to have no fear about the words that he has heard. The Lord has also heard the blasphemous words of the Assyrians. He will cause their king to return to his own land and there he will die by the sword. Thus says the Lord."

These cheering words of hope from the great prophet caused the people to stand firm and steadfast against the potential invaders. But the Assyrian leaders were not quite finished with the obstinate Jews in Jerusalem. When Rab-shakeh returned and reported to Sennacherib that all his efforts to demoralize and dishearten the people had failed, the angry king sent a letter to Hezekiah that not only insulted the king and his people, but also mocked the Lord their God.

"Do not let the Lord your God deceive you by promising that He will save you from the hands of the Assyrians," the letter began. "Behold! You have heard what the kings of Assyria have done to other lands, utterly destroying them. What did the gods of these nations do to save their people? How then can your people and your God expect to be spared?"

Hezekiah received the letter from the messengers, read it, and went into the Temple to pray.

Clay Prisms of the Annals of Sennacherib, inscribed in cuneiform, were found at Nineveh. The above gives the Assyrian account of the siege of Jerusalem.   The British Museum

homes! There you can live in peace and eat food from your own vines and fig trees, until I come to take you to another land just like your own. It is a land of corn and wine, of bread and vineyards and olive-yards, and of milk and honey. There you can live and not die! If you refuse this

"Blasphemy of Rab-shakeh" by José Villegas. *Biblia Sacra.* Hezekiah sent Eliakim, Shebna, and Joah to meet the Assyrian officer, who reviled the God of the Israelites, and demanded the surrender of Jerusalem. Lemercier and Co., Paris

"O Lord God of Israel! You and You alone are the God of all nations, because You made heaven and earth," he said. "Incline Your ear and hear, O Lord, and open Your eyes and see. Listen to the words that Sennacherib has sent to belittle and ridicule the living God.

"It is true, O God, that the kings of Assyria have destroyed other nations and their lands, and have cast their gods into the fire. But these were not real gods. They were only handmade imitations, carved from wood and stone. Now, therefore, O Lord our God, save us from this king so that the people of all nations may know that You and You only are the one true God."

Even as the king was praying, the Lord came to Isaiah with a message for Hezekiah. The prophet hurried to the Temple and gave the king the good news.

"The Lord has told me that Sennacherib shall not enter the city, nor shall he attack it in any manner," the prophet said. "The Lord will defend the city, not only for His own sake, but also for the sake of His servant David."

That night the Angel of the Lord moved through the camp of the Assyrians and destroyed the huge army, numbering one

"Defeat of Sennacherib" by José Villegas. *Biblia Sacra.* The Assyrians conquered most of the cities of Judah, but when

Sennacherib prepared to capture Jerusalem, his soldiers died mysteriously at Lachish.

Lemercier and Co., Paris

hundred and eighty-five thousand of the king's soldiers. When Sennacherib arose the next morning and saw all the dead lying around him, he gave up and returned to Nineveh. Twenty years later, Isaiah's prophecy concerning his death was fulfilled. While Sennacherib was worshiping in the house of his god Nisrock, two of his sons conspired against him and killed him with their swords.

The defeat of Sennacherib has been recorded in history as inexplainable unless a firm faith in God's miraculous power is accepted. An English poet describes the event in these words:

"The Assyrian came down like a wolf on
    the fold,
And his cohorts were gleaming in purple
    and gold.
Like the leaves of the forest, when Sum-
    mer is green,
That host, with its banners, at sunset was
    seen.

Like the leaves of the forest, when Autumn has blown,
That host on the morrow lay withered and strown.

"For the Angel of Death spread his wings on the blast,
And breathed in the face of the foe as he passed,
And the eyes of the sleepers waxed deadly and chill,
And their hearts heaved but once, and forever grew still!

And the might of the Assyrian, unharmed by the sword,
Has melted like snow at the glance of the Lord."

Based on the story in the Bible:
2 Kings 18:9 — 19:37, 20:20;
Isaiah 36:1 — 37:38; 2 Chronicles 32:30

A View from the Castle of Sennacherib. The busy, modern city of Mosul, on the Tigris (Hiddekel) River, may be seen from the grounds of the ruins at Nineveh, the renowned capital of the Assyrian Empire. © Matson Photo

4
MANASSEH SUCCEEDS HEZEKIAH

SOON AFTER HEZEKIAH HAD RECOVERED from his serious illness, he made the one big mistake of his life. He warmly welcomed the son of the king of Babylon and his envoys and royally entertained them when they arrived in Jerusalem. In order to make a good impression on them and to lay the groundwork for a possible alliance, Hezekiah proudly showed them all his treasures.

When Isaiah learned about Hezekiah's visitors, he hurried to the palace and asked the king, "Who were those men? What did they want?"

Hezekiah replied, "They were the prince and envoys from far away Babylon. They came here to bring me greetings and a gift from their king."

"What did you show them?" demanded the prophet.

Hezekiah answered, "I showed them all my treasures—my silver, my gold, my precious jewels, my spices, and my oil. There is nothing in my storehouses that I did not show them. They also saw all my herds of cattle and flocks of sheep."

Hezekiah's mistake in trying to lure the Babylonians to his side by a great display of his material riches, instead of presenting the spiritual face of Judah to them, brought a stern rebuke from Isaiah. The prophet spoke solemnly to the king.

"Listen to the word of the Lord," he said. "The day will come when the very kingdom that you are attempting to win over will cause the downfall of Judah. The Babylonians will conquer your kingdom, carry away all your treasures, and take all the people into captivity."

"The word of the Lord is good," Hezekiah answered, humbly. He realized now how unwise he had been. His only comfort was that this dire misfortune would not happen during his lifetime.

After a reign of twenty-nine years, Hezekiah died and his son Manasseh ruled in his stead. Hezekiah, the great and good king, had done his best to bring his people back to God. He had arrived on the scene too late, however, to alter permanently the chaotic course of the tottering kingdom.

"Manasseh Carried Captive to Babylon by the Assyrians" by J. A. Adams and J. G. Chapman. *The Illuminated Bible* (1846). Later, Manasseh returned to his throne.   Harper & Brothers

What a contrast between father and son! Manasseh—cruel, wicked, idolatrous—began his reign at the age of twelve and ruled over Judah for fifty-five years. The young king, easily influenced by those around him, yielded to their demand that idol-worship be re-established throughout the land. When he grew older, he boldly went about reversing all the good things that his father had done.

Manasseh's sins were many and varied. Altars to Baal were rebuilt in all the high places, and idols were set up all over the land. He encouraged the people to worship the stars, and he even built altars to the stars in the Temple courts. Little children, including his own son, were cruelly sacrificed to the gods. Prophets and others who remained faithful to the Lord were killed. The purge was so thorough that the streets of Jerusalem actually ran with blood. Manasseh richly deserved his reputation as Judah's most evil king.

One day, the Lord spoke to some of His prophets.

"Manasseh, king of Judah, has caused his people to do things more wicked than all the sinful nations that I have destroyed," He said. "Because of this, I will punish Judah so severely that the ears of all who hear about it will tingle. I will turn the people over to their enemies, because they have done evil in My sight. They will be enslaved, and their land will be plundered. Time after time, they have provoked Me to anger, even from that day when I brought them out of Egypt."

Manasseh lay in chains in a Babylonian prison, suffering pain and misery. As he reflected on his sinful and useless life, he became more and more conscious of the Lord God of his father, Hezekiah. In deep penitence, he confessed his sins, humbly asked the Lord for forgiveness, and prayed that he might return to Jerusalem. How merciful and forgiving the Lord is! He heard the cry of His prodigal child and answered his prayer.

When Manasseh returned to Jerusalem, he spent the last few years of his long reign trying to undo the evil that he had done; but his son Amon, who succeeded him on the throne, followed the early footsteps of his father. Amon's short, wicked reign of two years was marked by the resurgence of Baal worship in his kingdom. His servants conspired against him and murdered him, but their crime did not go unpunished. The people of the land executed all the assassins, and made Josiah, Amon's son, king in his stead.

Based on the story in the Bible:
2 Kings 20:12 — 21:26;
2 Chronicles 32:31, 33:1-25

PLACES

in the Story of Hezekiah

ASSYRIAN EMPIRE

This empire developed from the city of Asshur, on the upper Tigris River. Its period of greatness dates from the 9th century B.C., when Nineveh was its capital. The Assyrians captured Samaria and took the Israelites into captivity (722 B.C.). Nineveh was destroyed by the Babylonians (612 B.C.), and Assyrian power was forever broken.

NEW BABYLONIAN EMPIRE

This is the name by which the Babylonia of the 6th and 5th centuries B.C. is known to

historians. Babylon, its capital city, is located in the Southern Mesopotamia. Manasseh spent some time in prison here. The empire itself was a growing power during the days of Hezekiah.

LACHISH

Among the first of Judah's fortified cities to be captured by Sennacherib, Lachish is 30 miles southwest of Jerusalem. This is the point from which Sennacherib launched his siege of Jerusalem.

The Assyrian Empire reached the height of its glory about 750-613 B.C. Its great kings—Sargon, Sennacherib, Esar-haddon, and Ashurbanipal—annexed neighboring countries, continually expanding their territory in all directions.

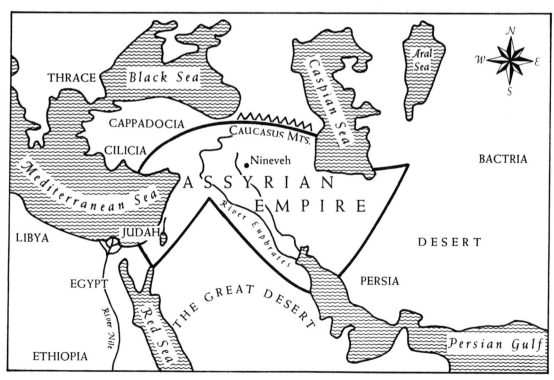

QUESTIONS
on the Story of Hezekiah

1

1 Describe the kingdom that Hezekiah inherited from his father.
2 Tell the reforms instituted by Hezekiah.
3 What was Hezekiah's far-reaching idea?
4 How did the people in Israel respond to Hezekiah's invitation? What was the reaction of those in Judah?

2

5 How many kings was the prophet Isaiah associated with during his long career?
6 What was the upsetting news that Isaiah gave to Hezekiah?
7 For how many years did the Lord extend Hezekiah's life? What important event occurred during this period?
8 Name one of Isaiah's best known prophecies.

3

9 What three steps did Hezekiah take to bolster the defense of Jerusalem?
10 Which of his defense projects was the most important? Can it be seen today?
11 What is the Siloam Inscription? When was it discovered?

12 What sum of money did Sennacherib demand from Hezekiah in exchange for immunity from attack? How did Hezekiah raise the vast amount of money?
13 What did Sennacherib do, as soon as he got the money?
14 What was Isaiah's message to Hezekiah regarding the outcome of the siege?
15 Why did Sennacherib give up the siege and return to Nineveh? What was his eventual fate?

4

16 Why did Isaiah rebuke Hezekiah so sternly?
17 Who succeeded Hezekiah on the throne? What was the new king's well-earned reputation?
18 What did Manasseh do while in a Babylonian prison?
19 What did Manasseh do when he returned to Jerusalem?
20 How long did Amon, Manasseh's son, reign? How did he die?

*Answers are found
on the following pages.*

ANSWERS

on the Story of Hezekiah

1

1 Hezekiah inherited a wicked, corrupt, idol-worshiping kingdom.

2 Hezekiah sought out and destroyed the altars, idols, and false gods. He also restored the Lord's Temple to its original brilliance and beauty, and he called for his people to come to Jerusalem for a consecration service.

3 Hezekiah's idea was to bring the people of both kingdoms together in Jerusalem for a joint celebration of the Feast of the Passover.

4 Hezekiah's couriers were greeted with boos, taunts, mockery, and laughter by the people in Israel. On the other hand, they were greeted warmly and politely by the people in Judah.

2

5 Isaiah served under four kings.

6 Isaiah told Hezekiah to put his house in order, because the Lord had told him that the king would not recover from his illness.

7 The Lord postponed Hezekiah's death for fifteen years. Manasseh, his son and heir apparent, was born during the third year of his extended life span.

8 Isaiah foretold the birth of the Lord Jesus almost eight hundred years before the event occurred.

3

9 Hezekiah's defense projects were:
   (1) to pollute most of the brooks and streams so that the enemy would not have sufficient drinking water;
   (2) to rebuild and strengthen the walls of Jerusalem; and
   (3) to dig a tunnel through solid rock so that he could divert the flow of water from a spring outside the walls to a pool inside the city.

10 Hezekiah's most important defense project was the digging of the tunnel, thus assuring the city's inhabitants an adequate supply of drinking water. The tunnel can be seen today, and a person can also walk through it, albeit with some difficulty.

11 The Siloam Inscription consists of six lines in Hebrew; it is neatly carved on the wall of the tunnel. The inscription is near the Siloam entrance and describes how the tunnel was dug. Archaeologists discovered it in 1880.

12 Sennacherib demanded three hundred talents of silver and thirty talents of gold, a tremendous sum with a cash value of $2,500,000. To appease the Assyrian king, Hezekiah had to strip the Temple and the palace of all their gold, silver, and other treasures.

13 As soon as the money changed hands, Sennacherib broke his promise and laid siege to Jerusalem.

14 Isaiah told Hezekiah not to worry about the outcome of the siege. The Lord would cause Sennacherib to return to his own country where he would die by the sword.

15 Sennacherib awoke one morning and found one hundred and eighty-five thousand of his soldiers dead. He gave up the siege, returned to Nineveh, and never attacked Judah again. Twenty years later, Isaiah's prediction about his fate came true. Two of Sennacherib's sons conspired against him and killed him with their swords.

4

16 Isaiah rebuked Hezekiah sternly because the king had proudly displayed his material riches to the Babylonian envoys and had neglected to show them Judah's spiritual riches.

17 Manasseh succeeded his father, Hezekiah, on the throne. His reputation as the most wicked of all the kings of Judah was well deserved.

18 While in the Babylonian prison, a chastened and penitent Manasseh confessed his sins, begged God to forgive him, and asked that he might return to Jerusalem.

19 Upon his return to Jerusalem, Manasseh spent the last few years of his long reign trying to undo the evil that he had done.

20 Amon's wicked reign lasted for only two years. His servants conspired against him and murdered him.

"The Defeat of Sennacherib" by Rubens. The Prado, Madrid. After the Assyrians mocked the God of Israel and threatened Jerusalem, the Angel of Death swept over their camp and slew one hundred and eighty-five thousand soldiers. The Prado

FURTHER FACTS
AND OUTLINES
for the Story of Hezekiah

SECOND KINGS

OUTLINE

Judah's History during the Reigns of Hezekiah, Manasseh, and Amon (chapters 18-21)

Hezekiah, King of Judah; Hezekiah vs. Sennacherib; Army of Sennacherib Slain by Hand of the Lord (chapters 18, 19)

Hezekiah's Sickness and Miraculous Cure; Death of Hezekiah (chapter 20)

Manasseh's Evil Reign; His Reforms (21:1-18)

Amon's Evil Reign (21:19-26)

ISAIAH

AUTHORSHIP AND DATE

Isaiah, son of Amoz and resident of Jerusalem, was an 8th century prophet of remarkable insight, a religious genius, and a man who lived close to God. He made his home in Jerusalem and was in contact with civil rulers and authorities, to whom he preached as well as to the commoner. The Mishna says Isaiah was killed by Manasseh and the Apocryphal *Ascension of Isaiah* says he was "sawn asunder." Some commentators have suggested that Hebrews 11:37 is a reference to Isaiah's death. He lived in the 8th century B.C., and his ministry extended approximately from 740 B.C., when he was called and anointed for his work (chapter 6), to 700 B.C.

DESTINATION

Especially to Jerusalem and Judah, though there are warnings to the Northern Kingdom and to surrounding Gentile nations (that is, Babylon, Moab, Damascus).

PURPOSE AND THEME

Isaiah writes with a passion of the righteousness of God and the necessity of faith (some have compared his book with the Book of Romans), the coming Messiah and the deliverance He will bring, the need for moral and religious reformation in Judah. As to the latter, Isaiah cries out against mere form in worship, morals, and politics; he declares that it is not enough to act as if one believed in holy behavior; rather, one must *be* holy. Isaiah prophesied during the reigns of Kings Uzziah, Jotham, Hezekiah, Ahaz. He speaks out fearlessly against evil and commends heartily righteous acts. Isaiah, the "Evangelical Prophet," more than any other Old Testament writer looks ahead to the coming Messiah (note especially 7:14 and chapter 53).

OUTLINE

Prophecies About Judah and Jerusalem (chapters 1-12)

The Moral Condition of Jerusalem and Judah (chapters 1-5)
  Sham and Sin, God's Indictment Against Judah (chapter 1)
  God's Judgments against Sham and Sin, and Subsequent Blessing (chapters 2-4)
  The Parable of the Vineyard, with Application (chapter 5)
Hope for a Divine Deliverer (chapters 6-12)
  Isaiah's Vision and Commission: Deliverance Available (chapter 6)
  Isaiah's Message to Ahaz, but Rejection of Deliverer (7:1 – 8:8)
  Isaiah Encouraged: A Righteous Remnant Accepts Deliverer (8:9 – 9:7)
  Isaiah's Nation Near Disaster: The Deliverer Rescues Nation (9:8 – 10:34)
  Isaiah's Future Hope for Israel: The Reign of the Deliverer (chapters 11-12)
God's View of International Affairs (chapters 13-27)
  Babylon and Assyria Attempt to Conquer by War and Torture: The Righteous God will not Tolerate Such (13:1–14:27)
  Philistia Puts Faith in Weapons and Military Alliances; In Point of Fact, GOD Controls History (14:28-32)
  Moab is Proud, but Pride Fosters Prejudice (chapters 15-16)
  Samaria (North Israel) Has Neglected Her Historic Spiritual Foundations (chapter 17)
  Ethiopia Needs to Learn that Confidence Can Be Had by an Adequate View of God (chapter 18)
  Egypt has a False Trust in Human Wisdom; but Egypt, with Her "Wisdom," and Assyria, with Her Might, will One Day Worship with Israel at the Altar of the Lord (the Missionary Thrust of chapter 19)
  Egypt and Ethiopia will Suffer Military Humiliation, a Lesson to Judah (chapter 20)
  Babylon's Imperialism (21:1-10)
  Short Oracles Concerning Dumah (perhaps a name for Edom), and Arabia (21:11-17)

Judah not Grateful for Help (chapter 22)
Tyre Suffers from Materialism (chapter 23)
The Universe, its Judgment and Redemption (chapters 24-27)

God Is Man's Only Hope (chapters 28-35)
  It is Folly for Judah to Put Her Trust in an Alliance with Egypt (chapters 28-29)
  It is Folly to Rely on Egypt (chapters 30-31)
  The Age of Justice, Jerusalem Women Warned, the Outpouring of the Spirit (chapter 32)
Destruction of Assyria Told (chapter 33)
  The Final Judgment and Redemption (chapters 34-35)

Historical Interlude on Events in Hezekiah's Reign (chapters 36-39)
  The Assyrian Threat to Jerusalem (chapters 36-37)
  Hezekiah's Illness, Healing, and Song of Gratitude (chapter 38)
  Hezekiah's Foolish Pride (chapter 39)

Israel's Future Glory (chapters 40-66)
  Comfort and Deliverance for the Captives (the Birth of Christ Announced) (chapters 40-48)
  Comfort and Assurance for Israel (chapters 40-41)
  The Lord's Servant (chapter 42)
  The Lord Redeemer, Israel's Final Restoration (chapter 43)
  God versus Idolatry (chapter 44)
  The Commission to Cyrus (chapter 45)
  Babylon's Idols versus God, the Destruction of Babylon (chapters 46-47)
  The Folly of Israel's Unfaithfulness (chapter 48)

The Suffering and Ministering Servant: Christ Portrayed (chapters 49-57)
  "I am the Lord your Savior, and your Redeemer, the Mighty One of Jacob" (chapter 49)
  Israel's Rejection of the Messiah, Yet His Faithfulness in Spite of Suffering (chapter 50)
  God Will Redeem and Restore Israel (chapters 51-52)

Via Sacra, Babylon. The Assyrians imprisoned Manasseh, idolatrous king of Judah, at Babylon. While in prison he repented and returned to the God of Israel. When he resumed his throne, he tried to reform his subjects. © Matson Photo

"The Prophet Isaiah" by Michelangelo. Sistine Chapel, Rome. In Isaiah's time, Judah was harassed by stronger nations. Isaiah's faith that God would protect His city, Jerusalem, enabled him to counsel wisely the Judean kings. Alinari

269

Response to the Challenge

by
Bob Richards

Hezekiah challenged the people of Israel to turn away from worshiping idols and to come back to the God of their fathers, Who alone was worthy of their worship and praise. The people responded, and a great reformation began—one that saved the nation from the advancing Assyrian conqueror, Sennacherib, as King Hezekiah prayed and then listened to God's instructions brought by Isaiah, the prophet. Bob Richards, who was twice the Olympics pole-vault champion (1952 and 1956) and who has maintained his interest in athletes and religion through the years, indicates what our response to present-day challenges should be in a chapter from his book, *The Heart of a Champion* (© 1959 by Fleming H. Revell Company, Westwood, N.J.).

OUR REACTION DETERMINES OUR DESTINY

DR. ARNOLD TOYNBEE, in his amazing ten-volume history of civilization, says that you can measure civilization by studying the responses of the people of history to the great challenges they have had to face; that history is only the record of how they faced one crisis after another. As we have responded, so has history taken its course. When we have responded negatively, progress has slowed down, cultures have disintegrated, empires have collapsed. When we have responded positively, mankind has leaped ahead; art, music, religion, and industry have flourished; life has been more abundant. The way we react to our challenges determines the destiny of our lives, our country, and our world.

I hardly need repeat the well-known statement that we live in the most challenging hour of all time. I think this is obvious to anyone who knows history or who knows the gigantic problems men are grappling with today. Depending upon the responses that you and I make, so will go the next ten, twenty, thirty years—if there are those thirty years. I couldn't possibly analyze *all* of the tremendous challenges of our time, but may I list what I think are the primary ones that you and I are facing in today's world?

Number one, *there is the challenge of using the genius of man for the creative things of life rather than for the destructive....* This one hit me not long ago while I was reading Albert Einstein's book, *Out of My Later Years.* Here is a man, perhaps the greatest scientist of all history, saying words to the effect that it was his hope that his theories would be used for the betterment of mankind, and that his chief sorrow was to see some of his ideas (which had led to the development of hydrogen energy and the hydrogen bomb) used not in their creative intent but used for destruction. Einstein went on to say that it seems as though there is a bent in human culture that uses the genius of mankind for that which maims and hurts....

Second, *there is the challenge of maintaining health in a day of mechanization.* This one struck me when I was at Purdue University, while I was there to give a talk. We were held up in the street by a car in front of us, a car waiting for a boy to come out of a fraternity house. Finally, the boy sauntered out, got into the car, drove fifty yards around the corner, and went to his second-period class. I couldn't help thinking how this illustrates one of the dilemmas of modern man. We have push-button gadgets, mechanization to the point that we are losing our physical dynamic. We are losing the virility that is so essential in building happiness and creativity in life. . . .

Third, *there is the challenge to maintain an emphasis upon the total personality in a day of specialization.* The more I see this, the more I am convinced that we sometimes see people only as functions, rather than as sacred personalities with intrinsic worth. Nowadays, a man is thought of a laborer, or as a soldier, or as a scientist. Each and every one of us is more than a function. Each of us is an emotional, moral, mental, aesthetic, spiritual being. You don't deal adequately with the problems of men until you realize that all these facets of the total personality must be developed. . . .

Fourth, *there is the challenge of maintaining personal relationships in an urban society.* As I go into urban areas, I am more and more impressed with the fact that we seem to be trying to depersonalize everyone and, in the process, we are dehumanizing people. I once had a church in Long Beach, California, and I used to go out and make calls. One day I knocked at a door and, since I did not know quite where I was, I asked the lady who opened the door, "Do you know where Mr. and Mrs. So-and-So live?" She looked at me and said that she had never heard of them. I found out later that she lived right next door to the people I sought. She had lived there for two years—and she didn't even know their names! But *they* didn't know her name, either. . . .

Fifth, *there is the challenge to maintain brotherhood in a day of prejudice.* I need not stress this one too much. I am quite sure that you are aware of the racial tensions in America and throughout the world. Every newspaper headline, every television and radio report—yesterday's, today's—are filled with this gnawing problem that is eating away at the heart of democracy. . . . The world is almost won, scientifically; it will possible within a

few years to fly around the world in very few hours. The world is that small. Yet it is torn asunder by prejudice—not only racially but religiously and politically, as well. The real challenge in this day is to maintain brotherhood, to stress the essential humanity of mankind. . . .

Sixth, *there is the economic challenge.* It is the problem of feeding the world and meeting global economic need. I was in India a few years ago. Coming out of my hotel room, I ran down the steps and grabbed my bags. Late for a plane, I jumped into a cab and, just at that moment, from the corner of my eye I saw a lot of human beings asleep on the sidewalk. I backed out of the cab and looked around. As far as I could see, on either side, there were people sleeping on the sidewalks. I found out later that thousands of people in Calcutta have no other home. . . . I need not tell you that, in terms of total additions to the population, a whole new nation is born every year. . . . and many of the new people entering the world every year are literally starving to death. They want an economic answer. To talk platitudes to them, even to talk of liberty and freedom to people who have known nothing but hunger, want, and slavery to economic needs, is to talk foolishly. . . . The tendency is to let the state solve this tremendous problem. . . . We must solve it with creative individuals helping and working together.

Seventh, *there is the challenge of meeting the dynamic of communism.* I put this one next to the economic challenge because I've just seen it in Moscow. I've just seen those young intellectuals marching down the street with outstretched arms, shouting, "We are out to win the world. We're out to win the world!" They are young men and girls, fresh out of school. . . . You can see them . . . in other places, eyes flashing with hatred, inciting mob riots. . . . You see this thing and you begin to realize that there is a deadly dynamic to communism. . . . I don't think it will ever be bombed away. It will be defeated only by a greater passion for a greater way of life. . . .

Closely related to this, *there is the challenge of maintaining a spiritual perspective in a day of materialism.* Not only communist materialism but a far more subtle form of materialism eats away the real genius of man. I am not just talking religion here, but I am saying that every great principle of democracy grows out of a spiritual framework. You don't have ideas in isolation; every idea has a root. And I maintain that the sacredness of the human personality, the idea of the rights of every person . . . are rooted in a Judaic-Christian heritage. These are part of our culture. Such a spiritual perspective is essential. I think that the only thing that can meet communism successfully is a point of view which insists that moral values are written into the heart of the universe, that truth triumphs over falsehood, that goodness triumphs over evil, that love triumphs over hate, that there is a purpose to life. . . .

May I speak for a moment from the world of sports? . . . I think that in some of these great sports stories you can see into the heart of human society. In sports the first demand is that the athlete respond quickly. Immediately!

I think of Herb Elliott, a great miler from Australia. Back in Australia, some years ago, Herb Elliott had a broken foot; he hadn't been running for several months. He watched John Landy run the mile under four minutes. He went up to Coach Percy Cerutty, one of the best coaches in Australia, and said, "Mr. Cerutty, I want to run the mile in less than four minutes." Cerutty looked at him and replied, "Son, do you know what it takes to run a mile under four minutes? Do you know what it is to run until you can hardly stand up, suck in hot air until you are almost unconscious? Do you know what it is to run that kind of a race?" Elliott said, "I don't care what it takes; I want to run the mile under four minutes." The coach said, "O.K., come out to the track tomorrow."

Cerutty didn't put him on the track. He took him out to a beach nearby, ran him uphill on the sand, and ran him over boulders and rocks. He ran him over the most difficult obstacle course he could find. The kid kept running; he wouldn't give up. Less than one year afterwards I watched him run the mile in 3:54.8 in the Coliseum. Later he ran it in 3:54.5, to smash the world's record. That's what happens when a man responds, when he gets a vision, when he believes there is something he can do. . . .

We must respond to these challenges with courage. . . . I think of the Babe. You know about Babe Didriksen, who won two gold medals in the Olympic Games. She was All American in softball, basketball, horseback riding, tennis, golf, swimming, and then—cancer. At the height of her career, cancer! She called in her pastor the day before she died and said, "Pray a little harder. I'm getting a little closer." The pastor prayed, and left. I played golf with her husband, and he himself told me how she then called him to her bedside and said, "Honey, I hope you will find someone to love you as much as I have loved you." And then, as he cried, she gripped his hand as tightly as she could and said, "Now, honey, don't take on so. While I've been in the hospital, I've learned one thing: A moment of happiness is a lifetime, and I have had a lot of happiness.". . . That's courage! It goes to the heart of things. To stress the quality of life rather then just quantity, to meet life's greatest tragedy with a smile—this is real courage.

We must meet these challenges with commitment. This is interwoven in every aspect of life. I have seen it in sports. The greatest athletes whom I know, pray. In this world of muscle and bone, I have heard them breathe a prayer that God will help them. . . . I remember Maxie Truex, a little 5-feet 6-inch 129-pounder, who said to me, "Bob, with God's help I am going to break every long distance record in America." And the very next year he did it! You'll never convince me that he runs with just his 129 pounds; he runs with everything he has—heart, faith, will, determination. . . . I could go on and tell you about so many others. . . .

I pray that you will respond to every moment of great inspiration and challenge but, above all, that you will respond to Christ's "Follow me," the greatest challenge of all human history.

Josiah

PERHAPS THE STORY OF JOSIAH is the most heroic, yet pathetic, in the Books of Kings. With the accession of Josiah to the throne, there came the last attempt at reformation before the final sweeping away of Judah into captivity. His first step was restoration of the Temple, which had been neglected and deserted. All that followed resulted from that act, for in the course of the work came the discovery of the Book of the Law.

The sacred writings had been neglected and the actual Temple copy lost. On reading the Book, Josiah discovered how far the nation had wandered from the Divine ideal and how terrible were the curses pronounced upon Judah for such wandering. He turned for counsel to the prophetess, Huldah, who recognized the sincerity of the king as well as the corruption of the people. She declared that the reformation would be unreal so far as the people were concerned.

Despite this, Josiah worked with enthusiasm and energy. He arranged for a public reading of the Book of the Law. He purged the Temple and the rest of the land of false idols and shrines. He then observed the Passover Feast, which had long been neglected. But, though Josiah was sincere and loyal to the will and word of God, the people simply followed his lead, without any sense of penitence or a return to the Lord, so Josiah's actions produced no results in national life. Therefore, there was no turning on the part of God from His necessary purpose of judgment. The fact is that when the Book of the Law was lost, nothing could save the nation or its people from ruin.—G. Campbell Morgan, *Searchlights from the Word.*

RUBENS: *The Defeat of Sennacherib*

PRECEDING PAGE

The Defeat of Sennacherib

by PETER PAUL RUBENS (1577-1640) *Flemish School*

Pinacothek, Munich

And it came to pass that night, that the angel of the Lord went out, and smote in the camp of the Assyrians an hundred fourscore and five thousand: and when they arose early in the morning, behold, they were all dead corpses. 2 KINGS 19:35

IN A GRAND MELEE of the earthly and the supernatural, of the contemporary with old Roman and Oriental costumes, of figures inspired by ancient statuary and others by Renaissance painting, Rubens has created this scene of incredible complexity and excitement. It is one of the great achievements of his particular genius that he was able to summon up such a vast and varied population for his pictures, and moreover to maintain such order in his seething mass of shapes that we are able to read the events at the same time that we are swept along in the action.

1
A GREAT DISCOVERY

THE LAMP OF JUDAH was slowly flickering out. Soon her day would be ended, and the once great nation would plunge into darkness, destruction, and despair. However, the people were to have one last chance to turn away from their wicked ways. Josiah, great-grandson of Hezekiah, that fervent reformist of fifty years earlier, sat upon the throne of Judah and made a final, fruitless attempt to bring his people back to God.

Because of the untimely death of his father, Josiah became king when he was only eight years old. For the next eight years wise counselors guided and trained him in his kingly duties; and Jedidah, his godly mother, taught him so well in religious matters that he sought the Lord in the days of his youth and found Him.

At the age of twenty, Josiah made a start toward the fulfillment of his first great dream. He roamed far and wide throughout the land of Judah, personally directing the destruction of idols, carved and molten images, and altars to false gods. Josiah made a clean sweep of the idolatrous practices in Judah, not neglecting to take care of the priests serving the false gods.

The young king did not confine his activities to his own kingdom. Ruthlessly and relentlessly he carried his purge of idolatry into the former kingdom of Israel. At Bethel Josiah paused long enough to destroy the altars and golden calf that Jeroboam I had placed there. Then he and his men spread out over all the northern territory in a zealous search for traces of idols and idol worship. When he had broken down all the altars, ground all the graven images into dust, and cut down all the idols in Israel, Josiah returned to Jerusalem.

After six years of tireless effort, Josiah felt certain that idolatry had been forever crushed throughout his kingdom and the land adjacent to it. The good king was now ready to enter the second phase of his planned program to bring the people of Judah to their knees in prayers of repentance to the one true God.

During the long, evil reign of Josiah's grandfather Manasseh, the Temple of the Lord had been woefully neglected and was badly in need of extensive repairs. One day Josiah called Shaphan the scribe to him.

"Go to the Temple," he said, "and tell Hilkiah the high priest to give the money, which the doorkeepers have collected, to the custodians of the Temple. They will use it to hire carpenters, builders, masons, and artisans, and to purchase lumber, polished stone, and other materials needed to repair and renovate the Temple. No accounting will be required of them as to how the money is spent, because they are honest and trustworthy."

The restoration of the Temple was proceeding on schedule. Meanwhile, inside the Temple, Hilkiah and Shaphan were busily engaged in dusting, rearranging, and looking through the Temple treasures.

"Come quickly!" Hilkiah suddenly exclaimed. "I have found the Book of the Law in the House of the Lord!"

Shaphan rushed over to look at it. Then he asked Hilkiah to give it to him so that he could show it to the king. While the scribe walked toward the palace, he read

JOSIAH

"The Piety of Josiah" by J. A. Adams and J. G. Chapman. *The Illuminated Bible* (1846). Josiah reverently obeyed the words of the Book of the Law when the sacred writings were found. He tried to save his people. Harper & Brothers

hurriedly through the scroll, which turned out to be part of the Book of Deuteronomy. He noted that it contained many of the laws and teachings of Moses.

Shaphan stood before Josiah and spoke excitedly.

"Look!" he exclaimed. "Hilkiah has found the lost Book of the Law in the Lord's Temple!"

The king examined the Book and then asked Shaphan to read it to him. The longer the scribe read, the more disturbed the king became. How great were the sins of omission and commission by the people of Judah! At the end of the reading, Josiah arose and tore his clothes, in anguish. He then appointed a committee, headed by Hilkiah and Shaphan, to consult with a servant of the Lord concerning the words in the newly-found Book. The king knew that, if it really was the Book of the Law of Moses, the people of Judah were in

deep trouble because of their many transgressions.

There were three prophets, including the great Jeremiah, who lived as contemporaries in this period; but the delegation went, instead, to the prophetess Huldah in Jerusalem. They showed her the Book and discussed the matter with her. Then she went into another room to wait for a message from the Lord. When Huldah returned, she spoke solemnly.

"Thus says the Lord," she began, "to the man who sent you to me: 'I will bring evil upon all your people, because they have forsaken Me and have offered sacrifices to other gods. My wrath has been kindled against this place, and it shall not be quenched. But, because your heart was tender and you humbled yourself before Me when you heard what I said in the Book of the Law, and because you tore your clothes and wept before Me, I will

276

gather you to your fathers in peace and you shall not see the woes and the destruction that I will bring to your kingdom.'"

The men brought Huldah's words to the king, and he knew what he must do. Although the fate of Judah seemed bleak and hopeless, Josiah was determined to continue his crusade for the redemption and rededication of his people.

In response to Josiah's call, the elders, the prophets, the priests, and all the people of Judah and Jerusalem assembled at the Lord's Temple to hear the reading of the Book of the Law of Moses. When the reading was completed, Josiah stood by his pillar in the Temple and made a covenant before the Lord to keep His commandments and His statutes with all his heart and soul, and to obey all the laws that were written in the book. All the people joined with him in this covenant.

The pinnacle of Josiah's reformation program came with the great celebration of the Passover. Preparations for the Feast went forward in strict accordance with the instructions contained in the book of the teachings of Moses. Priests and Levites were assigned their special duties. The people were divided into family groups and were given housing in the homes of the Levites. A large number of animals was rounded up for the sacrifices. Josiah gave thirty thousand lambs and goats and three thousand bulls; the princes of the kingdom gave two thousand and six hundred lambs and goats and three hundred oxen.

At last the glorious day arrived. King Josiah stood before his people and cried out: "Sanctify yourselves and prepare for the Feast of the Passover!"

After this announcement, there was a bustle of activity among the priests and Levites. The Passover lamb was killed and its blood sprinkled over the altar. It was then roasted according to the ordinance. Sacrifices and burnt offerings were made to the Lord, and the meat and unleavened bread were passed out to the people. After the Feast, the sons of Asaph, the singers, ended the festivities with songs of praise and thanksgiving to the Lord.

Josiah sat upon his throne, pleased, relaxed, and confident. Surely, the Lord's heart would relent after witnessing the magnificent celebration, and He would spare His people from the fate that Huldah had predicted for them. Poor Josiah! He little realized that the people were only giving lip-service to the worship of the Lord. The Judeans were biding their time until the good king died and they could tumble back into their evil, idolatrous ways.

Based on the story in the Bible:
2 Kings 22:1 – 23:23;
2 Chronicles 34:1 – 35:19

2
JOSIAH'S GRAVE MISTAKE

WHILE JOSIAH WAS MAKING HIS REFORMS inside Judah, the storms of war were raging outside the tiny kingdom. The Assyrians were making their last desperate struggle against the rapidly growing might of the Babylonians. Pharaoh-necho of Egypt was preparing to help deliver the death blow to the once powerful Assyrian Empire.

Josiah was about to embark upon a dangerous and unnecessary mission. His couriers had just advised him that Necho, pharaoh of Egypt, was on the move and that his armies would soon cross the Plain of Jezreel enroute to launch an attack against Assyria. Impetuously and unwisely, Josiah decided to intervene.

With his armies and chariots, Josiah made a rapid march to the north and caught up with Necho at Megiddo, a town overlooking the Jezreel Valley. When the king of Egypt saw the advancing Judaean army, he sent delegates to Josiah with a message.

"O king of Judah! Why have you come out to fight me?" he asked. "I have no quarrel with you. It is against the Assyrians that I am waging a war."

Stubborn Josiah turned a deaf ear on the envoys and told them that he was deter-

Megiddo (Tell el-Mutesellim). Many civilizations have occupied this site because of its strategic location. Josiah was killed here trying to block the advance toward Assyria by the Egyptian Pharaoh-necho (608 B.C.)   © Matson Photo

"Jeremiah Mourning the Death of Josiah" by J. A. Adams and J. G. Chapman. *The Illuminated Bible* (1846). Josiah had been loved and esteemed by his subjects, especially Jeremiah, whose lament was chanted by the singers.   Harper & Brothers

mined to fight the Egyptians. Necho's delegates had failed in their mission of peace, so they hurriedly returned to make their report to their king.

Josiah ordered out his army and met Pharaoh-necho's men at Megiddo, the scene of the great battle between Sisera and Barak during the days of Judge Deborah. The fighting was hot and furious for several hours. Then one of the Egyptian archers took careful aim and sent an arrow speeding toward Josiah. The felled king called to one of his aides.

"Take me back to Jerusalem, for I am badly wounded," he said.

With their king no longer able to lead them into combat, the army of Judah beat a hasty retreat, carrying their injured king with them. Despite the best medical care and attention, King Josiah died a warrior's death on the field of battle.

When the people of Judah learned of the death of their king, a great wail of anguish and sorrow rent the air. His son and successor, Jehoahaz, proclaimed a thirty-day period of mourning for Josiah. Jeremiah, a rising young prophet, wrote a lament for him, and the singing men and women chanted it, with tears in their eyes, at his funeral. The Bible pays this high tribute to Josiah, a great and good king:

"He did what was right in the sight of the Lord, and walked in the way of his forefather David, and he turned not aside to the right hand or to the left . . . There was no king before him like him, who turned to the Lord with all his heart, and with all his soul, and with all his might, according to all the Law of Moses; nor did any like him reign after him."

Based on the story in the Bible:
2 Kings 23:25, 28-30;
2 Chronicles 35:20-25

PLACES

in the Story of Josiah

JERUSALEM

The capital city of Judah, Jerusalem was the site of the Temple which Josiah found so much in need of repair. By his restoration of the Temple and leading his people in a study of Moses' Law and in obedience to it, Josiah re-established in Judah the worship of the one true God. The observance of the great Passover Feast took place in Jerusalem.

BETHEL

This town is about 12 miles north of Jerusalem. During Josiah's purge of idolatry the golden calf, set up here by Jeroboam I, and its altar were destroyed.

MEGIDDO

This important city in north central Palestine overlooks the Plain of Jezreel and is located about 15 miles east of the Mediterranean Sea. King Josiah of Judah was fatally wounded here when he made his senseless stand against Pharaoh-necho and the Egyptian army.

Airview of Megiddo Mound. At excavated areas, city gates and fortifications (AA), shrines, temples, and altars (BB), and evidence of stables (CC) from many civilizations were found. Oriental Institute, University of Chicago

QUESTIONS

on the Story of Josiah

1

1 How old was Josiah when he became king of Judah? How were his early years spent?

2 What did Josiah do when he was twenty years old?

3 What was the second phase of Josiah's program to bring his people back to God?

4 What great discovery did Hilkiah, the high priest, make during the restoration of the Lord's Temple?

5 What did Josiah do when Shaphan finished reading the Book?

6 What was the message that Huldah, the prophetess, gave to Josiah's delegation?

7 What did Josiah do when he heard the words of Huldah?

8 Did the people of Judah join with Josiah in his pledge of allegiance to the Law of the Lord?

9 What was the climax of Josiah's reformation program?

10 How was the Feast of the Passover celebrated?

11 Why was Josiah relaxed and relieved after the celebration ended?

12 Why was he doomed for disappointment?

2

13 What was the political situation outside Judah during the time when Josiah was making his religious reforms?

14 What unwise and impetuous decision did King Josiah make?

15 What was the message that Necho sent to Josiah?

16 Where did Josiah's army meet with the Egyptian army? What great battle had been fought there many centuries earlier?

17 What happened to Josiah during the heat of the battle?

18 How long did Josiah rule over Judah? Who succeeded him?

19 Who wrote a lament for Josiah? How was it sung?

20 What does the Bible say about the reign of Josiah, a great and good king?

*Answers are found
on the following pages.*

ANSWERS

on the Story of Josiah

1

1 Josiah was eight years old when he became king of Judah. During his early years he was instructed and guided by wise counselors regarding his kingly duties, and he received his religious training from his godly mother, Jedidah. He sought the Lord in the days of his youth, and he found Him.

2 When Josiah was twenty years old, he purged the land of Judah and adjacent territory of all traces of idolatry and the worship of false gods.

3 The second phase of Josiah's program was to repair and restore the long neglected Temple of the Lord.

4 Hilkiah discovered the lost Book of the Law of Moses.

5 Josiah tore his clothes and wept. Then he appointed a committee to consult with a servant of the Lord concerning the words written in the Book.

6 Huldah told the delegation that the Lord was very angry with the people of Judah, because they had forsaken Him, and that He would destroy the land and the people. However, Josiah would be spared the pain of witnessing the destruction because he had humbled himself and repented on hearing the words that the Lord said in the Book of the Law.

7 Josiah called all the people to Jerusalem and read the Book of the Law to them.

8 The people of Judah made a covenant with their king to obey the Law of Moses.

9 The apex of Josiah's reformation program was his great celebration of the Feast of the Passover.

10 The Feast of the Passover was celebrated in strict accordance with the instructions contained in the Book of the Law of Moses. The Bible says that no such Passover had been observed since the days of Samuel.

11 After the celebration, Josiah was relaxed and relieved because he felt certain that the Lord would relent and stay His judgment on the people.

12 Josiah was doomed for disappointment, because his people were giving only lip-service in the worship of the Lord.

2

13 Kingdoms around Judah were struggling for power. The mighty Babylonian Empire was rapidly becoming the dominant force among the surrounding nations. The Assyrian Empire was on the wane and, four years after the death of Josiah, Nineveh would fall to a Babylonian siege and the Assyrian power would be forever broken. The Egyptians were also weakening, but they were still strong enough to help give the Assyrians the kiss of death.

14 When Josiah learned that Pharaoh-necho of Egypt was advancing on Assyria, he decided to intervene.

15 Necho told Josiah that he had no quarrel with him or his people. He emphasized that Egypt was waging war with the Assyrians.

16 Josiah ordered out his army and he met Pharaoh-necho's army at Megiddo. Sisera and Barak had fought a decisive battle there, centuries earlier, during the time of Deborah, Israel's only woman judge.

17 An Egyptian archer mortally wounded Josiah with a carefully aimed arrow.

18 Josiah ruled over Judah for thirty-one

ANSWERS ON THE STORY OF JOSIAH

years. His son, Jehoahaz, succeeded him.

19 Jeremiah, a rising young prophet, wrote a lament for Josiah. The lament was chanted sadly by the singers with tears in their eyes.

20 The Bible says that there was no king like Josiah, either before or after his reign. He turned to the Lord with all his heart, soul, and might, according to all the Law of Moses.

"The Sabbath Breakers of Judah" by J. A. Adams and J. G. Chapman. *The Illuminated Bible* (1846). Josiah saw that many Judeans violated the Fourth Commandment of Moses, "Remember the Sabbath day to keep it holy." Harper & Brothers

283

FURTHER FACTS
AND OUTLINES
for the Story of Josiah

SECOND KINGS AND SECOND CHRONICLES

THEME AND PURPOSE

The story of Josiah's life is one of pious devotion to God and His purpose, in its early years, and of seemingly irresponsible actions in later life that resulted in his untimely death.

Eight years old when he began to reign, Josiah began to exhibit his pious disposition when he was sixteen. Four years later he started uprooting the idolatry that had infested Judah.

While this reform work was proceeding, in Josiah's twenty-sixth year the Book of the Law was found as the Temple was undergoing repairs. The authentic copy of the Law had been lost, but it was now found by Hilkiah, the high priest. Profoundly moved by reading the record of God's dealings with His people, Josiah gathered the representatives of the people into the Temple and made a solemn covenant to walk in the ways of the Lord. As Hezekiah had been assisted by Isaiah, so Josiah found in Jeremiah a strong support. For the last time in her long, turbulent history, Judah was raised to a high religious plane.

When Pharaoh-necho of Egypt began marching against the Assyrians, it was necessary for him to pass through Palestine. Although he assured Josiah that he had no hostile intentions with reference to Judah, for some unexplained reason Josiah sought to prevent Necho from passing through the land. This action resulted in the Battle of Megiddo, and Josiah was slain. Jeremiah, recognizing the loss to the kingdom, prepared a dirge in which Josiah was mourned as a great man fallen in Judah.

OUTLINES

SECOND KINGS

Good King Josiah and the great Reforms that He Put into Effect (chapters 22:1 – 23:30)

SECOND CHRONICLES

King Josiah's Good Reign and His Reformation; Killed at Megiddo in Battle with the Pharaoh of Egypt (chapters 34-35)

Courage Takes Time

by
J. Edgar Hoover

At first glance there may seem to be little in common between a dedicated F. B. I. man and the royal reformer, Josiah. But a careful reading of J. Edgar Hoover's evaluation of Sam Cowley, told in *Guideposts* (© 1960, Guideposts Associates, Inc., Carmel, N.Y.), reveals one very important common trait: moral courage. The distinguished director of the Federal Bureau of Investigation makes a distinction between *physical bravery* and *moral courage* that is often overlooked in the evaluation of a man's worth, to himself and to society, in today's world.

DEVOTION TO DUTY AND PRINCIPLE

I HAVE KNOWN some very brave men in my time. But there is a difference between physical bravery and moral courage. Bravery is a temporary manifestation. It flashes forth to meet a sudden challenge. Moral courage, however, has the dimension of *duration*.

The latter may be less spectacular than the sudden type of heroism, but it is more important because it endures. It's the month-to-month, year-to-year, steady, sustained devotion to duty and principle as opposed to self-interest that may never make any headlines, but without which the world would be a dark and dangerous place indeed.

What I am saying, I suppose, is that the greatest adventure in moral courage is a moral life. I truly believe this. Every life—yours, mine, everyone's—is an endless series of choices between right and wrong, good and evil. No one makes *all* the right choices. But the struggle to make as many right choices as possible goes on ceaselessly, and this is what makes life the great adventure that it is.

Now, what is the quality in a person that makes a moral life possible? It's discipline, isn't it? Self-discipline is precisely the quality that the criminal lacks. He can never say no to himself. He can never deny a selfish impulse. He steals, he robs, he cheats, he kills

because that seems to him the easiest way to get what he wants. The undisciplined person is always wondering what he can take from life with the least possible effort. It takes a controlled and disciplined person to wonder what he can give.

It is also a theory of mine that physical courage, in its highest form, rests squarely on a moral base. Let me tell you about a man whose life was a shining example of this.

His name was Samuel P. Cowley. He was not quite 30 years old when he entered the FBI as a Special Agent back in 1929—a big, young fellow, as solid and dependable as he looked.

At that time, when the Bureau was smaller, I made a point of knowing all my men personally, and so I knew all about Sam Cowley. I knew that he was deeply religious, that from 1916 to 1920 he had done missionary work in the Hawaiian Islands for the Church of Jesus Christ of the Latter Day Saints. I knew that he had attended the Utah Agricultural College, working as a salesman during the summer months to pay his tuition. I knew that later he took a law degree at the George Washington University. I knew that he was a Sunday school teacher, that he lived a clean, honest, hardworking life. *I knew, in other words, that Sam Cowley was already trying to make his life an adventure in moral courage—and I knew that this was the kind of man we needed.*

To come into the FBI in those days, you had to be an idealist. Sam Cowley's starting pay was $2,900 a year. The FBI had made no great reputation at that time. Except in special cases, its agents were not even allowed to carry guns. With his education and character, Sam Cowley could have earned far more money in a far less difficult and dangerous job. He chose not to consider these things.

Did this choice involve moral courage? I think it did. The Depression had not yet struck the country. There was easy money to be made almost anywhere. Like most young men, Sam Cowley wanted to raise a family, to give his wife and children a few luxuries. But he chose the FBI because he felt that the most important thing to do with his life was to fight against evil. His personal comfort and safety meant less to him than being on the side of good.

We brought Sam Cowley along as fast as we could because we needed him. We were fighting a crime wave that was a grim hang-over from the Prohibition Era. Bootlegging had put vast amounts of money into gangster pockets and had bred in them a contempt for the law.

Perhaps the most vicious of all was John Herbert Dillinger, bank-robber, jail-breaker, police-hater. His gang included a trigger-happy murderer known as "Baby Face" Nelson. Between September, 1933, and July, 1934, members of this gang killed ten men, wounded seven more, robbed four banks, and broke out of three jails.

In June I called Sam Cowley into my office. By this time I knew that he was one of our most determined and capable men, but I think my choice was based on something more than that. To me, Dillinger and his gang were the personification of evil. Sam was one of the finest characters I had ever known. I think that, unconsciously perhaps, I was trying to oppose this vile personification of evil with the highest example of good it had been my pleasure to know, because religion teaches us that good is stronger than evil.

I remember quite clearly the orders I gave to Sam. "Stay on Dillinger. Go anywhere the trail takes you. Try to take him alive, but protect yourself."

It was a tough assignment, grim and dangerous. The hunted man was constantly on the move. In his dogged pursuit, Sam Cowley crossed the country from coast to coast, from southern Florida to northern Michigan. He was almost never at home. He and his wife were planning to buy a house where their two small children could have their own play yard. Their plans had to be postponed.

The days lengthened into weeks. And if Sam Cowley was displaying moral courage, what about his wife? What were her thoughts every night as she tucked her two small boys into bed and waited for the phone call that might, or might not, come? It would have been very easy for her to show her fear, and by showing it to distract her husband, or even sway him from his hazardous task. But she never complained. Love can make you courageous—very courageous.

Everyone knows how Cowley and his men cornered Dillinger as he left the Biograph Theatre in Chicago. When the gangster clawed a gun from his pocket and started to run, three of our men fired five shots . . . and Dillinger fell dead.

Next day I wrote a letter of commendation to Sam, praising him for his persistence, patience and energy. As a reward, he was promoted to the rank of Inspector.

Some men might have been content to rest on their laurels, but Sam Cowley was not that kind of man. He considered his job unfinished so long as any members of the Dillinger gang were at large. In particular, he wanted to capture "Baby Face" Nelson . . . and four months after Dillinger's death Sam got his chance. In a gun-battle near Barrington, Illinois, one of our agents was killed and Sam Cowley was mortally wounded. He died early the next morning. But their mission had been completed, as that same day the body of "Baby Face" Nelson was found in a roadside ditch not far from Chicago.

So in one murderous moment, the FBI lost two of its finest men. And what is my point?

My point is that this sacrifice was not just a magnificent demonstration of momentary heroism. It was the culmination of that greatest of all adventures in moral courage—a truly moral life. As a friend of Sam's said at his funeral, "I have thought that his name should have been Peter. He was a veritable rock to those who knew, who loved and trusted him. His was the calm of a man who did his best and left the final decision to a Higher Power."

There, it seems to me, is the key, the answer to those who wonder what the secret of a moral life really is: it is simply to do the best you can and leave the rest to God.

Religion points the way. I honestly believe that if every child in this land went to Sunday school every week, if every adult went to church with the love of God and his fellow man in his heart, if each of us would make a conscious and sustained effort to live by the Golden Rule, a moral revolution would come not only to America, but eventually to the whole world.

This may seem visionary, but we can all hope for it and work for it and pray for it. I know I do. Every single day.

Jeremiah

THROUGH STRESS AND STRAIN, against hatred and hostility, Jeremiah declared the Word of God to a rebellious and stiff-necked people. His perseverance in the face of opposition was, like King Josiah's, heroic. Starting when Josiah was twenty-one years old, Jeremiah conducted a prophetic ministry in Judah for forty years. So far as producing any results in directing the people back to God is concerned, he was without success.

Jeremiah's prophecies, which had stirred the anger of the people, were literally fulfilled. The writings of this great man, as preserved for us, show that he had no joy in the sorrows that befell his people through their sins; rather, he felt the most acute suffering. Nevertheless, he must have had great satisfaction in the fact that he had been true to the Word of the Lord that was delivered to him.

The Word of God is always fulfilled, no matter by whom it is proclaimed. The man who never fails nor falters in the delivery of that Word is indeed happy, in the deepest sense. It is not so much the selfish joy of seeing things turn out as he has predicted. It is, rather, the high joy of realizing that he has been honored in being the messenger appointed to deliver the Word which cannot fail. —G. Campbell Morgan, *Searchlights from the Word*

MICHELANGELO: *Jeremiah*

Jeremiah

by MICHELANGELO (1475-1564) *Italian School*

Sistine Chapel, Vatican, Rome

To whom shall I speak, and give warning, that they may hear? JEREMIAH 6:10

THE BROODING FIGURE of Jeremiah seems to communicate the sorrowful mood of the prophet. He warned the people that they would be punished for their sins, but his words went unheeded. During his lifetime Jeremiah witnessed the tragic decline of Judah, the destruction of Jerusalem, and the exile to Babylon, all of which he had predicted. Michelangelo's prophet seems to carry the burdens of all mankind, forever.

1
JEREMIAH, GOD'S CHOICE

IN ANATHOTH, A SUBURB OF JERUSALEM, God raised up another of His men of the hour. When the boy-king Josiah came to the throne of Judah, another boy was growing up in the priestly town of Anathoth. His name was Jeremiah, son of Hilkiah and a descendant of Eli, the guardian of Samuel. The lad was destined to be a great prophet for the Lord.

Jeremiah was reared among people who were faithful to God. Members of the community spent much of their time in writing and teaching the great stories of Jewish history. Jeremiah sat at the feet of Levitical teachers, learning the Law of Moses and hearing inspired messages from Elijah, Elisha, and other prophets.

Jeremiah and Josiah were about the same age, and it was in the thirteenth year of the pious king's reign that the Word of the Lord came to Jeremiah and told him of his divine commission. The startled young man shrank back and hesitated, just as Moses had done centuries earlier.

"O, Lord God!" he exclaimed. "I cannot be your spokesman, because I am only a youth."

Aerial View of Anathoth. This Levite city lay northeast of Jerusalem in the territory of Benjamin. Jeremiah was born here, and in his youth he learned the Law of Moses from the holy men of the city. © Matson Photo

"Don't say that you are only a youth," the Lord replied immediately. "Before you were born, I consecrated you and appointed you as a prophet to all nations and all kingdoms."

The Lord then stretched forth His hand, touched Jeremiah's lips, and said: "I have put words in your mouth. You shall go wherever I send you and say whatever I tell you. Have no fear if the people become angry at the words that you speak, because I will be with you to guard and protect you."

During the first eighteen years of his career, Jeremiah spent a relatively quiet and peaceful life. He used much of this time in study and preparation for the stormy days that the Lord had told him were sure to come. He walked among the priests and listened quietly and attentively to their words of wisdom. His knowledge of the power and patience of the Lord God of Israel increased, day by day.

Jeremiah was filled with excitement. In the eighteenth year of Josiah's reign the godly king launched a prodigious religious reformation program throughout his kingdom. As soon as Jeremiah heard the news, he rushed to Jerusalem and watched with amazement the rapid restoration of the Lord's Temple to its original splendor.

Jeremiah's heart was filled with hope as he watched the young king make his next move in a determined effort to bring his people back to God. When the work on the Temple was finished, Josiah issued a proclamation forbidding the worship of idols and ordered their immediate destruction. The young prophet strongly endorsed this action and he became a wayfarer as he wandered the length and breadth of the land, exhorting the people to rally behind their king.

After six years all the idols had been destroyed, and the people had returned to the worship of the Lord. God rewarded Josiah's faithful service by giving him and his kingdom seven years of peace and prosperity.

Then . . . King Josiah was dead! His aides had brought their badly wounded king back to Jerusalem from the battlefield of Megiddo. Despite all efforts to save his life, he had died a few hours later. Jeremiah and all Judah were grief-stricken. A mournful nation paid tribute to their beloved king. As a climax to the service, the singing men and women slowly intoned the praised-filled lament written by Jeremiah in honor of his king.

Based on the story in the Bible:
Jeremiah 1:1-10

2
THE TRIALS AND TRIBULATIONS OF A PROPHET

THE DEATH KNELL FOR JUDAH was sounded when King Josiah died. All of his great reforms were quickly forgotten as the people resumed their mad dash toward their impending doom. Yet a merciful, loving God still yearned for His people to return to Him and was willing to give them another opportunity to repent.

Jehoahaz was chosen to succeed his father on the throne. His turbulent, wicked, three-month reign ended abruptly when Pharaoh-necho replaced him and put his older, more cooperative brother, Jehoiakim, in the royal palace. The

"Jehoahaz Put in Bands by Pharaoh-necho" by J. A. Adams and J. G. Chapman. *The Illuminated Bible* (1846). The Pharaoh deposed Josiah's son Jehoahaz, who had become king of Judah, and imprisoned him in Egypt. Harper & Brothers

deposed king was taken to an Egyptian prison where he remained for the rest of his life. Jehoahaz thus became the first Judean prince to die in a foreign land.

During the first year of King Jehoiakim's reign, the Word of the Lord came to Jeremiah.

"Stand in the Temple Court and speak to the throngs of people who come there to worship," God said. "Perhaps they will all repent and turn away from their wickedness. If they do, I will reconsider the punishment I have planned for them. Warn them, however, that if they do not heed My words and obey My laws, I will destroy the Temple just as I destroyed the shrine at Shiloh, and I will make the name Jerusalem a curse word among all the nations of the earth."

Jeremiah had just finished delivering his great Temple Sermon and, as a result, was in deep trouble. Instead of repenting when they heard his stern words, the people became an angry, shouting mob. Led by priests and false prophets, the people surrounded Jeremiah.

"Kill him! Kill him!" they shouted. "He has prophesied in the name of the Lord against this Temple and against this city."

When the princes heard the noisy tumult, they rushed out of the king's palace to learn what had caused the people to become so excited. Some of the priests and false prophets saw them coming. They ran to meet them and glibly said that Jeremiah deserved to die because of his prophecy against Jerusalem. The princes quickly restored order. They arrested the prophet and led him to the city gate for trial. Jeremiah made a stirring plea in his own defense.

"The Lord God of Israel sent me to the Temple Court to speak to these people," he began. "He told me exactly what to say,

"Jeremiah Prophesies the Fall of Jerusalem" by J. A. Adams and J. G. Chapman. *The Illuminated Bible* (1846). Jeremiah, in his Temple Sermon, admonished the people to return to God or Jerusalem would be destroyed.   Harper & Brothers

and the message heard today is His message. The Lord had hoped that His people would mend their evil ways and come back to Him and His teachings. By their refusal to do so, the people have left the Lord no alternative but to fulfill His harsh judgment against them. As for me, I am in your power and you can do whatever you will to me. However, one thing is certain. If you put me to death, you will have innocent blood on your hands and there will be innocent blood on this city and its people. I repeat: I am telling the truth when I say that it was a mission for the Lord that brought me here this day."

After a short deliberation, Ahikam, spokesman for the princes who served as court officials, arose and announced the verdict.

"This man Jeremiah is not guilty! Release him from custody at once!" he said.

Ahikam, son of Shaphan the Scribe, was one of the more powerful princes in the royal court. He was also one of Jeremiah's staunch friends. After the acquittal was announced, he and some of the elders who had remained loyal to the prophet escorted him to his home town of Anathoth.

During the fourth year of Jehoiakim's reign, the Word of the Lord came again to Jeremiah.

"Take a roll [scroll] and write upon it everything that I have said since the days of Josiah, when I first spoke to you, until today," He began. "It may be that, when the people of Judah hear the things that I intend to do to them, everybody will turn from their evil conduct; then I can forgive their wrongdoing."

When Jeremiah had finished dictating all the words that God had spoken against Israel and Judah, he had a personal word for his secretary.

"Baruch," he said, "because of the unpopular stand that I have taken on many issues, I am barred from entering the

"*Baruch*" by J. James Tissot. *The Old Testament*, Illustrated. Baruch went to the Temple and read aloud the words of the Lord that Jeremiah had dictated.   M. de Buffan & Co.

Lord's Temple. You must therefore go in my stead and, on fast days when people from all over the kingdom come here, read the words of the Lord that I have dictated to you."

Baruch did as directed. When he had

finished reading the hot, burning words from the scroll, he looked around. Only one person in the vast throng appeared to have been impressed. Michaiah, grandson of Shaphan, rushed to the palace to consult with the princes. After several minutes of earnest conversation, the princes agreed to send Jehudi, an officer of the court, to Baruch and invite him to bring his scroll to the palace and read it to them.

Baruch stood before the princes and began to read. As he progressed, they became more and more anxious and perturbed. When the reading was ended, one official approached Baruch.

"Although some of us are in open sympathy with you and Jeremiah and the cause that you espouse, we must report this matter to the king," he said. "When he hears what is written on the scroll, your lives will be at stake. Give me the scroll and hurry back to Jeremiah. We will not see the king until you have had time to find a good hiding place."

As the officials had expected, King Jehoiakim was furious when Jehudi finished reading the words that Jeremiah had dictated. He angrily grabbed the roll, cut it into ribbons with his knife, and burned it in his fireplace. When the flames had consumed the written words of the Lord, the king ordered the arrest of Jeremiah and Baruch. Happily, however, they could not be found because the Lord had hidden them well.

While they were still in hiding, the Word of the Lord came again to Jeremiah.

"Take another scroll and write upon it all the words that were on the first one," He said. "Also write this message for Jehoiakim. Tell him that I shall punish him severely because he dared to burn My

"Jeremiah" by J. James Tissot. *The Old Testament,* Illustrated. Jeremiah dashed a pottery vessel to bits to symbolize the fate of Jerusalem.   M. de Buffan & Co.

words. He shall be killed by an enemy and, through the winter cold and the summer heat, his body shall remain where it falls. Furthermore, I shall bring upon the people of Jerusalem and the people of Judah all the evil that I have pronounced against them."

Jeremiah's forthrightness had placed him in serious trouble again. Standing before the people with a potter's bowl in his hand, the prophet had smashed it to the ground and cried out, "Even as I have smashed this potter's bowl, the Lord God will break this city and all of its people."

When Pashur, chief officer of the Temple, heard this solemn warning, he arrested Jeremiah and put him in stocks for twenty-four hours. During the long, hot day, the prophet sat near the north gate of the city and listened to the mockery, jeers, and taunts of the people. As the sun sank in the west, so did his spirit.

Jeremiah was as discouraged as he would ever be. All his prophecies thus far had pointed to the death, doom, and destruction of his beloved nation. How he wished he could stop giving those harsh warnings! In the depths of despondency, he even had these thoughts: "I will not mention the Lord again! Nor will I speak any more in His name!"

Such thoughts were quickly erased from Jeremiah's mind, as he answered himself, "I know that the Lord's words are burning in my heart and that I am the one whom He has chosen to speak for Him."

Jeremiah's lonely vigil was over. When Pashur released him the next day, Jeremiah had a word of warning for the Temple officer: "Because you have prophesied falsely, you and all your family will be carried as captives to Babylon. There you will die."

Another of Jeremiah's trials and tribulations was ended. During his long and turbulent career, however, there were to be many more.

*Based on the story in the Bible:
2 Kings 23:31 — 24:7; Jeremiah 20:1-6,
26:1-19 and 24, 36:1-32*

3
THE FALL OF JERUSALEM

IT WAS ONE MINUTE BEFORE MIDNIGHT for the tiny kingdom of Judah. Jeremiah sat in the prison court and watched sadly as King Zedekiah prepared to make his frantic, last-ditch stand against the powerful Chaldean army. Jeremiah remembered vividly the tumultous chain of events that had brought Jerusalem to the brink of disaster.

The prophet recalled how the Babylonian Empire had rapidly risen to power under the brilliant leadership of its young king, Nebuchadnezzar. Jehoiakim's fruitless rebellion against paying tribute to Babylon had resulted in his capture and being carried away in chains. King Jehoiachin, his son, had inherited an impossible situation and had been able to resist Nebuchadnezzar's continued siege for only three months. Then he had opened the gates of Jerusalem and had surrendered not only himself but also his mother, his wives, his servants, and his court officials to the king of Babylon.

Jeremiah remembered that Nebuchadnezzar had not been satisfied with this token surrender. He had entered the city, had gathered much treasure from the Temple and the palace, and had selected ten thousand of Jerusalem's finest, most brilliant young men and one thousand of her most skilled artisans and craftsmen. King Jehoiachin's group, the captives, and the treasure had been carried off to Babylon. Before leaving Jerusalem, Nebuchadnezzar had placed Zedekiah, Jehoaichin's uncle, upon the throne of Judah. At the death

"The Chaldeans Destroy the Brazen Sea" by J. James Tissot. *The Old Testament,* Illustrated. The Chaldeans broke down the brass pillars, bases, and even the laver of the Temple and took the brass to Babylon.   M. de Buffan & Co.

"Zedekiah Is Bound in Chains" by José Villegas. *Biblia Sacra.* The Chaldeans captured Zedekiah and his sons. Nebuchad- nezzar ordered the sons slain and the king taken captive to Babylon, in chains.
Lemercier and Co., Paris

of Nebuchadnezzar, thirty-seven years later, Jehoiachin was released by Evil-merodach and dined at the king's table.

Jeremiah continued to look back on the past. Not long after the captives had been taken away, the Lord had appeared and told him to write a letter to His poor, disobedient people in Babylon. He would never forget the contents of the letter that the Lord had dictated.

"The voice of the Lord has told me to write to all of you who have been carried away into captivity," the letter began. "Build houses and live in them. Marry wives and have families. Give your sons and daughters in marriage, and live in peace in the land to which He has sent you. After seventy years the Lord will visit you again and will bring you back to Jerusalem. However, you must seek the

Lord, and you shall find Him when you search for Him with all your heart."

Jeremiah was still reminiscing. Time after time he had urged Zedekiah to surrender to the king of Babylon in order to save his own life, the lives of his people, and Jerusalem itself from destruction. His constant repetition of these warnings had finally cost him his freedom. Zedekiah had arrested him and charged him with treason. Yet, while still in prison, he had demonstrated his faith in the future of Judah by exercising his right of inheritance and purchasing some land from his cousin Hanameel.

Jeremiah's next recollection was the great folly that Zedekiah had committed in the ninth year of his reign. He had had the audacity to rebel against Nebuchadnezzar! The Babylonian king's reaction had been prompt and effective. A tight two-year siege of Jerusalem had brought its people to the point of starvation.

Jeremiah was aroused abruptly from his musing by the sound of a falling wall. The battering rams had done their job well. A breach appeared in one of the walls, and the mighty Chaldean army came pouring into the city. When Zedekiah saw that Jerusalem had fallen, he and his army fled through the north gate, heading east, the best escape route to the Arabah. Captured near Jericho, the king soon faced the angry sovereign who had placed him on the throne eleven years earlier.

Nebuchadnezzar showed no mercy to his rebellious puppet. Zedekiah's sons were executed before his eyes. Then the king himself was blinded, bound in chains, and taken to Babylon, where he remained in prison until he died.

The sack of Jerusalem was complete. The broken-down walls, the destroyed Temple, the wrecked palace, and the burned homes spoke eloquently of the pitiless fury of the king from the North.

Before his return to Babylon, Nebuchadnezzar issued a command to Nebuzar-adan, his captain and temporary military commander of Judah:

"Release Jeremiah, the political prisoner of Zedekiah, and treat him with kindness and respect. Also let him decide whether to come to Babylon with you or to stay here with the small group who will be left behind to look after the fields and vineyards."

Jeremiah was a free man once more and, when given the choice, he elected to remain in Judah.

Based on stories in the Bible:
2 Kings 24:1, 8-17, and 25:1-21;
2 Chronicles 36:5-20; Jeremiah 29:1-13,
37:11-15, 39:1-14 and 51:31-34

4
JEREMIAH'S STRUGGLE

BEFORE LEAVING JUDAH, now only a satellite of the powerful Babylonian Empire, Captain Nebu-zar-adan appointed a ruler over the tiny kingdom. He chose Gedaliah, grandson of Shaphan and a wise, godly man, to be governor of the people. Gedaliah set up his government in Mizpah, and Jeremiah went with him to help in the great task of rebuilding and restoring the land.

The good news spread rapidly. Soldiers and their leaders, who had scattered abroad after the fall of Jerusalem, heard it. Displaced persons, driven from their homes during the long Chaldean invasion, heard it. Nebuchadnezzar had left a segment of the people in Judah; a government had been established; order had been restored; and bountiful harvests were

Peasant Girl Picking Grapes in the Hills of Ephraim, a site of agricultural settlements. When Babylonia conquered Judah, Captain Nebu-zar-adan gave the poor people vineyards and fields in this productive area.   © Matson Photo

being reaped. Hope once again began to rise in the hearts of the refugees as they started streaming back to Judah. They assembled at Mizpah and stood before their governor. Gedaliah had the same message for each and every one of them.

"Do not be afraid to serve the Chaldeans," he said. "Remain in this land and submit to the rule of the king of Babylon, and all will go well with you. For my part, I shall remain at my headquarters here so that I can represent you when Chaldean officials come to visit us. As for you, return to your cities and rebuild your homes. Harvest grapes, summer fruit, and olives. Make wine and oil. Fill your storehouses with supplies."

After the happy people had returned joyously to the homes from which they had fled, the princes, the captains, and their armies pledged their loyalty to the governor.

Despite the seemingly peaceful and prosperous façade, dark clouds of adversity were gathering for Gedaliah and his people. The governor listened incredulously one day when Johanan, captain in the army, came to him.

"There is a traitor among us!" Johanan exclaimed. "Did you know that Ishmael has formed an alliance with the king of Ammon and is plotting to kill you? Let me go and kill him before it is too late."

Gedaliah refused to doubt the loyalty of Ishmael, so he said, "No, Johanan, I cannot permit you to perform such an act. Surely you must be mistaken about Ishmael."

Gedaliah little realized that Johanan's words of warning were well-founded. Instead of surrounding himself with guards and taking other safety precautions, the governor played right into the hands of Ishmael. Gedaliah invited him and ten of his friends to Mizpah for a state dinner honoring some Chaldean visitors.

Soon the governor's mansion ran with blood. During the night, Ishmael and the other traitors arose to fulfill their dastardly plot. They not only assassinated Gedaliah but also murdered all the other people in the house, including the Chaldean visitors.

Despite the massacre already committed, the blood-thirst of the traitors was still unsated. Early the next morning, before the murder of Gedaliah became known, Ishmael and his friends saw eighty mourning men going toward Jerusalem to offer sacrifices at the partially restored Temple of the Lord. Ishmael, pretending to be a mourner also, lured them into Mizpah. There his men sprang upon the unarmed strangers and began to slaughter them and toss their bodies into a deep pit. Ten of the men, however, bribed Ishmael to spare their lives in exchange for great stores of wheat, barley, oil, and honey that they had hidden in a field.

The news was out and spread rapidly. Ishmael had assassinated Governor Gedaliah, massacred seventy pilgrims, and was fleeing, with the entire population of Mizpah as hostages, toward his ally, King Baalis of Ammon. Johanan and the other loyal princes responded quickly on learning the terrible news. They began a hot pursuit of the fleeing traitors and caught up with them and their hostages at Gibeon. While the captives were being released, Ishmael made good his escape. As he raced across the Jordan to his ally, this royal rogue from the house of David disappeared into the sands of time and was never heard from again.

Jeremiah was face to face with his greatest struggle. After the death of Gedaliah, the people became more and more restless. One day Johanan came to Jeremiah and spoke what was on his mind.

"All of us fear that the Chaldeans will blame us for the murder of our governor," he said. "The people have become panic-stricken and have decided to flee into Egypt. Before we leave, however, we beg you to pray to the Lord your God and ask Him to show us what to do."

For ten days, Jeremiah sat alone and prayed that the Lord would make His wishes known. At the end of the tenth day, the Word of the Lord came to the prophet. Then Jeremiah summoned Johanan, the other captains, and all the people and gave God's answer:

"Thus says the Lord God unto Whom you sent me: 'If you remain in this land, I will build you up and not pull you down, because I have repented of the evil that I brought upon you. The time for mercy has come. Do not be afraid of the king of Babylon, for I will be with you and deliver you from him. However, if you go to Egypt, the sword that you fear here shall overtake you there. Everyone who goes to live in Egypt shall die by the sword, by famine, or by disease.'"

Although they had promised to heed the voice of the Lord, Jeremiah could sense that the mood of the people had changed during his ten-day absence.

"You are not telling the truth!" Johanan and others exclaimed. "God did not send you here to warn us not to go into Egypt. Instead, you and Baruch are plotting to turn us over to the Chaldeans. We are determined to go to Egypt, and we will take you with us!" Their destination in the Land of the Pharaohs was to be Tahpanhes.

The ringing voice of God's great spokesman faded into the silence of time when the people forced Jeremiah to go down into Egypt with them. The brave, fearless prophet died, with none to record the time and manner of his death. It was a fitting

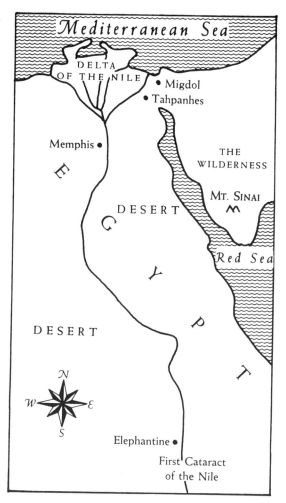

Four Jewish Colonies in Egypt were Elephantine, Memphis, Migdol, and Tahpanhes. Jeremiah was forced to accompany Johanan to Tahpanhes after Gedaliah was assassinated.

finish for Jeremiah who had spoken, all along, not to please the crowd but to give them God's burning message.

Based on the story in the Bible:
Jeremiah 40:7 — 43:7

PLACES

in the Story of Jeremiah

ANATHOTH

Jeremiah's birthplace, Anathoth, is 2½ miles northeast of Jerusalem.

MEGIDDO

Overlooking the Plain of Jezreel, this important town is about 20 miles east of the Mediterranean Sea and about 25 miles southwest of the Sea of Galilee. King Josiah was fatally wounded near here.

NEO-BABYLONIAN EMPIRE

This is the name by which Babylonia of the 6th and 5th centuries B.C. is known to historians. Under its best-known king, Nebuchadnezzar, Judah was taken into captivity.

BABYLON

Capital of Babylonia, this important city is located in southern Mesopotamia, north of the Persian Gulf. Most of the Hebrew captives were relocated here.

ARABAH

Also known as the Jordan Valley, this 100-mile plain extends from the Dead Sea to the Gulf of Aqaba. Zedekiah and his army fled through the north gate of the city and headed east, the best escape route to the Arabah.

JERICHO

This ancient city lies 17 miles northeast of Jerusalem and is 6 miles west of the Jordan. Zedekiah was captured near Jericho and taken back to face Nebuchadnezzar.

MIZPAH

This town in the territory of Benjamin is 7 miles north of Jerusalem. The Babylonian governor made his headquarters here after the destruction of Jerusalem.

GIBEON

Located about 8 miles northwest of Jerusalem, this city was the scene of action when Johanan caught up with the fleeing traitors and released their captives.

TAHPANHES, EGYPT

This is a city in the Egyptian Delta on the Pelusiac branch of the Nile, about 130 miles southwest of Judah's southern border. The Jews fled here following the murder of Gedaliah.

Ruins of Babylon. This ancient city, rebuilt by Nebuchadnezzar, was famous for the splendor of its palaces, temples, and gardens. It was the city of the Hebrew captivity (586-538 B.C.) until the Persian conquest.   © Matson Photo

QUESTIONS
on the Story of Jeremiah

1

1 Where was Jeremiah born? What was his early environment?

2 Why did Jeremiah say that he could not accept the divine commission? What did the Lord tell him?

3 Who was king of Judah during the first period of Jeremiah's ministry? What did this king do that gained him lasting fame?

4 How did the people of Judah react when they learned of the untimely death of King Josiah?

2

5 Who succeeded King Josiah on the throne? How long did he reign? What was his fate?

6 What did the Lord tell Jeremiah to do during the first year of Jehoiakim's reign?

7 How did the people of Judah respond to Jeremiah's Temple Sermon? What was the court officials' verdict?

8 What did the Lord tell Jeremiah to write on the scroll? Why did He tell him to write it?

9 Who took the scroll to the Temple and read it? What effect did its reading have upon the crowd? the princes? the king?

10 What was God's judgment against Jehoiakim for burning the scroll?

11 Why did Pashur put Jeremiah in stocks? What was Jeremiah's mental reaction to this treatment?

3

12 What happened to King Jehoiakim when he rebelled against paying tribute to powerful Babylon?

13 What did Nebuchadnezzar do when young King Jehoiachin surrendered? What was Jehoiachin's ultimate fate?

14 What did the Lord tell Jeremiah to write in a letter to the captives at Babylon?

15 Why did Jeremiah constantly urge King Zedekiah to surrender to Nebuchadnezzar? What happened to Jeremiah because of these urgings?

16 What was Zedekiah's folly in the ninth year of his reign?

17 How did Jeremiah show his faith in the future of Judah while he was in prison?

18 How long did Nebuchadnezzar besiege Jerusalem before the city fell?

19 What did Zedekiah do when he saw that Jerusalem had fallen? Where was he captured?

20 How did Nebuchadnezzar punish the rebellious king?

21 What did Nebuchadnezzar order his captain, Nebu-zar-adan, to do? Where did Jeremiah decide to live?

4

22 Whom did Captain Nebu-zar-adan appoint as governor of Judah? Where did the governor set up his headquarters? Who went with him to help him rebuild Judah?

23 What was the good news that reached Judah's displaced people and her scattered army?

24 What advice did Governor Gedaliah give to the returning people?

25 What was the incredible message that Johanan gave to Gedaliah?

26 How did Ishmael carry out his nefarious plan to assassinate Gedaliah?

27 Where did Johanan catch up with Ishmael, his friends, and his captives?

28 What did Johanan tell Jeremiah that the people had decided to do? What did he ask the prophet to do?

29 What was the message from the Lord that Jeremiah brought to the people?

30 What was the Judeans' response to the message?

Answers are found on the following pages.

"The Prophet Jeremiah" by Michelangelo. Detail. Sistine Chapel, Rome. Jeremiah witnessed the decline of Judah, the fall of Jerusalem, and the Exile. He had warned the people that these events would occur because of their sins. Alinari

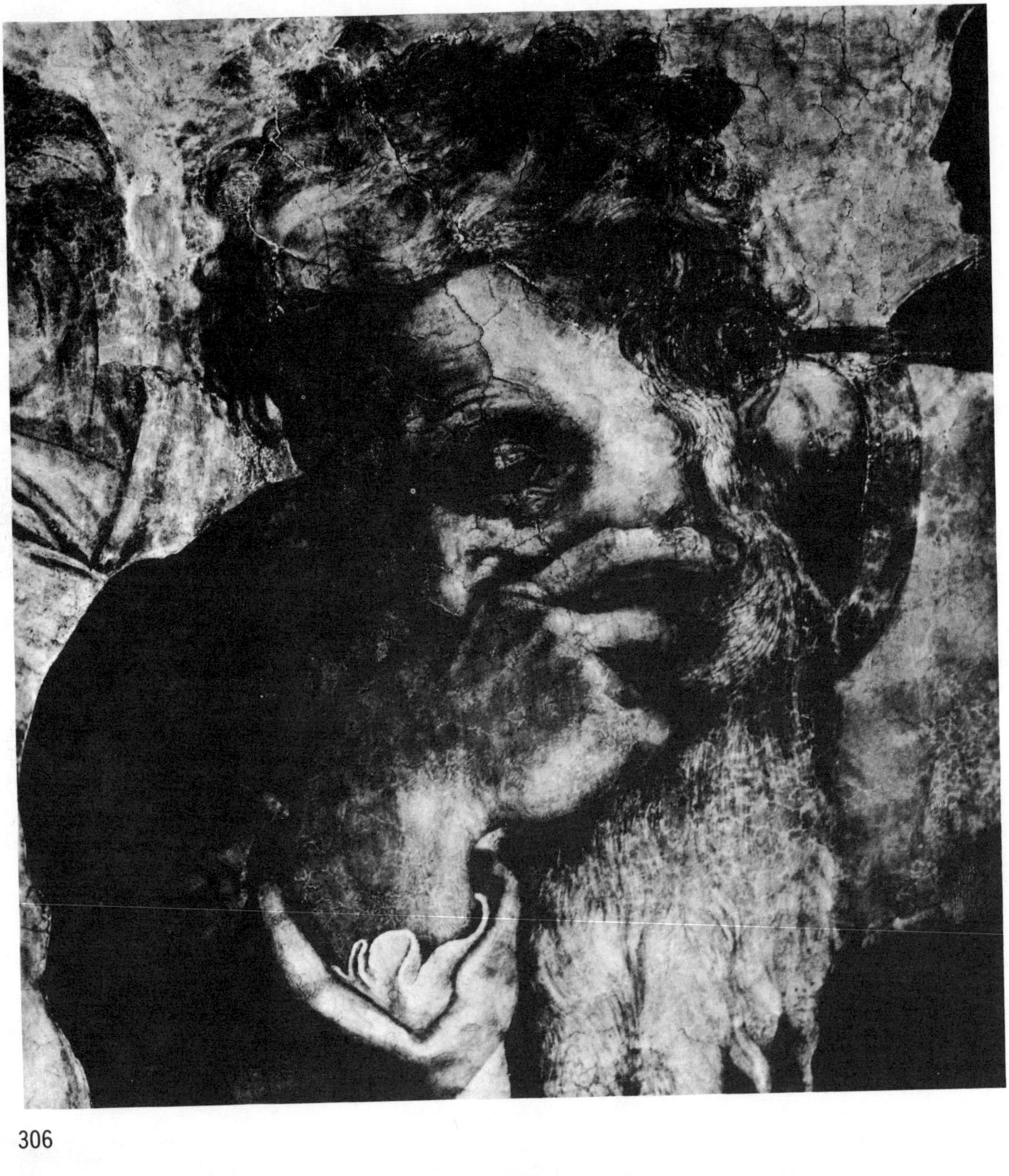

ANSWERS
on the Story of Jeremiah

1

1 Jeremiah was born at Anathoth. He was reared among faithful, God-fearing people who spent much of their time writing and teaching great stories of Jewish history.

2 Jeremiah said that he could not be a spokesman for the Lord because he was only a youth. The Lord told Jeremiah that He would put words in his mouth and promised to be with him, to guard and protect him, wherever he went and whatever he said.

3 King Josiah. He restored the Temple, destroyed false gods, and brought his people back to the worship of the one true God.

4 The Judeans were grief-stricken when they learned that King Josiah had been killed in battle. The mournful nation paid great tribute to their beloved king.

2

5 Jehoahaz succeeded his father on the throne. His wicked reign lasted for only three months. He was deposed by Pharaoh-necho and taken to an Egyptian prison where he remained for the rest of his life. Jehoiakim, his older and more cooperative brother, replaced him on the throne.

6 The Lord told Jeremiah to stand in the Temple Court and warn the people that, if they did not turn from their wicked ways, He would destroy the Temple and make Jerusalem a curse word among the nations.

7 When they heard the Temple Sermon, the people became an angry, shouting mob and threatened to kill Jeremiah. The court officials rescued Jeremiah, arrested him, gave him a public trial, and found him innocent of all charges.

8 The Lord told Jeremiah to take a scroll and write upon it everything that He had ever told him. The Lord hoped that the people would turn away from their evil ways when they heard all the things that He intended to do to them. Then He could forgive them.

9 Jeremiah's secretary, Baruch, took the scroll to the Temple and read it. The people were unimpressed when they heard the reading of the scroll. The princes listened with mingled emotions. The king was so furious that he cut it into pieces and burned it.

10 God's judgment against Jehoiakim was that he would be killed by an enemy and that his body would be left where it fell.

11 Jeremiah was put in stocks because he smashed a potter's bowl to the ground and warned the people that the Lord would smash Judah the same way if the people did not repent. The prophet became discouraged and almost bitter as he sat there, listening to the taunting jeers of the crowds.

3

12 King Jehoiakim was captured by Nebuchadnezzar and carried away in chains to a Babylonian prison.

13 Nebuchadnezzar stripped Jerusalem of ten thousand of her most brilliant young men (including Daniel and his three friends), one thousand of her ablest artisans, and took many of the treasures from the Temple and palace. Thirty-seven years later King Jehoiachin was released from prison by Evil-merodach and permitted to dine at the king's table.

14 The Lord told Jeremiah to write the captives and encourage the people to live in peace in the land where He had sent them, and to tell them that, after seventy years, He would visit them again and bring them back to Jerusalem.

15 Jeremiah urged Zedekiah to surrender so that the lives of many people could be saved and Jerusalem could be spared from destruction. The king arrested Jeremiah and charged him with treason.

16 Zedekiah dared to rebel against Babylon.

17 Jeremiah exercised his right of inheritance and purchased some land in his home town of Anathoth.

18 Jerusalem was besieged for two years before it fell.

19 When Jerusalem fell, Zedekiah and his army fled through the city's north gate and headed east, the best escape route to the Arabah. Zedekiah was captured near Jericho.

20 Zedekiah's sons were killed before his eyes. Then he was blinded, bound in chains, and carried to a Babylonian prison where he spent the rest of his life.

21 Nebuchadnezzar ordered Jeremiah's release from prison. The prophet chose to stay in Judah.

4

22 Gedaliah, grandson of Shaphan, was appointed governor of Judah. He set up his headquarters at Mizpah. Jeremiah went with him.

23 The good news that reached the scattered army and people was that Nebuchadnezzar had left a segment of people in Judah; that order had been restored; that a government had been established; and that the people were reaping a bountiful harvest.

24 Gedaliah told the people to remain in Judah and submit to the rule of the king of Babylon. He promised that all would go well with them, and suggested that they return to their own cities and begin life all over again.

25 Johanan told Gedaliah that Ishmael was planning to kill him.

26 Gedaliah invited Ishmael and ten of his friends to come to Mizpah and have dinner with him. During the night, they arose and assassinated the governor.

27 Johanan caught up with the fleeing traitors and their hostages at Gibeon.

28 Johanan told Jeremiah that the people had decided to flee to Egypt. He asked the prophet to find out if the Lord approved this decision.

29 Jeremiah told the people that the Lord disapproved their plan and warned them that everyone who went to Egypt would die by the sword, by famine, or by disease.

30 The people told Jeremiah that he was not telling the truth. They accused the prophet and Baruch of plotting to turn them over to the Chaldeans. They repeated their determination to seek sanctuary in Egypt and said that they would force Jeremiah and his secretary to go with them.

FURTHER FACTS
AND OUTLINES
for the Story of Jeremiah

JEREMIAH

AUTHORSHIP AND DATE

Jeremiah. He dictated the book to his secretary Baruch (36:1-8, 32). He prophesied from about 626 to 586 B.C. There is evidence of editing in the book of Jeremiah.

DESTINATION

Judah and Jerusalem, especially, but also the nations around Judah.

PURPOSE AND THEME

Jeremiah's purpose, under God, was to warn Judah that her sins would result in chastisement from the North (the Babylonians) in the near future. His prophecy did, in fact, come true and took expression in the Babylonian Captivity. (Jerusalem fell in 586 B.C.) Jeremiah also cries out against the sins of the surrounding nations. But there is a brighter side to his message; for example, his prophecies of the coming Messiah (chapters 23, 31, 33). Jeremiah 33:16 is a great Messianic promise: "In those days Judah will be saved and Jerusalem will dwell securely. And this is the name by which it will be called: 'The Lord is our righteousness.'"

Near the outset of Jeremiah's ministry, the good King Josiah instituted his famed reforms (begun about 621 B.C.), the Temple being repaired and idol worship outlawed. This cheered the people of earnest intent, such as Jeremiah; but he knew that surface reform was not sufficient, that the very hearts of the people must be altered. Repentance thus became one of his great cries. Idolatry must be replaced by revealed religion, God must be recognized as the Covenant God, God will judge Judah and Israel for sexual sins. This straightforward preaching fell on deaf ears; Judah was inflexible in her sinful ways. Exile and punishment came. But a day will come, said Jeremiah, when truth will prevail and the Covenant will be respected once more—this was to be the Messianic Age.

OUTLINE

Jeremiah Called and Empowered (chapter 1)

Jeremiah Condemns Judah and Foretells Babylonian Captivity (chapter 2-29)
  Judah's Apostasy (chapter 2)
  Judah Worse than Israel (chapter 3)
  Judah Threatened with Military Invasion (chapter 4)
  Warning: "You have eyes to see but see not" (chapter 5)
  Impending Punishment (chapters 6-9)
  Idols Shall be Done Away (chapter 10)
  The Tragedy of the Broken Covenant (chapter 11)
  Jeremiah's Complaint and God's Answer (chapter 12)
  The Linen Girdle (chapter 13)
  Judgment on Judah Inevitable (chapters 14-15)
  Jeremiah To Remain Single (chapter 16)
  Those Are Blessed Who Trust in God; Sin of Breaking the Sabbath (chapter 17)
  The Potter and the Clay; the Potter's Earthen Flask (chapters 18-19)
  Jeremiah Persecuted for His Prophecies (chapter 20)

Warnings to King Zedekiah, King Jehoi-
akim, and the Leaders of Israel
(chapters 21-23)
The Two Baskets of Figs (chapter 24)
The Captivity Foretold and Jeremiah's Life
Threatened (chapters 25-27)
The False Prophet Hananiah Rebuked
(chapter 28)
Jeremiah's Letter to the Exiles (chapter 29)

Jeremiah Foretells Restoration (chapters
30-33)
Return from Exile Promised (chapter 30)
Mourning To Be Turned to Joy (chapter 31)
The New Covenant (chapter 32)
Restoration under the Messiah (chapter 33)

Jeremiah Foretells Judgment (chapters 34-44)
Zedekiah, the Rechabites, and Jehoiakim
(chapters 34-36)
Jeremiah Suffers Imprisonment, Relieved,
Delivered (chapters 37-39)
The Remnant Seeks Guidance; Refuses
God's Guidance and Goes to Egypt
Taking Jeremiah; Jeremiah Rebukes
Idolatrous Jews in Egypt (chapters
40-44)

Jeremiah's Prophecies Against the Nations
(chapters 45-51)
A Parenthetical Passage: Jeremiah and His
Secretary Baruch (chapter 45)

Against Egypt (chapter 46)
Against Philistia (chapter 47)
Against Moab (chapter 48)
Against Ammon, Edom, Damascus, Kedar,
Elam (Persia) (chapter 49)
Against Babylon . . . Also the Restoration
of the Jews (chapters 50-51)

Jeremiah's Summary of the Captivity of
Judah (chapter 52)

SECOND KINGS

OUTLINE

Judah's History from the Reign of Jehoahaz
(Shallum) to the Captivity of the
Southern Kingdom (23:31–25:30)
Jehoahaz' (Shallum) Reign (23:31-35)
Jehoiakim's (Eliakim) Reign (23:31–24:7)
Jehoiachin's (Jechoniah, Coniah) Reign,
His Exile to Babylon (24:8-17)
King Zedekiah Carried Away Captive by
Nebuchadnezzar; Final Destruction of
Jerusalem (24:18–25:30)

SECOND CHRONICLES

OUTLINE

Kings Jehoahaz, Jehoiakim, Jehoiachin,
and Zedekiah are Wicked Rulers; the
Babylonian Captivity of Judah
(chapter 36)

LAMENTATIONS

AUTHORSHIP AND DATE

From ancient times Jews and Christians
have ascribed this work to Jeremiah, who
prophesied from about 626 to 586 B.C.

DESTINATION

Judah and any other nations or people who
would profit from Judah's mistake.

PURPOSE AND THEME

A supplement to the book of Jeremiah,
Lamentations is quite literally a *lamenting*
over Judah's sins and the subsequent destruction she suffered. Here is at once a sad cry for

what has happened to God's people (their
capture and the capture of Jerusalem under
Nebuchadnezzar, 586 B.C.) and an earnest
appeal for repentance. In this setting, suffering is judgment upon sin. The vanity of human
effort is underscored in chapter four.

OUTLINE

Sorrow over Captive Zion (chapter 1)
Judgment from God (chapter 2)
Hope for Divine Mercy (chapter 3)
Present Destruction Contrasted with Past
Happy State of Being (chapter 4)
Prayer for Mercy (chapter 5)

EZEKIEL

AUTHORSHIP AND DATE

Ezekiel the priest (1:3), a contemporary of Jeremiah, lived in the 6th century B.C. and appears to have prophesied from about 593 to 571 B.C.

DESTINATION

To his fellow Jews in the Captivity and those still in Palestine, but to foreign nations, also.

PURPOSE AND THEME

Ezekiel's home was Jerusalem and he was of a priestly line. He was the son of Buzi; with the deportation of Jehoiachin, Ezekiel himself was taken into exile to Babylon (1:1). Ezekiel had a wife and a home, according to 24:16-18; and 24:1, 15-18 informs us that his wife died on the day the siege of Jerusalem began. Much of his prophecy is recorded in the first person. His call to prophesy, having come in the fourth month of the fifth year of captivity (1:1-2), and the last date recorded in the book of Ezekiel being the first month of the twenty-seventh year (29:17), his ministry lasted at least twenty-two years. It is evident from 14:14, 20 and 28:3 that he knew the prophet Daniel.

Against this backdrop of acquaintance with people, events, and conditions, Ezekiel writes his strange prophecy. In figurative language he reveals to the Jewish people that their predicament is the product of their own sin; past and present rebellion is underscored. Man is indeed responsible for his acts. But God is ever faithful in spite of man's carelessness and thus He offers deliverance to the repentant. Ezekiel foretells the day when Israel will be reunited with her own king, and will worship the one true God in the reconstructed Temple. Judgments are pronounced upon foreign nations as well as Judah. These judgments have a twofold message: (1) doom on the wicked countries, (2) they will not prevent the redemption and restoration of God's chosen people. Such statements as "The soul that sinneth, it shall die," "Turn ye, turn ye, for why will ye die?" and the longer one in 36:25-27, are classic.

OUTLINE

Impending Judgment upon Judah and Jerusalem: Prophecies Given before the Fall of Jerusalem (chapters 1-24)

Introduction: Ezekiel's Initial Vision of God's Glory, His Call (1:1 – 3:21)

A Second Vision of God's Glory (3:22-27)

Symbolic Activities Dramatize the Destruction of Jerusalem (chapters 4-7)

Vision and Punishment of Jerusalem (chapters 8-11)

God "Gives Up" Jerusalem to False Teaching and False Prophets (chapters 12-14)

Punishment Inevitable and Necessary (chapters 15-17)

God's Just Dealings with the Individual (chapter 18)

Lamentation over the Princes of Israel (chapter 19)

Final Warnings before the Fall of Jerusalem (chapters 20-24)

Judgment upon Foreign Nations (chapters 25-32)

Against Ammon (25:1-7)

Against Moab (25:8-11)

Against Edom (25:12-14)

Against Philistia (25:15-17)

Against Tyre (26:1 – 28:19)

Against Sidon (28:20-26)

Against Egypt (29:1 – 32:32)

Restoration Foretold: Prophecies after the Fall of Jerusalem (chapters 33-48)

A New Covenant; God's Love for the Sinner (chapter 33)

God's Care of His Flock (chapter 34)

Devastation of Edom (chapter 35)

A Clean Heart and New Spirit for Israel (chapter 36)

Restoration of Israel Symbolized in the Vision of the Dry Bones (chapter 37)

The Prophecy Against God of the Land of Magog (chapters 38-39)

A Vision of Restored Israel Symbolized by Describing the New Temple To Be Built (chapters 40-48)

"The Prophet Ezekiel" by Michelangelo. Detail. Sistine Chapel, Rome. Ezekiel emphasized that man is responsible for his acts and will be punished for his sins, but that God will forgive the repentant sinner.

The Heart of a Champion

by
Bob Richards

After observing many famous athletes in action, Olympic Champion Bob Richards has come to the conclusion that the difference between the mediocre athlete and the champion lies in the champion's mental attitude that never gives up, whatever his physical circumstances may be. Richards elaborates on this theme and his own personal reliance on prayer in his book, *The Heart of a Champion* (© 1959 by Fleming H. Revell Company, Westwood, N.J.). Jeremiah the prophet fits Richards' description of a champion perfectly. Few men have faced more hostility and opposition in proclaiming God's Word, yet Jeremiah never gave up. Young and old alike can learn valuable lessons for today from this chapter in *The Heart of a Champion*.

THE SPIRIT THAT NEVER GIVES UP

ABOUT MY ONLY CLAIM to fame is that of being a "pole-vaulting parson." Or, as some others have put it, a "jumping padre." I think the best comment of all is the one made by a sports writer in Cleveland who said that I was the only preacher he knew of who was trying to lift himself into heaven on his own strength.

Be that as it may, I have had a lot of wonderful experiences in this world of athletics. In the past several years I have had the privilege of traveling throughout Europe and of hob-nobbing with a number of great champions. I've had the privilege of rooming with them, of talking with them about their ideas, their drives, what makes them tick. I've had the privilege of watching them as they broke one world's record after another. I've seen more than forty world's records broken in the past few years in athletic competitions. And I've come to believe that what it takes to make a champion in the game of athletics is what it takes to make a champion in the game called life—that life is pretty much made of the same tissue, that one realm is not different from another, that the principles for excellence in one realm are the same as in another, and that what it takes to succeed in the world of athletics is the same sort of heart and soul and quality of personality that it takes to succeed in life.

I'd like to share with you what I've seen in the hearts of a few champions. As I've worked in the world of religion, I know that it applies there. As I've gone on in the field of education, I've found that the same principles apply there.

In other words, what I'm trying to say is that every man needs the heart of a champion. It's a quality of mind, a mental resolve, an attitude that turns a man beyond the normal and the mediocre to accomplishing great things in all walks of life. Perhaps the most important thing that I've seen in the heart of a champion is this mental attitude that refuses to give up, no matter what the circumstances may be.

Now I know people may say that this is rather a trite value, but I have seen it over and over again. I've seen thousands of great potential athletes, fellows with bodies that you would believe would be undoubtedly the greatest coordinated body that a man could possibly want. I've seen fellows with spring in their legs. I've seen fellows with tremendous reaction times and coordination times, but they lacked just a little bit of a mental attitude, a philosophy that would help them get over a defeat or a discouraging situation. The difference between a champion and a mediocre athlete is the difference between one who gives up and one who doesn't.

Perhaps the best illustration of this is the story of Bob Mathias. I think Bob Mathias crystallizes in his personality this attitude of mind better than any champion I've ever seen. I saw him in London, England, as a young boy, seventeen years of age. I saw him as a schoolboy achieve probably the greatest honor that any boy could hope to achieve—the Olympic decathlon championship, won under the most adverse circumstances imaginable. I saw that boy go out there and throw the javelin when they had to have a flashlight to show him where the foul marker was. He pole-vaulted under the same conditions; they had to point a flashlight on the crossbar. And I saw that seventeen-year-old boy finish the 1,500 meters in a mud-bespattered condition on a horrible track ruined by the rain; and when he finished as the winner of the Olympic decathlon, probably the most gruelling, grinding event of all, I thought to myself, "Could any high-school kid hope to achieve more than what this boy has achieved?"

I thought he'd never surpass it, but he did it later in Helsinki, Finland. I saw him go out in the first day of the decathlon. In the broad jump, he pulled a muscle high in his right leg; and, if you know anything about pulled muscles in athletics, you know they are tremendous handicaps to overcome. Everyone wondered if Bob would quit, if he would give up. I heard afterwards that, when all the trainers and coaches went up to him and put their arms around him and asked, "Bob, what do you think you're going to be able to do? Do you think you'll be able to compete?" Bob reached up and he put his hand on his coach's shoulder, and said, "Don't worry, coach. Somehow I think I can come through."

Most fellows would have given up; they wouldn't have competed any more. But Bob went out there with that pulled muscle and

tried again. He not only came through, but he broke the Olympic record, and broke his own world's record for the greatest single performance of his entire career—and this with a pulled leg muscle.

It's that quality of mind that makes champions. No matter what the situation is, they have the ability to grit their teeth and keep on going. They don't quit. They refuse to give up. . . .

In Fresno, California, I was sitting in the stands with a boy by the name of Parry O'Brien. We were watching some high-school boys as they put the shot, as they pole vaulted, as they ran races, and I just casually said to Parry, "What do you do when you put the shot? Do you ever pray and ask God to help you?" Parry looked me right in the eye, 225 pounds of solid man, a brilliant boy, an intelligent fellow; he said, "Bob, a young fellow asked me that the other day, and I told him this, and I'd like to tell you the same thing: 'You can train your body to a peak of physical perfection; you can have it as strong as it is able to be. You can concentrate on shot-putting to the point where you know every minute thing that you're going to do. But when you get into that ring you need something just a little extra, something down deep within you that can give you that extra boost you need for world's-record-breaking performances. I always pray to God, because I've found in Him that power that helps me do just that little extra.'"

I watched Parry O'Brien as he went out on the track that night. I saw him get down on his third throw of the evening. He must have prayed, because as the shot left that hand and that grunt left his lips, Parry O'Brien put the shot for a new world's record, 59 feet, ¾ of an inch.

What had he discovered? Not only the lesson of hard work and physical perfection, but also the great lesson that every champion learns: to call on everything he's got, down to the deepest spiritual reserve in his heart and soul.

I experienced something like that at Helsinki, Finland. I went to Helsinki with a pulled muscle in my left leg. If you know anything about the pole-vaulting, as you leave the ground everything goes out of your left leg. You drive off the ground hard, you bend your hips in, and you start pulling up. If your left leg isn't right, you just can't leave the ground properly. I kept waiting for my leg to heal, but it just wouldn't, and four days before the games I had to go out and get in at least a workout. I tried to get off the ground, and it was just like a knife sticking me in the back of my leg. I couldn't even leave the ground.

I'll never forget the psychological reaction that hit me in that moment. I began to think that I was out of the Olympic Games. You can't realize what that is until you train four years for something. In four years I hadn't been out of shape for more than a month, training for the Olympics with all my heart and soul. And then to realize that—well, you were finished. I'll never forget; I walked off that field that day, my pole in my hand, and I never felt so blue and despondent in all of my athletic career. Brutus Hamilton, the coach, came up to me and gave me a wonderful inspirational word when he said this: "Bob, I want to quote a Scripture passage to you. '*All* things work together for good to them that love God, to them who are called according to His purpose.' " (Romans 8:28)

I said, "Thanks a lot. That helps me a great deal." I made my way up the pathway to our living quarters and walked into my room. The other boys were working out, and as I entered the room I happened to see Bud Held's open Bible on the desk beside his bed. You know, Bud happens to be one of the greatest javelin throwers America has ever produced. He has thrown it 270 feet. He is studying to be a Presbyterian preacher. When I looked down and saw that Bible, it made me mindful of a resource that I could yet use in the situation. I'm not ashamed to say it. I'd like to recommend it to all of you. In the quiet of the afternoon, in the silence of that room, I got down by my bed on my knees and I just prayed that God would help me. I've never prayed to win in my life. I never will, because praying to win seems so selfish and so silly, to me. But I've always, in my big competitions, asked God to help me. That spiritual power has never let me down.

We went to jump. The crossbar went up to 14 feet and 1¼ inches. Five fellows went over it. It went up to 14 feet 5¼ inches. A new Olympic record! Four fellows made it. It went up to 14 feet 9⅛ inches, and Denisenko of Russia couldn't get over it, and Lundberg of Sweden couldn't quite get over it; Don Laz and I were barely able to make it. They moved it up to 14 feet 11⅛ inches. The wind was blowing. We were getting tired. We had been jumping six hours, and I knew that this was about the end of the competition.

Well, Don missed his first one. I missed mine by a hair's breadth. Don didn't come too close on his second one, and I missed mine again, just by a trickle. Don went up and over his last one and hit it coming down, and I had one last jump. I don't know whether you've experienced this in athletics, but no doubt you've experienced it in business, or had a similar psychological feeling in other situations. You go back there to the end of the runway and look down at the pole vault crossbar and it looks to be about 25 feet high. You begin to get tight, and tense, and this old emotional excitement begins to well up inside of you. Your mouth turns dry and that feeling of weakness hits you all over. You just feel like —well, "I can't do anything."

To make matters worse, 70,000 people in that stadium simultaneously went: "Sssshhhhhhh." They might just as well have dropped the stadium on me. I started to go and then I just caught myself and said, "Bob, you won't jump 12 feet feeling like this." And once again in that quietness—it was so quiet I could hear my spikes scratching in the cinders beneath my feet—I just bowed my head, and with my pole in my hand I asked God somehow to help me do my best.

I can't explain it psychologically, but the emotional excitement died down. The tightness and the tension left me, and I began to feel relaxed. That crossbar began to come down to about 15 feet, where it belonged. And instead of feeling weak, I began to feel strong, and my faith began to well up. I began to have the confidence that I could do it. I started to take off—and the wind hit me and I had to stop. I started again and it hit me again. I began to feel a little tight. Once again I just bowed my head and prayed, looked up, saw that Olympic flag and I knew it was blowing in my direction. I knew the wind was with me and I took off, got a perfect take-off and started upward. And here's the unusual thing about the experience. In a split second it dawned on my consciousness what I was doing wrong—I wasn't pushing.

There's the value of prayer for me. *It enlightens you as to what you are doing wrong.* I started up and turned over and it seemed like everything within me said "Push!" I came up off that pole as I had never pushed before. And I cleared the crossbar by about 5 inches. Can you imagine the feeling? Four days before I was about to quit, to give up—and then to look up and see that crossbar on its pegs, to hear the roar of the crowd in your ears! It's an experience I'll never forget. When I hit the sawdust I practically went back up over the crossbar again, and in the next breath I thanked God for helping me. What I found was what a lot of champions have found—that when you've given everything, there's something else you can call on. I don't know what you call it. For me, it's God.

It's there, and it's what makes a champion. I've come to believe that no man will really find the greatest joys in life until he is willing to give everything he's got. There is a strange saying about life that goes like this: "If you don't give, you don't receive." It's only the man who puts himself into something—who pours out all his energy, his mind, his spirit—who reaps greatness and success in life.

Jesus put it beautifully when He said, ". . . Whosoever will save his life shall lose it: and whosoever will lose his life for my sake shall find it." (Matthew 16:25) Whoever tries to hold back shall lose life.

Here's where Jesus is, for me, the Champion of champions in the game called life. Here was One who, no matter what the circumstances, did not give up. When the world collapsed around Him, He maintained His spirit, His ideals, to the very end. Here was One who dared to believe that the impossible could be done, that men could be free from sin, that men could live new lives, that men could reflect the image of God in their personalities. Here was One who didn't quit when He hurt. He went to the cross to live forever, in the hearts of men and in the heart of the universe. Here was One who gave everything He had physically, mentally, and spiritually. He's the greatest inspiration of human life.

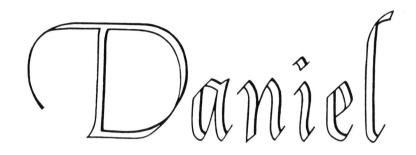

Daniel

IN THE HISTORY OF DANIEL, it is remarkable that, notwithstanding his position as one of the captive people, he came to occupy posts of power in three kingdoms—those of Babylon, Media, and Persia—and this without deflection from unswerving loyalty to the God of his fathers. In this regard, his very first experience placed him in danger.

Daniel was among the number selected for royal service, a peril for the age of youth—so impressionable and so likely to be influenced by the glitter of material splendor. But Daniel suffered no deterioration of character, either then or subsequently. These words give us the secret of that strength: he "purposed in his heart." This is a fine phrase, revealing a conviction made dynamic by the reinforcement of the will.

All that Daniel did in the three world kingdoms with which he became associated was of secondary importance. He was chosen of God to live among those kingdoms in order to see them in their relation to the Kingdom of God, and to interpret that relationship to those whom the prophet addressed then and to men for all time through the writing of his inspiring book.

Nebuchadnezzar, Belshazzar, and Antiochus Epiphanes challenged and defied God. Autocratic ambition sets itself against all rule and authority other than its own. If successful over human competitors, it attempts to fling off the authority of God by claiming Divine power and authority for itself. When it does this, it comes to its doom by the direct act of God. ". . . His Kingdom is an everlasting Kingdom, and His dominion is from generation to generation." (Daniel 4:3)—G. Campbell Morgan, *Searchlights from the Word*

1

FOUR YOUNG PRINCES

WHEN JEHOIAKIM SURRENDERED JERUSALEM to Nebuchadnezzar in 606 B.C., that king carried into captivity ten thousand of Judah's most intelligent young men. Among this group were four young princes, Daniel and three of his friends—Hananiah, Mishael, and Azariah. Nebuchadnezzar decided to train some of these youths for service in the royal court, so he called his chief officer, Ashpenaz.

"Select some of these young men to be schooled in the Babylonian language and the customs of our country," he said. "They must meet rigid qualifications. They must be handsome, skillful, physically fit, and educated well enough to take full advantage of their instructions. After they have been taught for three years, bring them to me and I will assign to them

"The Prophet Daniel" by Michelangelo. Detail. Sistine Chapel, Rome. Although Daniel spent most of his life in foreign lands, he still followed scrupulously his early religious training and kept his faith in the God of Israel.　　　　Alinari

their place and duties in the palace."

Daniel and his three friends were among those who were chosen for special training. Before beginning their studies, Ashpenaz changed the names of the four friends. He called Daniel "Belteshazzar," Hananiah he called "Shadrach," Mishael he called "Meshach," and Azariah he called "Abed-nego."

Daniel and his friends were soon confronted with their first real problem after arriving in Babylon. All students were supposed to eat the food and drink the wine from the king's table. The Jews, however, had strict rules as to what foods they might and might not eat. Daniel was determined not to defile himself by eating the king's rich food or drinking the king's wine, so he went to Ashpenaz.

"Is it possible for an exception to be made in the king's food program?" he asked. "My friends and I wish to be served vegetables instead of the king's meat and wine."

Ashpenaz politely, but firmly, denied his request. "You know full well what the king has ordered you to eat and drink," he replied. "If I complied with your request and you became weak and unhealthy, my head would be in jeopardy."

Although he had failed the first time, Daniel was not easily discouraged. He and his companions went to the steward in charge of dispensing the food and begged him to feed them vegetables and water for ten days. Daniel reinforced the request with a promise.

"After ten days, you can judge for yourself," he said, "and, if there is any difference in our appearance and that of those who eat the king's meat, then deal with us as you wish."

The steward agreed to the test and, when ten days had passed, he was amazed to note that the four friends appeared even more healthy than the others. Daniel and his companions were allowed to be vegetarians during their three-year course of study.

School days were over for Daniel and his friends, and they had learned their lessons well. With the Lord's help, they had mastered the culture and language of the Babylonians, just as Moses had mastered "all the wisdom of Egypt" many centuries earlier. In addition to the talents all four young men possessed, God gave Daniel the ability to interpret dreams and visions.

The four young princes stood before Nebuchadnezzar for an interview. The king was surprised and pleased when they answered his questions ten times better than any of his wise men and astrologers. As a result of this interview Daniel, Hananiah, Mishael, and Azariah were given high positions in the royal court at Babylon.

Based on the story in the Bible: Daniel 1:1-20.

2

DANIEL INTERPRETS NEBUCHADNEZZAR'S DREAM

SOON AFTER DANIEL WAS APPOINTED to his important position in the royal court, Nebuchadnezzar had a dream that caused him much concern. The reason he was so worried about it was that, when he awakened the next morning, he could not remember it. One day he became so troubled that he called in his wisest men.

"I have had a dream," he said. "Tell me what it was!"

The startled wise men responded with surprise to this unreasonable request.

"There is not a man alive who can do what you ask," they said. "Furthermore, no king or ruler in all the earth has ever made such a demand. If you will tell us your dream, we will interpret it."

Nebuchadnezzar retorted, furiously, "Surely you brilliant men must realize that, if I could remember my dream, I would not ask you what it was. One thing is certain. Heads will roll if you wise men

"Daniel and the Wise Men" by J. James Tissot. *The Old Testament,* Illustrated. Nebuchadnezzar could not remember his dream, and even the wise men were unable to help him, but God revealed the dream unto Daniel. M. de Buffan & Co.

"The King's Dream" by G. Rochegrosse. *Biblia Sacra*. Nebuchadnezzar dreamed of seeing a colossal statue—its head, body, and legs made of metal, its feet of clay—suddenly shattered by a thrown stone.

Lemercier & Co., Paris

TENIERS THE ELDER: *Daniel in the Lions' Den (detail)*

Daniel in the Lions' Den (detail)

by DAVID TENIERS THE ELDER (1582-1649) *Flemish School*

Bavarian State Picture Collections, Munich

My God hath sent his angel, and hath shut the lions'
mouths, that they have not hurt me: forasmuch as before
him innocency was found in me. DANIEL 6:22

TO A SEVENTEENTH-CENTURY ARTIST, this miracle—the best-known event of Daniel's career—posed a problem almost impossible to solve: how to show a group of lions being both ferocious and peaceable at the same time. The oddly human expressions of the animals in our picture bespeak Teniers' effort to convey to us that these lions are aware of the unusual role they have been forced to play and, if they seem ill at ease, we can hardly blame them for their pose of studied indifference.

don't come up with an answer soon."

No answer was forthcoming, so the king issued a decree that all the wise men in Babylon should be executed. Daniel and his three friends were among those who faced imminent death. When Arioch, the captain of the king's executioners, came to arrest the four Hebrews, Daniel spoke out boldly.

"Why is the king in such a hurry to execute all of his wise men?" he asked.

Arioch explained why the king was so angry. Daniel then took a brave step. He hurried to the wrathful king and spoke to him.

"O king, if you will give me a little time," he said, "I will tell you what your dream was, and I will also interpret it for you."

Nebuchadnezzar agreed to hold the executions in abeyance for a few days so that the Hebrew wise man might have the opportunity to solve the problem. Daniel rushed home and told his companions what had happened at the palace. Then all four youths prayed earnestly to their God, asking that He reveal the king's dream to Daniel. That night God did reveal the dream to His servant. When he awakened, Daniel knelt and thanked the Lord.

"Blessed be the name of the Lord, forever and ever," he said. "Wisdom and strength are His. He changes the seasons, He sets up kings, and He removes them. . . . I thank You, O God of my fathers, for making the king's dream known to me."

Daniel then went to Arioch and said, "Do not execute the wise men! Take me to the king, so that I can tell him his dream."

Daniel stood before Nebuchadnezzar and had his chance to prove once again that God's wisdom is far greater than that of man.

"O king," he said, "the Lord God of Israel has made known to you what will occur in the latter days. You dreamed, O king, that you saw a great statue. This statue, mighty and exceedingly bright, stood before you, and the figure was terrifying. Its head was made of gold, its arms and breast were made of silver, its stomach and thighs of bronze, its legs of iron, and its feet were made of a mixture of iron and clay.

"The interpretation of this dream is simple. The various metal parts of the statue represent kingdoms that shall arise in the latter days. You, O king, are the head of gold and shall have a long and prosperous reign. Other kingdoms will succeed you but they, too, shall pass away. As you saw in your dream, a stone was cut out by no human hands and was hurled at the feet of clay. This caused the other kingdoms to come crashing to the earth and break into small segments. Meanwhile, in the days of those kings, the God of heaven shall set up a kingdom that shall last forever, and all the other kingdoms shall be broken into pieces—like chaff that the wind drives away. The dream is certain, and the interpretation is sure."

Nebuchadnezzar was amazed. While Daniel spoke, the king's dream rose vividly before him. He came down from his throne and paid homage to Daniel.

"Truly, your God is the God of gods and the Lord of kings," he said, "because He has revealed to you the secret of this mystery."

King Nebuchadnezzar then appointed Daniel ruler over all Babylon, gave him many gifts, and made him chief of all the wise men. At Daniel's request, the king appointed Shadrach, Meshach, and Abednego to high positions in the kingdom; but Daniel remained in the court of the king.

Based on the story in the Bible:
Daniel 2:1-49

3
FROM HIGH RANK TO A FIERY FURNACE

IN THE YEARS THAT FOLLOWED NEBUCHADNEZZAR'S dream, many important domestic projects were completed in Babylon. The king dug irrigation canals throughout the Tigris district, and the land soon became "like a garden," rich in corn, fruits, and flowers.

His greatest achievement, however, was the construction of the "Hanging Gardens of Babylon," which were destined to become known as one of the Seven Wonders of the Ancient World.

Nebuchadnezzar felt very proud of himself. In spite of his great military and domestic accomplishments, he had not neglected to worship and to honor his god, Merodach. On a rolling slope, within sight of the Hanging Gardens, the king had erected a huge golden image of his god. The time for its dedication was drawing near.

In response to Nebuchadnezzar's command, all the princes, governors, counselors, captains, judges, treasurers, sheriffs, and the rulers of all the provinces came to Babylon for the dedication of the golden idol and to worship it. It measured six cubits at the base and pointed skyward for sixty cubits. Included among the throng were the three friends of Daniel—Shadrach, Meshach, and Abed-nego. They were startled when they heard the heralds going through the crowd, shouting the king's proclamation:

"Hear this, O people of all countries and all languages! The king has commanded that, when you hear the sound of music, you shall fall down on your faces and worship the golden image. If you fail to do so, you shall be arrested immediately and cast into a fiery furnace."

The three young Hebrews looked into one another's eyes, clasped hands, and made the instant decision that they would rather die than to worship the image.

The music burst forth and the massed crowd, like corn before a strong breeze, bent over and worshiped the image. Not so, the three young Hebrews; they stood straight and tall throughout the ceremony. Conspicious by their brilliant, official robes, they were quickly spotted by some Chaldeans who were already jealous of the high honors given to these young captives. The Chaldeans hurried off to make their report to Nebuchadnezzar.

"There are certain Jews, O king," they began, "to whom you have given positions of great responsibility—Shadrach, Meshach, and Abed-nego. These men have disobeyed you. They neither serve your gods nor do they worship the golden image that you have set up."

When he heard this report, the king's fury knew no bounds. How could these young men, whom he had treated so kindly, openly flaunt and disobey his commands? Nebuchadnezzar ordered that Shadrach, Meshach, and Abed-nego be brought before him at once. When they stood before him, the king stormed at them.

"Is it really true that you do not serve my gods, nor worship the golden image that I have set up?" he asked. "Even so, I shall give you a final opportunity to atone for your actions. If you bow down and worship the golden image when the music sounds again, I will forgive you and all

"The Three Young Men Condemned to the Fiery Furnace" by Matteo Roselli. R. Galleria Antica e Moderna, Florence. Nebuchadnezzar was enraged when Shadrach, Meshach, and Abed-nego would not worship the golden image.   Alinari

will be well; but if not, you shall be bound and cast into the fiery furnace within the hour. How can your God save you, then?"

Nebuchadnezzar's taunt at their God strengthened the determination of these young men to remain true to their religion. They answered the king, who had been so gracious to them, with quiet respect.

"There is really no need for us to discuss this matter, O king," they said. "Our God, Whom we serve, is able to deliver us from the fiery furnace; but whether He does or not, we will not serve your gods nor worship your golden image."

Nebuchadnezzar's face was purple with rage. He ordered the furnace to be heated seven times hotter than usual. Then he commanded the strongest men in the army to bind Shadrach, Meshach, and Abed-nego and cast them into the fiery furnace. The soldiers obeyed their king's command and cast the young men into the incredibly hot furnace. The men who carried the young Hebrews to the furnace, however, did not escape unscathed. When they opened the door to perform their gruesome task, a blast of exceedingly hot air burst forth and burned all of them to death.

325

Nebuchadnezzar sat near the furnace, observing all the details. Suddenly he arose and cried out in astonishment, "Weren't there only three bound men that we cast into the furnace?"

The counselors replied, "That is true, O king!"

The king then said, excitedly, "Look! I see four unbound men walking unhurt in the flames; and the figure of the fourth one resembles an angel of the Lord!"

Nebuchadnezzar then strode near to the door of the furnace and called out: "Shadrach, Meshach, and Abed-nego! You servants of the most high God! Come out of the flaming furnace and stand before me!"

The furnace door slowly opened and the three young men emerged from the midst of the fire. When the young Hebrews stood before the king, all the princes, governors, captains, and counselors who were gathered there gasped with awe. The intense fire had had no effect on their bodies! Their hair was not even singed, and their clothes were not so much as scorched!

Nebuchadnezzar spoke loudly, so that all those present could hear.

"Blessed be the God of Shadrach, Meshach, and Abed-nego!" he cried. "He sent His angel to protect and to save them, because they were determined to serve and worship no God but their own. I now, therefore, decree to the people of all nations and all languages: Anyone who says anything amiss against the God of Shadrach, Meshach, and Abed-nego shall be summarily executed, and his home shall be utterly destroyed."

After issuing this decree, the king then promoted Shadrach, Meshach, and Abed-nego to even higher positions in the kingdom of Babylon.

*Based on the story in the Bible:
Daniel 3:1-30*

"In the Fiery Furnace" by J. James Tissot. *The Old Testament,* Illustrated. Nebuchadnezzar found the three young Hebrews protected from the flames. M. de Buffan & Co.

4
THE FEAST OF BELSHAZZAR

WHEN NEBUCHADNEZZAR HAD RECOVERED from his seven years of insanity, he resumed control of his empire. Imagine his surprise when he learned that his son, Evil-merodach, had actually rejoiced because of his illness.

For this act of disloyalty, the son was cast into prison where he met Jehoiachin and became his friend. Evil-merodach succeeded his father on the throne, and his brief two-year reign was marked by his kindness to the captive king. He freed the king of Judah from prison and gave him all the privileges of the royal court.

The death of Nebuchadnezzar marked the beginning of the rapid deterioration of the power and prestige of the once-great Neo-Babylonian Empire. Belshazzar, the grandson of Nebuchadnezzar, now sat on the shaky throne of Babylon, and he was acting strangely for the king of a nation in the midst of a great crisis. The Medes and the Persians had besieged Babylon for two years, and the city was likely to fall at any minute. Belshazzar ignored all this and prepared a great feast for his wives and one thousand of his lords.

The feast was in full progress. Belshazzar, from the ruler's place at the head of the table, set the feast in motion by drinking a goblet of red wine. His goblet, like those of all the others, came from the treasures taken from the Lord's Temple at the time of the fall of Jerusalem. This desecration of the Lord's goblets was one more mark against the king and his people.

"Belshazzar's Feast" by Mattia Preti. National Gallery of Capodimonte, Naples. The laughter and gaiety of Belshazzar's banquet were stilled when a man's hand suddenly appeared and the fingers wrote strange words upon the wall. Alinari

Wine was drunk with reckless abandon. The feasting, gaiety, and revelry was approaching its climax when—suddenly—silence filled the room! The king and the people stared in awe-stricken terror at the fingers of a man's hand writing on the plaster of the wall. Belshazzar turned pale, and he was so terrified that his knees were knocking and his flesh crawling. He called for his wise men and astrologers to read the words and interpret them. But the words were written in a strange language that none of them knew.

Word of what was happening in the banquet hall reached the Queen Mother, so she hurried to her troubled, perplexed son and gave him this advice:

"There is a man in your kingdom who can tell you what the writing means. He is wise and understanding; his name is Daniel. He was so good at interpreting dreams, solving problems, and explaining riddles that my father appointed him chief of all his wise men, astrologers, and Chaldeans. Send for this man, and he will interpret the meaning of the words."

When Daniel appeared before the king, Belshazzar spoke eagerly: "If you can read the writing on the wall and tell me what it means, you shall be clothed in purple and shall have a chain of gold around your neck. You shall also be third in command throughout the kingdom."

Daniel answered gravely, "Keep your gifts and rewards for yourself and others. However, I will tell you what you wish to know."

Daniel first reminded Belshazzar how God had once punished his grandfather Nebuchadnezzar by causing him to lose his mind, roam the fields and forests like a wild animal, and eat grass like an ox. Only when he acknowledged that the Most High God rules all the kingdoms of men did the Lord restore him to his sanity and power. Daniel then continued solemnly:

"Even though you knew all about this, Belshazzar, you did not profit from his experience. You have drunk wine from the vessels of God's Temple, and you have praised false gods of gold, silver, iron, wood, and stone that cannot see or hear; yet, the God upon whom your very life depends, you have failed to honor. For these and many other reasons, He sent the hand to write the message on the wall. This is what the message says:

"'MENE, MENE, TEKEL, UPHARSIN.' And this is the interpretation:

"'MENE. God has numbered the days of your kingdom and will soon end it.

"'TEKEL. You have been weighed in the balances and found wanting.

"'PERES. Your kingdom has been divided and will be given to the Medes and Persians.'" (*Upharsin* is plural of *Peres*.)

Although Belshazzar was not happy about these ominous words, he kept his promise and clothed Daniel in scarlet and placed a chain of gold about his neck. He then proclaimed him the third ruler of Babylon.

It was later than they thought! While Belshazzar and his guests still sat in stunned silence, Darius the Mede had crashed through the walls of Babylon. He and his men were already racing toward the palace. Soon the floor of the great banquet hall was flowing with blood, mingled with the spilled wine from the banquet table, as Darius and his soldiers ruthlessly slaughtered King Belshazzar and all the people gathered there.

Thus it came about that the golden head of Nebuchadnezzar's dream-statue fell crashing to the ground, and the great Neo-Babylonian Empire was never again a power in the history of the nations.

Based on the story in the Bible:
Daniel 4:1—5:31

5
DANIEL FACES THE LIONS

VENERABLE DANIEL WAS HIGHLY RESPECTED in the court of Darius. He was honest and trustworthy, so the king placed him in charge of the royal treasury. There were rumors that Darius was planning to give Daniel even greater authority. These rumors aroused the jealousy of some of the nobles around the throne, so they tried to think of some plan to degrade the Hebrew statesman in the eyes of his royal master.

The jealous nobles had been unable to find any fault in Daniel. He ruled so wisely that the realm was enjoying its greatest period of prosperity. They, therefore, decided to try to strike at Daniel through his God, Whom he worshiped openly three times a day. The clever conspirators knew that they could not make a direct attack on Daniel, so they came to Darius with a wily proposal.

"Live forever, O king!" they began. "All the governors, the princes, the counselors, and the captains have met together and written a royal statute. It states that anyone who worships any god except yours during the next thirty days shall be cast into a den of lions. Issue the decree and sign the document, O king, so that, according to the law of the Medes and Persians, it cannot be repealed."

Little realizing what he was doing, Darius signed the document and issued the decree. The pleased plotters hurriedly left the king's court. They were certain that they now had Daniel in an escape-proof trap.

Daniel was about seventy years old when he faced the greatest test of his long and dedicated life. He had soon heard of the king's ill-advised and hasty decree, so he decided to return to his house. When he entered, he walked slowly to a window facing west toward Jerusalem, his beloved city that he had not seen since the days of his youth. He noticed the people in the courtyard, waiting anxiously to learn what he would do. There was, however, no real problem for Daniel. He would continue to serve his God. Standing in full view of all the people, he raised his hands, bowed down, and worshiped the Lord God of Judah.

The nobles shouted with glee when they saw what had happened. Daniel had done exactly what they had expected. They pounced upon him and led him back to the palace. Leaving a few men to guard Daniel, the others hurried inside for an audience with the king.

The spokesman for the nobles slyly asked Darius, "Isn't it true, O king, that you recently decreed that no one shall worship any god but yours for the next thirty days? Don't you remember the penalty for disobeying this decree?"

When the king answered both questions in the affirmative, the princes and the nobles shouted triumphantly, "We are here to tell you, O king, that Daniel, the Hebrew captive, does not obey either you or the decree! Instead, he worships his God three times a day."

King Darius was distressed when he heard the news. How could he have allowed himself to be cajoled into signing such a foolish decree? He tried desperately to think of some way that he

DANIEL

could save his faithful, trusted servant. Pressure mounted from the court, however, as the people continually reminded the king that the law could not be changed. Finally, there was nothing left for Darius to do but to command that Daniel be thrown to the lions.

Even as Daniel was falling, his heathen king uttered a strange prayer: "May the Lord God Whom you worship so faithfully and so constantly protect and save you during this ordeal."

The king then sealed the stone at the mouth of the lions' den with the royal signet and returned to the palace. There was no sleep for Darius that night. He fasted and permitted no music to be played during the long vigil.

"Daniel in the Lion's Den" by John M. Swan. *Biblia Sacra.* When Darius was king, Daniel's faith was tested again. He continued daily worship, despite a royal decree, and was thrown to the lions.　　　　　　　　　　Lemercier & Co., Paris

Basalt Lion. At the ruins of Babylon there is a basalt statue of a lion, marking the supposed site of the lions' den from which Daniel emerged unharmed. These animals are now extinct in this area. © Matson Photo

As soon as it was daylight, the king hurried to the den of lions and cried out, anxiously, "O Daniel, servant of the living God! Was your God able to save you from the lions?"

A deep sigh of relief surged through the king's body when he heard Daniel's reply: "O king, live forever! My God sent His angel to stand beside me all through the night. He also closed the lions' mouths so that they could not harm me."

The king was exceedingly happy and he ordered Daniel's immediate release from the lions' den. Then he commanded that Daniel's accusers, along with their wives and children, be cast into the den of lions. The hungry lions broke the falling bodies into pieces even before they reached the bottom of the pit.

Then Darius wrote a decree for the people of all nations and languages within his dominion:

"I have made a decree that every one in my kingdom shall fear and tremble before the God of Daniel, because He is a living God and His kingdom shall last forever. He delivers and He rescues; He works wonders in heaven and on earth; and He saved His servant Daniel from the power of the lions."

Daniel prospered, and his official court life continued during the reign of Darius and into the reign of Cyrus the Persian.

Based on the story in the Bible:
Daniel 6:1-28

331

PLACES
in the Story of Daniel

BABYLON

This important city in south Mesopotamia was the capital of the Neo-Babylonian Empire. It reached its peak during the reign of Nebuchadnezzar. Daniel and his friends spent most of their years of captivity here.

MEDIA

This mountainous country, located south of the Caspian Sea, was an ancient area in northwest Iran. It was in this kingdom, under the reign of Darius the Mede, that Daniel spent most of his declining years.

PERSIA

This relatively small country north of the Persian Gulf was dominated by the Median Empire until Cyrus the Great mastered Media and began his career of conquest. Daniel's long and illustrious life came to an end in the early years of the reign of Cyrus the Persian.

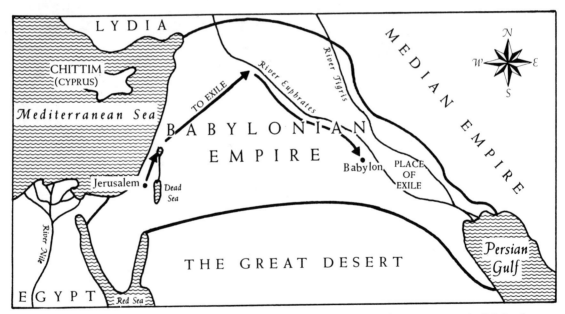

Route to Exile in Babylon. When Nebuchadnezzar besieged Jerusalem and overcame Johoiakim, along with Daniel he took many other intelligent young men to Babylon for special training. Daniel never returned to his native land.

QUESTIONS
on the Story of Daniel

1

1 What were the names of Daniel's friends? What were the Babylonian names given to the four of them?

2 What were the qualifications required in order for a young Hebrew to be chosen for special training in the language and customs of the Babylonians?

3 Why did Daniel and his friends refuse to eat the food and drink the wine from the king's table?

4 How did the vegetarian diet affect Daniel and his three friends?

5 How did Daniel and his friends fare at the king's interview? What additional ability did Daniel have that his friends did not possess?

2

6 Why was Nebuchadnezzar so worried about his dream?

7 What strange request did Nebuchadnezzar make to his wise men? What was their startled reply?

8 What punishment did Nebuchadnezzar decree for his wise men?

9 What did Daniel do when he learned of the king's decree?

10 What did Daniel tell the king that his dream was?

11 How did Daniel interpret this dream?

12 How was Daniel rewarded for making known and interpreting Nebuchadnezzar's dream?

3

13 What was Nebuchadnezzar's greatest domestic achievement? Why did it become so famous?

14 How did Nebuchadnezzar pay tribute to his god? What was the size of the golden image?

15 What did the king command the people to do? What was to be their punishment for failure to obey his command?

16 What was the instant decision that Shadrach, Meshach, and Abed-nego made?

17 What did Nebuchadnezzar do when he saw four men walking around in the flames?

18 What was the decree that the king issued concerning the God of the three young Hebrews?

4

19 For what was Evil-merodach's short reign noted?

20 How did Belshazzar desecrate the golden vessels from the Lord's Temple?

21 Why did the gaiety and revelry in the banquet hall suddenly become subdued?

22 What did the Queen Mother tell her son to do?

23 What were the words of the handwriting on the wall? What did Daniel tell Belshazzar that these words meant?

24 What happened to Belshazzar, his guests, and his kingdom that very night?

5

25 Why were the nobles in the court of Darius jealous of Daniel?

26 How did the wily conspirators plan to downgrade Daniel in the eyes of his royal master?

27 What was Daniel's reaction to the king's decree? How was he punished for disobeying it?

28 How did the Lord protect and save Daniel during his night in the lions' den?

29 What was the fate of Daniel's accusers?

30 Why did Darius decree that the people of his dominion should stand in fear and trembling before the God of Daniel?

Answers are found on the following pages.

"The Prophet Daniel" by Bernini. Church of Santa Maria del Popolo, Rome. At the entrance to Chigi Chapel is this marble statue of Daniel in prayer. The use of the lion identifies a prominent event in the life of Daniel. Alinari

ANSWERS
on the Story of Daniel

1

1 The Hebrew names of Daniel's friends were Hananiah, Mishael, and Azariah. Daniel's name was changed to Belteshazzar, and his friends' names were changed to Shadrach, Meshach, and Abed-nego.

2 To be chosen for special training in Babylonian culture, the young Hebrew had to be handsome, skillful, physically fit, and well educated.

3 Daniel and his friends felt that the rich food and wine from the king's table would defile their bodies.

4 The vegetarian diet made Daniel and his friends appear even more healthy than the other students.

5 The four young princes answered the king's questions ten times better than any of his wise men and astrologers. Daniel possessed the additional ability to interpret dreams.

2

6 Nebuchadnezzar was troubled about his dream because, when he awoke, he could not remember what it was.

7 The king asked his wise men to tell him what he had dreamed. The startled wise men replied that there was not a person alive who could do what he asked.

8 Nebuchadnezzar decreed that all his wise men should be executed.

9 Daniel went to the king and asked him to grant a stay of execution so that he could try to find the solution to the king's problem.

10 Daniel told the king that he had dreamed that he saw a mighty statue standing before him. Its head was made of gold, its arms and breast of silver, its stomach and thighs of bronze, its legs of iron, and its feet of a mixture of iron and clay.

11 Daniel told Nebuchadnezzar that the various metal parts of the statue represented kingdoms that would arise in the latter days. The golden head represented Babylon, which would be the first kingdom to topple. Then the other kingdoms would rise and fall. Meanwhile, in the days of those kings, the God of heaven will set up a kingdom that will last forever.

12 King Nebuchadnezzar appointed Daniel ruler over all Babylon, gave him many gifts, and made him chief of all his wise men.

3

13 Nebuchadnezzar constructed the Hanging Gardens of Babylon. They became famous because they were selected as one of the Seven Wonders of the Ancient World.

14 Nebuchadnezzar built a large golden image in honor of his god. It measured six cubits at its base and was sixty cubits tall.

15 The king commanded his people, at a given signal, to bow down and worship the golden idol. Anyone who disobeyed this command would be thrown into a fiery furnace.

16 Shadrach, Meshach, and Abed-nego pledged that they would die rather than worship the image.

17 When Nebuchadnezzar saw a fourth person walking in the flames of the furnace, guarding and protecting the young Hebrews, he went near the door of the furnace and called for them to come out.

18 Nebuchadnezzar decreed that anyone

who said anything amiss against the Lord God of Shadrach, Meshach, and Abednego should be executed immediately and his home completely destroyed.

4

19 Evil-merodach's short reign was marked by his kindness to a captive king of Judah.

20 Belshazzar desecrated the holy vessels by drinking wine from them and using them in making toasts to strange gods.

21 Quiet reigned in the great banquet hall. The awe-stricken people stared in hushed amazement at the fingers of a hand writing on the plaster.

22 The Queen Mother told her son to send for Daniel and he would interpret the handwriting on the wall.

23 The words on the wall were: MENE, MENE, TEKEL, UPHARSIN. Daniel told Belshazzar these words meant: (1) MENE, "God has numbered the days of your kingdom and will soon end it." (2) TEKEL, "You have been weighed in the balances and found wanting." (3) PERES, "Your kingdom has been divided between the Medes and the Persians."

24 Belshazzar and his guests were slaughtered, and the kingdom of Babylon fell to Darius the Mede.

5

25 The nobles were jealous of Daniel because he held such a high position in the king's court, and there were rumors that Darius would soon give him even greater power.

26 The conspirators hoped to downgrade Daniel by striking at him through his faithful worship of his God.

27 Daniel continued to worship his God three times daily. He was punished by being cast into a den of lions.

28 God sent His angel to stand beside Daniel and protect him. The lions' mouths were also closed so that no harm could come to him.

29 Daniel's accusers, along with their wives and children, were cast into the lions' den. Even before they hit the bottom of the pit, their bodies were crushed and their bones broken.

30 Darius told his people that the Lord God of Daniel is a living God who performs miracles, both in heaven and on earth. The king was particularly impressed with the way God saved Daniel from the power of the lions.

Byzantine Urn with Bas-relief. National Museum, Ravenna. Early Christian art, such as this sculpture of Daniel among the lions, often was employed to tell Bible stories. Alinari

FURTHER FACTS
AND OUTLINE
for the Story of Daniel

AUTHORSHIP AND DATE

Daniel, a contemporary of Nebuchadnezzar, Belshazzar, Darius, and Cyrus. According to both Jewish and Christian traditions, Daniel wrote the book in the 6th century B.C.

DESTINATION

The Jews, but also partly for the Babylonians.

THEME AND PURPOSE

God's sovereignty over the kingdoms of this world is the great overall purpose or theme of Daniel. To be sure, pagan Babylon lords it over Israel momentarily, but only because God permits her to be the instrument of His punishment of the Jews; but pagan nations will lose their power some day, for God is the real and ultimate ruler of the world. Indeed, secular power is limited now, as evidenced in the supernatural power of God to free Daniel from the lions and the three Hebrew children from the fiery furnace. Even Nebuchadnezzar is forced to recognize the superiority of God's power to his own monarchical power. In the last days God will in fact bring about the Kingdom which will never be destroyed. (In this connection note 7:13 on the second coming of the "son of man" with "the clouds of heaven.") How relevant Daniel's message is for us in the 20th century who fear the "kingdoms" of materialism, Communism, and general paganism!

OUTLINE

The Great Stories of Daniel (chapters 1-6)
    The King's Food and Drink Refused by Faithful Hebrew Young Men (chapter 1)
    The Great Image in Nebuchadnezzar's Dream (chapter 2)
    'Shadrach, Meshach, Abed-nego Delivered from the Fiery Furnace (chapter 3)
    Nebuchadnezzar's Dream about the Tree; Daniel's Interpretation of the Dream (chapter 4)
    Belshazzar and the Handwriting on the Wall (chapter 5)
    Daniel in the Den of Lions (chapter 6)

The Great Prophecies of Daniel (chapters 7-12)
    Daniel's Dream about the Four Beasts (chapter 7)
    Daniel's Dream about the Ram, He-goat, and Horn (chapter 8)
    Daniel's Prayer and Its Answer (chapter 9)
    Daniel Has Another Dream (chapter 10)
    Conflicts between Persia and Greece, and between the South and the North (chapter 11)
    The End Time: Tribulation but Resurrection (chapter 12)

LESSONS FOR TODAY'S LIVING

Under the North Pole

by
William R. Anderson

Prayer was the dominant force behind two outstanding men whose careers were separated by more than twenty-five centuries, Captain William R. Anderson of the nuclear submarine *Nautilus* and the Hebrew prophet, Daniel, trusted advisor to the rulers of three heathen empires. Captain Anderson, in his article under the above title in *Guideposts* (© 1965, Guideposts Associates, Inc., Carmel, N.Y.) tells how the greatest adventure of his life, commanding the *Nautilus* in its history-making voyage under Arctic seas to the North Pole, was planned in prayer and accomplished through the same power. Daniel made prayer such a habit of life that, in every great decision, God's answer to his petitions was his guiding light. Even facing death in a den of lions, Daniel persisted in his daily habit of facing Jerusalem and praying to his God. We have much to learn from these two great men who knew the importance of placing first things first in every area of their lives.

DIVINE HELP AND PROTECTION

IT WAS THE GREATEST adventure of my life—a task conceived in prayer, planned in prayer, attempted in prayer, and achieved in prayer. It was the 1958 voyage of the nuclear submarine *Nautilus* under the frozen Arctic seas to the North Pole. It was my privilege to command the *Nautilus* on that historic occasion and I am convinced that if we had not asked for and received Divine help and protection, we never would have made it.

That voyage from ocean to ocean across the top of the world was an event of critical importance in the history of our country. To understand this, one must remember the circumstances that prevailed at the time. In October, 1957, the Russians startled the world by putting the first man-made satellite into orbit. In November, they launched an even larger one. With two Sputniks circling the planet, it looked as if the Russians had seized a commanding lead in the Cold War. Throughout the world, confidence in America's weapons and military power was badly shaken.

During the summer, before the Sputniks went up, the *Nautilus* had carried out some experiments under the ice pack on the Atlantic side, north of the Greenland Sea. We had discovered that in places the ice was twice as thick as it had been assumed to be — and had bashed up our periscopes in the process. On my return to Washington, I had discussed with Captain E. P. Avrand, then Naval aide to the President, the possibility of the *Nautilus* making a polar transit. Now suddenly, in January, 1958, I received an urgent summons from the Pentagon to report for discussion of a subject "too sensitive to talk about on the telephone."

At the Pentagon I learned that the White House had inquired if it would be feasible for the *Nautilus* to attempt a voyage from the Pacific Ocean to the Atlantic by way of the North Pole. If successful, such a feat would produce a vast amount of scientific information and would dramatize the range and power of our small but growing fleet of nuclear

STEEN: *The Wrath of Ahasuerus*

The Wrath of Ahasuerus

by JAN STEEN (1626-1679) *Dutch School*

Barber Institute of Fine Arts, Birmingham, England

*And Esther said, The adversary and enemy is this wicked
Haman. Then Haman was afraid before the king and the
queen. And the king, arising from the banquet of wine,
in his wrath went into the palace garden.* ESTHER 7:6-7

AN INNKEEPER BY TRADE, Steen is more noted for his lively
pictures of Dutch family life than for his painting of religious
subjects. Here, with amusing results, he has merged the two:
Ahasuerus is none other than the heavy Dutch father, thundering
at his errant son (Haman), while the servants whisper in the
corridor, and the mother (Esther) looks relieved that the job of
disciplining the children has been taken out of her hands.

submarines. Clearly, such a voyage would lift morale of freedom-loving people everywhere.

When the President was advised that the Navy favored such an operation, he insisted on one thing: complete secrecy. The proposed trans-polar voyage of the *Nautilus* was one of the most closely guarded secrets in the history of the Navy. I don't think that more than a dozen people knew about it. My own superior officer in the submarine service didn't. My wife didn't. My crew certainly didn't. When we finally left Seattle, they thought we were on a routine training cruise.

This secrecy heightened my sense of loneliness and responsibility to a degree I have not known before or since. There was only one thing I could do to lessen it: pray. Whenever I did pray, I felt less alone, and I prayed often—prayed that whatever happened I would not fail my crew or let down our country.

We knew that the most difficult part of the voyage would come after we passed through Bering Strait and began to grope our way under the ice of the Chukchi Sea north of Alaska. The Chukchi Sea is shallow; its average depth is only 120 feet. If the ice was thick, could the big *Nautilus*—4,000 tons submerged and as long as a city block—get through? This was the question I lived with.

One thing I *didn't* have to worry about was the calibre of my crew. Of the 116 men aboard, no two were alike. Some came from big cities, some from small towns. Some had Italian ancestors, some English, some Irish. . . . To a man they were skilled, good-humored, responsible and brave. People say to me sometimes, "Weren't there a lot of psychological problems?" To such a question I can give an honest answer: No, we were too busy to be bored. And you aren't likely to get problems in a team where each man is an individual working in his own special way to achieve a common goal.

We made our first attempt to reach the Pole in June. For eight days, all went well. But suddenly, near midnight on June 17th, the voice of my conning officer, Lt. Bill Lalor, rang through my cabin speaker, sharp with urgency, "Captain, will you come here, please!"

Instantly I snapped up and raced to the control room. When I looked at the tracing of the sonar pen, I felt my heart pound. The ice above us was 63 feet thick and getting thicker. Only eight feet of water separated the jagged, granite-hard under-surface from the top of the *Nautilus*. As I watched, the margin dropped to five feet. Close under our keel was the bottom of the Chukchi Sea.

We were driving ahead at ten knots; there was no time to think. I had dodged torpedoes in the war, but I had never faced anything like this. There was not even time to pray. And yet I must have prayed, because in that splitsecond of time a decision was made—not *by* me but *for* me. I actually felt, on my left shoulder, something like a great, reassuring hand, pressing—*down*.

"Take her down 15 feet!" I heard my voice give the order. Then I stood there, bracing myself for the grinding crash of steel against ice or the sickening shock that would mean we had hit bottom. But there was none. I ordered the rudder put hard over, and slowly the *Nautilus* swung around, carrying 116 men away from the deadly ridge of ice. Few of them knew how close we had been—a prayer's breadth, I truly believe—to disaster.

So the ice defeated us on that first attempt. But later that summer we tried again. Cautiously, gingerly, we probed our way through the shallows of the Chukchi Sea into the deep waters of the Arctic basin. On August 3, cruising in comfort below 400 feet, we approached the Pole. Above us was the vast wilderness of ice, gray and chaotic. Below us the sea was more than two miles deep. In the control room, our navigators tensely made their final calculations.

Then, at 11:15 p.m., E.D.T., we reached the top of the world. Picking up the microphone of the public address system, I told the crew that we were at the Pole. "And now," I added, "I would like for all of us to give our thanks to Him who has guided us so truly, to pay a silent tribute to those brave men who have preceded us here, whether in victory or in failure, and finally to offer our prayers for lasting world peace."

There was silence for a moment. Then I

heard cheers in the crew's mess. Our navigator was noting down our official position: *U.S.S. Nautilus: Latitude 90 Degrees North; Longitude Indefinite.* If there really had been a north pole, our course would have taken us right through it.

Two days later, after 96 hours under the ice, we surfaced northeast of Greenland and were able to report our success by radio in a momentous three-word message: "Nautilus 90 north." I was picked up by helicopter, flown to Washington, greeted by the President, then allowed to fly to England to meet the *Nautilus* and share in the tremendous welcome she received on her arrival there. There is nothing in the world more thrilling than the feeling that your country is proud of you.

I also was grateful—grateful to the Power that watched over us, the Power that ordained and sustains and rules the universe.

Esther

IT IS INTERESTING TO NOTE that Esther's original name was Hadassah, which means "myrtle," while Esther is a Persian name which means "star," suggestive of the form of flower that the myrtle tree bears. The beautiful daughter of the Hebrew race at the court of a Persian king, a girl born in captivity, was called Myrtle. In all likelihood her father had named her Hadassah because the myrtle tree had become the sign and symbol of the race. The Persians called her Star to indicate that she was the flower of the myrtle tree, full of beauty, full of grace.

There are peculiarities in the story of Esther which have raised doubts as to whether it ought to have any place in the canon of Scripture. The name of God is never mentioned. There is found no reference to the Hebrew religion. The Temple never appears. No ceremonial of Hebrew worship is referred to. There is one reference to Jerusalem, in the sixth verse of the second chapter, but that merely accounts for Mordecai and shows whence these people had come. Perhaps the book is a fragment of secular history captured for its sacred purposes; perchance it was copied bodily from Persian history and incorporated in the ancient Hebrew Scriptures. While there is no name of God and no reference to the Hebrew religion anywhere, no one reads this book without being conscious of God. Its permanent value is that it is a revelation of God acting in providence. . . .

The doctrine of Divine providence is that God both possesses and exercises absolute power over all the works of His hands. . . . Esther is a book of pictures, and the teaching of these pictures is that of Divine providence: God amid the shadows, but at work. God hidden, unrecognized and undetected by the vast majority, but still at work. The book then reveals the method, the principles, and some of the results of Divine providence. . . .

The application of a story like this is not declared in words, but it glows in letters of flaming fire upon all the pages of the book: Reckon with God. Trust in God. Cooperate with God.—G. Campbell Morgan, *Living Messages of the Books of the Bible*

1
A NEW QUEEN REIGNS

WHILE THE PEOPLE OF JUDAH were still in captivity, a figure emerged from behind the scenes and took her place alongside other great women of the Bible. Her name was Esther. She was virtuous, lovely, and loyal to her people.

She was, in fact, ready to sacrifice her life for them. Who could do more?

King Ahasuerus, better known in history as Xerxes I, was proud of his mighty Persian Empire. He reigned over one hundred and twenty-seven provinces that extended from India to Ethiopia. One day the king summoned all his princes, all his military leaders, and all the governors of his provinces to his palace at Shushan. When these official visitors arrived, Ahasuerus started a series of celebrations and banquets that lasted for six months. With his head high, the king displayed all the riches, pomp, and splendor of his vast empire.

The official meetings were over. King Ahasuerus sat with his guests in the garden-court of the palace and watched his servants make final preparations for a great banquet. It would last for seven days, and every man, both great and small, in the capital city had been invited. The garden was gaily decorated. Golden goblets and silver cups, filled with wine, were distributed copiously throughout the large outdoor court. Meanwhile, back in the palace, Queen Vashti prepared simultaneously a banquet for all the women of the royal court.

It was during the seventh day of his banquet that the king thought of a crowning entertainment act for his guests. He would send for his beautiful wife and display her charms for all to see. Queen Vashti quickly thwarted this plan, however, and earned her niche in Bible history by daring to say a resounding "No!" to her besotted husband's immodest proposal. The queen, lovely to behold, defiantly refused to parade herself before the lecherous eyes of the drunken men.

"Mordecai" by J. James Tissot. *The Old Testament,* Illustrated. Mordecai, a Jew, lived in the Persian city of Shushan and was the foster father of Esther. M. de Buffan and Co.

"Esther Is Crowned Queen" by José Villegas. *Biblia Sacra.* King Ahasuerus had exiled his queen, Vashti, for disobed-ience. In the contest for a beautiful and talented girl to take her place, Esther was chosen by the king. Lemercier and Co., Paris

King Ahasuerus was livid with rage. How could Vashti have dared to treat him with such disrespect in front of all his guests? What should he do with her? The king asked for advice—and he got it.

"Punish Vashti swiftly and severely," his counselors told him. "Dethrone her and banish her from the kingdom before the word spreads that the queen has openly defied her husband. Our own wives might decide to treat us the same way if she goes unpunished!"

Then began the first recorded beauty and talent contest. The prize was fabulous. The winner would replace Vashti as Queen of all Persia! On learning of the king's plan to assemble in his palace the fairest girls in the land and to choose his queen from them, a Jew named Mordecai determined that his lovely cousin Esther, whom he had adopted after the death of her parents, should be a contestant.

Finally, it was Esther's turn to stand before the king. Ahasuerus was overcome by her beauty and stately mien. He announced immediately that the search for a new queen was ended. He then called Esther to the throne and placed the royal crown upon her head. Poised, beautiful, and wise, Queen Esther quickly won the love and respect of the Persian people.

Mordecai sat at the gate of the palace, deep in thought. How thrilled he had been at the choice of his adopted daughter as queen! He remembered how, early in her reign, he had uncovered a plot by two of the king's bodyguards to seize and kill Ahasuerus. Mordecai had reported the plot to Esther who, in turn, had told the king. After investigating and verifying the conspiracy, the king ordered his two body-guards hanged. The entire incident had then been recorded and the document placed in the royal archives.

With a start, Mordecai came back to reality. He could little dream how important a role the record of his loyalty was to play in his life.

Based on the story in the Bible:
Esther 1:1 — 2:23

2
A VILLAINOUS PLOT IS FOILED

QUEEN ESTHER WAS DEEPLY DISTRESSED. The lives of her foster father Mordecai and all her people were at stake. She knew that she must act swiftly and cautiously to have any hope of successfully interceding for them. Her brave, momentous decision was made without fear of the consequences.

"I will go to the king," she said to herself, "even if it costs me my life."

The events that led to Esther's dilemma can be placed squarely upon the shoulders of Haman, one of the first recorded anti-Semites. How he hated all Jews! He especially hated Mordecai because he stubbornly refused to bow to Haman and pay him homage. Haman had risen rapidly in the court of King Ahasuerus and now held the post of grand vizier, a position second only to that of the king. Despite his rank and power, however, Haman was to see his efforts serve only to reaffirm God's

"Mordecai and His Enemy" by J. James Tissot. *The Old Testament,* Illustrated. Haman, the grand vizier, hated Mordecai because he refused to pay him homage. Haman plotted to destroy Mordecai and all the Jews of Persia.   M. de Buffan & Co.

promise to Abraham in those faraway days at the beginning of the Jewish nation: "Those who bless you, I will bless; and those who curse you, I will curse."

By clever connivance Haman had maneuvered the Jews into a seemingly hopeless position. He had persuaded King Ahasuerus to issue a proclamation that on a certain date, to be determined by casting Pur (or "lots"), every Jew in the empire would be slain. The date finally chosen by casting the lots was the modern-day equivalent of March 13, some eleven months in the future.

When Esther learned of this cruel decree, she turned to Mordecai for advice. He warned her that all was lost for her people unless she could induce the king to revoke his proclamation. Three days later, Esther prepared for her life or death mission on behalf of Mordecai and the Jewish people. She had bathed in exotic spices and perfumes of the Orient and was clothed in her most alluring royal robes.

All of Esther's fears had been for naught. King Ahasuerus' eyes sparkled with delight as his winsome wife stood before him in his inner chamber. He stretched

"Esther and Ahasuerus" by Cavallino. Uffizi Gallery, Florence. Mordecai and Esther devised a plan to thwart Haman's decree to slay all Jews. To prepare the way, Esther first planned a banquet for Ahasuerus and Haman. Alinari

forth his royal scepter and, as Esther approached the throne to touch it, she knew that she had been received favorably.

"What is it that you want, my queen?" Ahasuerus asked, solicitously. "Name it and I will give it to you, even if it is half my kingdom."

Esther decided not to press her advantage, so she made a modest reply.

"O king," she said, "if it pleases you, my only request is that you and Haman dine with me today."

The king sent for Haman, and together they went to the dinner that Esther had prepared. After the feast was over and the three of them were drinking a rich wine, King Ahasuerus again asked his wife what she wanted. For the second time, Esther postponed telling her benign husband what it was that she really wanted. Her coy reply was to invite the king and Haman back to dinner again on the next day. She promised that she would then reveal to him her innermost desire.

Haman left the palace, proud and happy. A dark scowl crossed his face as he passed through the palace gate and saw Mordecai sitting there; but he decided to ignore the Jew this time and hurry home.

On reaching home, Haman sent for his wife Zeresh and some of his friends. Then he began boasting.

"Surely, I am the most fortunate man in the kingdom," he declared. "I have great riches and ten fine sons. The king has bestowed many honors upon me. Today, I—and I alone—was invited by Queen Esther to have dinner with her and the king. Moreover, the invitation has been repeated for tomorrow. Yet"—and the scowl appeared again— "all these things mean nothing to me, so long as Mordecai the Jew still sits at the king's gate."

Zeresh and his friends made a suggestion. "Build a great gallows," they said, "and, tomorrow when you see the king,

"*The Chronicles Are Read to Ahasuerus*" by J. James Tissot. *The Old Testament*, Illustrated. The king learned that, earlier, Mordecai had saved his life. M. de Buffan & Co.

ask him to have Mordecai hanged on it."

Haman thought that this was a splendid idea. He was so certain the king would approve his request that he had the gallows built that very night.

Meanwhile, back at the palace, the king was having a sleepless night. He finally ordered the scrolls from the archives brought and read to him, hoping that this would lull him to sleep. When the servants read the scroll telling how Mordecai had saved the king's life, Ahasuerus abruptly halted the reading.

"About this man Mordecai," he asked, "what honor has been conferred on him, or what tribute has been paid to him, for his loyal deed?"

Informed by his servants that nothing had been done for Mordecai, the king determined to honor him the next morning. The reading continued throughout the long, weary night; but Ahasuerus was never able to sleep. Shortly after daybreak

"Esther Accuses Haman" by José Villegas. *Biblia Sacra.* At the end of the second banquet that Queen Esther gave for Haman and Ahasuerus, she revealed to the king that Haman had issued the proclamation that would destroy the Jewish people in the kingdom.   Lemercier & Co., Paris

he heard a noise in the courtyard and asked his servants who was out there. Told that it was Haman, the king asked him to come inside.

In his eagerness for vengeance, Haman had risen early and rushed to the palace where he would ask the king to have Mordecai hanged. Before the cruel grand vizier could utter a word, as he entered the king's chamber Ahasuerus posed a question.

"What shall I do," he asked, "for a man whom I wish to honor?"

Believing he was that man, Haman had a prompt reply.

"The man whom you wish to honor," he said, "should be dressed in royal robes that you have worn and placed upon a horse that you have ridden. Then one of your most noble princes should lead the horse around the public square, proclaiming: 'This is being done to a man whom the king is pleased to honor!'"

When he heard the king's next words, Haman received the shock of his life.

"Here are my robes and horse," Ahasuerus said. "Hurry to Mordecai the Jew and do for him all the things you have mentioned. Be sure not to leave out anything."

The irony of it all! At the very hour he had planned on asking for Mordecai's execution Haman found himself leading the king's horse, with Mordecai astride it and dressed in the king's robes, through the streets of Shushan. After carrying out the king's command, Haman rushed to his home, with his head covered in humiliation. Mordecai returned to the king's gate, grateful for the honors given him.

Although Haman's wife Zeresh and his friends had given him no encouragement after he had related the events of the morning, Haman's spirits began to rise as he responded hastily to the king's reminder about the feast that Esther had prepared, and of the grand vizier's invitation to it.

The second feast was over. Esther and her guests were still at the table, relishing the fine wine she now placed before them. King Ahasuerus once more asked his queen what he could do for her. Esther arose, then bowed before him.

"O king," she cried, "I plead for my life and the lives of my people! Someone has used your seal and issued a cruel decree ordering all Jews throughout your empire to be slaughtered."

Ahasuerus was furious. When Esther had finished speaking, he thundered the question uppermost in his mind.

"Who is this person? Where is he who would dare such an evil deed?"

Esther replied, calmly but firmly, "My enemy and the enemy of my people is here, in this very room. That wicked Haman," she said as she pointed to the cowering grand vizier, "is the man!"

Events moved swiftly after Esther denounced Haman. The king's anger did not abate until his chief executioner reported the hanging of Haman on the gallows he had built for Mordecai. Ahasuerus then confiscated Haman's home and property; these were given to Esther. The king's next move was to appoint Mordecai as the new grand vizier. Esther then gave Haman's home and property to her foster father.

Ahasuerus could not revoke Haman's heartless decree against the Jews, because it had been sealed with the king's signet. However, he did permit Esther and Mordecai to write a new edict to offset Haman's. This decree gave the Jews the authority to bear arms and to defend themselves.

The day chosen by Haman for the extermination of the Jews passed into history. Many Persians, including Haman's ten sons, were killed one day earlier, as the Jews successfully defended themselves against their scheduled purge. They rested then, in preparation for their first Purim Festival. ("Purim" is the plural of the Hebrew word, "Pur," used to designate the "lots" cast by Haman.)

To the present day the Purim Festival, or Feast of Purim, is celebrated on March 14 and 15 by Jews throughout the world.

Esther herself continues to live in the hearts of her people, because she turned a day of almost certain tragedy and death into one of happiness and life.

Based on the story in the Bible:
Esther 3:1 — 9:32

"Mordecai's Honor" by J. James Tissot. *The Old Testament, Illustrated.* After Esther exposed Haman's villainy, the king appointed Mordecai grand vizier. Mordecai offset Haman's proclamation and saved his people.   M. de Buffan & Co.

PLACES

in the Story of Esther

SHUSHAN (SUSA)

This ancient Persian city, some 150 miles due north of the Persian Gulf, lay along the Coaspes river. During the days of King Aha- suerus (Xerxes the Great) and Queen Esther, it was one of the capital cities of the Persian Empire. All the events in the story of Esther revolve around this city.

Aerial View of Shushan (Susa). At the time of Esther, one of the Persian capitals was Shushan. This city is now in ruins, but excavations have uncovered an elaborate palace and citadel. Oriental Institute, University of Chicago

QUESTIONS

on the Story of Esther

1

1 Describe some of Esther's characteristics. What was she prepared to do for her people?

2 By what name was King Ahasuerus better known to history? How large was the Persian Empire during his reign?

3 Why did Ahasuerus summon all his governmental and military leaders to his palace in Shushan? How long did the official banquets and celebrations last?

4 What did Ahasuerus decide to do at the close of the official meetings?

5 Why was Queen Vashti deposed?

6 How was Vashti's successor to be chosen?

7 Who was Mordecai?

8 Whom did the king choose to be his new queen?

9 What did Mordecai do that would one day change the course of his life?

"*Queen Esther*" by Andrea del Castagno. Convent of Saint Appolonia, Florence. The beauty, goodness, and courage of Esther place her among the heroines of the Bible. The Feast of Purim commemorates her story each year.   Alinari

"Arrest of Haman and His Condemnation." Tapestry. Pitti Palace, Florence. Enraged by the disclosure of Haman's de- cree, which would also have affected Esther and Mordecai, Ahasuerus condemned Haman to be hanged. Alinari

2

10 What was Haman's position in the court of Ahasuerus?

11 Why did Haman hate Mordecai so passionately?

12 How did Haman plan to exterminate all the Jews in Persia?

13 What did Esther do when she learned of Haman's decree?

14 What happened during the king's sleepless night? Why did Haman rush to the palace early the next morning?

15 What was the angry king's first command after he heard Esther denounce Haman as her enemy and the enemy of her people? When was his anger abated?

16 Where did Mordecai live after the king appointed him grand vizier?

17 Why couldn't the king revoke Haman's cruel decree? What did Esther and Mordecai do to counteract it?

18 What happened to Haman's ten sons?

19 Why is the Purim Festival still celebrated to this day? What are the dates of this Festival?

20 Why does Esther continue to live in the hearts of her people?

Answers are found on the following pages.

ANSWERS

on the Story of Esther

1

1 Esther was virtuous, lovely, and loyal to her people. She was willing to lay down her life for them.

2 King Ahasuerus is better known to history as Xerxes the Great. During his reign the Persian Empire extended from India to Ethiopa and contained one hundred and twenty-seven provinces.

3 Ahasuerus called all the leaders of all his provinces to the palace for two reasons. His primary purpose was to show them the great riches, the pomp, the power, and the splendor of his vast empire. His secondary reason was to hold conferences with them and to entertain them with banquets. The official business lasted for six months.

4 When the official meeting and banquets ended, Ahasuerus decided to give a monumental public banquet that would last for seven days. All the men, great and small alike, in the capital city would be invited.

5 Queen Vashti was deposed because she refused to obey the wine-muddled command of the king to come to the courtyard and entertain his drunken, bleary-eyed guests.

6 Vashti's successor was to be chosen by bringing the fairest and most talented young women in the kingdom to the palace to compete for the honor of being the new queen.

7 Mordecai the Jew was foster father of his lovely young cousin, Esther. It was through

"Esther and Ahasuerus" by Filippino Lippi. Conde Museum, Chantilly, France. "And the king loved Esther above all the women, and she obtained grace and favor in his sight. . . ." (Esther 2:17-18)

Alinari

his efforts that she became a contestant in the search for a queen.

8 When Esther's turn came to stand before Ahasuerus, the contest was over. The king was dazzled by her beauty and impressed by her stately mien. He proudly placed the queen's crown on Esther's head.

9 Mordecai uncovered a plot on the king's life. He told Esther about it and she informed the king. An investigation proved the information to be true, and the two conspirators were hanged. The entire incident was recorded and placed in the royal archives.

2

10 Haman was grand vizier, a position second only to that of the king.

11 Haman hated Mordecai with a passion because the Jew was the only man in the city who refused to bow down before him and pay homage to him.

12 Haman prepared a decree, sealed with the king's signet, that on a certain day, to be decided by casting lots (Pur), all the Jews in Persia would be killed.

13 Esther consulted with Mordecai who told her that she must go to the king immediately and plead for her life and the lives of her people. Although she knew that the penalty for entering the king's inner chamber uninvited was death, she lost no time in preparing for an audience with Ahasuerus. Esther entered the room and stood before the king. He received her graciously and offered to give her anything she desired—even half the kingdom.

14 Scrolls from the royal archives were read to the king during his sleepless night. When the scribe read of Mordecai's part in saving the king's life and the king learned that his action had gone unrewarded, Ahasuerus was determined to pay high honor to Mordecai the next morning. Haman rushed to the palace early the next morning because of his eagerness to obtain the king's approval to hang Mordecai on a gallows Haman had built during the night.

15 The angry king commanded that Haman be hanged upon the gallows he had built for Mordecai. His anger was abated only when his chief executioner reported that Haman was dead.

16 Mordecai lived in Haman's former home following his appointment as grand vizier.

17 Ahasuerus could not revoke Haman's decree against the Jews, because it had been sealed with the king's seal. Esther and Mordecai hoped to counteract it by issuing a new decree, also sealed with the king's signet, giving their people the authority to band together and defend themselves on the day that Haman had named for their destruction.

18 Thousands of Persians, including Haman's ten sons, were killed on the thirteenth of the month Adar when they attempted to make Haman's decree a reality.

19 The Purim Festival is still celebrated to this day because Esther's last decree was that it should be celebrated yearly. Using the Gregorian calendar, the dates are March fourteenth and fifteenth.

20 Esther will live forever in the hearts of her people because she changed what could have been a tragic day of mourning for the Jews into a day filled with happiness.

"Mordecai Lamenting before the Gates of the Palace" by Botticelli. Pallavicini Collection, Rome. After hearing Haman's proclamation against the Jews, Mordecai put on sackcloth and mourned in front of the king's gates. Alinari

FURTHER FACTS
AND OUTLINE
for the Story of Esther

AUTHOR

Unknown. Mordecai has been suggested. The author could well have been a Persian (but certainly one with a Jewish point of view) because the book reflects first-hand acquaintance with Persian life and habits.

DATE

After the death of Ahasuerus (Xerxes I), who died in 465 B.C. The last half of the 5th century B.C. is the general date.

DESTINATION

To the Jews dispersed in parts of Persia.

PURPOSE AND THEME

The book tells the story of Divine deliverance of the Jews in the time of the Persian King Ahasuerus (485-465 B.C.). They were slated for death because of the wicked grand vizier (or prime minister) Haman; but, through Esther and Mordecai, they were spared. Mordecai replaced Haman as second in power to the king. Esther, depicted as a patriotic and heroic Jewess, stands as a symbol of loyalty and faith.

The origin of the Feast of Purim is made clear in the book. Although this is the only book of the Bible in which the name of God does not appear, the book shows clearly the *hand* of God at work in the life of His people, the Jews. Esther is the only Old Testament book not represented in the Dead Sea Scrolls.

OUTLINE

Esther Made Queen of Persia (chapters 1-2)
    The Queen Vashti Is Dethroned by King Ahasuerus (chapter 1)
    The New Queen Esther Is Seated on the Throne (chapter 2)
Haman Attempts To Kill the Jews but Fails; Mordecai's Help (chapters 3-10)
    Haman seeks To Destroy the Jews (chapter 3)
    Mordecai Communicates with Esther, She Intercedes, A Banquet with the King (chapters 4-5)
    Mordecai Honored by the King, Haman Dishonored and Hanged (chapters 6-7)
    Mordecai Promoted to Haman's Position (chapter 8)
    Jews Delivered and Victorious over Their Enemies, The Feast of Purim (chapter 9)
Mordecai's Greatness (chapter 10)

"Mordecai Honored" by José Villegas. *Biblia Sacra*. King
Ahasuerus honored Mordecai's loyalty by dressing him in the
king's royal robes and then having Haman lead him through
Susa on the king's own horse.

Lemercier and Co., Paris

It Takes Courage To Be Yourself

by
Vonda Kay Van Dyke

Vonda Kay Van Dyke, Miss America of 1965, and Esther, the young Jewish maiden who became Queen of Persia, share much more than the honor of winning two beauty contests separated by many centuries. Both Esther and Vonda Kay display a firm faith in God. Of Esther it was said that she "came to the kingdom for such a time as this." Of Vonda Kay it is said that she "helps young girls find their way through the maze of teen-age problems to a secure, constructive place in the world." By the very force of their character each of these two young ladies speaks with authority and charm to our world today. Some of Vonda Kay's secrets of success are revealed in two chapters from her book, *That Girl in Your Mirror* (© 1966 by Fleming H. Revell Company, Westwood, N.J.).

YOU ARE AN INDIVIDUAL

SOME GIRLS make a big fuss over their individuality, and in a way you can't blame them. It's quite thrilling to realize that you're distinctly different from everyone else you know. But before you season your conversation with too much "I," you had better stop and remember that you discovered something that's been there all the time.

That's right—from the day you were born you've been an individual. Your baby cries were not the same as any other baby's, and your view of the world through the bars of your crib was your very own. You learned to move around, to talk, to behave, to play, and to read—all in your own time and your own style. You received all the world's wonderful gifts in a unique way.

Now the time has come for you to start putting things back into the world, and no one else will do it in quite the same way. You can put things back into the world by expressing yourself, your individuality, to others—this is the real meaning of being yourself.

Now you know why it is so important for you to understand what kind of a person you are. You can hardly express someone else's personality, can you?

You can't be yourself by going off in a corner, either. That's not the way to express your individuality, but it's a good way to lose it! You can't function as a whole person unless you mix it up with people, lots of people. A personality isn't much good unless it is used and developed, and you won't learn anything about yours until you try it out on other people.

Are you afraid that you'll lose your precious individuality if you become one of the crowd? You may have a point there. It's hard to be yourself and please the crowd at the same time, but it might help you if you remember that you don't have to please the whole crowd all of the time.

It takes individual people to make up any group, or any gang, or any crowd, and they don't necessarily surrender their individuality by getting together. At least, they don't *have to* give it up, although some girls seem to be eager to do it.

If the crowd insists that you smother your own personality and go along with everyone else, then that's not the crowd for you. It doesn't matter if it's the "in" crowd—it won't last long. Any group needs the personality of each member or it has none of its own. Conformity is colorless, so go and find the crowd that will welcome you for what you are.

Be careful, though, that you don't go too far in the other direction. You don't have to conform, but you should try to be agreeable. Don't be the girl who is so obsessed with her individuality that she refuses to do what anyone else wants to do. She's not herself—she's a pest!

Even though you may have your ups and downs, the experience of being in a group will be good for you. Individuals have to learn to respect each other's wishes if they want to get things done, and a little difference of opinion won't hurt them.

Don't be afraid to be different. Sometimes you can express yourself in only one way, a way no one has ever tried. It isn't wrong just because it's new; it's wrong if it will hurt someone, and this is something you would have to consider no matter how you wanted to express yourself.

Some girls will tell you to go ahead and be different—if you've got the nerve. They seem to think people will stare, or boo, or ridicule you if you don't do things in the same old way. But they don't know much about people!

For some reason, I've been doing things differently since I was a little girl. When I was in high school I had the double distinction of being the only girl in the printing class and the only girl who had ever played the tenor saxophone in the school band. I didn't do any of these things simply to be different, but I didn't see why my interest in printing or my enjoyment of the tenor sax should be choked off because I was a girl. And no one poked fun at me—not the school principal, not the boys in the print shop, not the other members of the band. In fact, they seemed to think I had made the most natural choices in the world.

Life holds out so many wonderful opportunities to each of us that it's a shame to say "no" to some of them simply because we're girls. If you think women were created just to sit and spin, open your Bible to the stories of

Esther, Naomi, Deborah, Priscilla, and Mary. Imagine how much the world would have lost if they had said, "Oh, I can't do that—no woman has ever done anything like that!" when God called them.

I don't know why more girls haven't become ventriloquists, although I must admit I was first attracted to it because it was so unusual. I used to watch Paul Winchell and his dummy Jerry Mahoney on television when I was about six years old, and the idea of one man holding a conversation with himself caught hold of my imagination. It certainly wasn't something that everybody else was doing!

As my interest grew I began to practice until I could "throw" my voice so that it seemed to come from another part of the room. I remember how I used to sit at the dinner table and ask my father to "please pass the butter" in a voice that seemed to come from behind him. He would ask me to do it again for my mother, and then we would all laugh.

When my parents saw that I kept working on my technique, they gave me a small Jerry Mahoney dummy for my seventh birthday. What a day that was! For once, I could hardly think of anything to say when I opened that long box and looked in to find that red-haired, wide-mouthed, saucer-eyed, funny little doll lying among the layers of tissue paper. He was only a piece of wood in snappy clothes, and when I took him out of the box and held him on my lap he would have fallen in a heap on the floor if I hadn't held him up. Slowly I began to poke around the mechanisms on his back until I found out how to make his mouth open and close. It would take a lot of practice to synchronize the mouth openings with the words he would seem to speak, but already I could see my little dummy taking on a sparkle of life.

I couldn't wait, and I began to hold a conversation with the little fellow. It was clumsy and I didn't give him the same voice all the time, but right before my eyes that piece of wood took on a personality! He wasn't limp and lifeless any more—he seemed to be in constant motion! He looked over his shoulder, drew his head back in surprise, shook his head. I never had such a really good time!

Ventriloquism has always been a lot of fun for me. Of course, being a girl ventriloquist at the age of seven was certainly different, but I enjoyed the novelty of it and my friends took it in stride. I was simply the girl with the dummy—I had my hobby and my friends had theirs. That's the way friends should be, and you should be able to relax with them.

It's almost impossible to relax with a crowd and I hope you won't let this discourage you. One of the biggest obstacles to being yourself is your own worry that people won't like you when they get to know you. Sometimes, in an effort to become popular, a girl will abandon her own convictions and follow the will of the crowd because she thinks that is the only way to please people. Well, maybe it is—and where does that leave her? For the moment, she rates with the crowd, but where does she stand in her own opinion?

What you think of yourself is very important. Don't expect to be able to please everyone you meet, but always try to live up to the standards you set for yourself. If you are ever faced with choosing between your own self-approval and the approval of someone else, don't get cold feet. Stick to your principles!

You can live with someone else's frown, but you'll be miserable with your own.

If you have been completely honest with yourself, you'll know when you're about to do something that isn't right for you. You can often cover up with other people, but don't try to fool yourself. You can't make yourself believe you're something other than what you are.

I'll make you a promise. If you will take a deep breath and try to be your own genuine self for a few days—and then a few weeks—you'll wonder why you were ever afraid to do it. You'll be surprised to find how many people will welcome your fresh and candid personality, and you'll have a far better opinion of yourself.

Once you feel the warmth of people's friendliness, you'll want to be sure you're worthy of it. No matter how much progress you've made, you'll see areas that could use some improvement. After all, the girl you express to others should be the best possible girl you can make of her!

Now you're really getting somewhere. You know who you are and you've introduced yourself to the world. Well, don't just stand there—do something with yourself!

BE A GOOD WINNER

WHAT HAPPENS when you win something important? Do you feel that you've arrived? You haven't. When you get to the top, you've got a long way to go.

If you win that election for class president, do you just sit back and take it easy? No, you don't. Now you have to tackle those problems and find out how to be a good administrator. All that striving, all those outstanding abilities, and even the achievement of your goal, were only promises of the things you could do. Now that you've won your prize, you have to *show* what you can do.

A new concern came to me the day after I was crowned Miss America. I didn't know how Miss America should act. Was she different from Vonda Kay Van Dyke?

She was, as Dr. Billy Graham pointed out to us in a visit with my parents and me the second morning after the Pageant. I wasn't simply a young woman with a faith and some principles—I was an example to a lot of other young women. That gave me an enormous responsibility. What a humbling experience! Together we knelt and prayed for God's guidance during the year ahead.

Now things began to make sense to me. God could do something with my title, after all. It was going to take me to many new places and I was going to meet many new people. They would come to see Miss America, and I could introduce them to the God who is the source of my strength.

It's true that Miss America is a leader of

sorts, and she sets the standards for many young women who admire her achievement. But the leadership young people really need in their lives is something they can never find in any other human being. Young people need God, they need Christ as a constant Companion. That was what I hoped to be able to tell them. For a year I would have many opportunities to speak—and people would listen. I had to make those words count!

I couldn't always talk about my faith every time I opened my mouth. God isn't overbearing and I didn't want to represent Him that way. But lots of people had watched me on television during the Pageant and someone always asked me whether I still had my Bible with me. I always did, and those questions—some, slightly sarcastic—gave me the floor.

At the beginning of my reign, I made up my mind that I would go on trying to please God in everything I did. I wanted to be able to say that I had done my best for Him every day. And my greatest blessing was that I was able to say those words at the end of my year as Miss America.

I had wanted to be Miss America for one reason—I wanted to tell people about the Christ I love and try to serve. If I inspired one young person to find a new life—a truly exciting and abundant life—in Christ, then there was great value in the crown I wore.

Some people cry when a good thing comes to an end, but I had begun my year by crying for three days and I couldn't very well end it the same way. Besides, I've never known any good thing that comes to an end—it simply leads on to something else that's good. When you let God lead you along the way, you just don't run into any dead-ends!

I wasn't sad about placing my crown on a new Miss America. I had lived a magnificent year and I would take its memories with me into the years ahead. Again, I had a ball during the Pageant that ended my reign and I was able to appreciate what courageous girls those other forty-nine contestants were. This time I was backstage when the winner was announced and I saw the faces of the losers—

every one a champion! Oh, a few tears were shed, because queens are girls underneath their titles, but their applause was hearty and genuine. They were ready to go back to their states and fulfill their reigns as state queens, and they would do it wholeheartedly.

Near the end of the program I was scheduled to make a farewell speech that was supposed to last no more than one minute and thirty seconds. I had thought about that speech for several weeks before the Pageant, and I wrote it out many, many times. It was so hard to fit all my gratitude and happiness into those precious seconds. So many things had happened to me and I wanted to share them.

I kept crossing out extra words and finally was able to fit my message into the time limit. When I came out on the stage that night, I felt I was among friends I had known for a long time and my heart opened up to them. I wanted them to meet my Friend.

"My year as Miss America will not only be remembered by what I have taken from it, but by what I have become by it.

"This crown has offered many valuable gifts. It has sparkled with thousands of miles of travel. It has glowed with hundreds of priceless friendships, and it has reflected a bright new world of knowledge, with opportunities to grow both mentally and spiritually.

"These lasting, life-changing gifts deserve a thank-you to many wonderful people, but most of all to God for giving me an open mind and an open heart to take the gifts and use them.

"I ascended my throne last September with two statements: that my biggest responsibility was to live up to my Christian testimony, and that the Bible was the most important Book I owned. Tonight, I descend from my throne with the same thoughts and the same Scriptural promise which says: 'And we know that all things work together for good to them that love God, to them who are the called according to his purpose' (Romans 8:28).

"So, you see, I won't be stepping down. I'll be stepping up—*to a new year, a new life, a new challenge!*"

Return from Captivity

THE WALL OF JERUSALEM was built through the patriotism and high devotion of one man, Nehemiah, and through the fact that, by his influence and leadership, he was able to weld the people into a unity of heart and purpose and endeavor which carried the work to completion. The efforts of this man and the people were characterized by caution, courage, and passionate persistence against all opposing forces.

Perhaps this persistence was the most outstanding quality. The enemies of the work sought by all means to prevent its being carried out. After beginning in contempt and proceeding through conspiracy, they turned to subtlety. Nehemiah and his helpers were proof against every method. Nothing turned them aside until the wall was finished.

The wall was dedicated in solemn ceremony, and ". . . the joy of Jerusalem was heard even afar off." (Nehemiah 12:43) It was a great day, greater even than these people knew. The reformers had sought to bring the remnant, weak and small though it was numerically, back to a recognition of the deepest truth concerning the national life; namely, its relationship to God.

Their joy that day was the joy of the Lord, and this was indeed their strength. All the pomp and pageantry and material splendor of the days of the monarchy had passed; but, in devotion to the Law and to the purposes of God as manifested in the building of the wall, there was more of moral power than the old days had ever known, since the time when in their folly the people had clamored for a king like the nations around them.—G. Campbell Morgan, *Searchlights from the Word*

1

THE AMAZING PROCLAMATION OF CYRUS

D URING THEIR MANY YEARS IN EXILE the people of Judah returned to the worship of the one true God. The wisest and most learned scribes among them turned their attention to the study, compilation, and recopying of their sacred books.

Others became merchants and traders, who amassed great wealth. Still others were given high positions of responsibility and trust in the courts of both Babylonia and Persia. Their captors had been kind to them and had permitted them to remain together, wherever they were taken.

Despite all these things, the people from Judah longed to return to Jerusalem. An example of their heart-sickness and home-sickness is portrayed in a psalm (Psalms 137) written by one of them:

"By the rivers of Babylon,
  There we sat down;
Yes, we wept
  When we remembered Zion.
We hung our harps
  Upon the willow trees,
Because our captors
  Asked us to sing for them.
How can we sing God's songs
  In a strange land?
If I forget you, O Jerusalem,
  Let my right hand forget her skill."

"By the Rivers of Babylon" by J. James Tissot. The Old Testament, Illustrated. Although captivity had not been harsh for most of the people of Judah, many still yearned to return to their homeland city of Jerusalem. M. de Buffan & Co.

Cylinder of Cyrus. An edict issued by King Cyrus the Great permitting the captive people of Judah to return to Jerusalem and rebuild the city and Temple (538 B.C.) is recorded in cuneiform writing on this excavated stone.   British Museum

The hearts of the people of Judah were filled with high hopes and great excitement. If Jeremiah's prophecy was to be fulfilled, their days of captivity were drawing to an end.

King Cyrus, a just and kind man, sat upon his Persian throne and prepared to make an amazing proclamation. Reduced to writing, it read as follows:

"Thus says Cyrus, king of Persia: The Lord God of heaven has given me all the kingdoms of the earth, and He has told me to build Him a new Temple in Jerusalem. I, therefore, here and now grant permission for all of His people who will to return to Jerusalem and help rebuild the House of the Lord."

More than forty-two thousand eager, enthusiastic people responded immediately, glad of this opportunity to return to their homeland. They hurried to their homes and began preparing for their departure. Willing hands worked long and hard as they loaded the wagons that Cyrus had provided. In the center of the long procession stood one wagon that was heavily guarded and given special attention. It contained not only the five thousand and four hundred gold and silver treasures that Nebuchadnezzar had looted from the Lord's Temple at the fall of Jerusalem, but also a large amount of money that Cyrus had collected from his own people and from the Jews who had chosen to remain behind.

Led by Zerubbabel, the great caravan slowly but steadily wended its way along the route Abraham had traveled many centuries before when, at God's command, he had left Ur and journeyed toward a land that the Lord later showed him. After four long months and nine hundred miles, Zerubbabel's vast procession crossed over the Jordan and moved onward to Jerusalem.

At last the caravan came to a halt. The people gazed with mingled emotions at the ruins of the once proud, powerful, and beautiful Jerusalem. To the older among them the scene brought poignant memories of the grandeur and splendor of their beloved city. To the younger, who had never seen Jerusalem in all its glory, the sight of the rubble and broken walls made them realize the tremendous amount of work that had to be done in restoring the Temple and the city.

Before starting the rebuilding project, the people of Judah had to plant crops and vineyards so that they would have sufficient food and other supplies. Everyone, therefore, returned to his own city and farm. Only the priests, the Levites, the two hundred singing men and women, with some of the people—including Zerubbabel— remained in Jerusalem.

Based on the story in the Bible:
Ezra 1:1 — 2:70

2
REBUILDING IN JERUSALEM

HARVEST TIME WAS OVER, and the yield had been bountiful. With the task of providing food completed, all the people of Israel converged on Jerusalem the very first day of the seventh month to offer sacrifices to the Lord — and to make plans for rebuilding the Temple. An altar was hastily set up, and the Israelites celebrated the Feast of the Tabernacles for the first time after being carried off into captivity. They also sacrificed burnt offerings to the Lord each morning and each evening.

Almost a year passed and the foundation for the Temple of the Lord had not been laid. However, the Israelites' leader, Zerubbabel, and the chief priest, Jeshua, had not been idle. A descendant of David, Zerubbabel followed in the footsteps of Solomon as he began gathering material and supplies. He traded vast quantities of food, wine, and oil to the people of Tyre and Sidon for cedar logs. Miners were hired to quarry stone, and glaziers were hired to smooth it. Engravers were hired for the ornamental work. All of these workers were paid from the Persian money that Cyrus had given.

At last the day arrived when the foundations for the Temple were laid. The priests

"Rebuilding of Jerusalem" by J. A. Adams and J. G. Chapman. *The Illuminated Bible* (1846). In accordance with the decree of Cyrus, money was given to the Jews for the rebuilding of the Temple of the Lord in Jerusalem. Harper & Brothers

and Levites came to the site in their robes, with their trumpets and musical instruments. The singing men and women lifted their voices in song, using words like these from Psalm 100:

"Make a joyful noise unto the Lord;
   Serve the Lord with gladness;
Come into His presence with singing.
   Enter into His gates with thanksgiving,
And into His courts with praise.
   For the Lord is good,
And His mercy endures forever!"

There was great joy in Jerusalem that day, but there was also much sadness. The older priests, Levites, and people were grieved when they noted the great difference between the foundations of the new Temple and those of the Temple that Solomon had built. They cried so loudly that it was hard to distinguish the noise of joy from the sounds of weeping.

On returning to Jerusalem, the Israelites had found a nation of foreigners in the former Northern Kingdom. These people called themselves Samaritans, and their capital city was Samaria. They were descendants of the national groups that King Sargon and successive kings had deported from other lands and sent to the Northern Kingdom to repopulate it after the Ten Tribes had been carried away to Assyria. The Samaritans were a mixed race, and their religion was a mongrel religion.

One day a group of Samaritans stood before Zerubbabel and made what seemed to be a friendly proposition.

"Let us help you rebuild your Temple," they said. "After all, we worship your God and have made sacrifices to Him, from the time the Assyrian kings brought us here."

Zerubbabel knew that what they said was partially true; but he also knew that they did not worship only the Jewish God. They merely included Him, "the god of

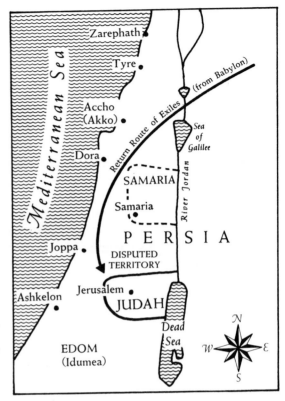

Return Route of the Exiles. A long procession from Babylon, composed of over forty-two thousand Judeans led by Zerubbabel, crossed the Jordan and proceeded to Jerusalem. Samaria is the territory shown as enclosed by dotted lines. The land of Judah is indicated as lying within the solid lines.

the land," in their worship of Assyrian idols and false gods. He gave them a prompt, curt reply.

"How dare you foreigners to think that you have a right to help rebuild the Temple!" he cried. "The Jews, and only the Jews, will build the House for the Lord God of Israel, even as we have been commanded by King Cyrus of Persia."

The Samaritans strode away angrily; and, from that very day, an enmity sprang up between them and the Jews that grew more bitter through the years and existed in the time of Jesus and beyond His day.

Zerubbabel's harsh, hasty reply cost the Jews dearly. Their enemies, the Samaritans, used every ruse they could think of to hinder the work of rebuilding the Temple. The Samaritans finally succeeded in their nefarious plot. They made

"*Haggai*" by J. James Tissot. *The Old Testament,* Illustrated. Rebuked by the prophet Haggai, the people resumed work on the Temple at Jerusalem and completed it.   M. de Buffan & Co.

false accusations against the Jews to the Persian king and persuaded him to issue a decree halting the construction of the Temple. For fifteen years, therefore, activity at the Temple site was at a standstill. The foundations were the only evidence that the Jews had made any effort to carry out the command of Cyrus.

Haggai and Zechariah, two of the Lord's prophets, were among those who had returned to Jerusalem with Zerubbabel. Haggai, particularly, became increasingly concerned because the people showed little or no desire to start back to work on their mission of rebuilding the Lord's Temple.

At the beginning of the fifteenth year of the Jews' lethargy and inactivity, Haggai could no longer endure the indifference of his people. He was determined to arouse them from their apathy, so he roamed from city to city and proclaimed this word of warning:

"O people of Israel! You have been unfaithful to the Lord God of our fathers. He put it into the heart of King Cyrus to permit you to return to Jerusalem and rebuild the Lord's Temple. You say that the time has not yet come to resume work at the site of the Temple. Still you have found that the time is right for you to build your own comfortable houses. You should be ashamed to look one another in the eye while the House of the Lord lies in ruins! Mend your ways, and do as the Lord has commanded."

In other messages Haggai reminded the people that the terrible famine from which they had just emerged was punishment by the Lord for their procrastination in fulfilling their primary mission. Zerubbabel and Jeshua heard and heeded the words of Haggai. A call for workers was issued. Response by the people was instantaneous. Soon there was great activity at the Temple site, as the building of the

"The Prophet Zechariah" by Matteo Civitali. Chapel of St. John the Baptist, Cathedral, Genoa. Zechariah worked with Haggai to inspire the rebuilding of the Temple.　　Alinari

Lord's House was resumed, immediately.

One day Tattenai, governor of one of the Persian provinces west of the Jordan, received some startling news. The Samaritans brought word to him that the Jews had violated the decree of his king and were progressing rapidly in the rebuilding of the Temple. Tattenai decided to make an official investigation of the matter immediately.

When the investigating committee arrived at the Temple site, they saw that the Samaritans had made a true report. The outer walls had already been erected, and the masons had almost finished laying the Temple floors. Tattenai and his secretary,

Shethar-boznai, hurried to Zerubbabel.

"Who gave you permission to finish this structure?" the governor asked harshly.

"Fifteen years ago, King Cyrus issued a decree, and sealed it with his signet, giving us permission to return to Jerusalem and rebuild this Temple," Zerubbabel replied quietly. "According to your law, this decree can never be revoked. Why don't you write King Darius and ask him to search the royal archives and verify my statement? Until you receive his answer, do not take any action against us while we continue our work."

Tattenai agreed that this was a reasonable request, so he and his committee returned to their province. When he reached his mansion, the governor dictated a letter to his secretary.

"To Darius, the king," it began. "Greetings and all peace! I want to let you know, O king, that the Jews have violated a royal decree and are rebuilding the Temple of their great God. I have been to Jerusalem and have seen it with my own eyes. Zerubbabel, the governor of Judah, sought to justify his action by telling me that King Cyrus issued a decree about fifteen years ago that gave him and his people permission to return to Jerusalem and rebuild the Temple. Now, therefore, if it pleases the king, let a search be made in the royal archives to see whether such a decree was issued and sealed by King Cyrus. I shall withhold any action against these people until I receive your reply."

In the course of time Tattenai received an answer from his king.

"I have searched the royal archives and have found the decree issued by Cyrus," Darius began. "The governor of Judah spoke the truth when he told you such an edict had been issued. Now, therefore, Tattenai, governor of the Province beyond the River Jordan, keep away from Jerusalem and let the work on the House

Darius and Xerxes. One of the remaining relief carvings on the walls of the royal treasury at ancient Persepolis shows Darius the Great on his throne, with his son Xerxes standing directly behind him.
Oriental Institute, University of Chicago

of the Lord continue. Furthermore, I have decreed that you and the governors of other provinces in Canaan help these people in every way possible. If they need money, give it to them from your treasuries. If they need food, give it to them day by day. If they need young bulls, rams, or sheep, give them without fail.

"I also decree that anyone who changes one word of this edict, or fails to obey it, shall be impaled upon a beam that has been pulled from his house. These orders must be obeyed implicitly. May the Lord God Who has caused His name to prevail in that land strike down any king or any nation that tries to destroy the Temple of the Lord. I, Darius, King of Persia, have spoken."

Tattenai and the other governors did what Darius had ordered. With their assistance Zerubbabel's workmen completed the Temple five years after the work was begun. How proud the people were, and how beautiful the new Temple was! Even the elderly people, who had expressed doubt at first, conceded that the prophecy of Haggai was true: "The new Temple shall exceed in splendor the one that Solomon built."

Although there was great happiness at the dedication of the new Temple, there was also a note of sadness because the Holy Place was empty. The beautiful golden Ark, with its two golden angels on the lid and the stone tablets inside, disappeared while the people were in captivity and has never been found.

Yes, the Lord's Temple was rebuilt— but the walls of the city still lay in ruins.

Based on the story in the Bible:
Ezra 3:1 — 6:22, Haggai 1:15 — 2:9

373

EZRA GOES TO JERUSALEM

EZRA, A DESCENDANT OF AARON, was a priestly scribe and a high official in the Persian court of Artaxerxes. This scholarly scribe was well versed in the laws that God had given to Moses, and he was anxious to go to Jerusalem and teach them to his people.

About sixty years after the Temple had been rebuilt, Ezra stood before the king and asked for permission to go to Jerusalem. Artaxerxes responded favorably to his request and issued the following decree:

"From Artaxerxes, king of kings, to Ezra the priest, and a scribe of the law of the God of Heaven, perfect peace and greetings:

"I decree that all the people of Israel under my jurisdiction may, if they so desire, return to Jerusalem with you. In addition to the gold and silver that I and my advisers have freely given to you for the Lord God of Israel, I authorize you to accept voluntary offerings from all the people in my kingdom. Furthermore, you may carry with you the rest of the Temple treasures that Nebuchadnezzar brought to Babylon.

"I, Artaxerxes the king, have also issued a decree and sent it to the treasurers of all my provinces across the River Jordan: Whatever Ezra, the priest and scribe, shall require of you for the Lord's House, give it to him from the royal treasury. Give him up to one hundred talents of silver, one hundred measures of wheat, one hundred jugs of wine, one hundred bottles of oil, and an unlimited amount of salt.

"Finally, I decree that the people of Judah shall be tax-exempt until such time as I notify you."

After reading the decree, Artaxerxes turned to Ezra and said, "When you return to Jerusalem, appoint judges and magistrates to judge over the people who know the laws of your God, and teach those who do not know them. Then, whoever does not obey the laws of your God, let judgment be speedily executed against him, whether it be by death, banishment, confiscation of his goods, or by imprisonment."

Ezra was surprised and pleased by the king's kindness and generosity. He fell to his knees immediately and thanked God for having put it into Artaxerxes' heart to want to help beautify the Lord's Temple, and he also thanked the Lord for the mercy that the king had extended to him.

Ezra sat near the bank of stream Ahava and recalled the excitement and activity of the days just passed. The Persian people, and his own people who had chosen to remain behind, had been far more generous with their voluntary offerings than he had anticipated. The people had assembled quietly and orderly near the Ahava and had just concluded the three-day period of fasting and praying that he had proclaimed.

Ezra's reverie was interrupted by one of the leaders who came to tell him that the caravan was ready to move out. The procession soon began its long trek to Jerusalem. Ezra followed the route taken by Zerubbabel eighty years earlier; and, four months later, he and his weary travelers stood before the ruined walls of Jerusalem. God had heard their prayers and had brought their long journey to a safe conclusion.

Upon their arrival at Jerusalem, Ezra and his group camped outside the city for three days. On the fourth day they entered the city, and Ezra led the caravan to the Lord's Temple. There he and the treasure-bearers entered the Temple, and Ezra gave the silver and gold and the rest of the looted treasures to the Temple custodians.

When Ezra came outside the Temple, he saw that the returned exiles were already preparing to offer burnt offerings to the Lord their God. Altogether, they offered twelve bulls, ninety-six rams, seventy-seven lambs, and twelve male goats.

After the burnt offerings were finished, Ezra proceeded with the third part of his commission from King Artaxerxes. He sent messengers to all the governors of the provinces on this side of the Jordan and requested from them the help that their king had promised. The Persian governors responded immediately, and the messengers soon returned to Jerusalem with a huge stock of supplies and a large amount of money for the House of the Lord and for the people.

A short time later, however, Ezra was aghast and broken-hearted. It had taken only a few days' investigation for him to learn of the unholy and chaotic conditions that existed in Jerusalem and the rest of Judah. To demonstrate his deep grief because of the actions of his people, Ezra tore his clothes and sat silently in front of the Temple from early dawn until just before the evening sacrifices. As he had anticipated, the crowd before the Temple grew larger and larger as the day progressed. The sun was sinking when Ezra arose and gazed sadly but compassionately upon the tremendous throng gathered there. Then he knelt down, lifted his hands, and prayed fervently to the Lord his God.

"O my God, I am ashamed and I blush to lift my voice up to You because our sins have increased and our guilt has ascended as high as the heavens," he began. "From the days of Abraham, Isaac, and Jacob to this very day we have sinned against You. During the years You have punished us, our kings, and our priests by delivering us into the hands of our enemies, by permitting us to die by the sword, by the looting and the plundering of the land, and by letting us be taken into captivity.

"And now, O God, for a brief period of time You have shown mercy to us and have put it into the hearts of the kings of Persia to allow a few of us to return to the land of our fathers and rebuild Your Temple. Yet, despite Your goodness to us, we have again broken Your commandment by marrying foreign women and adopting their customs.

"What can we say after this, O Lord our God? For the second time we stand before You, guilty of our iniquities against You. Why, O Lord, should You not be so angry with us that You would utterly destroy all of us?"

After Ezra had ended his prayer of confession, the people wept bitterly and repented of their sins. The men with foreign wives made a covenant with God to send them and their children back to their homelands.

Ezra does not reappear on the scene until about fifteen years later, after the walls of the city had been rebuilt. During all this time, however, he was busily engaged in carrying out Artaxerxes' final suggestion. He roamed the length and breadth of Judah, appointing magistrates, re-establishing law and order, setting up schools and synagogues in the smaller towns, and teaching the laws of Moses to those who did not know them.

Based on the story in the Bible:
Ezra 7:1 — 10:44

4

NEHEMIAH BUILDS THE WALLS OF JERUSALEM

ONLY A FEW STORIES IN THE BIBLE are told by the men and women who actually participated in them. Nehemiah was one of these men. His autobiography reveals a man who was deeply religious, brave and persistent, energetic and patriotic. A skilled engineer and wise administrator, he was another of the Jewish captives who had risen to an honored, trusted position in the Persian court.

In the twentieth year of the reign of Artaxerxes, Nehemiah's brother Hanani came to the palace at Shushan bringing sad news. When Nehemiah heard the report about conditions in Jerusalem, he sat down and wept. Then he fasted for several days and, after that, he prayed daily for four months that God would reveal to him what course of action he should take. Near the end of his prayer vigil, Nehemiah was firmly convinced that it was God's will for him to go to Jerusalem.

One day as he was standing before the king, tasting the king's food and wine, Artaxerxes noticed his downcast face and asked, "Why are you so depressed and melancholy?"

"Live forever, O king!" Nehemiah answered promptly. "Why shouldn't I be depressed and sick at heart? The city where my ancestors are buried lies in ruins. Its walls are crumbling in the dust, and its gates have been destroyed by fire."

The king then asked, kindly, "What do you want to do, Nehemiah?"

Again the answer came quickly. "If it please the king, and if I have proved loyal and faithful to you, I earnestly request that you give me a leave of absence so that I can return to Jerusalem and rebuild its walls," the king's cupbearer said.

The Lord was with Nehemiah that day. Artaxerxes not only granted him a leave of absence but also appointed him governor of Judah for the length of his stay there.

A few days later, Nehemiah and Hanani left for Jerusalem. They were accompanied by a military escort, and Nehemiah carried several important documents from the king. These included his commission as governor, letters to the governors of the Persian provinces beyond the river requesting safe conduct across their

"Nehemiah and King Artaxerxes" by J. James Tissot. The Old Testament, Illustrated. Nehemiah had prospered while in exile and had become the king's cupbearer. M. de Buffan & Co.

376

"Nehemiah Looks upon the Ruins of Jerusalem" by J. James Tissot. *The Old Testament,* Illustrated. When Nehemiah returned to Jerusalem, he examined its ruined walls and made plans to rebuild them and thus fortify the city. M. de Buffan & Co.

territory for Nehemiah and his party, and a letter to Asaph, the keeper of the king's forest, ordering him to provide for Nehemiah all the timber needed in his reconstruction work.

Ezra had been in Jerusalem thirteen years when Nehemiah and his group arrived. After presenting his credentials to the officials, the new governor of Judah wandered through the city. He could hardly believe his eyes as he observed the weather-beaten ruins of Jerusalem. What a great task lay ahead of him! Although the Jews had been back in Jerusalem for almost one hundred years, Nehemiah could see nothing that had been done to restore the city, except the building of the new Temple.

After Nehemiah had been in Jerusalem for three days, he decided to go outside the city and inspect the damaged walls. Since he had not yet told anyone what God had put in his heart to do at Jerusalem, he planned to make this inspection secretly and at night. Nehemiah and a few of the men who had come with him from Shushan slipped silently outside the city, and his secret midnight mission was underway. After his survey of the battered walls was finished, the governor and his men quietly returned to the city through the same gate from which they had departed.

The next day Nehemiah called his people together and announced the real purpose for his return to Jerusalem.

"Look all around you, O people of

Samaritan Priest with Ancient Scroll. Because they were offended when their offer to help in the rebuilding was rejected, the Samaritans split with the Jews at the time of the restoration of Jerusalem and organized their own sect. © Matson Photo

Israel!" he cried. "What do you see? Your broken-down walls make you an easy prey for your enemies. Their forays, in turn, have made it impossible for you to clear the debris from Jerusalem and to rebuild your homes. Our first task is to make Jerusalem a fortified city. Come now, let us build the walls!"

Nehemiah was a good organizer. He divided the walls into sections, and then shrewdly assigned to every man the task of rebuilding the section nearest to his own household. There was a flurry of activity along all the walls of the city. Stones were being salvaged from the ruins, and the timber that Asaph had sent was being made into lumber. Other workers were at the stone quarries cutting new stones for the walls.

When the enemies of the Israelites saw the progress being made on this building project, they became very angry and used all the wiles at their command to hinder or actually halt the work. At first, they tried taunts and jeers.

Sanballat, governor of Samaria, called out in mocking tones, "What are you feeble Jews trying to do? Do you really think you can finish the wall?"

Tobiah the Ammonite, who was with the Samaritan governor, also called out to the weary workers, "What if you do build the wall? Even a fox could brush up against it and knock it down!"

Their bitter mockery caused Nehemiah to utter a harsh prayer against the enemies of his people. He prayed for God to put a curse upon them and to let them be carried away into captivity.

Failure piled on top of failure for the enemies of the Jews as they vainly attempted to thwart the building of the walls. Finally, there was only one thing left for them to do: form an alliance and launch a surprise attack against Jerusalem. The enemies talked over their strategy: "We shall advance upon the Israelites so swiftly that we shall be in their midst before they know it. Then we shall kill all of them—and *that* will stop the building of the walls!"

Rumors spread throughout Jerusalem that Sanballat, Tobiah, the Arabians, the Ammonites, and the Ashdodites had banded together to fight the Jews. The people were panic-stricken. Nehemiah moved boldly and resolutely to meet the crisis. First, he called the people together and calmed their fears.

"Do not be afraid of them," he said. "Remember that God is great and good, and He is on our side. Return now to your posts, arm yourselves, and be prepared to fight for your lives—and the lives of your wives, sons, and daughters."

The people were reassured by Nehemiah's soothing words, so they resumed the building of the walls. Each worker went back to his job with a construction tool in one hand and a weapon in the other. Meanwhile, Nehemiah was speedily completing plans for defense of the city.

A state of emergency was declared. No workers living outside the city were permitted to return to their homes at night. Lookouts were posted at every gate, and all were armed. They also carried trumpets so that an alarm could be sounded if the enemy approached the city. All the men were under orders, on hearing the signal, to converge swiftly on the place from which the sound came. The people were divided into two groups. One group worked on the walls, and the other group stood guard—from the rising of the sun until the stars appeared.

When the coalition of enemies learned that their plans were known, and that the Jews were prepared to make a strong stand against them, the aggressors reviewed their strategy and decided to return to their own lands. The Lord had once more acted on behalf of His people.

One day Nehemiah proudly announced: "We have built the walls . . . because the people had a will to work!"

The walls had been completed in the incredibly short span of fifty-two days, and the people of Judah were now streaming back to Jerusalem to participate in the dedication ceremony. Sacrifices were offered to the Lord. The celebration then continued with prayers and thanksgiving, with singing, dancing, and the playing of musical instruments. There was such great joy in Jerusalem that the sound of rejoicing that day could be heard miles away.

The massed crowd sat in solemn silence and waited for Ezra to make his reappearance. They soon saw him come through the Water Gate and walk slowly to the steps of the wooden pulpit that had been built for him. Flanked on each side by three laymen from the crowd, Ezra opened the book of the Law of Moses, that the Lord had given to Israel, and began teaching these laws to the people. From early in the morning until midday, this great teacher read and thoroughly explained the laws to his people.

After the first day's instruction, Ezra excused most of the people from further sessions so that they could celebrate the Festival of the Booths. The elders, the priests, the Levites, and the heads of households faced six more days of intensive training. On the eighth day of the New Year, all the people returned to their homes.

Ezra, the teacher and prophet, and Nehemiah, the patriot and statesman, formed a perfect team as they worked together closely to strengthen and consolidate Judah, and to restore the religious and moral life of its people. The efforts of these great co-laborers marked the turning

"The Procession on the Wall of Jerusalem" by J. James Tissot. The Old Testament, Illustrated. A great throng gathered to celebrate the dedication of the wall.   M. de Buffan & Co.

point in the history of the Jews and prepared the nation for the coming of Jesus, the Son of God.

Before the singing of the angels is heard above the hills of Bethlehem, however, it is necessary to cross a History Bridge of about four hundred years in order to learn what happened in Israel and the rest of the world between the time the Old Testament ends and the New Testament begins.

Based on the story in the Bible:
Nehemiah 1:1 — 13:31

PLACES
in the Story of the Return from Captivity

THE PERSIAN EMPIRE

Cyrus, the founder of the Persian Empire, came to the throne about 559 B.C. Taking advantage of rebellion in the Median army, he defeated Astyages, king of the Medes, and entered his capital city, Ecbatana.

In an amazingly short time Cyrus extended his borders westward and northward. He continued his western march into Asia Minor until he reached the fabulously wealthy kingdom of Lydia, whose western border was the Aegean Sea. While Croesus, its king, was waiting for help to come from his two allies, Babylon and Egypt, Cyrus struck and added Lydia with all its riches to his growing empire. (Even to this day the expression, "as rich as Croesus," refers to an extremely wealthy man.)

Having gone westward to the Aegean Sea, Cyrus turned eastward toward the Tigris-Euphrates Valley and moved his armies in the direction of Babylon. He had a series of victories north of the capital, and Babylon itself fell to the Persian armies in 538 B.C. After liberating the Jewish captives from the Babylonians, Cyrus fulfilled a prophecy made by Isaiah about two hundred years earlier. This great prophet had foretold the return of the Jews to Jerusalem and had specifically named Cyrus as the Persian king who would free them.

It was during the reign of Darius the Great that the Persian Empire reached the apex of its power and splendor. His two million square-mile kingdom extended from the Indus River Valley in the east to the Aegean Sea in the

The Persian Empire. The Persian kings—Cyrus, Darius, and Xerxes among them—had conquered vast territories and established a great empire. Arrows indicate the journey of Nehemiah from his home in exile in Susa to Jerusalem.

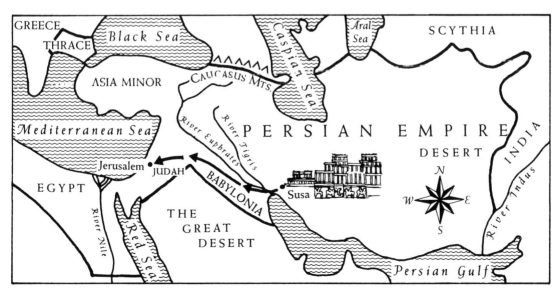

Ruins of the City Gate of Samaria. Sargon did not deport Israeli peasants; he brought non-Jews to settle with them in Samaria. Orthodox Jews disowned the Samaritans because they were a mixed race. © Matson Photo

west, and from the Jaxartes river in central Asia to Libya in North Africa.

TYRE AND SIDON

These two Phoenician seaport cities are about 22 miles apart. It was in them that Zerubbabel contracted for most of the supplies and skilled labor that would be needed to rebuild the Temple.

SAMARIA

Former capital of the Northern Kingdom, this city had become the capital of the province of Samaria. Bitter enmity sprang up between the Samaritans and the Jews during the days of Zerubbabel and still existed at the time Jesus began His ministry.

JUDAH

This district was all that remained of the once powerful Jewish Empire, established by David and Solomon. The tiny kingdom that Zerubbabel and the first group of returnees controlled was far different from the Judah of old. Its borders had shrunk so much that they were not over thirty miles apart in any direction.

JERUSALEM

During the days of Cyrus, Darius, Xerxes I (Ahasuerus), and Artaxerxes, this capital city of Israel was the center of activity for the Jews who returned from captivity. Zerubbabel brought the first group of Israelites back in 538 B.C. They built a new Temple for the Lord. Ezra and another group of exiles arrived in Jerusalem in 458 B.C. and, in 445 B.C., Nehemiah brought a third group back to their homeland. Led by Nehemiah, the people rebuilt the walls of Jerusalem in the record time of fifty-two days.

SHUSHAN (SUSA)

Nehemiah asked for and received permission from Artaxerxes, at the palace in this ancient Persian capital city, to go to Jerusalem and rebuild its walls.

AMMON

Across the Jordan, east of Judah, lies the province of Ammon. The Ammonites were another of Israel's bitter enemies. Tobiah the Ammonite joined forces with Sanballat, governor of Samaria, and other enemies of Judah to wage war on Israel during the time when Nehemiah was rebuilding the city's walls.

QUESTIONS
on the Story of the Return from Captivity

1

1 What effect did their many years in captivity have on the people of Judah?
2 How were the Jews treated by their captors?
3 Who was Cyrus? What did he do?
4 Who led the first group of Israelites back to Judah? How many people were in the caravan? How long did the journey take?
5 What was the reaction of the people as they gazed upon the ruins of Jerusalem and of the Lord's Temple?

2

6 What did the people of Judah do on the first day of the seventh month (New Year's Day)?
7 How did the people celebrate the completion of the laying of the foundation for the new Temple?
8 Why did Zerubbabel curtly reject the

Tomb of Cyrus the Great, founder of the Persian Empire. The burial place of Cyrus, "King of Babylon and all the countries," is preserved at Pasargadae, his capital. It is in Iran, north of Persepolis. Oriental Institute, University of Chicago

Samaritans' offer to help rebuild the Temple? What was the result of his rejection?

9 Why was work at the Temple site discontinued for about fifteen years?

10 Who aroused the people from their apathy toward the building project? What did he tell the Israelites?

11 Why did Tattenai write to Darius, the Persian king? What was the king's reply?

12 How long did it take Zerubbabel and his workers to build the new Temple?

13 Why was there a feeling of sadness among the people when the restoration of the Temple was completed?

3

14 Who was Ezra? Why did he want to go to Jerusalem?

15 What was Artaxerxes' response to Ezra's request for permission to return to Jerusalem?

16 Where did Ezra's group assemble? What did they do for three days prior to their departure?

17 What were the first three things Ezra did upon his arrival in Jerusalem?

18 Why was Ezra heartbroken over the conditions that he found in Judah?

19 What did Ezra do to bring his people to repentance?

20 When did Ezra again appear on the Bible scene? What did he do during this intervening time?

4

21 What were some of the characteristics of Nehemiah?

22 What did Nehemiah do when his brother Hanani brought him the sad news about conditions in Jerusalem?

23 What were the documents that Artaxerxes gave to Nehemiah to take with him to Jerusalem?

24 What was Nehemiah's real purpose in returning to Jerusalem? How did he make certain that the walls would be strongly constructed?

25 What did the enemies of Israel conspire to do when they saw the rapid reconstruction of the walls?

26 How did Nehemiah meet their threat?

27 How long did it take Nehemiah and his men to rebuild the walls? Describe the dedication ceremony.

28 Why were the people of Judah silently waiting for Ezra to make his appearance on the speaker's platform?

29 How did the team work of Ezra and Nehemiah affect the Jewish people?

30 What is a History Bridge?

*Answers are found
on the following pages.*

ANSWERS

on the Story of the Return from Captivity

1

1 The long years in captivity strengthened the faith of the Israelites, turned them back to the worship of the one true God, and created in their hearts a burning desire to return to Jerusalem.

2 The captors of the Jews treated them kindly. Unlike the tribes of the Northern Kingdom whom the Assyrians had scattered to the four corners of the earth, the people of Judah were permitted to remain together, united and unified. Their scribes were given the opportunity to study, compile, and re-copy their sacred books. Other members of the Jewish community became merchants and traders; some amassed great wealth. Still others rose to high positions in the courts of both Babylonia and Persia.

3 Cyrus was the king who founded the Persian Empire. After conquering Babylonia,

Eastern Stairway to the Great Hall, Persepolis. Relief sculptures on the stairway show envoys from subject nations bearing gifts for King Darius. In the distance are arches of the palace doors.

Oriental Institute, University of Chicago

he issued a decree which permitted the Israelites to return to Jerusalem.

4 Zerubbabel led the first group of over forty-two thousand people back to Judah. The nine-hundred-mile journey took four months.

5 The people had mingled emotions when they viewed the ruins of Jerusalem. The older Jews, who remembered the beauty of the city, were saddened at the sight. The others were impressed by the great amount of work that would be required to restore the city.

2

6 The people of Judah came to Jerusalem to offer sacrifices to the Lord, to celebrate the Feast of the Tabernacles, and to make plans for rebuilding the Temple.

7 There was great joy in Jerusalem as the people celebrated the laying of the foundation for the new Temple. The priests and the Levites came to the site in their robes, blew their trumpets, and played their musical instruments. The singing men and women sang beautiful songs from the Psalms.

8 Zerubbabel rejected the Samaritans' offer because he did not intend to have a partly heathen nation participate in the building of the Lord's Temple. The result of his rejection was fierce enmity between the two nations.

9 By making false accusations against the Jews, the Samaritans were successful in having the king of Persia issue an order halting the construction of the Temple.

10 Haggai the prophet aroused the people from their apathy and rekindled thir desire to build a new Temple. He told them that they were unfaithful to God and disloyal to the command of Cyrus by their failure to rebuild the Lord's House.

11 Tattenai wrote Darius that the Israelites were disobeying a decree of the king and were rebuilding the Temple. The governor added that Zerubbabel tried to justify his action by saying that Cyrus had issued an earlier decree authorizing the construction. A search of the royal archives was requested in order to verify the existence of such a decree. Darius replied that Cyrus' decree had been found, and he ordered Tattenai to leave Jerusalem and not interfere with the work of the Israelites.

12 It took Zerubbabel and his workers five years to build the new Temple.

13 There was a feeling of sadness among the Israelites at the dedication of the Temple because of the absence from the Holy Place of the beautiful Golden Ark which disappeared during the Captivity and was never found.

3

14 Ezra, a descendant of Aaron, was a priestly scribe and a high official in the Persian court of Artaxerxes. He had thoroughly studied the laws and ordinances that God had given to Moses, and he was anxious to go to Jerusalem to teach them to his people.

15 Artaxerxes granted the prophet's request and authorized any of the people of Judah, who so desired, to return to Jerusalem with him. The king also approved the collection of voluntary offerings and instructed that they be given to Ezra for use in the Lord's work. The remainder of the looted Temple treasures were turned over to the priest, and the treasurers of all the provinces in Canaan were ordered to give Ezra anything he needed for the furtherance of his work among the people of Judah.

16 Ezra's group of returnees assembled near the stream Ahava. The people fasted for three days and prayed that God would give them a safe journey to Jerusalem.

17 Upon his arrival in Jerusalem, Ezra gave the silver and gold to the Temple custodians and presented the remainder of the looted treasures to them. Next, he offered burnt offerings to the Lord. Then he sent messengers to the governors of all the provinces and requested from them the help that Artaxerxes had promised.

18 Ezra was heartbroken because, in the short space of eighty years, the people had again turned away from God and had broken His commandment by marrying heathen women and adopting their customs.

19 Ezra first demonstrated his deep grief by tearing his clothes and sitting silently before the Temple from early dawn until just before the evening sacrifices. As the day progressed, the crowd before the Temple grew larger and larger. Just as the sun was sinking, Ezra arose and gazed sadly but compassionately upon the throng gathered there. Then he knelt down and lifted up his voice in a fervent prayer of confession to the Lord. When the prayer was ended, the people wept bitterly and repented of their sins. The men with foreign wives made a covenant with God to send the wives and their children back to their native lands.

20 Ezra appeared again on the Bible scene about fifteen years later. This time he was with Nehemiah, who had just finished rebuilding the walls of Jerusalem. During this fifteen-year interval, Ezra had roamed the length and breadth of Judah, appointing magistrates, re-establishing law and order, setting up schools and synagogues in the smaller towns, and teaching the laws of Moses to those who did not know them.

4

21 Nehemiah was deeply religious, brave and persistent, energetic and patriotic. He was a skilled engineer and a wise administrator.

22 Nehemiah sat down and wept when his brother brought him the sad news about conditions in Jerusalem. Then he fasted for several days and, after that, he prayed daily for four months that God would tell him what he should do.

23 The documents that Artaxerxes gave to Nehemiah were: his commission as governor of Judah, letters to the governors of the Persian provinces requesting safe passage for Nehemiah and his party, and a letter to Asaph, the keeper of the king's forest, ordering him to provide for Nehemiah all the timber he would need in his construction work.

24 Nehemiah's real purpose in returning to Jerusalem was to rebuild its walls. He made certain that the walls would be strong by shrewdly assigning to each man the construction of that section of the wall nearest his own home.

25 The enemies of Israel conspired to wage war against them in order to halt the rapid construction of the walls.

26 Nehemiah met the threat of his enemies by reassuring his people that God was on their side and that there was no need to fear. He sent them back to work with a construction tool in one hand and a weapon in the other. He then declared a state of emergency, cancelled all leaves for workers living outside the city, posted guards at each gate, and divided the people into two groups. One group worked on the walls and the other group stood by, armed and ready for instant action.

27 Nehemiah and his people rebuilt the walls in the incredibly short span of fifty-two days. The dedication of the walls was the occasion for another day of great rejoicing in Jerusalem. Sacrifices were made to the Lord, and the priests raised their voices in prayers of thanksgiving. The ceremony continued with singing, dancing, and the playing of musical instruments.

28 The people of Judah were waiting for Ezra to teach them the Law of Moses. The great teacher soon appeared and, from early morning until midday, he read and thoroughly explained the laws to his people.

29 The efforts of Ezra and Nehemiah marked the turning point in the history of the Jews. These two great men strengthened and consolidated Israel, restored the religious and moral life of its people, and prepared the nation for the coming of Jesus, the Son of God.

30 A History Bridge, as used here, covers the events that occurred in Israel and the rest of the world during the four centuries between the time the Old Testament ends and the New Testament begins.

FURTHER FACTS
AND OUTLINES

for the Story of the Return from Captivity

EZRA

AUTHORSHIP AND DATE

Unknown, but perhaps Ezra ("helper"), a priest and a scribe, was author or compiler. He used sources for events he did not witness himself. Ezra lived in the 5th century B.C.

DESTINATION

The Jewish exiles already returned and those yet to return from Captivity.

PURPOSE AND THEME

The story is told of the Jewish restoration from the Babylonian Captivity, including re-establishment in Jerusalem and Judah. In fact, Ezra gives us almost all the information we possess on the Jews from the Captivity of Babylon under Cyrus (539 B.C.) to Ezra's entrance into Jerusalem in 457 B.C. Note, too, the relationship of the last of 2 Chronicles and Ezra 1:1-4. The book is written from the religious point of view, the Jews being viewed as a kingdom of priests and as a holy nation to walk in the bright light of the Law.

There are two quite distinct returns from the Babylonian Captivity: the one under Zerubbabel (chapters 1-6); the other, years later under Ezra (chapters 7-10). God's overruling providence is seen in Cyrus' letting the Jews rebuild their Temple (chapter 1); yet, they prefer the comforts of their homes in Babylon to the unsettled conditions of Judah (chapter 2). Though they started well (chapter 3), they allowed opposition to stop the rebuilding project (chapter 4). But once again, after some years, the project was taken up, due to the revival that came because of the preaching of Haggai and Zechariah, and the Temple was finished in 516 B.C. (chapters 5-6). Ezra comes to Jerusalem, at the command of King Cyrus, to inspire and discipline the people according to Jewish Law (chapter 7). He brought with him more exiles (chapter 8) and struggled with the problems of relocation, especially mixed marriages between Jews and pagans (chapters 9-10).

OUTLINE

The First Return from Exile and the Rebuilding of the Temple under Zerubbabel (chapters 1-6)

Cyrus Releases Exiles To Rebuild the Temple, Yet Jews Prefer the Comforts of Babylon (chapters 1-2)

The Rebuilding of the Temple (chapters 3-6)

Altar Built, Temple Foundations Laid (chapter 3)

Samaritan Opposition: Delay of Some Years (chapter 4)

Haggai and Zechariah Inspire Return to Work (chapter 5)

The Temple Completed (chapter 6)

The Second Return from Exile under Ezra (chapters 7-10)

Preparation and Return to Jerusalem Under Ezra (chapters 7-8)

Ezra Mourns and Prays over the People Who are Living Unseparated from the World (mixed marriages); Ezra's Reforms (chapters 9-10)

NEHEMIAH

AUTHORSHIP AND DATE

Perhaps Nehemiah ("Jehovah comforts"), a layman and the governor of Judah for about twelve years, was author. Ezra and Nehemiah were originally one book. This can be said: Memoirs of Nehemiah and other sources were used by the compilers who completed his work, perhaps in the 5th century B.C.

DESTINATION

The Jews who had returned to Jerusalem from Captivity.

PURPOSE AND THEME

The book tells the beautiful story of Nehemiah's deep concern for the people of Jerusalem and for the city itself. This concern expressed itself in prayer for the rebuilding of the city walls—in spite of great opposition. Nehemiah, as governor of Jerusalem, and Ezra, as a priest in Jerusalem, instituted reforms among the people, also inspired revival. The message of the book is seen in the execution of a goal through prayer and tenacity (even firmness) in the face of frustration.

OUTLINE

Restoration of the City Walls of Jerusalem under Nehemiah (chapters 1-7)
   Nehemiah Hears of the Problems of His People in Jerusalem, Grieves, and Is Sent to Jerusalem (chapters 1-2)
   The Walls Rebuilt, Despite Opposition and Greed (chapters 3-6)
   Nehemiah Provides for Rule over Jerusalem (chapter 7)

Reformation and Revival under Ezra and Nehemiah (chapters 8-13)
   Ezra Serves as Teacher of the Law (chapter 8)
   Reformation and Revival (chapters 9-10)
   Problems of Repopulation of Jerusalem Handled (chapter 11)
   Dedication of the City Walls (chapter 12)
   Nehemiah's Return to Jerusalem (chapter 13)

HAGGAI

AUTHORSHIP AND DATE

Haggai ("my feast"). An old tradition says Haggai was a Levite and that he returned to Jerusalem from the Babylonian Captivity with Zerubbabel.

During the second year of the reign of King Darius of Persia (520 B.C.), two prophets preached and recorded the essence of their messages; namely, Haggai (Haggai 1:1) and Zechariah (Zechariah 1:1). The two prophets are mentioned together in Ezra 5:1 and 6:14.

DESTINATION

The people of Jerusalem, Zerubbabel the governor of Judah, and Joshua the High Priest (1:1, 13-14; 2:2, 21).

PURPOSE AND THEME

The completion of the Temple is the theme of Haggai. Work on the Temple had begun the year after the people had returned from the Exile; but now the people were discouraged.
The prophet cries out against the prevalent idea that God's work is of secondary importance and must await economic solution. The economic problems are, in fact, God's judgment; when the people put God's work back in its rightful place, *then* problems will find solution. Haggai is raised up to challenge the people to finish the great building project. Messianic inspiration is included and comfort, too. Zerubbabel is said to be God's choice of a governor of Jerusalem and a type of the Messiah (2:23).

OUTLINE

First Message: Negligence in Completion of the Temple (chapter 1)
Second Message: Courage, Messianic Promise (2:1-9)
Third Message: Disobedience Means Absence of God's Blessing (2:10-19)
Fourth Message: Comfort—God will Fulfill His Promises (2:20-23)

"The Prophet Zechariah" by Michelangelo. Detail. Sistine Chapel, Rome. Zechariah lived and preached in Jerusalem after returning from exile in Babylonia. He was a contemporary of the prophet Haggai. Alinari

ZECHARIAH

AUTHORSHIP AND DATE

Zechariah ("Jehovah remembers"), son of Berechiah and grandson of one Iddo (probably same as in Nehemiah 12:16). If the Zechariah of Nehemiah 12:16 is the same as this Zechariah, he was a priest. Zechariah began his prophetic ministry two months after Haggai in the year 520 B.C. Chapters 9-14 may have been written later than the suggested 520 date.

DESTINATION

Jews who had returned from the Exile (1:2, 3; 7:5), Joshua the High Priest (3:8), and Zerubbabel the governor (4:6).

PURPOSE AND THEME

Like Haggai, Zechariah's aim was to challenge the people to finish the building of the Temple. Zechariah was greatly concerned with the spiritual implications of the challenge. He also makes some of the most revealing and inspiring Messianic declarations in prophetic literature.

OUTLINE

Introduction (1:1-6)
Zechariah's Visions (1:7—6:15)

Vision of the Horses: God's Judgment on the Nations and Jerusalem; the Temple To Be Rebuilt (1:7-17)

Vision of the Four Horns (Assyria, Egypt, Babylon, Medo-Persia): These Enemies Will Be Punished (1:18-21)

Vision of a Man Measuring Future Dimensions of Jerusalem: God's Salvation Will Mean Enlargement (chapter 2)

Vision of High Priest in Dirty Clothes: He Pleads for Mercy and Receives It (chapter 3)

Vision of the Candlestick and the Two Olive Trees; Obstacles To Building the Kingdom To Be Removed by God's Spirit (chapter 4)

Vision of the Flying Roll: Divine Judgments (chapter 5:1-4)

Vision of the Ephah and Weight of Lead: Iniquity, God's Restraining of Sin (5:5-11)

Vision of the Winds: God's Judgments (6:1-8)

Vision of Restoration: Messiah's Deliverance (6:9-15)

Question of Fasting: God Would Rather Have Obedience (chapters 7-8)

Destruction of the Nations and Deliverance of the Kingdom—Israel (chapters 9-14)

The Messiah Will Rule, Other Nations Perish (chapters 9-10)

The True Shepherd (Messiah) and the False Shepherd (chapter 11)

Israel's Future Repentance and Turn to God (12:1 – 13:6)

Purification of Israel; Future Glory of Jerusalem (13:7 – 14:21)

"Malachi" by J. James Tissot. *The Old Testament,* Illustrated. The Old Testament closes with the Book of Malachi, written four centuries before Christ.   M. de Buffan & Co.

MALACHI

AUTHORSHIP AND DATE

Malachi ("messenger of Jehovah"), of whom nothing is known, wrote his book apparently after the Temple had been reconstructed, perhaps in the 4th century B.C.

DESTINATION

To the Jews who have returned from Captivity, also to priests (1:6, 2:1).

PURPOSE AND THEME

The aim is to make clear the sin and apostasy of Israel and to underscore the judgment of God (1:3, 4) that comes to the sinner, but the blessing that awaits the repentant. That the people have not always honored God, that priests have become lax in doing their liturgical assignments, that priests have also caused the people to err because of false instruction, that mixed marriages (with heathen people) have taken place—all these sins are decried. That God is sovereign is also spelled out, and Malachi's teaching about God is important. The grace of God, past and present, is unfolded (1:2; 2:4, 5; 3:6). The Messiah will come to fulfill His purposes and cleanse His people. The people must obey the Law of Moses and thus prepare for the Great Day of the Lord. Note the reference to tithes and offerings in 3:8-10.

Malachi is the link between the Old and New Testaments, and his is the last voice until John the Baptist. About four hundred years lapsed between Malachi and John.

OUTLINE

Israel's Sin and Apostasy
(chapters 1:1 – 3:15)
The Priests' Sins (1:1 – 2:9)
The People's Sins (2:10 – 3:15)

Blessing for those who Repent (3:16 – 4:6)

Does Faith in God Insure Success in Business?

by

John E. Mitchell, Jr.

To run a big business in the United States or to rebuild the wall of an ancient city requires a good administrator. Rightly to solve the problems arising from either of these enterprises requires faith in God. Nehemiah acted on such firmly rooted faith in every step he took in the restoration of Jerusalem's walls, centuries before Christ. John E. Mitchell, Jr., Christian industrialist of Dallas, Texas, illustrates his stand from personal experience as he projects the need for faith in God against the background of the 20th-century business world in a chapter from his book, *The Christian in Business* (© 1962, Fleming H. Revell Co., Westwood, N.J.).

A LITTLE THING—BUT BIG

ONE DAY IN 1947 the Purchasing Agent of our company came into my office with a problem. He held in his hand a screw about three-fourths of an inch long. It was little, but it was important. We were using several hundred of these special, patented screws in every cotton cleaning machine we manufactured, and normally ordered them in lots of a million or more at a time. There was no substitute for this screw, and there was only one source of supply, a New York concern which I shall call the Klein Manufacturing Company.

Now, instead of the usual six months' supply, our stock had dwindled to a scant two weeks' supply. The P. A. said that the Klein people were several months behind with their shipments on our orders. This was not their fault, he added, but was due to an acute steel shortage; they could not obtain the steel wire necessary for producing the screws.

And so our company faced the bleak prospect of a shutdown. For more than fifteen years we had not laid off, even for one day, a single regular full-time worker for lack of work. Now, that record was about to be ended by a general layoff which, if it should last long enough, would work a severe hardship on our employees. Furthermore, since the threatened shutdown would come just when we were approaching our peak production and shipping season, we would lose more than a million dollars of business that would be canceled by customers who could not wait.

The Purchasing Agent had worked hard on the problem. He had written many letters and had sent many telegrams; also, he had made several long distance telephone calls, finally putting the matter squarely up to the president, Mr. Klein, himself. Mr. Klein had written us: "We are sorry to say that it looks very much as though we will be unable to take care of you in accordance with your requirements. It is very distasteful for us to have to give you this information in view of the fact that you have been one of our loyal customers for the past fifteen years, but in this respect you are in no different position than several score of our other friends. Like yourselves, over the years we have been supplying such well-known concerns as Philco, RCA, Ford, Frigidaire, Pullman Standard Car, New York Central, General Electric, Westinghouse, and many other prominent manufacturers too numerous to mention. . . ."

When the P. A. left my office, I stared glumly at the little screw which he had left with me, wondering how so small a thing could cause so great a crisis.

Finally—and I am afraid it was a last, desperate resort—I decided to take the matter "upstairs" to the Chief Executive. In other words, I prayed to the Lord for guidance and help. The reader will judge for himself from the rest of this story as to what extent the prayer was answered.

My reasoning, which I will readily admit was rather farfetched, went something like this: There must be *some* steel wire available —enough to produce *some* screws for *some* customers—and the Klein Company, if properly convinced of our dire need, would surely place us high on their priority list. Further, *somewhere* in New York City there must be *some* person who was preëminently qualified to present our cause to Mr. Klein. Who this person was, I had not the slightest idea. But it occurred to me as a rather forlorn hope that *some* New York banker could probably tell us how to proceed to find such a man. To locate such a banker was in itself a problem.

I decided to start with Mr. Milton Brown, President of the Mercantile National Bank in Dallas. Upon hearing our story, he suggested that we call the executive vice president of one of the largest banks in the world—a gentleman whom I shall refer to as Mr. Marshall. In ten minutes' time Mr. Marshall was on the phone. Then I began to feel how presumptuous it was for a little manufacturer deep in the heart of Texas to be bothering a great banker in New York City about so trivial a matter as a barrel of screws. However, I had gone too far to back out; and so, after due apologies, I told my story to Mr. Marshall. Could he by any chance help me find someone in New York City who could listen to my story and then relay the facts to Mr. Klein with such urgency and persuasiveness as to

manage to get some of these screws for us?

To my amazement, it then developed that Mr. Marshall himself was well acquainted with the Klein Manufacturing Company. He knew Mr. Klein personally. Mrs. Marshall and Mrs. Klein were good friends and, if I remember correctly all the facts at this late date, he even had some official capacity with the company. Furthermore, he had once been asked by another company, much larger than ours, to do what he could to obtain some of the same kind of screws for them. At this point, I exclaimed, "Mr. Marshall, do you realize how remarkable this is? In ten minutes' time I have located on the telephone, over 1600 miles away, the one man among seven million people in New York City who can really help us. Were you successful in getting some screws for your other friends?"

"Yes, it so happens that I was able to help them out," replied Mr. Marshall, "and I shall, of course, be glad to do what I can for you and for my friends at the Mercantile Bank there in Dallas."

Two or three days after this conversation, we had a telegram from Mr. Klein indicating that he now understood from Mr. Marshall how urgent our need was; that, fortunately, his company had just received a small shipment of wire and they were giving our order special preference; that 100,000 screws would be shipped by air freight within a week, with other shipments to follow rapidly until our order was completed. His promise was kept to the letter; the screws arrived just in time. Not a single hour of production was lost. No one was laid off. No orders were canceled.

Immediately we proceeded to telephone Mr. Brown of the Mercantile Bank to thank him for his part in solving our problem. Then we wired Mr. Klein to thank him. We of course wrote a warm letter to Mr. Marshall expressing our gratitude to him. (Incidentally, we were greatly pleased a few weeks later to read that Mr. Marshall had become the president of his great bank.) Finally, we took the matter up with the One who had engineered it all, the Lord Himself, and said "thank you" to Him.

I realize that many people would regard the

events I have just related as merely a chain of remarkable coincidences. Such folks would no doubt scoff at the idea that God can be interested in anything so trivial as a nearly empty screw barrel. To think He *is* interested in such matters, they would say, is childlike and presumptuous.

What is wrong with being childlike? Does not God commend childlikeness in us—yes, demand it? Jesus says, "Suffer little children . . . to come unto me: for *of such* is the kingdom of heaven. . . . Except ye be converted and become as *little children,* ye shall not enter into the kingdom of heaven" (Matthew 19:14; 18:3). And "without faith it is impossible to please Him: for he that cometh to God must believe that He is, and that He is a rewarder of them that diligently seek Him" (Hebrews 11:6).

It seems to be the universal testimony of God's servants, both in the Bible and out of it, that He does hear and answer their prayers. Sometimes the answer is "Yes," sometimes "No," and sometimes it is "Wait a while." Doesn't an intelligent, loving father of today do the same thing with *his* son? Sometimes *he* says "Yes," sometimes "No," and sometimes *he* says, "Let's wait a while, son." Is God inferior to an earthly father in wisdom or in what is to our ultimate best interest? As sensible children of an all-wise Heavenly Father whom we love, because "He first loved us and gave himself for us," we should readily submit to His will, whether or not it coincides with our own desires.

Does faith in God guarantee success in business? Of course not. There are some kinds of business in which a Christian has no business at all. But assuming that a given business is one in which a Christian can engage with good conscience, will he be sure of success just because he is a Christian? Of course not.

To answer "Yes" would be to assume that God is under obligation to reward every Christian with money for every "good" thing he does. If such a philosophy prevailed, men would soon be near to bursting with "goodness," holding out their hands for the prize money and thanking God—and themselves—

for being better than other men. Prigs of this kind would be both counterfeit Christians and sorry businessmen, in the bargain.

Surely no sincere Christian would regard God as a sort of glorified servant, like Aladdin's genie, ready whenever the lamp is rubbed to accede to his every whim.

The only bearing that real Christianity has on business success is to ask: How is this success being achieved? What is the man doing with it? Is the Lord Christ honored and served in the whole matter? How does His servant endure success? And how does His servant stand up under disappointment and failure? If, due to factors quite beyond his control, a Christain experiences some great disappointment or some serious setback in his business, how does he adjust to such a disappointment or setback? Does he accept the experience in good grace, thank God for it and rejoice in the knowledge that "all things work together for good to them that love God"? Will he tackle the new situation with courage, energy and enthusiasm, asking for guidance and wisdom that he may proceed in a way satisfying to the Lord?

It is possible, I think, for a Christian to be a successful failure. It is possible for him to deal with a financial failure in his business in such a way that the outcome will be a spiritual victory. I offer as an exhibit the story that my father used to tell, many years ago, about a plumber in St. Louis. This plumber and his partner, due to circumstances beyond their control, went broke. The bank, of which my father was a director, charged off about $15,000 when the bankruptcy settlement was made. In due course the bank officials forgot about the matter.

However, Mr. A, the plumber, did not forget. One day, about five years after the bankruptcy, he showed up at the bank and told the cashier that he wanted to pay $100 on his note. The cashier called in the president, who explained that Mr. A was under no legal obligation to make any further payments on the indebtedness. Mr. A knew that; yes, he also knew that so far as any moral obligation was concerned his former partner was as much involved as he. But regardless of all this, he wanted to pay off the whole debt himself and, if the Lord favored him with good health and good business in his new enterprise, he would do it. And he did! It required three or four years to pay off the entire balance but, toward the end, the payments got bigger and closer together.

The bank's officers tried to persuade him to accept a portion of the debt as a "gift," but he would not hear of it. Finally, when the last payment was made and Mr. A left the bank with his note marked "Paid," he could know that he had indeed walked the second mile. No doubt he was pleased to reflect that the A Plumbing Company was now a flourishing enterprise and enjoyed splendid prospects for future business. Certainly, he had the assurance that all the people at the bank and all their friends would favor him with their plumbing business. But I like to imagine that to Mr. A the greatest satisfaction of all was to hear the Voice speaking quietly to his heart these words: "Well done, good and faithful servant: thou hast been faithful . . . ." (Matthew 25:23).

What is success for a Christian business-man? As a *businessman,* the Christian must submit himself to judgment by the same standards that apply to all businessmen: Does he operate his business at a profit? But, as a *Christian,* he must also submit himself to God's standards. He must walk humbly before his God, seeking on all occasions the Father's will, consulting Him in prayer, serving Him by being of service to other people, enduring hardships with valor and thankfulness, taking successes with gratitude but with humility and caution, giving Him the honor when things go well, and placing the blame upon himself, where it usually belongs, when things go wrong.

There could be no finer praise for a worker, whether a company executive or a man in coveralls, than the statement made concerning one of God's servants thousands of years ago: "And Enoch walked with God: and he was not; for God took him" (Genesis 5:24). Enoch's was an eternal success. That is the kind of success that God guarantees for each of us, if we want it earnestly enough to submit ourselves, without any reservations, to His will.

A HISTORY BRIDGE
between
THE TESTAMENTS

TWO CONTEMPORARIES, Nehemiah the builder-statesman and Malachi the writer-prophet, bring to a close the historical and prophetic records of the Old Testament. Our only accounts of the four centuries between their work and the birth of Jesus come from the Apocrypha and from secular historians—especially, Josephus, the Jew.

The Peaceful Persian Rule

For two hundred years after the period covered by the Book of Nehemiah, the Jews continued under the enlightened Persian rule. They were allowed complete religious freedom. They participated in the government, holding such high posts as lieutenant-governor. Religious law, as taught by the priests and the scribes, began to regulate the daily life of the Jews.

The Jewish community itself appears to have been practically self-governing. The High Priest, as interpreter of the Law and representative of the Lord, was the supreme authority, supported by a Council of Elders. Temple services were resumed, along with the observance of feasts and fasts. The little colony of Jews grew in numbers and in wealth. They served God with greater faithfulness than ever before in their history. There was no idol-worship, and in this they had a common bond with the Persians. The Jews who returned from Babylon were firm in their belief in the One God and that, in a special way, they were His people and His alone.

During these peaceful years there was much literary activity among the Jews. Their religious leaders worked with patience and perseverance to put into order the ancient manuscripts of the written law—a task begun in the days of Ezra. They were no less zealous in collecting into one code the laws which had passed from father to son and were, therefore, known as the Oral Law. Much of this work was excellent and valuable. Some of it, however, was marred by a harshness and narrowness that stamped it as the fruit of man's ideas, not God's; many of the rules laid down were almost impossible to comply with and later became targets of Christ's denunciation.

These were the years, too, in which the office of High Priest began to be sought by men of worldly ambition—so great was its political power in the Jewish community—rather than by men of religious piety and fervor.

Alexander the Great Brings Greek Culture

Between the years 333 and 323 B.C. Alexander the Great, a Greek of Macedonia, as part of his world conquest swept aside the Persians, taking one of their great capitals, Babylon, which he planned to restore, and established himself as ruler over the Jews and their land.

Syria, which then included Palestine, was a part of the great but waning Persian Empire. City after city fell before the relentless advance of Alexander's armies, including Syria's capital city, Damascus. The great northern seacoast citadel of Tyre, however, offered formidable resistance.

When Alexander appealed to the Jews for help in his campaign against Tyre, they replied through their high priest, Jaddua.

He boldly told Alexander's messengers that they could not give him aid because they had pledged Darius III, the Assyrian king, that they would not take up arms against him during his lifetime. The Jews, instead, found a way to help Tyre by sending provisions to the beleaguered city.

Without the benefit of Jewish aid, however, Alexander finally conquered Tyre in 332 B.C. His next move was to march against Jerusalem, Josephus the historian says in his account of the event, to punish her citizens for helping the Assyrian king.

When news of Alexander's march reached Jaddua, he was filled with anxiety. What could he do to prevent the wrath of so mighty a conqueror from falling on his people?

"The Entry of Alexander the Great into Babylon" by Charles LeBrun. The Louvre, Paris. After defeating Darius III at Arbela, Alexander and his army went in triumph to Babylon, where he was welcomed by the populace.　　　Alinari

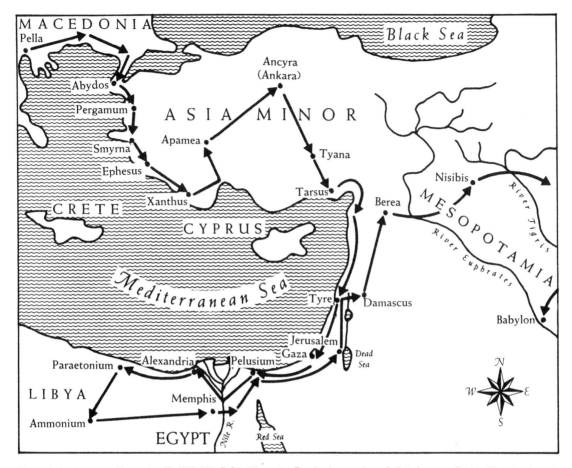

Alexander's Journey. Alexander III (356-323 B.C.), King of Macedonia, extended his kingdom to the limits of the Persian Empire in a series of victories over Darius III. Later, he advanced farther eastward into India as far as the Punjab area.

Jaddua could not defend the city by arms, but he ordered the people to pray to the Lord their God that they might be delivered from their great peril.

God appeared to Jaddua in a dream and told him that he should boldly open the city gates. Then he was to have the ordinary priests attire themselves in white robes, while he himself was to dress in the official robes of the High Priest. He was then to lead the procession through the city gate to meet Alexander.

On awakening, Jaddua joyfully obeyed God's commands. He waited patiently until informed that Alexander was approaching the city. Then the High Priest led an unusual procession out of the main gate.

Alexander was amazed, as were all who accompanied him. Never before had they seen a procession like this! When Alexander saw the brave leader, Jaddua, marching toward him in purple and gold robes with the name of God emblazoned on the miter [elaborate headdress], he saluted the High Priest and paid homage to the name on the miter. This act brought cheers for Alexander from the Jews, who quickly surrounded the youthful king.

Those in Alexander's company who

399

saw his impulsive act thought he had gone mad. One of them spoke what was in the minds of all: "Why do you, who are honored by everyone, choose to adore the High Priest of the Jews?"

"I do not adore the High Priest," declared Alexander, "but rather the God who has honored this man with the high priesthood."

The young king then took Jaddua by the hand and, surrounded by the jubilant crowd, they entered Jerusalem. Alexander then proceeded to the Temple to offer a sacrifice. His mission of vengeance had turned into one of genuine appreciation for the Jews.

Alexander decreed that there should be no interference with the civil and religious customs of the Jews. Further, he exempted them from paying tribute during the sabbatical year, when no crops were planted. Jews were recognized as equal citizens with the Greeks and were encouraged to settle in Alexander's new city of Alexandria in Egypt. Even in the army, the Jews were permitted to practice their religion.

It was Alexander's policy to plant Greek colonies in territory not yet settled or in already established cities like Damascus. Citizens in Greek cities benefitted from Greek education in language, literature, sculpture, and drama. Many of the Jews caught the Greek spirit but, on the whole, remained true to the one Invisible God instead of worshiping the ancient gods of the Greeks, such as Zeus and the galaxy around him.

Palestine as a Pawn

Alexander died in 323 B.C., leaving no heir, so his vast dominions were divided among his generals. One seized Egypt and another took Syria. Palestine, the center of Alexander's empire, was caught between the two and became a pawn that set off bitter strife and warfare for twenty years.

In 320 B.C., led by Ptolemy Soter, Egypt invaded Jerusalem on a Sabbath. Because no Jew would take up arms on this holy day, the city was easily overcome. During this period of Egyptian domination, constant warfare raged over Palestine. The Jews fled their homeland in large numbers, and many of them joined earlier immigrants to Egypt, where they were treated well.

The Jews learned the Greek language

Palestine Became a Part of Alexander's Empire and remained under Hellenic domination until his untimely death in 323 B.C. It was then annexed to Egypt, which was ruled by the Ptolemies.

quickly, and it soon became the native tongue of their children. Jews in Alexandria had synagogues where the writings of Moses and the prophets, translated into Greek, were read on each Sabbath day. According to tradition, Ptolemy Phil-adelphus, son of Ptolemy Soter, commissioned seventy-two Jewish scholars to translate the Holy Scriptures into Greek. This translation, called the Septuagint (LXX), did much to spread the Scriptures throughout the Western world.

Hellenist Jews Adopt Greek Culture and Customs

The Greek culture brought in by Alexander continued its pervasive influence at all levels of Jewish life. For the most part, this culture was not the intellectual brilliance of Athens but that of the soldier and the travelling merchant.

The theaters, the gymnastic games, and the Greek joy in physical living proved tempting to the Jews. Many not only imitated their conquerors' dress and customs but also began to pay less and less attention to their own religion. Even priests left their altars to play in the games, and sacrifices were offered to Greek gods.

On the whole, it was the wealthier Jews who chafed at the restrictions of the Temple laws against Sabbath amusements, against the eating of certain foods, and against other worldly activities. The poorer Jews were shocked at the violation of these laws. Soon there arose two distinct Jewish groups—the Hasidim, who were revolted by Greek paganism, and the Hellenists, who were all pro-Greek.

The Hellenists naturally gained the favor of their Greek overlords. They were given important posts, such as that of tax-collector. At that time, as well as throughout the life of Jesus, tax-collecting was "farmed out" for lump sums to men known as "publicans." These men proceeded to raise the required sum, plus whatever else they could wring from the purses of the people for their own income. Through such posts the Hellenists became a rich and powerful group.

Zealous for the national importance of their country, the Hellenists cared little for their religion. They even sought to increase their national power through the adoption of Greek institutions rather than through the observance of the Torah. They openly disregarded some of the Hebrew laws and began scheming to get possession of the important office of High Priest.

Syrian Oppression under Antiochus Epiphanes

During the impotent reign of Ptolemy V, troubled times came to Egypt. The powerful Hellenists then made their move. They had become dissatisfied with their treatment under the Egyptian régime, so in 198 B.C. they invited Antiochus III, King of Syria, into Jerusalem. In this easy fashion Palestine passed from the hands of the Ptolemies into the power of the Seleucids, named for Seleucus, another of Alexander's generals who founded Antioch and made it the western capital of his kingdom.

Antiochus appreciated this gesture from the Jewish Hellenists, even though he may not actually have needed their support. He had just defeated a large Egyptian army, virtually bringing his conquest of Egypt to a successful close. Nevertheless, Antiochus showed his appreciation by granting freedom to the Jewish religion and bestowing many privileges upon the Temple. This golden era of freedom was short-lived, however, for the accession of

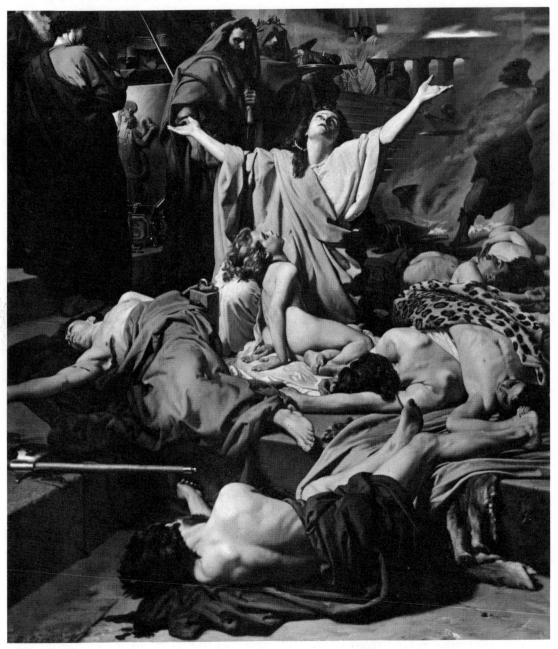

"The Maccabees" by Antonio Ciseri. Church of Santa Felicita, Florence. Persecution of the Jews by Antiochus led to rebellion under Mattathias and his sons. The martyrdom of seven brothers and their mother is shown above.

Alinari

Antiochus Epiphanes to the throne in 175 B.C. began a reign of terror.

Mistakenly assuming that the Hellenists represented the majority of the Jewish people, Antiochus Epiphanes tried to impose the Greek culture of his nation upon the Jews by force. He went so far as to establish a gymnasium in Jerusalem and to introduce Greek customs into the games and all athletic events.

Because Antiochus desperately needed money to maintain his mercenary forces over conquered peoples, he accepted a bribe offered by the head of the Hellenist party, Jason, for appointment as High Priest. With the king's help Jason was successful in obtaining the high priesthood, even though it meant deposing his own brother, Onias, from the office and banishing him. Jason further debased his sacred position by contributing money toward idol worship.

The next High Priest came to his post by offering a larger bribe than Jason's. He was Menelaus, a man so low in morals that he later robbed the sacred Temple treasury in order to get funds for paying his bribe! Feeling insecure in his stolen post, Menelaus next sought to strengthen his position by procuring the murder of Onias, the rightful High Priest. This he accomplished, even though Onias sought sanctuary in a Greek temple where (according to both Jewish and pagan custom) a man was free from harm. Even the Greeks were aroused by this savage act and had the assassins punished. Menelaus, however, again bribed the king and went free.

This callous disregard for decency caused a riot by the Jews. Later, when it was rumored that Antiochus Epiphanes had been slain on the battlefields of Egypt, there was widespread rejoicing in Jerusalem. The rumor was false, and Antiochus heard of the celebration by the Jews. He swept into the city with his army and massacred thousands of the Jewish people. This mass murder was followed by many sacrilegious acts. He stole the gold from the treasure rooms of the Temple. He ordered the Torah and other Scriptures to be burned, and—as a final devastating blow to Jewish law and pride—ordered a sow to be sacrificed on the sacred altar. In 168 B.C. Antiochus proscribed every Jewish rite and outlawed the Jewish religion. The Temple was turned into a heathen shrine dedicated to Zeus.

The more spiritual leaders of the Jews, the Hasidim, remained true to the faith of their fathers. The Hellenists, however, soon degenerated into heathenism. Even the High Priest Menelaus himself, a hireling of Antiochus, turned against the faithful members of his own religion and ordered soldiers to search out the pious members of the Hasidim and to kill them for performing their religious rites. There was little resistance, because the Hasidim were scholars, not soldiers.

The Maccabees: Mattathias and His Sons

The faithful among the Jews had been persecuted to the limit of their endurance. Revolution was simmering, and it finally flared up in 167 B.C. in the little village of Modin, twenty miles northwest of Jerusalem. Soldiers ordered swine sacrificed to the god Zeus on the sacred altar of the village. Mattathias, an aged priest, not only refused openly to do so; he killed a Greek soldier, as well as a Jewish Hellenist who also had offered to make the sacrifice, and then broke down the altar.

403

Modin (distant view). Mattathias, priest of Modin, slew a soldier and a Hellenist Jew to prevent a pagan sacrifice of swine on the sacred altar. He fled with his sons who became the leaders of the resistance.   © Matson Photo

Mattathias, with his five sons, fled to the mountains and there raised the banner of rebellion. Soon pious Jews and their families rallied to his standard and moved with him into the desert and the hills. The elderly priest had five sons: Johanan, Simon, Judas Maccabeus, Eleazar, and Jonathan. This family, which took the lead in checking the influence of Greek thought and customs on the Jewish religion, is known by two names—the *Hasmoneans*, from its noble ancestors, and the *Maccabees*, although the latter designation is properly applied only to Judas Maccabeus, the "Hammerer."

The struggle for freedom waged by the Maccabeans is almost unparalleled, for sheer heroism, in all the long annals of human history. Mattathias, the father, died almost before the revolt got started. His third son, Judas Maccabeus, took command of the insurgent forces and held high the banner of resistance.

Because he knew the territory so well, Judas was able to seize mountain passes where a small band of men could hold off an entire army. At first he avoided a direct confrontation with the forces of Antiochus in the open field of battle; but, gradually, as his men continued to inflict heavy losses by such tactics as slaughtering several detached divisions of the Syrian enemy, Judas came to the point where he was willing to risk open combat. The king's general, Lysias, met Judas with an army of 50,000 men. Judas, with a force

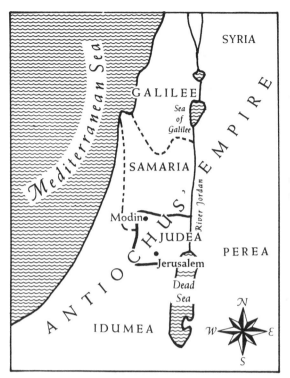

Antiochus' Empire. Antiochus III, king of Syria, a descendant of Alexander's general, Seleucus, won Palestine from Egypt (198 B.C.). The efforts of Antiochus IV (or Epiphanes) to Hellenize the Jews caused the great Maccabean rebellion.

Antiochus sent his invading armies into Palestine again and again, only to suffer defeat at the hands of Judas and his courageous followers. Only once were the Syrian forces able to penetrate as far as the walls of Jerusalem. A bloody battle followed, in which the Jews were hopelessly outnumbered and the youngest of the Maccabean brothers, Eleazar, was killed. Before the Syrian general, Lysias, could launch an assault on the walls, however, he received news from Antioch, the capital of Syria, about the death of Antiochus Epiphanes. So vital to his own interests was this message that he quickly offered terms of peace, which Judas

"The Triumph of Judas Maccabeus" by Rubens. Museum of Fine Arts, Nantes. Judas, third son of Mattathias, succeeded in restoring religious liberty to the Jews.   La Bibbia

one-fifth the size, routed his foe. Lysias returned with 65,000 men, but Judas earned his surname "Maccabeus" (the "Hammerer") that day as he pounded the army of King Antiochus Epiphanes from all sides and forced it to flee in disgrace.

The first concern of Judas, as he marched with his men in triumph to Jerusalem, was to repair the Temple and restore the worship of God. On December 25, 165 B.C., three years after the desecration of the Temple, sacrifices in accordance with the law of Moses were resumed. This reconsecration of the Temple was celebrated thereafter as an annual feast of eight days, occurring at the time of the winter solstice, called the Feast of the Dedication (John 10:22).

gladly accepted, and then departed—leaving the Jews in possession of their capital.

Judas next had to face trouble from one of the Jews. Alcimus, an Aaronite, asked the Syrians for appointment as High Priest and, by promising to turn Jerusalem again into a Greek city, received troops to support his claim. Demetrius I, who had succeeded Antiochus Epiphanes, sent one of his generals, Nicanor, against Judas. Nicanor had to retreat to Jerusalem, where he threatened to burn the Temple if Judas himself were not surrendered to the army. At this point the Hasidim rallied to the support of Judas, who decisively defeated the Syrians at Adasa. Nicanor lost his own life in this battle.

As political head of Palestine, Judas sent messengers to Rome asking for aid against Syria. His request was partially granted; the Roman Senate dispatched word to Demetrius to stop fighting the Jews, described as allies of the Romans. The Senate's message reached Demetrius too late to save the life of Judas Maccabeus, one of the most illustrious men in the world's long history. He died at Elasa, where his valiant army suffered defeat at the hands of the Syrian general, Bacchides.

The High Priest Alcimus immediately started a reign of terror in Jerusalem, directing it at the Maccabeans, now under the leadership of Jonathan, a brother of Judas. Leaving the capital, Jonathan led a force east of the Jordan to avenge the murder of his brother Johanan by the sons of Jambri. On his return Jonathan set up a rival government twelve miles from Jerusalem. When the High Priest Alcimus died, Bacchides decided that the conquest of Judea was complete, so he returned to Syria. Finding that the land still was not at peace, Bacchides took positive action. He gave Jonathan the legal authority to maintain an armed force at Michmash.

In the civil strife between two rivals for the Syrian throne, Jonathan became the ally of Alexander Balas against Demetrius I. When Alexander defeated his rival, Jonathan was established in 152 B.C. as a high priest, a prince of Syria, and as both the military and civil governor of Judea. For several years the country was free from invasion, and Jonathan used this breathing spell to consolidate the liberties of his people. Due to disturbances in Syria, Jonathan was able to conquer several cities in the Maritime Plain and south of Judea. He re-established treaties with Rome and Sparta. He strengthened the fortifications of Jerusalem, completely cutting off the Syrian garrison with a high wall. Various strategic points throughout Judea were fortified. These firm steps toward complete independence for the Jews were halted, however, by an act of treachery. Trypho, commanding general of young Antiochus V, inveigled Jonathan into a fortress and captured him. He was later executed by Antiochus.

Simon, the only survivor of the Maccabean brothers and in some respects the noblest of all the sons of Mattathias, succeeded Jonathan. He had served loyally under his two younger brothers and had proved his patriotism by a life of self-denial and unselfish devotion to his country's cause. During his brief rule of seven years as High Priest and civil governor, the nation attained the independence for which he and his brothers had so heroically struggled. A born diplomat, Simon found aid for his cause in the civil strife sweeping Syria. Recognition of the independence of Judea was the price he exacted from Demetrius II in exchange for a pledge to assist him in his efforts to gain the Syrian throne.

In the year 143 B.C., at a great assembly of priests and people, princes and elders, it was decreed that Simon should be perpetual High Priest and ruler "until the great prophet should appear." This, in effect, made the office of High Priest hereditary in Simon's family. In memory of the occasion, a tablet of brass in Simon's honor was placed on a wall of the Temple. The Jews celebrated this consummation of their struggle for freedom by designating the year 143 B.C. as the beginning of a new era, from which all documents were dated.

Descendants of the Maccabees

John Hyrcanus became High Priest and civil ruler after his father, Simon, met a violent death at a banquet. A man of war, John Hyrcanus was ruled by an obsession to restore the territory of the Jews to its extent during David's reign. This ambition did not look promising at the start of his reign because, at his first encounter with the Syrians, he was defeated by Antiochus VII. After the death of Antiochus in a campaign against the Parthians was followed by a succession of weak monarchs on the Syrian throne, John Hyrcanus was able to pursue his policy of expansion unhindered.

During a prosperous reign of thirty-one years Hyrcanus extended the boundaries of the nation on both sides of the Jordan River. He besieged and captured the city of Samaria, destroying the rival temple which the Samaritans had built on Mt. Gerizim. He established a brilliant court, issuing coins as High Priest and head of the Congregation of the Jews; but he did not take the title of "king." His rule was also noteworthy for its road-building program and the expansion of commerce.

Although John Hyrcanus was High Priest as well as ruler, he neglected the office and work of the priesthood to such an extent that the pious Jews became alarmed. In placing his emphasis on nationalist rather than religious goals, Hyrcanus incurred the enmity of the Pharisees, a new pious group which had assimilated the Hasidim.

Originally, the Pharisees comprised a group of pious laymen who took the place of priestly teachers or scribes in teaching the Scriptures to the people. Champions of the Oral Law, they came to represent the religious beliefs of the majority of the common people in that day. They accepted the new doctrine of the resurrection and life after death. They also introduced many Temple practices into the homes. Theirs was a democratic attempt to wrest the Jewish religion from the aristocratic control of the Temple priests, the Sadduccees.

On their part, the Sadduccees constituted the nationalist party. To them the nation was everything. National honor, dignity, and freedom had to be preserved at all costs. The Sadduccees were purely political in their aims. Yet it was from this party that the High Priest was chosen. Other officials were largely drawn from this group, and to them the king looked for support.

The will of John Hyrcanus provided that the reins of government should be placed in the hands of his widow and that the high priesthood should be inherited by the oldest of his five sons, Aristobulus. This despicable character, known to history as Aristobulus I, soon had his mother starved to death in prison. He then raised his brother Antigonus to joint rule with him and, almost in the same breath, cast his other three brothers into prison. Suspicious of Antigonus, he soon had him slain. For the first time a member of the ruling house then took the title of "king." The brief reign of Aristobulus I (104-103 B.C.) is remembered for little besides his friendship with the Greeks.

After the death of Aristobulus, his widow Alexandra released his three brothers from prison. The oldest of these, Alexander Jannaeus, she married. He thus became both king and High Priest. Basically a military man, he extended the frontiers of Judea but was repulsed in an early campaign against the Egyptians. If Cleopatra's counselors had not advised against it, Judea at this time might have become a province of Egypt. With the departure of the Egyptian army, Alexander remained in control.

The military activity of Alexander and his inactivity, if not actual hostility, with regard to his high priestly office, revived the smoldering opposition of the Pharisees. At the Feast of Tabernacles ceremonies Alexander actually made blasphemous ridicule of his priestly duties, and this so enraged the worshipers that they hurled at him the offerings they had brought for the altar. Alexander's natural baser instincts took charge. He ordered his soldiers to slay the worshipers, and soon the Temple area was strewn with sprawling bodies of the dead.

For the Pharisees, this was the match that ignited the fires of a bloody civil war. Before it was over, six years later, an estimated 50,000 Jews had died. The Pharisees asked aid from the Syrian ruler, Demetrius III, who defeated Alexander. Many of the Jews had second thoughts on this matter, however, because they felt that their country might again fall under the dominion of the Syrians. They rallied to Alexander's support and he defeated his foes. His victory turned into another blood bath, because he executed as many of the Pharisees as he could capture and inflicted punishments of the most terrible nature on all others who had helped them.

Before dying in a siege of a Greek city in Palestine, Alexander bequeathed his kingdom to his wife Alexandra, along with the advice to make peace with the Pharisees. A remarkable woman, she decided to make leaders among the Pharisees her chief advisers. She defended Judea against various foreign enemies, but it was her domestic policy that highlighted Alexandra's rule. Guided by her brother Simon, she developed Judea from within along lines favorable to the Pharisees. Her nine-year reign (76-67 B.C.) was largely constructive.

Transition to Roman Rule

After Alexandra's death, civil strife again broke out in the quarrel of her two sons, Hyrcanus II and Aristobulus II, over succession to the throne. The queen's will had named her older son, Hyrcanus who was already High Priest, as her successor. Aristobulus, the aggressive younger brother, organized a rebellion and unseated Hyrcanus but provided him with a generous private income as he retired to private life.

The dispute appeared to have been settled and, except for the interference of an ambitious Idumean named Antipater, would have been at an end. He decided that Hyrcanus ought to be returned to the throne and, with the help of King Aretas of Arabia, organized an army that besieged Aristobulus in the Temple Mount.

At this point, events took another turn that was to make Judea tributary to Rome.

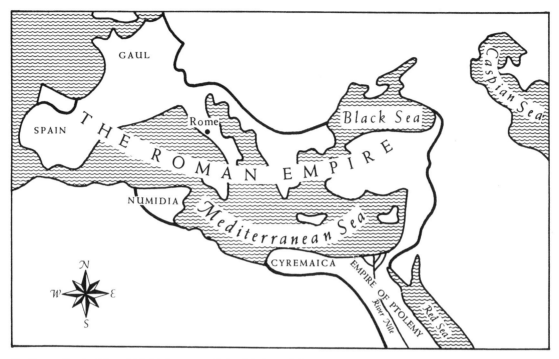

The Roman Empire (about 60 B.C.). From a small city, fighting only for survival, Rome became a world power, ruling the Italian peninsula and European provinces on the Mediterranean and Aegean seas, plus northern Africa and western Asia.

After successive conquests of Egypt and Syria, Pompey's army headed toward Jerusalem. The two brothers decided to let Pompey arbitrate their dispute. The Pharisees also sent a mission to Pompey asking that neither brother be allowed to rule Judea, but that the country be placed under a High Priest and a Council of Elders. Meanwhile, Aristobulus decided to continue the revolt, first at the fortress of Alexandrium on the hills of Samaria and later in Jerusalem, after Pompey had ordered surrender of the fortress. The Roman general then besieged the city. Various sections surrendered and, finally, all was taken except the Temple Mount.

After stubborn and bloody resistance to a long siege, the Temple Mount was surrendered to Pompey in 63 B.C. To the horror of the pious Jews, the irreverent Gentile forced his way into the Holy of

Holies to learn what the Jews worshiped with such devotion. To his amazement he found the place completely empty. The Jewish leaders were gratified, however, that he did not touch the Temple treasures. However, Pompey did make Judea tributary to Rome and he greatly reduced the size of her territory. Moreover, he re-established Hyrcanus as High Priest, but without the title of "king." Aristobulus, together with his wife and children, were carried in chains to Rome. Many other Jews, transplanted by Pompey to the Imperial City at this time, became the nucleus of the Jewish community in Rome.

Antipater's reason for supporting Hyrcanus in his quarrel with Aristobulus soon became apparent. He wanted a weak man as ruler of Judea. The wily Idumean soon became chief adviser to Hyrcanus and, by his influence, drew Judea more and more into the orbit of Rome. Because of the aid given by Hyrcanus and Antipater to Caesar in his struggle with Pompey, the Roman emperor gave many rights and privileges to Jews throughout the empire. Hyrcanus was given the title "ethnarch of Judea" and Antipater was named as the country's "procurator." The walls of Jerusalem, destroyed by Pompey, were rebuilt. Cities taken from Jewish rule by Pompey were restored to the control of the Jews. Hyrcanus and Antipater supported Cassius following the death of Julius Caesar and, after Cassius and Brutus died, aided Mark Antony. Antipater's death at this critical period dealt a blow to the career of Hyrcanus. Antony recognized the real power in the land by appointing Antipater's two sons as tetrarchs, or governors, over Jewish territory—Phasael in Judea and Herod in Galilee.

The Maccabean princes did not easily surrender their right to rule. Three of them had escaped from Pompey's Roman guards—one, Alexander whose wife was his cousin Alexandra, daughter of Hyrcanus II—had actually made his escape en route to the Imperial City. Aristobulus II and his other son, Antigonus, had made their leap for freedom from Rome itself. Aristobulus and Alexander both died as the result of ill-fated revolts. Now, the honor of the Maccabees rested in the hands of Antigonus.

The last of the Maccabean princes was highly successful at first. In the attack on Jerusalem, he drove Phasael to suicide as the city fell. Herod fled to Rome, going by way of Egypt. Mark Antony heaped honors on Herod, and the Roman Senate gave the wily Idumean the title, "King of the Jews." Meanwhile, Antigonus had consolidated his power in Jerusalem, where he continued ruling for three years (40-37 B.C.) as "king and high priest."

Herod the Great, King of the Jews

With Roman backing, Herod determined to make the title recently bestowed on him a reality. He returned to Jerusalem and laid siege to the city, which fell after five months. Antigonus was beheaded by Mark Antony, at Herod's request, in 37 B.C.

Earlier, Herod had married Miriamne, daughter of Alexander and Alexandra. He thus formed a connection with the Maccabean house. At Miriamne's request the king appointed her brother, Aristobulus III, as high priest at the age of seventeen. Because of the lad's popularity with the people, Herod had him drowned while bathing at Jericho during the same year as his appointment, 35 B.C. The king passionately loved his wife Miriamne, reputed to have been one of the most beautiful women of her day, and he was intensely jealous of her. Yet she was put to death at Herod's command in 29 B.C. because of scandalous reports on her to the king by his evil sister, Salome. The following year Herod had Miriamne's mother, Alexandra, executed.

The direct line of the Maccabees was thus wiped out. The line could have been carried on, however, through Alexander and Aristobulus, the two sons of Herod and Miriamne. The popularity of his sons, coupled with reports of conspiracies against him, caused Herod to have both of them executed. This is the same Herod who later was to order the slaughter of children under two years of age because of his fear that Jesus, the newborn "King of the Jews," might take his place.

410

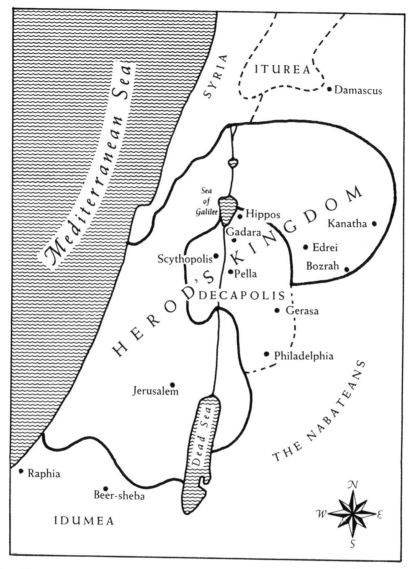

Herod's Kingdom. The Maccabees extended the boundaries of Palestine but, under the Romans, the family of Herod came to power. Herod the Great (73?-4 B.C.) was finally appointed as King of the Jews by Mark Antony and the Roman Senate.

Despite his bloody deeds, Herod the Great brought to the Jewish nation an aura of external magnificence. He established a brilliant Hellenized court. He tried to please the Jews by rebuilding their Temple, a task in which he succeeded so well that the great building was thereafter called Herod's Temple. He showed that he had no real understanding of the pious Jews, however, by establishing a theater and an amphitheater for shows and games. Only the Hellenists applauded this move. To make his military position secure, he built strong fortresses up and down the land. He lavished wealth on the building and furnishing of his own palace, which

411

Frank Mountain (Herodium). Herod the Great is reputed to have been buried with great pomp in a tomb at Herodium, located southeast of Bethlehem. His kingdom was divided among three surviving sons.

© Matson Photo

became a showplace. He built the city of Caesarea, naming it for the emperor.

But Herod never won the hearts of his conquered people. They always remembered that he was an Idumean, or Edomite, and therefore to be regarded as a usurper. Too, they never forgot that he was, in fact if not in name, a servant of Rome. This is the man who was on the throne of Judea, dying of an incurable disease, when Jesus was born in Bethlehem about the year 5 B.C.

NOTES

NOTES

NOTES

NOTES

NOTES